# ODYSSEUS

## ON THE RIVER OF TIME | BOOK ONE

To Glynis
for her fascination
with so many
things in life

Carl

# WORKS BY CARL HARE

POETRY
*On the River of Time*
Book One: *Odysseus*
Book Two: *Spenser* (forthcoming)
Book Three: *Archer* (forthcoming)

*A Weathering of Years*

PLAYS*
*The Eagle and the Tiger*
*John Gabriel Borkman* (adapted from Ibsen)

* Both these plays are in the National Library of Norway.

A wanderer is man from his birth.
He was born on a ship
On the breast of the river of Time.

— Matthew Arnold, "The Future"

In dedication

and with love

to my late wife, Clara

# TABLE OF CONTENTS

# About the Trilogy

Why write an epic poem?

Why? Because a shock, a sudden realization, can force you to respond, and if it is important enough and large enough, it can lead to a form expansive enough to express its implications.

As the Prologue suggests, this work was provoked by the accidental purchase and reading of Edmund Spenser's collected poems. Later, I discovered in his treatise on Ireland that Spenser advocated the starvation of the rebellious Irish to conquer them fully—in essence, given that almost the entire population could be considered in this light, suggesting genocide. But I also realized that even while he was writing this tract he was still working on the allegories of the high virtues in his epic poem, *The Fairie Queene*. How could one of the great poets in the English language, who could speak with the tongue of angels, hold simultaneously in his mind such contradictory attitudes with such conviction?

From the seed of this question grew the themes that pervade this work: the nature of our most basic perceptions; the Other; the Mask as an integral part of our lives; the implications of the consequences of our actions; and the continuity over the millennia of these human perceptions and drives. And as each of us journey through our individual lives, so the work concentrates on the journeys of three extraordinary men from different periods spanning almost three thousand years of human life—one mythical, one historical, and one fictional.

There are thus three stories related here in the three books of this epic trilogy: the first tells of the last voyage of the Greek hero Odysseus to propitiate the God Poseidon; the second, of the last four months in the life of the poet Edmund Spenser; and the third, of the director/actor Ray Archer's tours across Canada, his creation of a work about the country, and its tour in Ireland.

But why write in the form of a long narrative poem? Given the stories of these three men, the narrative would be lengthy. But the long poetic narrative has always been considered one of the major forms of our expression. And the ability of poetry to give resonance to the action of its heroes and to reveal the quality of an age has earned it that importance.

Here, then, is such a narrative. All three men endure journeys both external and internal; all three must face critical moments that in different ways change them significantly. And each story's form of expression reveals in its utterance the time in which its protagonist lives—a suggestion of the Greek epic poem; the Spenserian stanza for the Elizabethan period; and free verse for today— with further variations that link the separate tales to form a mosaic of word and action and character.

And that is why what you are about to read is an epic poem.

# ACKNOWLEDGMENTS

The inception of the idea for this work happened the year that *Kings*, my son's one-man performance of the great poetic adaptation by Christopher Logue of the first two cantos of *The Iliad*, occurred in 1993. Twenty-three years ago. And so my first acknowledgment must go to that remarkable poet, and my second to my son Kevin's brilliant reading of that work, which still reverberates in my mind today. Then there is the old bookstore in Winnipeg where I found the copy of Spenser's collected poems, and the Spenser I discovered in the story of his life. For ten years the ambivalence of his attitudes worked in my mind while I completed other projects, until finally I had the time to think more deeply about the issue and how it might be addressed.

Then, in ways I can no longer remember or fathom, the idea of the epic poem began to unfold, leading to the concept of the trilogy and the appropriate figures and ages for each quest, and a plan grew, which went through many changes from 2004 to 2007. To begin with, the three books were actually one huge work: Canto 1 of the first immediately followed by Canto 1 of the next, and so on. But finally the three stories were separated completely into the trilogy as it now exists. Even before this evolution took place, I had already began to plunge into the histories and the ways of living of the three eras that I had chosen, so that I had started to experience what the characters had done, where they lived, and the implications of their actions. Specific acknowledgements I will leave to each of the three books, but I will make a general and grateful acknowledgement to the vast help found through books and online that sharpened my perceptions and made the work legitimate.

The whole work was first called "Journeys," and I am indebted to Jim Munro of Munro's Books in Victoria for suggesting, tactfully and with humour, that I find a more interesting title. Matthew Arnold I must acknowledge for providing me in his poem "The Wanderer" the title which sums up this work more beautifully than I could have done myself.

But my major gratitude must go to my late wife Clara, who, along with our family, had to put up with the hours I spent away in libraries or at the computer, and when on holidays my continuing to write in hotel beds, on benches at Disneyland in California, in various rooms when we visited our children, and in coffee houses. She was the first to read the whole work, even while she was sick, and the first to show faith in it.

My gratitude also to Sharon Thesen, who was the first to read the epic after Clara, and who not only made acute observations but has stood by me as the work has continued through the years.

And, finally, to two editors and friends, whose work on the text has been so valuable. My thanks to Douglas Campbell for his painstaking examination of the text over many hours as a copy editor, keeping me on the right literate track. And to Carolyn Zapf, my long-time editor and writer of texts for me to direct, who has worked unstintingly on these books, always making penetrating observations and shrewd comments. My deep gratitude to her.

# PROLOGUE

Dust
and the odour of old books
linger on the packed sway-backed shelves,
drift among the heaps
of journals, magazines and maps
scattered on the worn, uneven floorboards
of this prairie bookstore
on this prairie summer day.

The shaded incandescent lights,
suspended with their caps
like the green eyeshades of old bookkeepers,
lose the battle with the brilliant sunlight
projected through the casements
of another era
to make the bindings and the covers
glow with the life that they contain.

Within this gleaming maze,
sidestepping piles of books to navigate the aisles,
distracted both by literature and store,
I spy in a far corner,
just before the light angles into darkness
*The Poems* (the prose, I later learned,
tactfully left out) *of Spenser*
and my student days rush hurly-burly back.

*The whiles the woods shal answer—*
an alien word and world
*Upon a bed of roses she was layd*
heard as an erotic patchwork
*As faint through heat, or dight to pleasant sin*

encrusted in words archaic
even for that rhetoric time—
*And your eccho ring.*

And now—for who knows
what reason … a prairie guilt
over something left unfinished?
a twinge to read the whole
of a vast quirky epic,
to join the few crumbs of it
half-digested so long ago?—
I buy the poems of Edmund Spenser.

To say the least,
this had not been my intent.
The faded store stood close
to where the Fringe Festival
displayed its variegated wares
and where my son's one-man *Kings*,
touching in a modern poet's words
*The Iliad*'s great opening strife,
played in the transfigured room
of an aging downtown hotel.

Bookstores are for browsing—
a nibble of a novel here
a taste of fancy there
and the hoped-for discovery
of some succulent curious volume
of ancient and forgotten lore—
and with this intention
I had sauntered in.

Well, that's how I remember it—
the store can be checked out
if it still exists—
but the luminous image of the place
still glows in the recesses of my memory;
I can still feel the wry twinge,

the impulse to acquire,
and the book now rests in my hand.

How our butterfly events
shape our future acts
when seen through the twisting prism
of our mazing past.
Who can really read our fractal patterns
except as a convenient history
in which one slight event
can change our lives?

The reading of his poems,
the reading of his life,
leads to this moment,
leads to this need
to sing of journeys,
his and two others,
all from different times and places,
of a poet who can hold together in his mind
Magnificence and Genocide,
of an ancient Greek hero,
"he who inflicts or receives pain,"
and an aging artist
pursuing his own unfolding quest,
all enmeshed in our chaotic life,
to trace the filaments of this web
like the subtle strands of the spider
hovering in the quiet dusk.

# ODYSSEUS

# Preface
## ODYSSEUS

The ending of *The Odyssey* is a masterpiece of telling, letting one struggle after another occur right up to the final scene: Odysseus arriving disguised as a beggar before being recognized by dog and servant and his son; his massacre of the suiters in the banquet hall; the terrible revenge upon the disloyal female servants; the sparring with the suspicious Penelope until he reveals the secret of their bed; Athena delaying dawn for the husband and wife, but Odysseus having to tell Penelope of the prophecy that he must make a second journey; and the climax of the civil war with the families of the suitors, ending with the peace ordered by Zeus himself.

Homer makes sure the prophecy's importance is stressed. Before they go to bed, Penelope insists on hearing it, and Odysseus tells her. Any response to the prophecy is shelved as the couple find themselves at last in bed together. And so in one sense Odysseus's story has come to a close with his return, revenge, and the new peace. But still hanging over him are the ominous words of the prophecy.

It is the fulfilling of the quest set out in the prophecy that is at the heart of this book. Poseidon has demanded that Odysseus must carry an oar on his back, travel to many cities, and eventually find a land that knows no salt; in that land he will meet a stranger who will ask him if the object on his back is to winnow the grain; when he hears these words, he must then plant the oar in that place and make obeisance to Poseidon. Only then will Odysseus be able to live a long life, after which "a gentle painless death" will come far from the sea—or, given the ambiguity of the original Greek, by someone far from the sea.

Such is the prophecy. But suppose Apollo discusses the punishment with Poseidon, who is about to destroy the island of the Phaeacians, his children with whom he is angry, and makes an ingenious suggestion that will intertwine both punishments? That possibility is also at the heart of this book.

Of all characters in literature, Odysseus is the one who has most fascinated the ages. Each generation of artists and scholars tends to view him from their own perspective, as W.B. Stanford has shown in *The Ulysses Theme*. My own imagining of Odysseus sets him in his own age, a time filled with danger, where rulers of small lands govern in perpetual wariness of each other. It is perfectly natural for Nestor, the ancient ruler in Pylos, after having banqueted Odysseus's son Telemachus, to ask if he sails as a trader or as a pirate. It is not surprising, then, that Odysseus has been viewed as a trickster, a liar, ruthless, willing to frame someone who has slighted his honour. He is all these things; but he is also wise, honours his friends, remains faithful to his family and the island he rules, and has struggled to survive against all odds. You will see him in all these lights.

As you may suspect, the gods play their part as well. In this telling, they never appear except in dreams and oracular utterances. But they reflect the uncertainties of that period, where mortals face both the dangers of those about them and the fickleness of those who seem to rule over them. We sometimes forget that in this mythology the entire tragedy of the Trojan War and its aftermath began with the vanity of three goddesses competing over which among them was the most beautiful. And, of course, the gods' games have long-lasting consequences.

The Trojan War ended twelve years before our story begins, and what we see is the aftermath of that war on peoples and veterans. Our time knows only too well the vagaries of conflict and its consequences, and consequences you will see.

## Canto 1

# CORINTH

Golden the light
As Helios urged on his blazing charge
To the verge of the broken horizon,
Golden the harbour as the sable sharp-beaked ship
Knifed toward the dock
And rubbed its dark side against the worn stones,
The small forest of long oars upright.
In the proud prow stood wary Odysseus;
Beside him his son, brave Telemachus,
Medon, Ithaca's eloquent herald,
And Halitherses, shrewd seer and friend.
As the ship had slipped into the embracing harbour,
On the dock they saw a tall figure,
Robed, his white hair and beard shining in the golden light,
And behind him a rank of glittering warriors.
A hand touched the king's arm:

"Polyidos."

"Euchenor's father," replied Odysseus to his seer,
Still keeping watch at the nearing dock.
"You were right. And he knows we are coming,
As you knew he would."

Now, ship docked, Medon first stepped on to the glowing stones,
The other three, poised, waiting.

"Citizens of Corinth, subjects of the Argolid,
Odysseus of Ithaca, famed hero of the War with Ilion,
Now long past,
Greets you and asks that you receive him as a friend."

As Medon's strong voice still reverberated,
King, son, and seer joined him before the Corinthian host.
Now moved to face them the renowned seer, Polyidos,
Ancient and stiff, yet still with proud authority,
Who slowly knelt before the isle-sceptred sovereign.

"Far-famed Odysseus, true vanquisher of that ill-fated kingdom,
Receive with all gratitude the thanks of Corinth,
And welcome!"

Odysseus, without a word, raised the old man
And embraced him in his powerful arms.
A great shout arose from Corinthians and Ithacans alike,
Flooding the harbour with their cheers
As the group stood burnished in the sun's last rays.
Then from the ship was led a virgin bull, gold horned,
And a great skin of the best Ithacan wine,
And the throng moved formally, in respectful procession,
To a small altar discreetly near the dock.
There the reverent warrior, holding the shaggy head
With one hand, his great bronze sword poised,
Looked skywards as he spoke:

"All knowing Zeus, Guardian of Justice,
Powerful Poseidon, who keeps dominion over land and sea,
Mighty Apollo, dread with prophecy,
And wise Athena, protector of righteous men,
Hear our prayers, and let us travel through these lands
In peace and union with our various peoples
As you have bid us do."

So saying, he slashed the dedicated throat,
And blood flowed quickly as the life ebbed away
And the sun began to sink beyond the horizon.
The wine, mixed with clear water, was passed among them,
The first portion spilt for the Gods.

Now, permission given, surges of motion
Surrounded the still ship as supplies were unloaded,
And all made ready for the lengthy trek.
A Corinthian guard, with two sons of faithful Dolios,
Mantilios and Dorindor, remained at the dock;

The rest, Corinthian and Ithacan alike,
Followed the procession as it started for the citadel.
Odysseus and his troop saw, some distance away,
The great rock that reared above the busy harbour;
Like a diadem upon a lofty forehead,
Or the inaccessible nest of some great bird,
The citadel perched at the top, its squat walls
Caught in the last rays of the setting sun.

As the procession trudged along the stone-lined way,
Polyidos, abreast Odysseus and his son
At the front, spoke quietly, saving breath
For the long winding climb ahead.

"Noble Odysseus, you have indeed been favoured by the Gods
With a fine son—I can see your lineaments in his face
And he is filling out as such sons should
And stands taller than his father:
A fitting inheritance for future greatness."

Proud Odysseus smiled and glanced toward his son,
Who had flushed with the compliment
But showed no expression otherwise.

"I have indeed been blessed," he said,
"And my son Telemachus has already proved his worth,
Both in Ithaca and on this journey."

Again a blush betrayed Telemachus's deep feelings,
But still the watchful son kept silence,
And his thoughtful father let his look fall briefly
On the ancient man still labouring at his side.

Now the way led to the base of the towering rock
And skirted it to start a tortuous ascent
To the great citadel glimpsed high above.
Shadows had now lengthened and joined
As dusk provoked the flare of torches
To mark the narrow road cut into living rock.
Few words were spoken, all their effort used
To climb the steep and winding trail.
At length, a massive wall rose before them,

Inset with huge bronze doors that now gaped open,
Inviting them to enter there the glowing cavity.
A few more paces brought them to the steps,
The palace uncertain in the flickering light,
And then they found themselves in the great hall.

On a dais before them, behind which loomed
The dim shapes of the lions of the Argolid
Facing each other, crouched in the shadows,
Sat a gray-haired man, robed in ornate cloth,
A bronze crown encircling his deep-grooved head
And his rich staff of office in his hand.
He did not rise when they confronted him,
But instead beckoned Odysseus to him.

"Welcome, great warrior and old friend!
Forgive my absence from the dock;
But, as you see, I have paid a price for Ilion."
Now the keen-eyed Odysseus noted
The hollow in the gown where a leg should be,
And looking in the pain-ravaged face,
He said, with heart-wrenched voice,

"My fellow warrior, great Escalios,
I did not know what fate apportioned you
When we last parted on that fire-torn night in Troy!
I greet you with all love."

Now he and his friend gripped each other's arms,
Both too moved to speak
As Time stopped then to give them rein to their emotions.

Later the feast, prepared for them with joints
And other sacrificial meats, carried ahead.
On one side of Odysseus was his friend, Escalios,
On the other, white-haired Polyidos;
Telemachus was near Escalios;
Halitherses beside Polyidos.
Apart from them mingled the Ithacan crew
And the lords of Corinth, all youths like Telemachus.
Again, libations to the Gods were made
With pungent wine mixed with sweet honey,

And sizzling fat portions carved out for them.
The great lords sliced long choice cuts from the thighs
And the feast began in earnest.
Then Escalios called out to his bard,
Had him seated with his own table
Enriched with breads and wine, meat and delicacies,
Had his lyre brought forth from its revered place.

"Come, Myconides, sing to us of the long war
For our guests, a great hero and old friend."

Honey-voiced Myconides respectfully acknowledged
His lord's request and saluted the seated guests and host.
He lifted up his lyre and, moving to the centre of the space,
Caught in the ever-changing flare of torches,
With a vibrant sweep of the strings
He began his song.

First was the deep insult that provoked the war,
Paris's theft of Menelaus's wife, ravishing Helen,
Failed embassies, the massing of the Achaeans,
The sacrifice of Iphigenia,
Agamemnon's own beloved daughter,
The armada's crossing, and the ten years
Of grueling war. His voice deepened, his lyre throbbed,
As he sang of the vicious struggle at the ships,
The burning and savage combat,
The death of Patroclus, the wrath of Achilles,
Hector's mutilation, Achilles's death by Paris's bow,
The Trojan horse, the entry to the city,
And the wrathful sack of the doomed citadel,
The tribulations of the remnants' return home,
And the vile murder of Agamemnon.

As the song soared through the palace,
Telemachus observed his father and his hosts.
In the uncertain flames their faces, shadowed
Or revealed, glowed as they once more
Lived through the battles and ordeals,
And each more than once obscured his face
To conceal the tears and sobs that so wracked
Their bodies and their wrenched, scarred souls.

The intensity of their grief smote him
But he could not turn away, bound in fascination
And sympathy by the song and by its effect.

The final note hovered in the air; then all was silence.
Odysseus rose and carved a great slice from the thighs.

"Myconides, take this gift in gratitude.
I have heard these harsh ordeals sung before,
And by great bards, but this is the first time
That I have listened with those who were there
Or whose loved ones have not returned."

And he placed the offering on Myconides's plate,
Who modestly received it.
Turning to his host, the moved warrior took his arm:

"Good Escalios, you lived through this song with me,
Which still gave but a faint shadow of what you were,
An indomitable warrior and unshakable comrade.
The price you paid should be overwhelmed
By the glory of your exploits and name."

Escalios smiled grimly, still held by the king:

"You're right, my friend, I did relive that time
Reignited by the power of Myconides's song,
But glory will not now return my leg,
Nor," glancing at Polyidos, "his son."

The old man, who had been watching his companions
Throughout the song, nodded then his head in acknowledgement,
And said,

"Renowned Odysseus, who fought in the densest battle,
I knew my son would die there if he went.
I told him of his choice: to remain here and waste away
From a cruel disease, or to sail across the great sea
And fall by a Trojan's hand. He chose the honourable way
And has not returned, and I revere his choice and action.
But though I foretold his death, I could not see the manner of it.
Escalios did not see it—he was fighting among the ships
Away from where my son did battle.
If you saw it, would you tell me its course?"

Weary-warred Odysseus sighed, then began:

"Ah, Polyidos, I had hoped
That Myconides's excellent song
Would give us enough of the war, and indeed,
It brought back to me those terrible events.
But I cannot spurn your request, for I was there,
As you say, in the thick of it, and I did see his end,
And therefore I will tell you all
To the best of my ability.
It was the fatal night when battle went both ways,
With Hector fierce and indomitable, a scourge on the plains,
And our own warriors raging against his host.
Like a torrent rushing forward, impetuous and turbulent,
Sweeping all in its river bed before it
As it foams and rages toward the sea,
Only to meet the high tide's waves that crash against the swart rocks,
The huge impact shaking the earth and seabed,
Neither force overcoming the other,
But the waters reared high by their collision;
So too the great armies met near the Scaian Gates and the oak tree.
Arês the Hungry had his fill of death then;
Many gasped out their life on the ground,
Slashed open, skewered, crushed underfoot.
Hector then was like a God, rushing upon us:
Even as a typhoon catches all in its path
And hurls its debris forward to destroy more,
Its violent winds screaming and full of death,
He broke through our lines, creating havoc.
We would have been chased back to our ships,
Routed and defeated, if I had not taken courage
And exhorted Tydeides Diomedes to join with me
To stay the advance; we raced forward,
Dealing destruction as we went.
Chariots we dislodged, Thymbraios and his driver Molion
Dead in the dust; and Hippodamas and Hypeirochos next.
Stripping these of their armour, we swept on,
Diomedes fatally wounding Agastrophos on the hip
While I slaughtered men about us.
As Tydeides found the now dead Agastrophos
And was about to strip him of his blood-stained armour,

Hector, who had seen the fray, charged forward with his men.
Brawny Diomedes threw his spear, hitting the top of Hector's helmet
So hard that, stunned, he was driven far back among his men
And fell to the ground on his knees, supported by his hand, dazed.
Tydeides saw where his spear had landed after the glancing blow,
And ran to retrieve it, and as he did so, Hector regained his senses
Staggered to his chariot, and escaped with his life.
Shouting insults after him, Diomedes began to strip the armour,
But as he lifted the helmet away, Paris, the prince Alexandros,
Standing behind a pillar at the tomb of Ilos Dardanides,
Took aim with his bow, and his arrow ran through Diomedes's
Foot as he knelt, and pinned it to the ground.
The two exchanged insults while I by Diomedes
Fought to protect him as, with excruciating pain,
He wrenched the arrow from his foot,
Then hobbled to his chariot and drove back to the ships.
I was now left alone. Like a pack of wolves,
On the track of a mighty stag and, now surrounding him,
Voraciously attack, so the Trojans came at me.
The battle that ensued still rings clearly in my mind:
First I leapt at Deiopites, wounding him in the shoulder,
Then cut down Thoon and Ennomos, stabbed Chersidamas
Under his shield as he stepped out of his chariot,
Only to lie clutching the dust. Then I wounded
Charops Hippasides; but his brother Socos arrived
And hurled insults and his spear at me;
His insults did me no harm, but his heavy spear pierced my shield
And belt, ripping the skin from my flank.
I knew it was no mortal blow, and replied to Socos
Both with my voice and with my spear.
He had already turned to retreat
As my spear drove through his back and out his chest.
I spoke triumphantly over his corpse and pulled out his spear,
Then retrieved mine. My wounds began to bleed;
The Trojans saw this, and like a pack of hyenas,
Advanced on me; I retreated, calling out for help
At the top of my lungs. Luckily Menelaos heard me,
And bringing Ajax and his men, rescued me.
Among them was your fine son, Euchenor,
Who engaged bravely with the enemy,

Sending many of them into the dust;
But Paris, still wielding his bow, took aim
And caught him with an arrow near the jawbone
Under the ear; your son died quickly and with honour.
Without his help I might have gnawed dust with the rest."

Polyidos sighed,

"My gratitude, valiant Odysseus, for your eloquence
In making clear that great battle and my son's end.
You may have noticed that there are few if any older men
Here; these youths are the children of the warriors
Who sailed from here and never returned."

Now Escalios, who had watched Odysseus closely, spoke.

"Ah, my friend Odysseus, how you bring alive that desperate night!
I had not known so vividly the details of the battle
In your area, but now am grateful to know it better.
But, tell me now, why have you come?
And what are your plans now that you are here?"

Odysseus looked at him, and for a moment
A haunted expression flickered across his face,
Quickly suppressed. As torches played on him,
He replied to his friend and veteran.

"You have every right to know why we have come
And where we go. You have by this time heard
It took me ten years to reach Ithaca,
All ships and spoil gone, ten long hard years seeking home.
Halitherses can tell what happened after I returned
As I secured my kingdom and my queen again.
When all was in place, I then raided towns along the coast,
Replenished my wealth and slaves. My son sailed
With me, and he showed his valour as a warrior
And his promise as a statesman."

Telemachus bowed his head in acknowledgement
And continued to watch and listen carefully.

"A short while ago, as I rested with my wife and son,
A harsh tremor shook the island; buildings toppled,

Inhabitants died under the rubble,
And my people were distraught and grieving.
Then a huge wave swept ashore, forging more havoc.
Halitherses came to me, and I asked him to divine
The significance of these dire events.
Sacrifices were solemnly performed,
And their smoke rose, succulent, to the heavens.
But Halitherses himself can tell us
The true meanings of these dreadful omens."

Halitherses looked gravely at the group, then said,

"It came to me, even as the smoke rose higher:
My senses abandoned me, the world shifted,
And a voice, terrible in its brightness and still intensity,
Filled my head:

> 'The time has come for the prophecy
> To be fulfilled. Odysseus has delayed too long;
> Poseidon's anger is expressed without doubt
> In what he has wreaked upon earth and sea.
> Odysseus must travel to Delphi,
> Discover her word on what he must do.'

"Then the earth became itself again,
And I told Odysseus what had taken place."

Odysseus, nodding to his seer, took up his narrative.

"I knew then that I had stayed too long.
Only Penelope, my faithful queen and wife,
Knew the secret that I had kept on my return,
And which now I must relate to you, my host,
And to my own people, my own son.
Know then, that Tiresias, the famed blind prophet,
Spoke to me at the dark verge of Hades,
In that shadowy land beyond the seas."

A gasp of shock and horror in the hall;
Telemachus gazed at his father in astonishment,
A wrench in the way he saw and knew him; all changed.

"He foretold what I must do once I returned home:

In order to allay the great enmity
And wrath against me of great Poseidon"—

Again uneasy murmurs rippled through the hall—

"That I must leave my land to rove through endless towns of men,
Resting on my shoulder an oar, strong, well crafted, until
I discover a land that knows no salt,
Whose people are ignorant of the sea,
And of our graceful ships, sharp prowed, slim oared.
In that land then, a man will join with me,
And as we walk, he'll ask whether across my shoulders
Is a winnowing fan to work the grain.
At once I must plant in the earth my long-borne oar,
And sacrifice ram, bull, and virile boar
To the dread lord of land and sea, Poseidon.
Then can I go home, to offer the best I have
To all the Gods, the eternal rulers of the heavens.
Only then may I live out my life in full,
Death coming to me far from the sea, taking me
Gently and painlessly after the long passage of years,
With all my people, blessed with peace, surrounding me.
These were the prophet's words; and when I came to Ithaca,
And knew once more my lovely wife, Athena herself
Appeared before us to remind me of the prophecy.
Yet prudence pushed me to delay, as you have seen,
Until the God spoke through the gifted Halitherses.

"Then I assembled the company you see before you,
And, leaving my kingdom in the care of Mentor,
My trusted friend and worthy guardian,
And taking painful leave of my dear wife,
From whom so long before I had been absent,
And now bereft again, her son with me,
We set sail for Delphi.
Our ship was swift and certain, our crew strong and capable,
But Poseidon still showed his resentment to me:
The sea turned black; grey clouds scudded before us,
Wind lashing the waves to heights of froth-tipped frenzy.
Long did the crew labour, their oars straining against the waves,
Fighting down the coast for many a weary hour,

Until we gained entry to the sheltering points of land,
Sailing with the distant peak of Mount Ranachaion
As a blessed beacon toward our destination.
Even as we came closer, the seas subsided,
And, exhausted, we let sail take our ship
Forward in the new favourable breezes.
The sun now appeared, and we sped along
Through the shining waters, enthralled with the huge peaks
That reared on either side.
Soon we entered the great Gulf of Corinth
And, rounding a point, saw in the distance Mount Parnassus,
Its dark shape seen through the clear ivory moonlight
That flooded the now sleeping sea.
The crew took in their fill of the majestic sight,
Then rested to prepare for the new day.

"Dawn came, spreading her calm blush over the still sea
And touching lightly the land and bay before us.
As we rowed into the sheltered bay, the sun's first glints
Struck the peaks of the sacred mount, which glowed radiantly,
A splendid beacon to our ordained destination.
Our prow and keel hissed onto the sandy beach;
Immediately we disembarked, leaving half the crew
To stand guard over the precious ship until our return.
Then, Halitherses, guided by the Gods, led our way,
Medon, Telemachus, and myself following close behind,
The others at our heels, armed and wary.
The land was cultivated—olive trees for the first part—
And a road—more a trail—wound through the tended land,
Which spread as a green plain to the verge of the rearing peaks.
But soon the country grew rough as we reached the base
Of the great mountain range; thick dark forests covered
The now rock-strewn terrain on huge ridges.
Up these we toiled, following the trail.
Through the trees we could hear the sounds of many birds,
Ever the caws of ravens and crows uppermost.
Occasionally through the trees we glimpsed
Rough, savage-looking men, who quickly slunk back
Into the thick foliage when they saw they were discovered;
And, looking back from a height, at the curving beach,

Bright in the sun, with our ship dark upon its breast,
We saw small groups of men following us below.
We took quiet note of them but continued on our way.
The trek was long and weary, up one ridge, deep down another,
Then a steep climb again; but still we ascended,
The towering walls of Mount Parnassus
Ever closer, then beside us as we trudged farther.
Engulfed by the vast peaks, we felt the weight
Of the centre of the world toward which we travelled,
Awesome in its immensity and significance.
Finally ahead arose the massive wall
Of the sanctuary's precincts,
Its stones sharp etched in the blazing sun's rays,
And all cradled in the immense crags of the Phaidrades.
As we drew near, an eagle circled high above us,
Soaring over the steep-sided slopes,
Where trees struggled against the harsh stone.
Halitherses smiled at the propitious sign,
And we arrived at the bronze gates.

"Above the gate, dark silhouette against the sky,
Stood a lone man, clad in priest's clothing.
As we drew near, he called out,

'Welcome strangers: be aware that this is a sacred place;
Only those who are ordained to ask Apollo their question
Through the sacred office of the Pythia may pass farther.
Therefore, tell me, who are you, that she may determine
Whether you are fit to hear the divine words of her lord.'

"On hearing this, I stepped forward before Halitherses,
As he had advised me, gesturing in friendship.

'Odysseus greets you, and comes in supplication,
Ordered by the great God himself to come to his servant
And ask for his dread message. To this end
I bring here the allotted palanon and sacrifice.'

"And I motioned my men to bring forward
A golden tripod with its shining bowl,
And the sacred snow-white, gold-horned ram
Which with difficulty we had brought from the ship.

The priest nodded and disappeared; and the gates ground open.
Inside, we saw, looming on higher ground,
The sacred temple of Lord Apollo,
With the paved road winding up to it.
Priests, their hair long, their eyes wild and haunted,
Took from us the tax and the sacrifice,
Then led us to the Spring of Kastalia,
Emerging from its cleft rich with plants, trees, and shrubs,
Where we purified ourselves for the encounter;
Then we climbed the great Sacred Way to the temple,
And on Apollo's altar, its stones worn from its holy usage,
The priests slit the throat of our sacrificial ram.
Now before us was the ramp leading to the entrance
To the temple, whose huge façade, stoned and carved,
Increased the sense of mystery and portent
Which I increasingly had felt,
My skin tingling with its promise.
The others were instructed to remain at the entrance;
Only I, as the theopropos, could go on.
And, apprehensive, I entered the temple's adyton.
There, in darkness streaked with narrow shafts of light,
And in the centre of this inner sanctum,
Rested the great omphalos stone,
Marking the centre of the earth,
Its conical shape covered with strange sculptural designs,
Which in the smoky haze seemed to writhe in indescribable ways
Around each other and the stone itself.
Near the omphalos, upon a golden tripod,
Set precariously above a deep cleft
From which sweet fumes emerged and dazed our senses,
Sat a woman, her hair still wet from Kastalia's waters,
Where she had purified herself. Her dark hair, long and soaked,
Hung lank over her shoulders; her chiton, even in the uncertain gloom,
Was dazzling white. But there seemed a strange, uncertain disorder
To her clothes, and her eyes seemed enormous in their wide-eyed dilation.
She sat stiffly, saying nothing but chewing bay leaves
Handed to her by one of the priests, hovering about her,
And drank water from the Kassotis Spring proffered by another priest,
Her face white and haunted.
A priest who stood beside her, tall and majestic, addressed us:

'Theopropos, behold the sacred Pythia,
Devoted servant of our Lord Apollo.
Ask now what knowledge you desire of the God.'

"By now the sweet fumes that engulfed the holy space
Were working on me: the priest's voice reverberated as from afar,
Echoing in my head, as I heard, or felt I heard, a faint buzz
Deep in my mind. But, with great effort, I spoke, my tongue thick and lazy:

'Oh revered Pythia, who speaks for your lord, mighty Apollo,
God of foresight, mender and killer of men,
Who deigns to hear us through your gifted ears,
Receive the humble and ordained question
Of a humble suppliant, Odysseus.'

"At the sound of my name the Pythia started,
And the priests around her exchanged quick, secret glances.
Then I spoke of the prophecy, twice given me,
And of the signs that showed Poseidon's wrath
And brought me to Delphi and to her.

'My question, then, oh handmaiden of divine prophecy,
Is this: Where does Poseidon direct me?
Where should I travel to fulfill the prophecy
And assuage his dreadful wrath?'

"Silence, except for the faint buzzing in my head.
The Pythia suddenly began to take great wracking breaths,
Breathing deeply the fumes that wreathed around her from the cleft below,
And then jerkily arose, her arms raised stiffly above her,
Her eyes blank, her mouth slackly working.
Then sounds began to issue from her, impossible noises,
Deep registered, then soaring high, shrieks and moans
Interspersed with unintelligible words, or what seemed like words.
While she continued this way in her trance,
A whispering filled the adyton, as priests around her
Repeated what she said, or shrieked, or moaned,
Memorizing the entire episode.
Finally, with one last echoing cry
She collapsed, held up by priests hovering close to her,
And was led away into the darkness past the omphalos.
The chief priest now silently directed me to follow him,

And we left the adyton, my head still swimming, dazed.
At the top of the ramp outside, my head began to clear,
And I heard the priest tell me to wait to receive the final word.
I joined the others, who pressed me to tell what had happened,
And I did so, although by now that whole incident seemed a dream.
Time now slowed; the afternoon drew on,
And as we waited I glanced up at the two tall crags,
Rhodine and Phleboukos, which glinted in the still bright sun,
And there I saw, wheeling in ominous and majestic flight,
Great vultures, who swooped to the base of the shining rocks,
Then later rose again, others of their kin descending in their place.
I turned to a priest who guarded the sacred door
And asked him why the vultures congregated at the crags.

'They feast on the guilty bodies of the sacrilegious,
Who earlier were hurled from the peaks, their shattered forms
Left as punishment and warnings to transgressors.
We guard always against blasphemers,
For below us there is much unrest, with pirates
And bands of brigands preying on those who seek our sanctuary.'

"Despite myself I shuddered, as into my head
Came the sight of young Astyanax, Hector's son,
His body hurtling down the cliff's dire length
Accompanied by the agonized screams
Of his grief-stricken mother, Andromache,
And the bright air grew dark around me for a moment.
I pushed the thought from me, shaken;
And we all waited in silence,
Only the birds calling to each other
Heard in the distance.
Finally, the chief priest appeared and beckoned
Both to me and to Halitherses, whom he recognized as seer.
We again entered the adyton, its fumes still lingering in the air,
And again that quiet buzzing filled my head,
But now the priest alone was present,
Standing erect beside the sacred stone.

'Hear what the Pythia answers from Lord Apollo, Odysseus:

Now the past presents the future;
Travel back to gain the ground;

    One forced way must lead to rupture,
    Alone in heights is meaning found.'

"And he faded back into the darkness behind the omphalos,
Leaving the two of us to stumble from the adyton
Into the pure air outside the temple.
I was puzzled by the Pythia's coiled answer,
But Halitherses pierced its meaning."

Odysseus turned to Halitherses and nodded;
The sage spoke with his seer's voice:

"Always the Pythia's words are coined two sided
And her meanings true from the face that falls toward us,
Or even from the hidden face.
I heard in the oracular words
Some of her truths; others must come to Odysseus
As his quest discovers them.
First, he is commanded to retrace journeys from the past
In order to determine where next he needs to go;
For this first excursion, we can accompany him,
But for the last, he must go on alone,
Finding his way past peaks and valleys to his destination.
What will take place on his last journey is unclear,
Except that it will not be easy, but hazardous, extreme,
Testing his great fortitude and courage."

"This is what Halitherses determined"

(Odysseus took up the thread again)

"In thoughtful discussion as we began our journey back.
First we bade farewell to the priest who led us from the sanctuary,
Rejoined our companions left outside the walls,
And then we started down the trail,
Relating what had happened as we went.
It was now deep in the afternoon;
The sun's rays caught the upper reaches of the peaks,
But now the shadows thickened through the pines and firs.
I suggested that we camp in some secure space
And make the full descent in the next day's dawn;
But Halitherses stopped abruptly, his face drawn and white.

'Our ship and crew are now in danger, soon to be attacked
When night and darkness cloak the verge and shore.
We must return at once, with no delay!'

"Hearing this, I urged all to hasten down the slope.
Swiftly and silently we moved;
Around us the shadows lengthened further,
Only the tips of the great mountains warmed by light.
In the woods on either side, all was quiet; no breeze stirred
As dusk began to deepen into darker light.
Now night creatures began to stir; owls drifted overhead,
Their strange cries echoing among the crags;
At times we heard the sound of animals breaking through the brush.
We had to slow our pace, feeling our way down in the steep black,
Until, over the peaks appeared the moon, full and bright,
Casting our way in sharp relief. We increased our speed,
Trotting carefully along the narrow way.
Then, suddenly, Telemachus reached his hand upon my arm,
Signaling all to stop."

"I had heard sounds close by the way"

(Telemachus took up the tale)

"Not made by animals or birds,
But stealthy, with the quiet clink of metal, and the breathing
Of quiet whispers. I pointed up ahead to where I had heard
The sounds. My father nodded, then silently broke our group
Into two parts, I leading the first, he the second.
We drew our swords, concealing them and our shields;
My group moved forward, spaced to seem like our whole company;
My father's drifted quietly into the shadows at the sides,
Keeping a short distance from us
As we trotted onward, seemingly oblivious to the ambush.
Suddenly rough men leapt from each side, yelling fiercely
And brandishing their weapons. We parried their blows,
Then ran forward as if we were fleeing.
They followed us, shouting triumphantly.
But then suddenly we stopped and turned,
With disciplined training fusing our spears,
Our shields interlocked. The first men were impaled on our fierce points,
And as the others moved forward to take their places,

My father and his men attacked them from the rear.
The onslaught was swift and deadly. Their gang was strong
But undisciplined; and in the moonlight and in the shadows,
They could not tell friend from foe, nor could they retreat
Or escape."

"All died,"

Odysseus interjected, looking proudly at his son,

"Pierced by our spears, hacked with our blades,
Their throats cut lest any find return to warn their friends.
We lost no men—and Telemachus did not say how well he fought,
Leading his men so cleverly and killing three himself.
It was clear this ambush was to prevent us getting to our ship,
And so we increased our pace, quickly descending the long steep slopes
To the luxurious plain below. No one hindered us,
And soon we heard from the beach the sound of shouts,
The clash of weapons. When we came to the shore
We stopped in the shadow of the verge to take in the scene.
In the harsh moonlight we saw our men defending the ship
Against a large band, rough and undisciplined as had been
The ones we fought. It was evident that our men had kept their ranks so far,
But they were outnumbered and were tiring.
The night was clear; the light was good;
I used my bow."

Telemachus interrupted, his voice betraying
The awe he felt for his father's prowess:

"As we stood in the shadow,
My father drew his great bow, that which no other man could draw,
And let fly his arrows. Each reached its mark;
Even as in the gales of autumn, ripping the leaves from the storm-tossed trees,
So too did men fall to his deadly arrows. But the gang,
Engrossed in the fight before them, did not notice their companions fall,
And even as they fought on, our band descended on them.
Now there was greater carnage; caught in our vice,
They fought viciously; but shield, spear, and sword
Proved too much for the ill-ordered rabble,
And soon all were dispatched, their blood seeping
Into the defiled and corpse-strewn sand."

Odysseus then nodded to his son and took up the story:

"When we took stock of our own men, we found
That none had been killed, but some now bore wounds.
And I was proud of how we had battled,
And of the men who trained and fought with me,
Men like the stout sons of Dolios, my faithful shepherd.
Even as we made our survey, we heard yells in the distance,
The sign of more approaching. Quickly we pushed our ship
Away from the protesting sand, and those able
Rowed us to the sanctuary of the bay's calm water.
That night a guard was set; all others slept;
And when the glimmering dawn awoke us,
We fed and rowed out into the embracing gulf.

"Now I called a conference, to determine where we should go;
And Halitherses gave us good council,
Saying that if I must deal with the past,
Where better to begin than where the Great War first began,
In Sparta and Mycenae, and in the towns so involved with them,
Finding what had happened to them, and gaining knowledge
That could lead me on to the next part of my journey.
We all agreed, and pointed our dark, sharp-pointed prow
Toward Corinth, here arriving as you know."

Silence lingered in the hall when Odysseus ended his tale.
Escalios sighed, then turned to the veteran warrior.

"Odysseus, you have lost none of your eloquence,
That persuasive voice that compelled us to battle
Or to agree to your cunning schemes;
Without you the Achaeans could not have held together
Despite the glittering power of Agamemnon and Menelaos.
But now, old friend and dear companion, tell me,
What will you do now? And how may we help you in your quest?"

Odysseus turned to study the face of his pain-diminished friend:

"Hospitable and noble Escalios,
The first part of my plan is clear;
The rest still hides, shrouded in the dark veils of my moira.
My companions and I will travel through the Argolid,
Finding for ourselves the outcomes of that now-distant war.

As we go, our future trek will reveal itself,
And when I must go on alone, solitary in my mission.
But to make this journey, I crave your help.
My island, as you have heard, is inhabited by goats and sheep;
It is too rocky and too rough to support the luxury or necessity
Of horses. Therefore I ask you to provide in your generous way
Such animals as can carry us on this quest.
Chariots are not appropriate
For the terrain over which we go,
But both for greater speed and for the length of our travels,
Horses can make our way lighter and more propitious.
We will leave our black-prowed ship here, with your permission,
As well as our wounded, whom we entreat you to tend,
And when we come back we will gratefully return your gift."

Escalios immediately and with no hesitation, grasped his companion's arm
And said,

"Think no more upon this; it is done. Your wounded are welcome;
And tomorrow you shall have the best choices from our corral.
I myself would dearly love to join you,
But, as you see, my days of riding are now gone.
But, in return, I ask one favour: that some of our young men
May travel with you, both to see our lands
And to associate with you, your son, and companions;
Such an opportunity does not come frequently
For us here. They are experienced riders
And can help you with the horses and train your men
Better to use their animals if danger comes your way."

The relieved Odysseus, smiling, did not speak,
But, nodding, embraced his chair-imprisoned friend.
Then the cheers of the young men of Corinth
Raced about the hall, and they clasped the hands and arms
Of the relieved Ithacan company,
Who also joined in the happy melee.

Now the assembly came to an end;
Servants with torches led the weary band
Along the shadowy stone walls to their beds,
And helped convey the wounded to their places,
And silence captured the citadel, no sound

Except that of the nocturnal raptors heard
Outside the tall narrow windows,
Through which the moon cast sharp shafts of cold light.

*Buzzing*
*Faint*
*Louder*
*Moon shafts polluted with dark specks*
*Flies*
*Millions of flies*
*Swarming through the windows*
*Circling in the light*
*Engulfing every space*
*Now deafening*

*In his own cold radiance*
*Apollo shines amongst his filthy cohorts*
*Face terrible in its unutterable beauty*
*His look inscrutable*
*Divine*

*Something*
*Thoughts*
*Echo through the mind*

"Odysseus
Most cunning of the Achaeans
Twister of truths
Knowledge will drive you
Even after redemption
In your journey
You will find what knowledge is"

*Flies swarm before their lord*
*Mass before the eyes*
*Blotting out the sublime form*
*Their innumerable ungainly hideous eyes*
*Close*
*Close*
*Then a black stream through the windows*
*God and filth gone*
*Only the moon's ivory shafts*

*Buzzing shifts*
*To noise of battle*
*The ships again*
*Some burning*

*In the thick of the fight*
*The spear tearing the side*
*Pain felt dimly in the fierce struggle*
*Anger*
*Yelling insults*
*Hurling spear into the retreating back*
*Wrenching it from the writhing body*
*Rescue and retreat*
*Away from battle now*
*Time distorted by growing pain*

*Then warriors returned*
*The story of the night related*
*Who survived*
*Who was slain*
*In a small pocket of hearing*
*Euchenor's name*
*How he fell*
*Near the ships*
*Elsewhere in the battle*

*A lie to Polyidos*
*A good lie*
*But a lie*

*A cliff*
*A conference*
*Agamemnon and Menelaos*
*As usual*
*Uncertain what to do*
*My advice*
*No line of Hector to survive*
*To endanger all of us again*
*Agreed*
*The young boy dragged to the cliff*
*Clothes filthy from the charred city*
*His face white*

*Confused*
*Trying to be brave*
*His mother*
*Hair dishevelled*
*Clothes torn*
*Stained with the sacking of the city*
*Struggling wildly*
*Held firmly by strong*
*Unsympathetic arms*

*Her eyes dark and wide with terror*
*See her son dragged to the crag's edge*
*Hurled roughly over*
*No cry from his astonished mouth*
*Nor from hers*
*Until his body shatters with a thud*
*Heard even on the crag itself*
*Then the agonized cry rips from her lungs*
*Her grief and horror palpable to all*
*But especially to me*
*Who feels the terrible sorrow*
*In my own bones and nerves*
*A pain excruciate*
*More than the wounds I had endured*

*Warriors pull her away*
*A noble hero's faithful wife and mother*
*Before so beautiful and graceful*
*The finest of the Trojan women*
*To be a slave and concubine*
*The feeling of that disgrace*
*The ruin of the woman*
*Child and father*
*The destruction of the doomed city*
*Blazing*
*Its citizens rent and raped*
*Survivors    slaves*
*Overwhelms me with its shame*
*A long scream echoing*
*Echoing in my riven mind*
*Until I cannot breathe*

Odysseus, sweat soaked, gasping, jerked awake.
The pale pink tendrils of the dawn
Reached through the windows
To soften the stone walls.
He arose quietly and left the room.
Servants were already up and busy;
They took him, bathed and oiled him,
Dressed him, and led him out
Upon an outcrop by the citadel.
He stood, looking out over the short plain before him
At the docks and at the dark waters of the gulf,
At the sun-tipped mountains beyond,
And all around him.
He knew now some of the dread lord's meaning,
And the knowledge that pierced his dream
Left him with new thoughts, new feelings.
Always before he had acted from thoughtful policy
And in the rage of battle had been lifted
By his own thrill and skill of action;
Never had he considered deeply the feelings
Of those he killed, robbed, or enslaved.
A new perspective opened before him,
An alien countryside of pain and insight.
The God's prophecy and words struck home,
Vivid and ironic.
He sensed that this journey would be harder
Than he had anticipated, and the way forward
Full of uncertainties and hidden stings.
Silently he stood, gazing out upon the vivid scene
As the sun rose to drench the citadel and country
With its brilliant rays. He viewed the narrow isthmus
And the two dark waters on either side,
Mountains gleaming everywhere;
The memories of sailing the fickle eastern sea
Returned to him, but he put them quickly from his mind.
And then he went to join the others.

Later that morning his company assembled at the stables,
Where a Corinthian, husky, gnarled, greeted them
And had horses, prancing, spirited, led out to them.

Telemachus and the men looked at each other apprehensively;
Odysseus tactfully took charge, addressing the veteran horse master:

"Your Corinthian horses deserve praise indeed.
They remind me of those fine beasts of the chariots
On the fields at Ilium, fearless and deadly,
The best aid to their masters and drivers.
Yours deserve good riders to equal their prowess.
But we, who come from a horseless island,
Have little skill in riding. We therefore ask you to be patient
And to teach us to come to the standard that Corinthians cherish."

The horse master, somewhat taken aback by this unfortunate turn of events,
But flattered by the subtle Ithacan, replied,

"Renowned Odysseus, acknowledged master of battle,
I thank you for your compliments. It will be difficult,"

Glancing at the men.
                    "But I will do my best
To bring your company to excellence in this craft."

And so the training began, with many mishaps and mistakes:
Men fell from their mounts, could not guide them,
Nor could they make the close connection
So needed between such horse and rider.
But over the days their confidence stiffened,
Their muscles lost their soreness from the alien stances,
And the beginnings of a sensed rapport developed.
Soon as well, the wounded healed and joined them,
Working hard to catch up with the rest.

Odysseus himself worked with his steed,
A huge animal, strong and intelligent, a leader of the herd;
And his experience from adventures past
Soon brought the two together; so much so
That the Corinthians marvelled at his skill.
During this interval he spent time also with Escalios,
Recalling their adventures together,
How they had both been in the Trojan horse
And let the army of Achaeans through the gates,
But also finding out the path that he should follow

As they made their way to Mycenae,
And what they might encounter on their journey.
When they were not training with the horses,
Medon, Telemachus, and Halitherses joined them
In the consultations; but Telemachus also had made friends
With a young nobleman of Corinth, Polymedes,
And the two spent the nights talking, each relating
The kind of life that went on in their respective lands,
And Telemachus keeping his younger friend spellbound
With his account of journeys made to find his father.
So the days passed profitably, with hard training
And evenings filled with new companionship,

But at night:

*Darkness inside the shell*
*Bodies*
*Armour covered*
*Packed together*
*Sweating in the stench polluted air*
*Heat from the sun*
*Merciless*
*All men I know*
*Ruthless warriors*
*Veterans*
*Capable*
*Trusted*

*Long hours waiting*
*The Trojans finally arriving*
*Their interminable discussions*
*The careful deceptions working on them*
*Despite Cassandra's desperate warnings*
*Veiled by Apollo*
*Then finally agreement*
*When Laocoon's priests*
*Were crushed*
*He and his sons writhing*
*In the huge serpent's inexorable coils*
*And the moving of the giant structure*
*Each jolt bruising the men*

Slivers from the roughened timbers
Thirst when water gone
No food
Silence vital
Weapons carefully held from clinking
The growing noise of crowds
The change from beach and plain
To city streets
Difficult to listen and to think
In the fetid air
Roars of celebration
Music
Dancing
Cries of triumph
And the heat grew worse

Sounds gradually dwindling
Silence

Then the voices of our wives
Heard calling
Only Helen could have imitated them
Anticlus
Desperate for his woman
About to cry out
My hand over his mouth and nose
Others holding his limbs and body
No noise
No life left
No betrayal
More silence

Then carefully
Carefully
The bolts slipped back
The hatches quietly opened
First a fraction
No one there
Then swung wide
Ropes thrown down
The shimmy to the ground

*Quickly*
*Silently*
*Move through the streets*
*Shadows at their edges*
*Seeing people drunk*
*Unconscious in the gutters*
*Not stopping to cut their throats*
*Reach the great gate*
*Creep up the stairs*
*Quietly slit throats of tipsy guards*
*Unbar the gates*
*Work the mechanisms*
*Open them wide*

*On the wall*
*Signal by Helen*
*Playing both sides*
*In the black silence of the plain*
*Light flickers briefly*
*Then goes out*
*A soft rustling and padding heard*
*Then shapes appear out of the darkness*
*Massive lines of warriors*
*Who quietly move through the gate*
*In readiness for what will come*

Two nights before the planned departure, after feasting,
Escalios took his friend aside and spoke in private to him.

"My friend,"
              Escalios began,
                              "sharp-eyed as you are,
You will have noted that our youths train not with horses
But with arms."

Ever-vigilant Odysseus, who had seen glimpses
Of men at work with their long wicked spears,
Their bronze swords, richly chased, sharp edged,
Clashing against the round shining shields,
Heavy with ornament, of intricate design,
And archers straining their bows skyward

As they quickly drew arrows from their thick-packed quivers,
Soon was aware that their Corinthian escort
Had more in mind than social intercourse.
He nodded but said nothing, listening carefully.

"Know then, the terrible cost of our return.
Great storms, sent from the vengeful Gods,
Scattered the fleet, as you know to your cost,
And many who survived to the edge of the storm
Perished on cruel rocks, following the false beacon
Set by Nauplios—may he in Hades suffer
Eternal torments!—in revenge for the killing
Of his son, Palamedes the traitor, as you yourself exposed.
Nor did his villainies end there, but spread on land
Persuading queens and wives to lovers and to murder.
Our great lord Agamemnon, as you know,
Butchered by Clytemnestra and Aegisthus,
His death avenged by matricide and retribution;
Orestes, now our king, maddened, only cured
Through trials, family revelations, and dangers
Beyond comprehension.
And Diomedes, our greatest warrior, Achilles excepted,
Returned to false accusations, betrayed by his wife,
Saved only by temple sanctuary, then fleeing,
Coming here to join other heroes wronged,"
                                        (here Odysseus gasped)
"Then helping them, through fierce expeditions,
To regain their lands—but not his own.
Great-hearted Diomedes has left Hellas
To find his fortune in the western lands
Far, far from his better homeland memories."

Silence, and darkness, save for the flickering torches
That partially revealed their somber faces,
Lay heavy in the still chamber, pregnant with memory.
After a time, the veteran warrior stirred and spoke.

"Escalios, harsh news you give me,
With surprises I wish had not been sprung.
Ignorant I have been for ten lonely years
As I struggled to return to wife and home,
And for the two years past I have not heard

What had transpired on the mainland,
Other than the Atreus tragedy
And what Telemachus had gleaned
From Pylos Nester and Spartan Menelaos.
But tell me, what now is happening
Here in the Argolid? Who rules, and where?"

Escalios's voice dropped lower, barely a whisper now:

"Most of our land is ruled by King Orestes,
Who has given Tiryns to Pylades, his dear friend,
Whose wife is now Electra,"
                                    (Odysseus raised an eyebrow
But said nothing)
                    "but Argos, ostensibly his city,
Since he became king when young Cylorabes,
Son of Sthenelos, whom you know well,"

(Odysseus nodded)
                    "died early in his reign,
Is still ruled by Sthenelos's other son, Cometes,
Who through Nauplios's seductive means
Became the lover of Aegiala, wife of Diomedes,
With the result you know. Be wary
If you go there; they know that Diomedes is your friend
And you could threaten them.
But of more import is Mycenae
And what the king, Orestes, has in mind.
For our lord has ambitions."

"War?"
            interrupted the wise veteran, sharp eared.
"I saw your men in training. This is no social jaunt
When they accompany us."

Escalios smiled.

"I knew you would see clearly what is happening,
And now you shall know all.
Orestes now commands the Argolid,
Or most of it, at least. And he has shown himself
Capable as a ruler, more in control
Than his illustrious father ever was."

Both men smiled knowingly.

"And now he looks northward for new lands:
Arcadia he now covets."

"Arcadia!"
              exclaimed Odysseus, brow creased,
"I have not travelled there, but I have heard
How fierce and inhospitable that rugged country is.
Few if any joined us for the War with Ilion,
And all entreaties were rejected."

"You have said well,"
                     Escalios replied,
"But Orestes, still driven as before,
Fixes upon its conquest. And I tell you, my friend,"

Earnestly peering in his companion's face
Seen in the uncertain torch light,

"Think clearly when you see him,
For he will ask you without doubt
To join his expedition. And I think
That he will not allow you to leave otherwise."

Silence again, shadows flickering on stone walls.
Again neither stirred, both deep in thought.
Then spoke Odysseus, his words chosen carefully.

"Again my grateful thanks, Escalios.
Pythia's words already take on flesh.
I will consider well what you have said.
My situation, as you know, must take in Telemachus;
But you will hear in future days
What my actions are. For now we will be silent.
And never fear, dear friend, of my betrayal—
Your words I will hold close, and none shall harm you."

All had been said; both separated; and that night
Each struggled with his thoughts, aware
That again events were growing to envelope them
And all their world.

Finally, on a sun-drenched day, the troop,

Both Corinthian and Ithacan, were equipped to leave.
As they prepared to mount, their armour gleaming,
Their horses snorting, impatient to be on their way,
Odysseus took leave of Escalios, who had been carried
Outside to witness their departure. He stood,
Supported by his retainers, proud and straight,
And after bidding farewell to his Corinthian youths,
Splendid with their horses, he turned to his friend.

"My good friend, greatest hero and adventurer among us,
May the Gods lighten your journey, and may you
Learn all that you need to speed your quest."

Odysseus embraced him gently, saying,

"Escalios, both your friendship and your generosity I cherish.
I will return with your Corinthian youths
And all that you have given us, I promise.
And may the memories of our visit linger with us both."

Then he mounted his horse, leading the way,
And all the others mounted,
And the troop, glorious in its number and youth,
With the veteran Ithacans leading with Odysseus,
Started down from the citadel, and Escalios saw them
Descend to the plain, the glitter of their procession
Diminishing as they wound their way onto the road
That led them deep into the lands of the Argolid.

# Canto 2
# THE ARGOLID

Soon the glittering troop came to the edge of the verdant plain,
Entering a narrow valley through which the river ran,
Longopotamo, its banks lined with wild pear trees and myrtles,
And as they rode, Odysseus and Telemachus conversed,
The other senior Ithacans discretely hanging back
To let son and father talk without hindrance.
Odysseus began:

"My son, you have noticed many scars upon my body,
Many the result of battles in the War with Ilion
And others which you yourself witnessed struck—
And returned with interest"—

                (both chuckled in the memory)

"In our coastal raids before we undertook this journey.
But one—you've seen it on my thigh, a harsh slash
Upon the flesh—is one that gives me fondest memories,
One which betrayed my true self to our faithful nurse
When I returned to Ithaca, disguised.
I have not told you until now how it was inflicted
But our trek to Delphi brings back that youthful time.
Know then, that my grandfather, the wily Autolycus,
Famous for guile and theft, who gave me my name
Odysseus—the Son of Pain—took me to hunt
Upon the brow of Mount Parnassus, accompanied
By his sons, my uncles, but without Laertes,
Your grandfather and my respected father.
My uncles were very like their father,
Exuberant and gamesome, ready to risk all
For the excitement and the danger,
Balancing on the cliff's edge, fighting each other
Like lion clubs mauling among themselves at deadly play—

Not like their brother, my father, more grave and serious.
I will not relate to you our glorious ascent
Among the tree-laden ridges of the holy mountain
Until we reached a deeply wooded glen,
A huge boar bursting from its dark thicket,
Raking my thigh with its white tusk
As I speared through its shoulder and laid it in the dust.
Then could I wonder at my family's prowess,
My uncles skillful in their binding of the wound,
My grandfather's magic craft to staunch the blood,
And, later, their munificence with gifts that I took proudly home.
Almost three decades now since that precious time,
And with the war and my long-delayed return
I have lost word of them and their exploits.
No time for us to find and meet with them on this quest;
Perhaps another journey."

And for a brief, brief instant
Odysseus, travel weary, sighed, then turned back to his son,
Who had listened closely, yet a new image forming of his father.

Now the track narrowed, the horses filing one by one,
Across a difficult and rocky ground, surrounded on all sides
By dark pine-crowned hills, above which hawks and eagles soared.
For some miles along this rough stony path all conversation ceased,
Until the way broke out to a small plain, broken by low hills
And crisscrossed by innumerable small streams, now mostly dry.
Westward on this plain, its cyclopean walls looming,
Standing on land elevated from the surrounding plain,
Cleonae, merchant rich, spread its flourishing structures.
As the troop bypassed the vibrant city, Telemachus
Drew abreast of his renowned father, and they talked again.

"Telemachus,"
Odysseus spoke quietly, so that no other heard him,

"Mycenae we will see before night falls, and we must prepare
For what will follow then. You have heard, no doubt,
From your new friend, Polymedes, the terrible story
Of King Agamemnon's return and murder,
And the matricide of Orestes, his son, now king there

After the Athenian trial where he was proclaimed justified
In the cruel slaughter that he perpetrated.
Orestes now rules over these lands fully, as his father did;
But I have heard that his ambition grows
And he harbours plans to have his kingdom grow
Through Arcadia—that is why you see your new friends
Outfitted, not for peaceful journeys, but for war,
Their armour and their weapons with them,
Ready to join his forces in Mycenae.
Sometime after we arrive there, Orestes will ask us
To join him in his fierce campaign.
Given our vulnerable state, the choice may not be ours,
But if it is, I do not wish to force you to a war
That you may not wish to join. Keep in mind
That Arcadia is no easy prize to win:
It is a rough and mountainous country,
Full of independent cities and with warlike peoples,
Who know their country intimately
And can be counted on to hold their own
At great cost to themselves and those who fight them.
You may not wish to tell me now, so soon after this hearing;
But I must know your wishes before Mycenae."

Telemachus, face flushed, eyes shining,
Answered his father:

"I have suspected some plan was afoot
As I watched Polymedes and the others
Training apart from us with different weapons.
He could not tell me anything of this concern
But his hints and slips made me realize
That this troop riding with us is for a purpose
Not understood till now. And with your revelation
I see where all this leads. And, father,"

(Here he turned to Odysseus as they rode,
Looking straight into his eyes)

"Long have I envied you your exploits in the Trojan War,
With no chance to show my own prowess
Except in the coastal raids and in the Delphi skirmishes.

This opportunity I cannot refuse; I must accept it,
And willingly will follow you into its heart,
If you, wise and wily as you are, conclude it best."

Odysseus smiled wearily but proudly.

"You have the spirit of your fathers—and your mother.
We will agree to it. But soon we must tell the others—
Quietly, for these plans are all in stealth, for maximum surprise.
Soon we will come to Nemea, stopping there to rest;
Then will we reveal what we have talked about,
And persuade our followers to fight with us."

By this time they had crossed the plain,
And they came abruptly to a narrow pass,
Through which they wound, rocky hills looming on either side,
The road more rugged than before.
Suddenly they came to a small circular plain,
In the midst of which arose a shining temple.

"The Vale of Nemea,"
$\qquad$ said Halitherses reverently,

"Where Zeus is worshiped for his great son's victory,
Mighty Heracles, who here battled the unconquered Nemean lion,
And with his bare hands cracked its neck bones in strangling it."

"We will rest here and pay our respects to the Lightning Thrower
And his glorious son,"
$\qquad$ said Odysseus.

All dismounted, and libations made to the God and demi-God.
Then Odysseus quietly drew his men together
And told them of what was to come.
There was no hesitation; all agreed, greedy to win renown
And spoil in such a vast endeavour.
In full knowledge the whole troop mounted again
To leave the sacred vale.

The road presently grew more rugged yet, more difficult,
And they passed through a steep defile, narrow and rough,
And when they came out they found
Before them and a little to the west

The hill rising to the great isolated rock and citadel
Of Mycenae, its huge cyclopean walls surrounding it
On all sides except the south, precipitous.
Then Polymedes spurred his horse to ride up to Odysseus.

"Great sir,"
      he began,
            "if you would not mind,
Let my men and me approach the guard first;
They know us from previous trips; this will smooth our way."

The warrior acquiesced, and the Corinthians wheeled up
To take the lead. Soon they came to the outbuildings
Of the acropolis, busy with the workings of the town;
Many looked up from their labour to see the horsemen
And regard the strangers' horses following behind.
Now they came to an outpost, guards posted,
Where they stopped for Polymedes to negotiate their passage.

"Officers of Mycenae, please tell our king, Orestes,
That we bring with us the great King Odysseus and his friends,
To greet him."

      The officer saluted and gave orders
To two of his men, who, with him, glanced back to see
The famous hero; then the two left for the citadel.
But even as they went, through the huge lion gates
Came a small noble delegation to greet the troop
Which had been seen approaching from afar.

"Welcome, famed Odysseus,"
        one of them, tall and distinguished, said,
"Be pleased to come with us to meet our lord,
Who is delighted that you come."

      The company dismounted,
And followed as the delegation walked with Odysseus, his son,
Medon, and Halitherses up the gradual road to the great gate.
For a moment Telemachus paused
To look up at the imposing structure,
With two lions reared high upon the arch,

Then caught up, the troop moving up the ramped stairway,
Turned and climbed steeper steps,
Wound through the streets, and approached the palace
With its massive stairs and spacious courtyard.
The building itself loomed large but stark, brooding as the walls.
They crossed through the propylon to the vestibule,
Then entered the main hall. Here they saw a central hearth,
Its fires dimmed, and beyond that, against an immense wall
On which were carved the two lions raging still,
Was set a royal dais and two thrones,
Cloths of vivid red thrown over them. Before them,
Clothed in black robes, but with glittering diadems
Caught in the shafts of light from openings above,
Stood Orestes and his queen, Hermione.
Odysseus quickly studied the king as he strode forward:
Taller, older than he would have seemed from his age,
His face still shadowed by what he had been through.

*He's filling out,*
            Odysseus thought,
                        *much of his father*
*Seen in attitude and stance, but with his mother's driven gaze.*

But Telemachus almost stopped and gasped,
For it was not the king that he saw first,
But Hermione, a tall woman
Of unutterable, unbearable beauty,
Who stood gravely watching them approach.
He had met her mother, Helen, on his Spartan journey,
And there had noted her unearthly beauty;
But her daughter, still youthful, had a mysterious air
That her mother, mature and world weary, did not possess.

As they came before the dais, Orestes raised his hand
And spoke in a voice hoarse but with authority:

"Welcome, illustrious Odysseus, great hero,
Support and staff of my father, Agamemnon,
In the War with Ilion. I am sorry that he himself
Is not here to greet you in gratitude and joy,
But we both know that is not possible."

Odysseus nodded gravely.

"Let me in his place give your accomplishment full recognition,
And all hospitality to you and your gallant entourage."

Odysseus gracefully replied,
                                "My thanks, great king,
I knew your father well, and still feel the tragedy
Rained down upon the ill-fated house of Atrides;
But now I see that the line has not failed
With such a noble king as you upon the throne—
And indeed"
                    (his sharp eyes searching Orestes's lineaments)
"I see the father living still in his admirable son."

Orestes flushed, but said nothing as Odysseus went quickly on.

"Allow me to present my companions. First, my son,
Telemachus."

                        The two young men acknowledged each other
As well-bred men must do; but each quietly took in the other:
Orestes the elder, but with a mien much older, more worn
Than the younger man; both promising the fierce strength
Of their powerful fathers.

The others introduced, Odysseus then turned toward the lovely consort.

"Hermione, gracious queen, you were but a child
When I first saw you. But now you are as beautiful
As your wondrous mother, Helen, whom all the world admired."

Hermione coloured slightly,
But graciously received the compliment.
Formalities completed, Orestes
Invited his travel-weary guests
To refresh themselves, then return for feasting in the night.
Quarters were appointed, servants were assigned,
And the honoured guests were cleansed in marble baths,
Oiled and clad in fresh garments.
Back to the great hall they went, where the fires
Of the central hearth blazed, and torches lined the splendid walls.
Sacrifices made, libations poured and drunk,

Feasting began in earnest. Odysseus sat with Orestes,
Telemachus beside Hermione.
For a time, little of consequence was said,
The sating of hunger and of thirst
More paramount. Then Orestes turned to his guest,
Asking him the reason for his visit.
Wary Odysseus repeated his tale
As he had for Escalios,
His utterance holding all in thrall
As does the power of a great singer's voice soaring
On the graceful wings of a fine song.

Moved, Orestes sighed, sat silent for a moment.

"Tomorrow we will speak more of this. But now,
Please grant me one boon. As you know, I was young
When my father left for Ilion; I remember him
Imperfectly, like the flickering of this fire.
You of all men, excepting my uncle Menelaos,
Knew him best. Tell me, if you will, what he was like."

Odysseus stayed silent for a moment, sipping wine.

"My lord, I also knew you as a young boy,
And I know too well how time shreds our knowledge of the past.
But I will try to tell you of your father
So that his image can live in harmony with you.
Agamemnon was indeed a forceful ruler:
Only he could have brought all Achaeans together
For the huge expedition to the shores of Ilion;
Only he could have kept them there for ten long years
Filled with battle, plague, and death;
Only he could have razed a great city to the ground,
Led the greatest war we have known.
As a man he was of mighty build, a fierce warrior,
Who killed more than his share of brave heroes.
He lacked nothing in courage and authority,
A man to be proud to have as father."

Odysseus ceased; silence crept through the hall
Against the crackling of the hearth's fire.
Finally, Orestes spoke, his voice still huskier with emotion.

"I was told, great Odysseus, of your persuasive voice,
But not till now did I realize its radiant power.
My deep gratitude for giving me my father,
Now live again, fixed in my mind by your eloquence."

Murmurs now could be heard as those at the feast,
Relieved that the two kings were so much in accord,
Returned to feasting and to conversation.
But then Odysseus, waiting for a tactful time,
Addressed his fellow king again.

"Most honoured Orestes, forgive my curiosity;
I have had little word reach me since my return,
And I know only of your blessed triumph
Vindicated by Athena's judgement,
Wise Goddess and friend of us both, in the trial at Athens.
If you feel willing, please recount to me what happened to you
After that great moment."

The murmur stopped; all looked toward the king,
Across whose face, as with the fire, flickered haunted memories.

"Good Odysseus, to no one else would I recount those days,
But as you were my father's greatest ally, on whom success
At Ilion depended, and who has grieved over this great king's loss,
I will tell you all, holding nothing back, so that you will know
The harsh cost of this kingship to our house of Atrides.
Know then, that although the trial acquitted me,
And Athena ordered the Erinyes to cease their harassment,
Even then my mind continued in disorder,
My wits broken and cracked like fallen tiles,
No pattern or meaning to my dread thoughts.
At times I found I could think lucidly,
Seeing clearly my dear friend Pylades,
And my sister Electra, so close to me;
Then my vision changed, shifted to distorted images,
Nightmares in the day, where I saw again
My mother pleading, my sword plunged in her breast,
Her blood washing over her polluted robes
As her shrill cry echoed in the palace.
I saw again the two slaughtered bodies
Heaped together, and then as if in an embrace,

Some ghastly repetition of their shame,
Their unlawful and unholy coupling.
And when I bathed, slaves gently washing me,
The water would turn red, and beside me I could see
My father's body, slashed and bloody, still in its death throes.
Sleep became, as before, a horror, as did waking hours.
In desperation I travelled to Troezen, seeking in the waters
Of the Horse's Fount some purification in that place
Where holy Pegasus struck with his hoof and waters answered.
The Troezen citizens, seeing me defiled, would not receive me;
I had to stay in a building built to keep me separate.
But their cleansing was to no avail; my fits of madness
Still drove me ever onward. Finally, I returned to Delphi,
Where the Pythia foretold that I would be rid of these horrors
If I could fetch from Tauris the statue of Artemis.
This answer disturbed me almost as much as my madness—
In Scythia, as is well known, strangers are not welcomed,
And those who stray within its borders are put to death,
Thrown into the sacred fire in the temple of Artemis.
But I had no option but to go,
And faithful Pylades came with me.
In Tauris we were captured, taken before the priestess
With the certain knowledge of our imminent death.
But, in a strange and wondrous way, as we were questioned by her
We learned by common knowledge that she was my sister,
Fair Iphigenia, who was supposed
To have been sacrificed at Aulis,
But now was mistress of the temple, bound to Artemis.
She herself knew nothing of how she had got there;
The last thing living in her memory
Was the delegation sent by her father,
With you, Odysseus, at its head, who was to bring her to Aulis,
Supposedly to wed the great Achilles.
I was but a boy when the sacrifice at Aulis took place
And did not see it happen; but a whole army did.

"After our astonishment and joyous reunion,
She proved herself resourceful and brave:
Under pretext of the need to purify it
After its defilement by the presence of strangers,

She brought Artemis's statue with her to the beach;
Then she came with us to our ships off shore.
But storms delayed our return to Mycenae,
For we were blown off course and around the Peloponnesos,
Eventually forced to land in Delphi, where we brought the statue.
While we were thus occupied, a messenger came to Electra,
Falsely saying that Pylades and I
Had both been sacrificed there in Tauris.
Aletes, son of Aegisthus and my mother, hearing that our line
Was now extinct, seized the throne, and Electra fled
With the messenger to Delphi to find out about our deaths.
We arrived on the same day, and when my sisters met,
The false messenger accused her of my murder. Electra,
In her fury and her grief, seized a burning brand
And would have killed her own sister, had not I
Appeared and intervened. We dispatched the messenger;
Then all of us returned to Mycenae,
Where I at last confronted Aletes
And killed him, returning the throne to its rightful heirs.
The statue I took to Athens, as I had promised;
And there it was installed, and its priestess:
For Iphigenia, who for so many years had seen
Innumerable victims slaughtered at its altar
Heard within herself the Goddess call
To keep her image pure in that lawful city.
Then, returning to Mycenae, I joyed
In the marriage of Electra to Pylades, my dearest friend.
Now, sane again, my kingdom strong, secure,
My thoughts turned to marriage for myself,
And thus to Hermione, promised to me by Tyndareus,
Her grandfather, her father gone to Ilion and to war."

"But," he said, turning to his queen inquiringly,
"Perhaps you should now tell your side of this story."

"As you wish,"
                  replied Hermione, after hesitation.
"You remember, King Odysseus, how as a child,
I was sent to live in Mycenae with my aunt
While the war raged in Ilion, both parents caught on either side.
After the terrible deeds done here, my betrothed maddened,"

(Here torn looks of anguish they exchanged)

"Neoptolemos, Achilles's famous son, arrived to claim me,
Asserting that I had been promised to him in the war
By my thoughtless father Menelaos,
And producing witnesses to testify
That he had done so. The citadel in chaos,
Orestes insane on his sick bed, there was nothing we could do;
And Neoptolemos took me, against my will,
Across the dark seas to his palace in distant Epirus.
There I became,"

                she said, tears welling in her lovely eyes,
"His wife, but shared his bed with his concubine,
Andromache, widow of ill-fated Hector, great prince of Troy.
She, poor woman, haunted still by her great misfortune,
Had already borne him a son, Amphialos, and a second child
Was on the way. It was clear that this arrangement could not last:
I was childless, and could be cast away as queen,
To be another slave, another concubine. But the Gods relented:
Neoptolemos became haunted
By a fear of Apollo's retribution
For his arrogance in demanding
Reparation for his father's death.
He made preparations for a lengthy stay,
Determined to win the God's favour, and sailed for Delphi."

"And,"

        said Orestes, interrupting her,

                    "here is where our tales merge.
When I had regained my sanity and kingdom,
I realized that Neoptolemos had taken her away
And I determined to recover her, my prior claim the stronger.
As it came to pass, I arrived in Epirus just after he had left,
And Hermione herself asked me to take her away.
Then we returned, and I assembled troops and quickly sailed to Delphi.
There the Delphians I persuaded that
Neoptolemos, arrogant as ever,
Had come, not out of piety to gain the favour of the God,
But to rob his temple. Outraged, the Delphians joined my troops
And we screened ourselves among the foliage of the laurel trees
Outside the temple, our weapons drawn.

As Neoptolemos emerged from the temple, we attacked.
A formidable warrior, as you can attest."

(Here Odysseus nodded knowingly)

                                    "He fought back bravely,
Killing many, but he was finally overwhelmed,
A mob madly hacking at his body, covered with countless wounds.
And so,"
            he said, with a grim smile,
                                    "I won back my wife,
My kingdom, and my house."

                        "And now,"
                                    Hermione said,
With a smile far more contented,
                                    "that house continues
With our son, Tisamenos."

"And may it continue longer,"
                        responded the gallant Odysseus,

And king and queen both smiled at him gratefully.

Now, only the embers of the central hearth glowing,
And the sputtering torches almost expended,
The darkened figures took their leave, each to allotted sleep.
But for Odysseus, sleep brought no rest.

*Hulking*
*The ruler stood*
*Legs planted arrogantly*
*Swart-faced*
*Beard tailored*
*For maximum effect*
*Eyes watchful*
*Deep set*
*Under forested brows*
*Deep organ voice*
*Cacophony*
*When angered*
*Laced leather*
*Strained on the massive chest*

*Gold and bronze*
*On helmet*
*Greaves*
*Huge ornamented sword*
*Arms built to kill*
*Body thick*
*Powerful*
*Deadly*
*For thrust of spear*
*Will stubborn*
*Or vacillating*
*Ambitious*
*Greedy*
*Wind blown*
*Hard to keep on course*
*But showed concern*
*At times*
*Not a man to trust*
*As friend*

*Iphigenia*
*So young*
*Tall for her age*
*Lissome*
*Large dark eyes*
*Open wide*
*Guileless*
*My plot*
*My deception*
*Her look when told*
*Marriage to Achilles*
*Journey to Aulis*
*Found the slave*
*Also tall and lissome*
*Both drugged*

*Iphigenia smuggled aboard*
*A secret ship*
*Sent to Tauris*
*A legend spread in Tauris*
*Suddenly discovered at the altar*

*Drug dazed*
*Made priestess*
*But no one knew*
*Especially her parents*

*The slave*
*Dressed and veiled*
*The bridal sacrifice*
*Still drugged*
*Supported to the altar*
*Throat cut beneath the veil*
*Blood soaking the white robes*
*The white skin*
*Neither parent*
*Could watch*

*And no one knew*
*No one*
*Still knows*
*But me*
*And Artemis*
*No way to tell then*

*And so*
*Clytemnestra's hatred*
*Aegisthus's triumph*
*Agamemnon's doom*
*Consequences*

As Eos spread her warm fingers
Caressing the mountain peaks and searching through
The shadows of the foothills and the plains,
Odysseus stood on the terrace edge
Looking at the vast plain and, beyond, the sea
Emerging in the dawn's mild light.
Through the plain cut a new road, rivers bridged with stone,
In the hazy distance incomplete, construction-littered.
Lush fields and olive groves patterned the fecund tract.
Down that road lay Argos and Tiryns,
Their fate pondered by the cunning warrior
Who knew Orestes would reveal what he had planned.

Then, turning, he studied the steepening hills,
The distant peaks past which lay Arcadia,
Rugged, foreboding, unknown.
What strands the Fates wove in both directions
He waited to discover and untangle.
Helios and his fiery horses now
Began their arcing passage through the sky
And Odysseus left the verge to meet his fellow king.

After their greeting in the hall, Orestes led his guest
To a smaller room, secure from lurking ears,
And there he spoke directly to him.

"Odysseus, I do not underrate your clear-sighted wisdom:
You know a martial force rode with you,
And I am sure Escalios told you what he knew."

Odysseus nodded, but said nothing for the moment.

"But know this: I revere my father,
Who thought he sacrificed a daughter and avenged a brother
To level Troy; but also sought to bring back booty,
Fill his treasury with the wealth of Ilion,
And celebrate his wealth and power.
But my path, which may lead to honour and to glory,
Is much different, although I learned from his deeds
That greatness here involves alliance with other Achaeans,
However scattered and contentious they may be,
But more is necessary. We need"
                        (Odysseus noted the plural)
"To unite the whole Argolid with a single ruler,
To eliminate the rifts and feuds and raids
That plague us, to let this country grow in peace and bounty,
Formidable in size and wealth: a mighty Argolid.
But,"
        he continued, glancing out a window to the north-west,
"This country could be more, my dream more mighty.
From those mountains and beyond lay tribes
More distant from us and more troublesome—
You remember how few answered my father's call,
How difficult they were in counsel."

Again, a silent nod.

"We need a country without friction at its borders,
And certain knowledge that peace can be kept there.
Therefore, Arcadia must be taken for the Argolid.
Then, with our strong ties to Sparta,
Much of the Peloponnesos is in our influence.
But, for this to happen, I need strong leaders for my warriors,
Men with experience and courage, exemplary, heroic.
You, the architect of Troy's downfall, are by far the best of these.
I ask you to join with me and general this great campaign."

For a long moment there was silence, each watching closely
The other to reveal himself. Then Odysseus, who already knew
What he wished to say and do, replied.

"Orestes, I respect your great ambition and fine plan;
Even your astute father, who could call on all Achaeans,
Would not conceive a plan so far seeing and so wise.
The scope of it excites me, and I'm sure my son, Telemachus,
Would find it equally exciting and would be the first to volunteer.
But, as I have told you, I am not free to act as I wish—
Apollo and Poseidon both direct my destiny.
And only when my penance is fulfilled may I be left
To do whatever next my moira ordains."

At this Orestes's face darkened, and Odysseus saw
He was controlled by the same black anger
That was the flaw seen in Agamemnon.
Odysseus knew that Orestes could not afford
To let him, his son, and men live to betray his plan
If they refused to serve him. But still he spoke.

"Also, my fellow king, for twenty years my bed was empty
Before I returned from Ilium; only two years
Have passed for me at home, and now I must voyage again,
With yet another onerous task to fulfill."

Orestes's eyes were black, his mouth a thin white slit,
His lips the edges of two sharp knives.

"Yet there may be a way for me to serve you,
If only for a time. The prophecy has said that I

Must visit many towns and cities; it does not say
*How* I must visit them."

The hardness in Orestes's face relaxed slightly.

"Therefore, I could serve your campaign for the first part
Before I journey on to Sparta."

Orestes considered what Odysseus had said, then replied,

"But your own words would lead to larger service.
There are many towns and cities in Arcadia to serve your need,
And greater glory is the outcome."

In response, the wily veteran chose words carefully.

"What you say is true in part, my respected lord,
But time is also paramount, for Poseidon will not wait long,
And if he is angered, both your plans and mine will go awry.
But,"
  he continued, before Orestes could respond,
"Apart from what I do in this campaign,
Where early victories can strike fear into an enemy,
And assist the later battles, if you will agree
To my participation in that limited way,
I will do you a service much more close to home,
And one as important, as I guess."

Orestes, now less angered and more thoughtful, replied,

"I would be loath to lose you part way through,
But if this other service is important, then I might consider it."

Odysseus, having laid the bait, now sprang the trap:

"The Argolid itself is almost yours—I have seen the road you build
To join the plain and sea with you—but yet only 'almost.'
Argos"
   —here Orestes came alert—
        "remains in hands
You cannot trust. And without Argos
Your country and your highway are in peril."

Orestes bit his lip and then replied,

"Argos is indeed in wrong hands. Yet my own hands are tied.
I cannot move on it without outrage in the country
And a possibility of civil war. What could be done, then?"

Odysseus smiled and said,
                                "Give me your promise
That I will be released from your campaign
After the winning of Arcadia's eastern part,
And I will guarantee that Argos will be yours."

Perplexed, the young king said,

"I do not see how Argos can be mine,
But if you can convince me that it will be,
I will make such a promise."

Odysseus smiled again.

"I will convince you by the act, not by my words.
You will know when it is done; better
You are ignorant till then. But when it does happen,
I have your word?"

Silence. Then Orestes spoke.
                                "My word."

And the two kings eyed each other levelly.

A few days passed, with feasting and fine hospitality;
But Odysseus quietly met with his son and men
And with their escort of Corinthians to lay his plans.
During this time Telemachus was also occupied,
Entranced in the company of the queen, Hermione.
Royal women he had known—
Penelope, his mother, Helen, and other consorts he had met
While searching for his father—but here was someone
Closer to his own age, in the full bloom of mature youth.
She, for her part, was intrigued and flattered
By a man still young and innocent but powerfully built
And lit by the glow of his father's reputation.
But at all times she made sure that they saw each other
Only at feasting, or with her slaves and ladies in attendance.
For Telemachus this was not enough; in the throes

Of a first passion he suffered, knowing well
The eyes of both Orestes and his father were upon him
And that no good could come of such involvement.
So, during the day, he sparred with his friend Polymedes,
Gaining skill in sword and spear and horsemanship.

His father, seeing his son's condition and his fierce training,
One day went riding with him, just the two, alone.
For a time they cantered in silence, savouring
The crisp morning air, the scents of pine and olive,
Shrub and flower as they traversed the lower hills and plain.
Then the father, glancing at his son, began.

"Hermione is lovely, is she not? A true daughter
Of her mother, Helen, most beautiful of women."

His son, face flushed, nodded his agreement.

"Do you know why I went with Agamemnon to the war?
Not for any enmity with Ilion, so distant from us,
But through my own stratagem, caught in my own web.
The power of Helen's incomparable beauty,
Herself then younger than Hermione,
Also conquered me; I was a suitor with many others,
And could see that I was not favoured by her or her father,
Tyndareus, not ruling so great a country as others,
And, also, that civil war could break out among her suitors,
A true catastrophe among our peoples.
I therefore advised Tyndareus that all the suitors
Take an oath that they would defend and fight for
Him chosen as her husband against any wrong
Done against him in regard to the marriage.
But in return I asked for—and got—Penelope, your mother,
Whose beauty can't compare with that of Helen
But whose deep abiding love fostered mine.
Then, as you know, Helen chose Menelaos.
And then came her kidnap and the call to arms
To fulfill the oath taken by all.
I tried to avoid my own device,
Pretending madness, but was discovered
When Palamedes put you as an infant
In front of my oxen as I ploughed a barren earth,

And I was forced to stop and to reveal myself.
Twenty lonely years passed then,
But always I have had your mother in my heart,
Even now, torn from each other once more
To fulfill this final quest."

Odysseus now fell silent, and they spurred to a gallop;
But Telemachus understood what his father meant
By these words, and though his feelings raged still in him,
He knew that he would now endure.

Word spread that Odysseus and his company
Would soon leave to visit Pylades and Electra
And the Corinthian company return home.
Following the still incomplete road by Argos
On a day still freshening, the diminished band set forth,
Showing off their new-mastered horsemanship.
Across the plain they cantered, easily travelling
The new-made road. Soon the majestic citadel dwindled,
Vanishing in the shimmering air.
Now signs of new construction showed in the piles
Of rock and rubble lining each side of the road,
And next workers toiled around them, levelling the land,
Packing the dense earth and hoisting stones to line the way.
As they continued farther, they broke through the dust and haze
And saw rich Argos close at hand, its buildings
Gleaming in the late morning light. Veering off the road
They travelled through the streets past rich merchants' houses,
Ending at the acropolis at the palace front.
A captain of the guard there confronted them,
Asking who they were and for what purpose they arrived.

"Tell the king Cometes that an old companion of his father,
Odysseus, comes to pay his respects to his honoured son."

The guard withdrew; and presently returned
To invite them to dismount and enter in.
They did so, leaving their mounts in the hands of slaves
Who quickly had appeared to do this service.
The hall they entered was not so magnificent
As that found in Mycenae, yet rich decoration
Filled its walls, and at the end a dais held

Two thrones enriched in gold, with great fur rugs
Spread over it, spilling onto the floor.
On them sat Cometes and Aegiala,
Once wife to Diomedes, and now mistress-queen.
Both smiled with hospitality and greeting,
But their eyes were wary and mistrustful.

"Welcome, mighty Odysseus,"
                              began Cometes,
His voice higher than it seemed it should be,
Given his bulky frame and opulent robes,

"It is an honour that you grace our threshold.
We had heard that you were come to King Orestes
But are surprised that you have deigned to visit us.
What brings you to the Argolid and here?"

Odysseus, smiling, said,
                          "My fellow king
I have a task ordained by Phoebus Apollo
That will take me through many towns and cities,
Many countries, before I can complete it.
This quest has therefore brought me to the Argolid
Where I am happy to be meeting so many
From the war, or their descendants. In this way
I visited our fellow king, Orestes, and am now
On my way to Tiryns, to Pylades and his wife Electra.
But passing here, I felt I must see the son
Of my old fighting friend, Sthenelos,
And hear what news, if any, of his father."

"The news is ominous,"
                        replied Cometes, relieved to hear
Why Odysseus had come, yet not altogether ready
To receive his guest at face value.

"We have heard he may be slain in a campaign
He waged in Cilicia, at Soli, but we have heard nothing more
As yet."

        Odysseus looked grave.
                              "Bad news indeed!
Let us hope that as it lives as rumour, it may die as one as well.

I should grieve if it were true. A friend to have in battle,
None better, excepting the incomparable Achilles,
And Sthenelos's own close friend, and mine as well,
Diomedes."

            At this Aegiala paled and Cometes's
Own face darkened, but for the moment he said nothing.

Odysseus continued,
                "But where is Diomedes,
So at home here? And where is his wife? I have not met her,
But she was never far from her husband's thoughts
And he spoke often to me of her. Where is she now?"

Aegiala reddened, and her eyes grew black with hate;
Cometes himself, suffused with rage, snarled,

"How dare you hurl sly insults at us and breach our hospitality!
You know full well that Diomedes is not here
And that his wife is now my queen!"

Odysseus, still mild, replied,
                 "I had heard rumours
Of what you say, but could not believe them."

Now, stern, commanding:
                "I could not think
That the wife of a man who, as a warrior,
Fought even with the Gods and won, would betray him
With the son of the man who was his dearest friend;
And that this son would leach the honour of two such great men
Both for his lust and his ambition!"

Enraged, Cometes called aloud a signal and drew his sword.

"I did not think you came in peace, sly-tongued as you are,
And will not let you live past your insults!"

As he spoke, guards filled the edges of the hall,
Ready to advance on the small Ithacan band.
Then Odysseus nodded to his son, who on a horn
Concealed till then, blew a clear and powerful note.
Even as the battle joined within the hall,

Sounds of further struggle could be heard outside.
Cometes, maddened, rushed at Odysseus, swinging his sword wildly.
Odysseus barely parried the blow, so fierce it was;
But, turning it, he thrust his sword upward
Through his assailant's stomach and to his heart.
Cometes lurched forward and fell face down.
The battle surged around both the victor and the fallen.
A guard thrust his spear toward Telemachus,
Who, sidestepping, grasped it and pulled the man
Onto his sword, to leave him gasping on the ground.
But the small band was outnumbered
And forced to move together as a compact body.
Aegiala, when she saw her lover slain,
Screeched in anguished rage, and, gripping a dagger
She had concealed, sprang at the unsuspecting
Odysseus, who, engaged with another guard, at the last instant,
Out of the corner of his eye saw a movement
And with instinct honed from war-torn experience,
Slashed sideways, cutting through her breast and shoulder.
She dropped, writhing, to the floor as he, cut slightly
By the soldier in the encounter, was rescued by his son.
At the same moment Polymedes and his men burst in;
Like ants on their colony's mound
Who swarm against the attacks of another host,
So those of Argos met the Corinthians,
But in a brief time the guards were all cut down.
For a moment all was silence except for the laboured breathing
Of the warriors; then Odysseus took stock, counting
Ithacans and Corinthians alike: two of his men were dead,
And several of the others, who had begun their deadly fight
Outside the hall. Odysseus noted servants still cowering
Near the dais, and had his men drag them to the centre of the hall.

"What is your name?"

        "Menodes,"
                replied the stricken man.

"Listen well, Menodes. You have seen what happened here;
I and my friends were suddenly attacked without cause,

When I said nothing but the truth. My herald,"
                                        here he gestured
Toward Medon,
                    "will take one of you to the acropolis
To describe—truthfully—what happened here.
We will follow shortly after, once the rest of you
And others you can call on, have started to remove the bodies
So that all, including our own fallen, can be given
Honourable rites."

            A nod to Medon sent him to choose
The most appropriate, who was Menodes himself,
Who had been in charge of other servants.
Together they left the hall, with two Corinthians,
Passing among citizens who had begun to cram the streets,
Hearing the battle that had taken place. All followed them
To the public place, where Medon, taking the servant with him
To a prominent place where they could be seen,
Addressed the agitated crowd of citizens and merchants,
Some frightened and bewildered, others angry, dangerous.
His magnificent clear voice rang over the multitude,
Whose noise abated and grew silent.

"Citizens of Argos, I come before you as a herald,
Before the coming of my ruler, Odysseus,
Hero of the fall of Ilion and friend to all the Argolid.
I will not tell you what has happened,
But let one of your own describe what occurred
When my companions met with King Cometes,
So that you will learn the truth from one who saw it."

Medon brought before him Menodes, who,
In a voice shaking from fright, described as fully as he could
The meeting with the king, what had been said,
And the battle that transpired, with the deaths
Of Cometes and Aegiala and their guards.

"Did my master ask you to speak of this truthfully?"

"Yes,"
        whispered the servant.

"Louder, so that all will hear."

"Yes, he did,"

Menodes managed in a louder voice.

"And have you done so?"

"I have."

As a stream's current finds in its path a rock or branch,
And in its progress past the obstacle makes a sound
Peculiar to that moment, and such different sounds together
Form a dialogue of water's splashing, gurgling, spray,
So now mutterings flowed through the crowd,
Some of amazement, others frightened, still others
Full of anger and mistrust.
Medon saw the temper of the crowd and spoke again.

"You have heard from your own the truth of what took place.
Now let Odysseus himself speak to the matter."

A hush spread and the crowd parted to let Odysseus,
Striding alone, the others discretely beyond the square,
Cross to the speaking place and turn to them.
As he prepared to speak, a voice cried out against him.
As tributaries of a river, small streams and creeks
With their quiet water discharging into the parent river
When overburdened in the spring by waters from
The snow-capped peaks raise their voices as their waters
Rush forward to meet the river, which now roars
With wild abandon in its swollen state,
So too the crowd, driven by the extreme act,
Roared out its shouts of anger and despair.
Odysseus knew the danger he was in, but signalled
To his men to stay still where they were;
And as the noise of the crowd increased, and movement
Could be seen within it, he prayed to his patroness
And often saviour, Pallas Athena, to give him the power
To sway the crowd to what he said. As in the past,
He felt himself grow stronger in mind and voice.
He spoke, and he was heard above the multitude,
Who quieted, awed by his now commanding presence.

"Citizens of Argos,"

            he began,

                    "hear me before you begin

To judge what I have done."

                     A surly mutter wound through
The crowd, but they remained still, listening closely to his words.

"You have heard what happened from the lips of a man
Who saw the whole thing and was instructed by me
To tell the truth of what he saw. And he has done so.
Do you think that if I wished to kill the king
I would have done so in this fashion, in front of all,
And then sent his own man to describe it for you?"

Again, muttering, but now more indecisive.

"You know who I am and what I have done,
And you know that I helped the Argolid to defeat Troy.
In that long war I was close to two of your greatest heroes,
Diomedes, who, next to Achilles, was our finest warrior,
And Sthenelos, father to Cometes, and himself formidable
In battle. Both these men I revere for their courage
And their loyalty, and I am proud to have been their friend."

From the crowd someone shouted,

                    "Diomedes was a traitor;
It was right that he was banished!"

"On what grounds was your greatest hero thought a traitor?
Is it not that Nauplios persuaded Diomedes's wife, Aegiala,
That Diomedes would bring home another woman in her place?
And did not Aegiala then take Cometes as a lover and become his queen?
And why would Nauplios say what he did? In revenge for his son,
Palamedes, who was discovered to be a traitor at Troy,
And was executed for it. Nauplios has spread lies throughout
The Argolid, causing friction everywhere; and he it was
Who lighted false beacons, luring our Achaean boats
To destruction on the rocks of our own homeland.
Is this the act of a man who wishes good to you?
As for Aegiala, where was her constancy and faith?
My own wife, Penelope, waited faithfully for me

For twice ten years; Aegiala less than ten.
Is this a woman whom you would call queen,
Unfaithful to her husband, banishing him, your greatest hero,
And leaving you with much lessened force
To protect your city and your business?"

Here merchants began to glance at each other in the crowd
As his words sunk in.

"As for Cometes, do you think his father, Sthenelos,
Would have approved of what he did to his best friend,
Taking his wife, banishing him, and ruling in dishonour?"

More murmurings and mutterings in debate amongst themselves.

"You have heard what I said to Cometes and his woman,
And you have heard how we were attacked—an attack premeditated,
Planned before we had arrived. Only the intervention of our friends
Saved us. Is this the way of honourable rulers? Is truth not mentioned here?"

Again, ripples through the crowd, some for, some against, his provocation.

"But now justice has been done; and though I grieve for Sthenelos,
Having had to take the life of his reigning son,
For Diomedes vengeance has been taken."

Before any word could be spoken in the crowd
He quickly spoke again.

"Now you are rulerless, unprotected, a rich prize
For lawless bands who will soon hear of your predicament."

Merchants exclaimed aloud, fearful of their goods and lives.

"But surely you can see what you must do—your eyes
Can tell you without much effort. Look in the distance,
Where the dust of construction fills the sky.
A new road, allowing easy passage of your goods both north
To Corinth, and when finished, south to Nauplia.
And who builds this road? Orestes, fit successor to his father,
The mighty Agamemnon—a man who found vengeance
For his father's murder, even in the punishment of his mother,
And, after long suffering, has been judged innocent
By Athens and by the Gods. Now he rules in the Argolid,

Bringing prosperity and peace to this region,
Even as his new road shows. What better king to rule you?
And what worse king to fear if you deny him?
I did not come with this in mind, he said hastily,
Forestalling thoughts in that direction, for I was
But passing through here on my way to Tiryns
To see King Pylades and his queen, Electra,
And thought only to pause for greetings in rich Argos.
But as we all can see, things do not necessarily turn out
As we would like them to. Now that this has happened,
I suggest that you appoint a delegation to go to Mycenae,
Telling him what has happened and what you intend.
If you wish, my herald Medon will accompany you
Along with some of our Corinthian friends.
You will see that Orestes knew nothing of this,
But I am sure that if you place yourself under his rule
He will act justly and bring you even greater wealth.
What say you to this plan?"

A roar of approval erupted from the crowd,
Which Odysseus let continue for a while,
Then took charge again.

"Since this is your wish, I will leave you to find
Your delegation. All I wish to do now is to give final rites
To all who died here today, as the Gods would wish."

An admiring murmur spread through the now docile citizens,
And as he left the square, loud cheers accompanied him.
The remnant of the day was spent in building funeral pyres
And deciding on the delegation,
And that evening all rites were performed solemnly
With Argos watching and involved with their own griefs
For the guards and their late rulers.

That night, Odysseus lay in the palace,
As did his men and the Corinthians,
Those who were not placed as sentinels.
But no peaceful sleep came to him.

*A good stratagem*
*The Corinthians*

*Disguised*
*Well before us*
*In Argos*
*Waiting*
*For the moment*
*Knowing it would come*

*Aegiala's eyes*
*Black*
*Hate-filled*
*Strong-willed*
*A fit companion for Diomedes*

*Diomedes*
*Tall*
*Thick-muscled*
*No fear of anything*
*Or anyone*
*Crafty*
*But loyal to his friends*
*Fearsome in battle*
*Strong*
*Swift*
*Dense-packed fight*
*His sword flashes*
*Sweeps*
*Cuts through a warrior's neck*
*Head in the dust*
*In one blow*
*Cuts back*
*Carving another's midriff*
*Plunges through another body*
*And out the other side*
*So fast*
*Wherever he is*
*Screams*
*Flight*
*Then caught on his spear*
*Red dust around him*
*Our night excursion*
*The two of us*

*Catching the spy*
*Tricking him to speak*
*My companion*
*With one sweep*
*Cuts off his head*
*Diomedes moves to the tents*
*We kill quietly*
*No sound from sleeping victims*
*Twelve with slit throats*
*Their king*
*Rhesus of Thrace*
*Slain last*
*Black pools staining the moonlight*

*Sthenelos*
*Burly*
*His son much like him*
*Vicious*
*Effective in battle*
*The two*
*Liked killing*
*Liked killing together*

*Palamedes*
*Too intelligent*
*Caught in the war*
*Caught me in the war*
*That finished him*
*A harder excursion*
*Than with Diomedes*
*Lugging the gold*
*To hidden spots in his tent*
*Forging the letter of betrayal*
*The look on his face*
*When accused*
*When the letter found*
*When the gold found*
*He knew what had happened*
*He knew who did it*
*He looked at me*
*As the sword plunged in*

*He died still looking*
*The eyes*
*The eyes*
*Knowing*
*Even in his agony*

*His father*
*Bright too*
*Took revenges*
*His tongue*
*His greatest weapon*
*Clytemnestra to Aegisthus*
*Two families stained*
*Through his words*
*Aegiala to Cometes*
*Another triumph*
*And the false beacon*
*So many ships splintered*
*So dark an ending*
*After victory*
*But he couldn't get me*
*And now he has died*
*As he killed others*
*On the rocks*
*Gasping*
*Broken body*
*Drowning*
*May his agony have been long*
*But it won't bring back*
*Twenty years*
*Twenty long years*

*Years*

Swirls of business the next day:
Delegations of merchants and others seen,
Haggling over who would represent the city,
And, over all, waiting for Mycenae to respond.
That afternoon, Medon returned, along with
The remainder of the Corinthian host,
And announced the imminent arrival

Of Orestes and his own retinue.
Argos quickly gathered to greet him.
From afar they saw the dust arise on the road,
And, as profuse as ants swarming with purpose
Along their wide pathways, an irresistible force,
Orestes's forces could next be seen;
And soon his warriors rode in, a formidable procession.
Then he himself arrived, splendid in his chariot,
His armour gleaming, and his great staff of office
Clutched firmly in his hand. Beside him, dazed
By the honour, rode the servant, then the delegation, and behind them
Marched the remainder of his host, which halted
With him, their great bronze spears foresting the square.
Odysseus met him, and the Argos delegation,
Doing appropriate honours to the ruler of Mycenae.
Orestes warmly greeted them, then turned
To address the citizens of Argos,
Who had watched his host arrive with apprehension.

"Citizens of Argos, hear me speak. Today's dawning
Brings a new world to you; and you, and you alone,
Must decide what that world will be.
I was astonished when I heard of what had happened here,
With the death of your king and queen; I can say
Before the Gods that I had no inkling of this tragedy,
Nor did I do anything to instigate it.
I have heard from your witness and your delegation
The truth of what took place, and it is clear
That Odysseus, famed hero of all Achaeans,
Acted in self defence and is in no way at fault;
By your own words he is innocent in this case."

No sound from Argos; all listened closely,
Not willing to betray themselves by looks or speech.

"I have come because your delegation has invited me,
And asked that I become your ruler."

Again, no sound, not even breathing.

"I have considered this offer, and here is what I say:
I will be your king, but only if you, here, now,

Agree to this, so that all will know that it is not done
By me, or by a few, but by you all, willingly."

Again, silence, with eyes slewing toward the warriors' lines,
Then to each other.

Then Odysseus stepped forward.

"Orestes, Ruler of Mycenae and the Argolid,
Permit me to speak here for a moment?"

Orestes, uncertain of the mood, nodded to him.

"May I suggest to those who represent the city
That they ask by a show of hands if you shall be king?"

Orestes paused for a moment, then again acquiesced.

Odysseus turned to the members of the delegation,
Caught up short, and nodded mildly to them.

Their leader understood, and stepping forward
Called out,
              "Shall Orestes, son of Agamemnon,
Ruler of Mycenae, be our king? Those who think he should,
Raise now your hands."

Some merchants' hands rose quickly; then,
As snow on a mountain peak begins to slide,
A small amount at first, and slowly,
But soon accumulates and grows, roaring down
The mountain slope, overcoming trees and obstacles
With ease; so too the hands began to rise as each man
Looked at others, and soon an avalanche of upraised arms
Proclaimed that a new ruler had been chosen.

Orestes, flushed with the acclamation, cried out,

"Citizens of Argos, I accept your decision—
And you will not regret what you have done!
The new road you see soon approaching you
Is but the first link in a chain of developments
That will increase our peace and our prosperity.
What my intentions are will soon reveal themselves,

And you will not be unhappy with them.
But now, I ask you to leave, while your representatives
And I work out our mutual future."

This said, he gestured to them all to leave,
And his army stepped aside to let them through.

That night, the palace was alight with celebration;
Those of the Argolid joining in the feasting,
And after, Orestes drew Odysseus aside.

"My friend, you have done what you said you would,
And in a way that I would not have conceived."

Both smiled, but Odysseus said nothing, waiting.

"You have my word that once the first campaign is done,
You may continue on your quest. And,"

        he continued,
Not waiting for reply,

      "now you may continue on
To visit Pylades and my sister in Tiryns. I stay here
To consolidate my rule and work out the details,
But within a few days I shall join you.
And you have given me the opportunity I needed
To begin my campaign without it advertised,
For my journey here with part of my host
Is seen as only proper for my becoming ruler here.
But when I arrive at Tiryns with these men,
The others will have come quietly, from different ways,
And will join us after we have left the citadel
Close to the mountains, unobserved.
And while we stay with Pylades, the three of us
Can work out the campaign's stratagems."

Odysseus nodded, saying,

      "As usual, you show wisdom,
And I will fulfill what I have promised fully,
Starting with those days of consultation."

More conversation took place between them,
But on a lighter note; the decision had been made,
And the Fates alone knew what outcome there would be.

The next day Odysseus and his retinue left Argos
To ride across the plain to Tiryns. Soon it came to view,
The mound with the massive citadel rising from the land
As a mammoth whale breaks the surface of the ocean.
Officers came out to greet them cordially and lead them
Through the outer fortifications—the narrow incline,
The great gate, and up to the palace, like a crown
Placed at the top.
Dismounting, they were led to the great hall,
A space near in grandeur to Mycenae's.
Again, the fire pit centred the room;
On the walls beside the torches were decorations,
Scenes of Gods and men, heroic actions, legends,
But at the room's end, on the wall, the great lions, as before,
Carved facing each other, claws upraised, mouths gaping,
While before them on a marble dais, shining white
Against the burnished colours of the animals,
Sat in two thrones of sturdy bronze, fretted with gold,
The king, Pylades, and his queen, Electra.
They rose as their guests advanced through the hall,
And sharp-eyed Odysseus noted the swarthy face,
Short stature of the king, compact and muscular.
Electra, taller than her consort, stood proudly,
But seemed worn thin, a wraith in her rich robes.
When she saw Odysseus a ghost of a smile
Flitted across her features, and she spoke first.

"Welcome, old friend, companion to my father,
I still remember you from those long days past,
Even so young as I was then."

She looked at him closely, then sighed,

"Yes, you look older now, and your face shows
The strains of battle and the years; but still you are
Formidable."

      "Thank you, dear lady, I too remember.
But that young girl is now a lovely queen,
Worthy of her great father."

The ghostly smile appeared again.

"Oh, do not flatter me. I know too well
What the years and these events have done to me."

"Whatever they have done to you,"

                        gravely spoke Odysseus,
"Your true worth still shines through, and I see before me
Fulfilled the promise that I saw in that small girl."

Electra flushed slightly, and turned to Pylades,
Who had been watching with great interest this meeting.

"My husband, here is the man I told you of,
Who is remembered by Achaeans for his prowess
And as the agent for the fall of Ilion,
Renowned Odysseus himself."

Pylades smiled and welcomed him with unaffected warmth.

"Since Electra told me of you I have wished to meet you,
For who could match your wisdom and your travels,
Wondrous to hear related. And now I see the man
Fits his reputation. Welcome, and be considered friends, not guests,
While you partake of all that we can offer you."

Odysseus, astute reader of men's character,
Saw he meant all he said, and he knew now
Why Pylades had deep ties to Orestes,
Following him through all adversities,
Giving him sound counsel, fighting for him,
And why now Electra was his wife,
For Orestes would trust no other man
To be her husband, frail as she had become
In mind and body.

"I thank you for your friendship and your praise,"
He smoothly said,

                  "honoured by hearing it from the lips
Of one himself so noble."

                  Pylades acknowledged
The counter-compliment, but a humorous smile
Played on his lips, infectious, Odysseus sharing in it.
Introductions were then made for Telemachus

And the others of the company; then quarters
Were assigned to each, with promise of a banquet
In the evening. The palace was a maze
Of rooms and corridors; and once Odysseus had his room
A servant came, inviting him to meet alone with Pylades.
The two met in a long loggia, and for a time
They walked quietly, no speech disturbing the quiet place.

Then Pylades said, quietly,
                              "Orestes has sent a messenger
To tell me what occurred at Argos, and that you
Have agreed to join in the campaign.
It seems to me,"
                 he smiled,
                              "you have still
The cunning and the power to sway kingdoms."

"I do what I must,"
                    Odysseus smiled back,
Then told him of his quest.

                              "That is why
I can stay only for the first campaign,
Both for my sake and for yours, to satisfy the Gods."

"Your path is tortuous,"
                          sighed Pylades,
"But of all men, you only could attempt it.
At least you will not tarry long
Before the war begins. Orestes, as you know,
Delays in Argos to cement the change,
And will in several days join us with his present host;
But in these last few weeks he quietly has sent
Expeditions of supplies now scattered through the plain,
And his other forces, in small groups, now make their way
To a secluded, quiet valley in the north
Near to the border to Arcadia.
When he arrives here, we shall pass some days
In banqueting and contests, the excuse for
The number he has brought with him.
Then, when he has word all are in place,
We all will march to that valley.

We do have plans for Arcadia
Which we must check with you, take your advice.
But,"
         he said, stopping to look Odysseus in the eye,
"What do you now think of our chances in that country?"

Odysseus, level-eyed with him, replied,

"What you and Orestes wish will not be easy.
The terrain is mountainous and with narrow passes,
The tribes strong, rough, and treacherous.
They fight without fear—if not us, then themselves—
And each space one wins will be paid for dearly.
Let us hope our own troop can fight as well,
And that there be enough of them to last."

Pylades nodded.
               "Nothing you say surprises me,
Nor do I disagree with anything you say,
But the gain is worth the cost. That is why
You are the key to our success, for, with your experience,
Your skilled strategy, your proven leadership,
The cost should be less than otherwise.
But we will speak again after he comes,
And we three work out the strategy more deeply."

So saying, he led Odysseus back to his quarters,
Leaving him to ponder what had been said.

That night the rites were performed simply but well;
Then the feast began with dignity and warmth.
Odysseus sat next to Electra,
Pylades next to Telemachus, who, clear-eyed as his father,
Saw how Pylades, who gave him full attention,
Still quietly attended to his wife, absorbed in talk,
Eager to hear all she could of her father
In the war, his courage and his exploits;
And as she heard, she seemed to grow younger,
Her cheeks flushed, her expression glowing
At the praises of her father Odysseus
Carefully bestowed.
Pylades clearly showed his pleasure

At his wife's new-found happiness;
Yet still he held the son in quiet conversation
Laced with humour, leavened with wisdom,
To impress deeply his new guest, still but a few years
Younger than himself. Telemachus also found his way
Of looking at things, so different from the Ithacans',
Strange but fascinating: sometimes the subject
Would arrive circuitously, ornately wound in
Curious description and phrasing; at other times
He spoke with startling directness, without reservation,
Surprising the young Ithacan, more accustomed
To conventional phrasing at the courts he visited.
But, involved deeply in the conversation as he was,
He still noted how Pylades quietly found out about him,
Winkling out fragments of his life in Ithaca:
How he had grown up, the tensions in his home,
His mother's loyalty and craftiness against her suitors,
And the way his father had returned, unknown and disguised,
To wreak vengeance on those who had abused his house
And to regain control of his island kingdom.

The banquet ended with new friendships deepened,
And all left, warmed by this strengthened spirit.
Odysseus did not go straight to his quarters;
Instead, he walked upon the great grounds of the palace,
Where he could look out while he thought.
The night was clear, the moon big and full,
And in its light he saw the dark plain in relief,
Its trees and fields in stark light and shade;
The sea now clearly seen between steep mountainsides
To the south, its surface silver in the ashen rays;
And in the east, the mountains jutting from the plain
In folds of foothills, deep clefts, and peaks snow-tipped,
Edges traced by the unforgiving moonlight.
As he looked at the immense and convoluted shapes
He sighed, considering the journey through them
Yet to come. He stood at the edge for a long time, thinking,
Then made his way back to bed and hoped-for sleep.

The next day his troop began to exercise again,
Preparing for the contests which had been announced

To mark Orestes's stay at the palace.
Telemachus was in the forefront, again working fiercely,
Trying all the sports with full exertion,
And would not spare himself. Odysseus,
Who himself participated in a less obtrusive way,
Noted his son's efforts and smiled sympathetically,
Knowing the source of his son's frenzied work.
Pylades took part as well, showing his fine strength
And agility, the Corinthians and the Ithacans
Watching him with admiration and surprise.
That night at the feast Telemachus sat with Electra,
Odysseus with Pylades. The young man at first
Was uncomfortable with the grave, fragile woman;
But soon her questions, sensitive and penetrating,
Made him more at ease, and in response he asked her
To tell him of the Argolid, which he had not visited before.

Late one afternoon Orestes and his entourage arrived.
As great schools of salmon surge up the turbulent stream,
Their silver spines and rainbow-coloured scales
Flashing with brilliance in the radiant sun,
So Orestes's cohorts marched through the plain
To Tiryns, chariots, horses, and warriors
Resplendent through the dust raised by their progress.
Around the citadel arose a second city—
Like stooks of wheat stacked row on row
Over a vast field, so did the tents of warriors
Spread throughout the fields and olive groves.
All greeted Orestes and his queen Hermione,
But Odysseus and his clear-eyed son noted well
The warm embrace between Orestes and his dear friend
And the cooler meeting of the two queens.
That night the rites become more complex and ornate:
A great bull, raised for the purpose, sleek and fat,
Horns gilded, was led forward; Orestes himself
Grasped the hefty two-edged axe, raised a prayer
To Zeus, ruler of all Gods and men,
And with one blow cut through the massive neck.
Slices of choice meat were offered to the other Gods as well
Along with libations to the Olympian pantheon,

And then the better cuts were distributed
Among the honoured hosts and guests.
Throughout the camp the rites and sacrifices
Also took place, piety and hunger satisfied together.

At the feast Orestes and his host sat together;
On either side of them their wives, with Odysseus
Beside Electra, his son beside Hermione.
Acutely conscious of the lovely queen's proximity,
Telemachus began to enter into conversation.

"Good queen, you appear to know your husband's sister
From before your marriage; would you be so gracious
As to tell me how?"

                    A moment passed.
Hermione glanced at him and for that moment
Her manner grew cold, her eyes narrowed slightly;
Then, she became composed again
And with a silky smoothness, friendly but detached,
She answered him.

"When the War with Ilion began, I was young,
And with my mother gone,"
                              here her face tightened,
"I was sent by Menelaos to Mycenae
To be brought up in the care of my aunt,
Queen Clytemnestra. It was there I knew
Electra, a few years older than myself.
But we did not know each other intimately,
Although always in close proximity.
She seemed more distant; her sister's sacrifice
Preyed always on her mind; and when Aegisthus
Became Clytemnestra's lover, and Orestes, still a boy,
Was spirited away, she withdrew further from us,
I myself felt in danger, and for more than one reason.
She shivered slightly, and Telemachus saw that beauty
Brought with it its own hazards without choice.
My childhood, like Electra's, was thus turbulent,
But these seas tossed us apart and not together.
Then, as you know, came Orestes's return
And all that followed. Now we are sisters again,

Joined with two friends but with the chasm
Of our childhood still between us."

She finished, and both sat silent as the feast
Went on around them. Then Odysseus's son
Broke the moment.

     "I thank you, Hermione,
For revealing what has passed between you,
And I feel great sorrow for what you have endured."

She smiled at him, but now he found a social mask
Lay on her face, and further intimacies were lost.
The evening concluded with slight, trivial conversation
And Telemachus knew the spell had now been broken.

Over several days the camp prepared for the contests.
Land close to the citadel was cleared and made level
For the races and for all events.
Dawn finally came when all gathered, a huge congregation,
To watch and to participate. Orestes and Odysseus
Declined to compete, but the rest of the Achaeans
Sought eagerly to show their prowess and gain glory.
The chariot race was held first, dust swirling up
As horse, chariot, and rider swept round the course.
The race was narrowly won by Orestes's favourite charioteer,
A man then honoured by his satisfied ruler.
In the horse race Telemachus, Polymedes,
And choice Corinthians and Mycenaeans were entered.
Despite his inexperience, Telemachus kept with the others;
As the hoof beats thundered and the dust rose higher,
The onlookers could not make out who led,
But as the horses strained to the finish,
Polymedes came first, Telemachus a close third.
Then the runners plummeted down the field,
And here Telemachus came second, his Corinthian friends
Far behind. When the wrestling then took place,
Telemachus again showed his strength and courage;
All fell before him. Then Pylades stepped forward.

"My young friend, let you and me now try our luck."

Both now grasped at each other, but Pylades
Showed not only his agility but his quickness
And his strength, and Odysseus's son unexpectedly
Found himself pinned beneath the smiling king.
Orestes laughed and cheered his friend, victorious,
And happily bestowed the wreath upon him.
But when the contest for the javelin took place,
Telemachus proved the greatest of the throwers
And the deadliest of aim; and, finally satisfied,
Received his wreath even from his father's hands.
The final contest was in archery, where many showed
Their prowess and their accuracy. When all had finished,
A Corinthian showed his great aim and distance.
But after the winner had received his prize, Odysseus
Stepped forward and said mildly,

"My fellow kings, would you give me the pleasure
Of trying my hand outside the competition?"

Orestes and Pylades, surprised, agreed.

Odysseus then placed a wreath far along the course,
Double the distance that the winner had attempted.
All looked with disbelief at what he did.

Then he said, again mildly,
                              "Perhaps we could make
A wager on the outcome of my shot?"

The two kings laughed, but then agreed to bet.

"Then let it be this: if I lose, I will acquiesce
In anything you say regarding what we do presently;
But if I win, then you will take my advice completely."

The other two paused for a moment, now more sober;
But looking at the target far away, they then agreed.

Odysseus took his bow, which no other man could handle,
Strung it again, and selected from among his arrows,
Which themselves were longer than any of the others.

"Athena, my beloved patroness, help me in this moment,"
He muttered as a prayer, quietly, unheard.

Then he drew the bow until it reached as far as it could bend,
Took aim, and let the arrow fly. It streaked away, swift,
The air whistling through its feathers, arched high
Into the sky; then, as a falcon sighting its prey below it,
Plummets down to seize the hapless victim in its claws,
So too the arrow with unerring accuracy
Plunged into the ground in the dead centre of the wreath.
All stood amazed; no sound was made; then a roar
Was heard, louder than when waves in a great storm
Crash into rocks, thundering their own destruction,
All lauding Odysseus and his splendid deed.

Orestes turned to him and said,
                                    "Now we know why
You are the legendary hero of the Trojan War—
Who could conceive of any other doing what you did;
And who would deny the legend of your craftiness as well?
You have won the wager, and we will listen to your counsel
As we would have anyway. You and your son
Are truly champions."

                    And all roared their approval.

That night the feasting and the revelry reached its height
And little sleep was found throughout the camp.

The next day, the three kings met to work out the campaign.
Odysseus listened carefully to Orestes and Pylades,
Not interjecting but taking note of all that they had planned.
Then he questioned them to make clear what they had said,
Not only for himself but for themselves
To truly understand what they intended.

"You speak of armed conquest of Arcadia.
Is the country under one ruler?"

Orestes frowned, but Pylades was the one who answered.

"There is a King of Arcadia, but from what we are told
He rules only the central highlands."

A nod from wily Odysseus, who then went on,

"And the regions of the high mountains
Are owned by separate tribes?"

"Yes, our spies tell us that they live in small citadels,
More small villages than towns, clinging to the sides
Of their harsh mountains, and therefore have
Strong natural defences against any who oppose them."

"I see. You have, of course, good guides
To see us through the mountain passes?"

Orestes, impatient of the questions, snorted,
But Pylades smiled and replied unperturbed,

"Of course. We have faithful guides who know
The mountains intimately and every trail."

Odysseus again nodded in pleasant acknowledgement.

"Forgive me for what I am about to say,
For as you know, I am unaware of events
In Arcadia over the last twenty years"—

The two kings looked at him warily—

"But when I was in the war I was good friends
With my fellow warrior Agapenor,
King of Arcadia, who was with me
In the Trojan horse, and was great in battle,
As were his warriors from his kingdom.
Have you entertained or talked to him?
For he would be a formidable opponent."

The two kings relaxed, and this time Orestes spoke.

"We forget, great Odysseus, that you still do not know
All that transpired following the defeat of Ilion.
On the return journey Agapenor's ship
Was blown by great unceasing winds to Cyprus.
This drastic change of course he believed
Came from the Gods themselves, and accordingly
He settled there to start another kingdom."

Odysseus was startled by this information,
Paused for a moment, then went on.

"Who, then, is now King of Arcadia?"

Again, Orestes made reply.

"The throne has descended to Aepytus,
Who has ruled since Agapenor did not return."

"What is he like?"

"We have had few dealings with him
But we understand that he is less the king
Than your old friend, but rough and not willing
To make friends. He also has ambitions to
Expand his kingdom and take in the tribes."

Odysseus thought for a moment before speaking.

"Thank you for your gracious answers to my questions.
With your permission, let us adjourn this conference.
I will sleep on what you have told me
And we can consider this next day what we might do."

The two kings were reluctant to cut short the meeting
But they agreed to the seasoned warrior's request.

That night Odysseus paced alone under the stars
For a long time contemplating what should be done.
As on a day in which the sky is filled with clouds
That layer by layer scud by, greying the landscape,
Until for a brief moment the bright rays of the sun
Pierce the gloom and light up all around,
So thoughtful Odysseus abruptly saw his way
And went to his bed satisfied.

*The darkness of the belly of the horse again*
*Aware of the huge man beside him*
*Silent but powerful*
*The warrior in battle*
*With the brute strength of an Ajax*
*But so swift*
*So sudden*

*And his men*
*Aloof*
*By themselves*
*But a terror in a fight*
*Vicious like their king*

At the council the next day
Odysseus told his fellow kings
About a dream that he had had
That came from Gods.
This in itself astonished them,
But when he described the plan
That wove itself from that dream
They were amazed at its audacity,
But with his great persuasive gifts
He brought them round to his own stratagem,
And they left the meeting with heads ashake
But understanding now the full brilliance of the man.

Several further days went by, Orestes sending contingents
Of his troops laden with supplies out quietly to meet
With others who discreetly were assembling
In the secluded valley where all were to meet.
Finally, the morning came when the main army
Was ready to leave Tiryns on the march toward Arcadia.
The camp was struck; men were assembled by late afternoon;
The two kings said farewell to their queens
Who stood together as two solitudes;
Odysseus, Telemachus, and their Ithacans
Drew into line with the Corinthians and those others
Of the Argolid; then, as a huge river slowly flows
Downstream, its width stretched far to the horizon,
Its oily waters gleaming in the setting sun,
So too the army set out, weapons and armours ablaze
In the light, great wagons of supplies groaning behind
In the huge clouds of dust, toward their destination—
The looming foothills and mountains of Arcadia.

## Canto 3

# ARCADIA

The route toward the mountains followed a wide trail,
Not like the new road forged from Mycenae.
Orestes's golden chariot lurched forward,
Flanked on one side by Pylades
And on the other by Odysseus.
Close behind rode Telemachus and his companions
Interspersed with their Corinthian friends
And with Odysseus's herald and his seer,
And then, like a great snake writhing in the dust,
The army marched through the haze of its own making.
Past the tended fields and olive groves they wove,
Even as the sun's chariot galloped in its fiery path
Over the western mountains toward which the huge procession drove.
Finally, as dusk clothed all in shadows,
They came to where their camp was to be set,
In the arms of a small mountain southwest of Argos,
And the army, like a well-trained animal,
Set to its chores: tents were set up,
Large fires blazed, and preparations finished
For the evening feast. The kings stretched and relaxed,
Standing by the flames until their accommodations
Were prepared. There was much noise throughout the camp,
Soldiers laughing and shouting to each other,
And from the hills and mountains below which they nested
In their groves of trees, it appeared as if the stars now twinkling
In the firmament were reflected in the tiny fires below.
But while all seemed both purposeful and carefree,
A stream of officers came to Orestes's tent,
Instructions were quietly passed on, and many of them
Disappeared past the dark verges of the camp.
Then, as the night grew late and feasting finished,

The camp grew dark and quiet, save for the guards
And fires at its large perimeter.

The next day a much smaller group set out:
The kings, their entourage of the Corinthians
And Ithacans, and a hundred horsemen.
This time Orestes was mounted on his horse,
His chariot left at camp. Through a pass north
Of the camp and on the other side of the mountain
Where Argos fringed its base the troop rode and marched,
Then started down the long valley and the borders
Of Arcadia. Their pace was slow and stately;
The paths were narrow and not often trod,
With the ranges of gaunt and barren mountains on each side.
At noon they stopped to rest beside the river
Which sped along the southern base,
And in the afternoon they brushed through the green vegetation
Until the valley narrowed and slopes appeared before them.
Here they encamped, with their fires blazing high
And their tents spread out beside the river.
Guards kept watch throughout the night.
The next day they came to a fork
Where both the valley and the river split,
Each leading to a new valley. A distance
And between the forks they saw a village,
Fortified, with warriors watching them
From the wooden parapets. A bridge crossed
The northern fork, affording access to the western valley
And to the village. On that side a troop of warriors
Stood waiting for the strangers to arrive,
Rough shod, with leather helmets and armour,
Grasping swords and spears. Orestes let Medon
Go before as their herald, and he approached
The band with signs of peace.

"Hail, men of Arcadia and this home of yours!"

One of the men stepped forward, burly
But of average height, and spoke without a customary greeting.

"Why are you here and what do you want?"

"We come on a pilgrimage and to meet with your king,
Great Aepytus. With your permission we wish to pass on
To meet with him and to fulfill our task."

The man grunted and looked sharply at the group.

"Why should I believe you? Who are you?"

Medon gestured at the kings clustered behind him.

"Behold the King of the Argolid, mighty Orestes,
And with him the peerless hero of the Trojan War,
King Odysseus of Ithaca and friend of your former king,
Terrible Agapenor. We come in peace
To fulfill our obligation, and we wish no harm
To you or to your country."

A thin man, older than the chieftain,
Moved to his side and spoke quietly in his ear.
A scowl, but then a reluctant acquiescence.

"We will not stand in your way for now.
Go forward, but be sure that on your trek
You will be watched throughout."

Medon thanked him courteously, and the band
Stepped back as the horsemen and the warriors
Rode past. Their way now led west,
Following the winding river almost at its edge
As it wound through a more barren valley,
The stone sides of the hills rearing above them
As they moved slowly down the narrow trail.
By the day's end the terrain opened out
Into a far-reaching sloping plain, thick forested,
And there they camped at its borders,
Their fires and guards enclosing them.
The third day they found their way more difficult
As they worked through the trees and brush,
Still skirting near the now fast-moving river,
And followed the plain upward and then to its side,
For it was the lap of a towering mountain,
And they found themselves in a narrow valley
Between this giant and its southern neighbour.

That day they forged on, going by the rocky façade
Of the mountain, to see before them the huge range
That they must cross over, its forested side looming ahead.
At its base they camped that night,
And the next morning earlier than before,
They set out again. Soon they came to a pass
That led them past the ramparts of the first range
And along the feet of the vast bare mountains.
Now they began to climb laboriously
Rising to cross the colossal spine and then
Following a tortuous route to break through
To the great highland plain of Arcadia.
That night they camped down below an eyrie
Well-fortified, and on the final day
They descended the steep slopes and made their way
North to their destination, Mantinea,
At the foot of the slopes overlooking the broad plain.

At the gates of the fortified town,
Its parapets bristling with defenders,
Medon again stepped forward to hail the walls.

"Citizens and warriors of Matinea,
The kings of Argos and Ithaca, the great lords
Orestes and Odysseus, greet you in peace
And ask for audience with your leader."

A figure appeared above the gates, which stayed
Firmly shut. He was more richly robed than
The rough leader of the previous village,
But his demeanour showed that he would be
Formidable in battle.

"I greet the two noble kings and ask
What you do here and where you go."

Medon gestured to Odysseus.

"Hear the victor of the Trojan War,
Odysseus, tell you himself why we have come."

The shrewd king dismounted from his horse
And moved to stand ahead of his herald,

Alone before the massive gate.
He was dusty with the journey on the plain,
But as he spoke he felt Athena touch him,
And he seemed to grow in stature
And his voice grew resonant and strong.

"We come to meet with your king Aepytus,
With a pious request that I must make
To him and you. Know then, that
Poseidon has decreed that I make a new journey
To appease him for the wrongs that I have done him.
My journey must take me through the cities
Of this vast land before I can achieve what
Is required of me. This I have begun,
Meeting with my fellow king, Orestes.
But even as I slept under his hospitality,
Athena came to me in a dream and told me
That I must show more propitiation
By building two sanctuaries here in Arcadia,
One near you at Calliae in a wooded grove,
Which I intend to dedicate to the dread God
And to Athena herself, and one farther north
Near Orchomenos, at Phineos,
For Poseidon only. I told my fellow king
Of this sacred dream, and he in his piety
Agreed to assist in the creation of these sanctuaries.
Thus we have come to ask your king to join with us
In this holy act. And of you I ask
That you will send a messenger to Aepytus
With our request."

There was a long pause as all stood spellbound,
Both on the walls and among the troops before it.
Then another man, standing beside and
Slightly behind the ruler, moved closer to speak to him.
After a brief consultation, the town's guardian nodded,
And turned to address Odysseus.

"Odysseus, noble lord, you have spoken eloquently
Of your quest, and it would be sacrilegious for us
To deny your request, as it has been already honoured

By King Orestes. We will grant your petitions,
But only if you will accept our hospitality tonight,
You and your fellow king and your commanders,
And feast with us. Your camp you may set up
Beside our town."

He then withdrew, to appear when the gates were opened.
He engaged in conversation with the kings
Before returning to the town to prepare for the feast
While the camp was set up and the leaders got ready.
Then Odysseus, Orestes, Pylades, Telemachus
And his friend, Medon, and Halitherses,
Returned to the town. The giant wooden gates,
Studded with bronze, creaked open, and again
They were greeted by the ruler of the town,
Whose name was Agamedion, and his cohorts.
The sacrifice and rites accomplished,
All settled down to enjoy their first true feast
For several days. As they sat and ate, they talked
Of affairs in Argos and in Greece; then
Odysseus turned to Agamedion.

"A fine feast—I congratulate and thank you for it."

Agamedion inclined his head slightly.

"It is only befitting the hero of the fall of Ilion.
If you would, please tell us of that famous time,
Your travails on your long return,
And more on the quest that brings you to our land."

Odysseus sighed, looking at the fierce flames
Devouring the huge logs and sending
Their shadows flickering about them.

"I will attempt to tell you of these things
In such a way that we will not spend the whole night
On my tales."

And as the others listened, some for the first time,
Others who had heard him speak before,
The eloquent warrior told his story,
And in the shifting light of the flames and torches

His listeners, all of them without exception,
Were held in rapt attention by his glorious speech.
Finally, after he had told of the prophecy
And of his recent dream that had led them hither,
He paused for a slight instant, then said,

"But I have not told you of my friend and your former king
Agapenor, whom I have known for more
Than two decades past, when we were both suitors
For the hand of the incomparable Helen,
And when we fought together in that fated war.
He was truly a formidable warrior and great hero,
And the men from Arcadia showed themselves
Worthy of the renown that they earned with him
In battle. I am sorry that he is not in this land
So that I could renew my friendship with him."

On hearing this the Arcadians shifted uncomfortably;
Then Agamedion spoke quietly to his now alert guest.

"As an Arcadian I am proud to hear of our
Countrymen's exploits and fame, and of your
Friendship with our former king, Agapenor.
However, I must suggest that you keep such talk
To yourself when speaking with our present king—
He is not happy to hear that king's name.
You would do well to avoid that subject
Even though King Aepytus well knows your fame
And your acquaintance with the former king."

Keen-witted Odysseus looked at him levelly and smiled.

"I thank you for your advice, good Agamedion.
It saddens me that the noble history
Of your land's involvement in the War with Ilion
Cannot be sung about the country as it is elsewhere,
But I am not here to provoke conflict
But, as you know, to perform two pious acts,
And then, when the time is ripe, to continue
On my pilgrimage."

Agamedion smiled in return,
Then turned to speak to King Orestes,

Who with Pylades had been listening carefully
Throughout this exchange.

"My lord, the messenger has been sent to
King Aepytus, who, I am sure, already knows
Of your presence in the country."

All present there smiled knowingly.

"You should have his reply the day after next.
In the meantime, I humbly invite you
To enjoy our hospitality during this time."

Orestes nodded and gracefully accepted.
The banquet then finished with all content,
And the troop returned to the camp.
That night Orestes sent a secret messenger
Who left on horse, concealed in darkness,
Even as a panther pads silently through the night,
Unknown to its unsuspecting victim.

The next day passed in pleasant activity
As the Arcadians and their visitors
Vied in sports and gained mutual respect
For their prowess and abilities.
As had been predicted, the following morn
A messenger arrived to bring the news
That King Aepytus would meet them as requested
In the woods of Calliae. Immediately
The camp was struck, thanks and gifts were given
To Agamedion and his town, and the troop
Set off down the slope of the mountain
To the great highlands plain itself.
The slope itself was steep and long
And it took the remainder of the morning
To traverse its narrow winding trails.
But once on the more level ground they gave
Their horses their heads, and the entourage
Galloped down the immense expanse.
On one side was the enormous range of mountains
They had struggled over to reach here;
On the other, mountains more huge and grand

Towered, their high peaks wreathed with clouds.
The landscape of the plain was harsh,
Clusters of dark trees gripping the brown soil,
And marshes straggling out from shallow streams.
In the afternoon they reached their destination,
Located before a sharp ridge that jutted out
From the forbidding range behind it,
Its forest struggling up steep slopes.
They quickly made camp within the forest,
Overlooking Calliae, the small town,
On a level meadow, a ripe site
For the proposed sanctuary, and
Awaited the arrival of Aepytus the next day
As he had ordained.

By the time that blushing Dawn arose
And Helios had lashed his horses now
To begin their race across the sky
The troop waited mounted, in ranks upon the meadow,
Ready for the king and his entourage.
Before noon Aepytus arrived, and with him
Many cavalry and soldiers, at least twice the number
Of his guests. He rode to the centre of the meadow
And there stopped, but did not dismount from his horse.
Sharp-eyed Odysseus noted this and spoke quietly
To Orestes; then the two kings trotted forward
To meet with the Arcadian king.
Odysseus quickly noted the essential features
Of the man—short but stocky, much like himself,
Swarthy, with beetling brows, flat nose, and wide mouth,
Cunning more than intelligent, with a ruthless eye,
More like a bandit leader than a king.

He said nothing on their approach; Orestes
Nodded to Odysseus, who then spoke:

"Greetings, King of Arcadia, from your fellow kings,
Orestes of Argos and Odysseus of Ithaca.
We come in peace and on a pious pilgrimage,
Which we are sure the messenger has told you."

Silence from the king, whose eyes flicked over them
And all the troop, assessing their strength.

"We ask you to join us in creating here
A sanctuary for the great Gods Poseidon
And Pallas Athena, as commanded by them
In my dream."

Aepytus smiled—or what appeared to be a smile,
Too close to a sneer to be comfortable—
And then for the first time spoke:

"I do not hold much with dreams and what they say.
As for a sanctuary here, this is my land,
And I see no reason to let foreigners develop it."

Orestes and Odysseus looked shocked by these words;
Halitherses, slightly behind them, was distressed.

Orestes now spoke, in a voice still peaceable.
"You do not wish us to honour the Gods here?"

Aepytus snorted contemptuously.

"You can honour the Gods anywhere you like,
So long as it is not in my country."

Orestes now purred his next question:
"What of an alliance, with this spot honouring our bond?"

Aepytus laughed harshly.

"Why should I ally myself with you, so foolish
As to invade my country with this piddling force,
When, as you see, I hold the upper hand here.
As invaders, I should hold you prisoners for ransom
Rather than the guests you unwisely claim to be."

Orestes smiled gently, saying,
"It would be well for you to think otherwise
And to greet us with more hospitality."

Aepytus gaped at him, then laughed uproariously.

"Why should I? I have the power here."

A feral grin, and then a snarl.

"I do not need your friendship, but I like your wealth.
Let's see what you two may be worth at home."

Orestes calmly replied,
                    "Let us see indeed."

And then he nodded. A horn sounded in the troop;
And from the verge of the forest round the meadow,
A sea of spears appeared that moved slightly forward,
And behind them a vast rank of bowmen,
Their bows raised in readiness. The Arcadians
Gasped in surprise; Aepytus turned red with rage,
But saw himself and his men helpless against such odds.

Orestes now moved his horse close to Aepytus,
And with a gaze now like a basilisk's
He held the eye of the astonished king.

"It is fortunate that you have shown your true colours
In how you have treated us. It would be simple now
To get rid of you and keep Arcadia for ourselves.
But that is not our intention."

Aepytus could not turn away from that gaze,
So implacable, steadfast, and merciless,
And he now realized how this man had the strength
To kill his mother and her lover and to endure
The agonies that followed such a terrible act.

"We *have* come to set up this sanctuary
Just as we have said. And we have come
To form an alliance, as we have also said.
It is now up to you to choose, either to do so,
Or to relinquish your throne and life on this spot."
And Aepytus, now sweating, knew in his heart
That Orestes meant everything he said.

Odysseus now moved to the other side of the king.

"If you choose the former, you must swear allegiance
Here and now, before your company, so that Arcadia

Will know what you have done and honour it.
Consider then what you will do."

And both kings stared at him relentlessly.
Aepytus knew that they would not wait long;
His body sagged slightly; and then he answered them.
"I will acknowledge you, but know I do it under force."

"No!"

      snapped Odysseus, his voice cutting like his sword,

"You must acknowledge King Orestes fully,
With no conditions, and with your full heart.
Nothing less will work for you and these nations."

As bullies, after they have tormented those that they despise,
Find that their intended victims have more strength
Than they supposed, and turn on them in wrath,
Must then show in shame their true cowardice
And acquiesce to the blame they owe,
So now Aepytus, fully conquered, had to vow
His full allegiance before all his men
To King Orestes and the Argolid.
And when he had, with shame-faced utterance
Made his vow, his men watching him with hard eyes,
Odysseus spoke again.

"Now King Aepytus, send out messengers from here
Up and down your kingdom, to proclaim to all
The new alliance between ourselves and you."

And he was forced to send from his force
Such messengers, and he knew then that as a king
He could now exist only through the power
Of the Argolid, for without the backing
Of Orestes, his life would now be nothing
In his country.

Now spears and bows were lowered, and to the space
Came priests of the two Gods to be honoured here.
All from the different countries stood to witness
The sanctifying of the meadow, and the sacrifices
There made. As the sacred bull was sacrificed,

Odysseus severing the head with a great blow
From his sword, Halitherses looked at Aepytus
And gasped, then quickly regained his composure.
But sharp-eyed Telemachus, standing near him,
Had seen what happened, and put it aside
In his mind for later. The other sacrifices
And the hymns to the two dread Gods were made.
Then all removed from the now holy space,
Leaving it to the architects who had come with the force
To work out all the details of the buildings
There to be constructed.
The combined forces now descended to Calliae,
Where soon preparations for a large feast began
And Orestes's army could make their camp.

That night great fires lit the sky, reflecting from
The rocky peaks above, and all feasted well.
Odysseus made sure that Aepytus's commanders
Were mixed among the Argive leaders
And that the Arcadian men were also found
Among the greater army. He, Orestes,
And their companions sat with Aepytus
And his closest followers around one
Of the great fires, the sparks from which arose
And showed on the one hand the plain fading
To infinity, and on the other
The harsh rock and the dark trees below which
They found themselves. Aepytus, sullen and afraid,
Said little as the feast progressed, but filled his cup
Continually. Odysseus sat on one side of him,
Orestes on the other, and as the flames
Made their faces red and their expressions
Shift with the blazing iridescence,
The astute king brought him to converse.

"King Aepytus, now that we are allied,"

The Arcadian's eyes blazed from beneath
His jutting brow, then shifted to look at the flames.

"Permit me to ask you about your realm."

Silence from the man brooding at his side.

"Your kingdom rests within this plain, does it not?"

Aepytus bridled.

"But the tribes that occupy the other side of this great range,
From south to north, still are unsubdued?"

The surly king opened his mouth to deny the question,
But seeing Odysseus's knowing look, he realized
That he was aware fully of the condition of this land.
He swallowed his deep rebellious anger
And gave a quick reluctant nod. Odysseus continued:

"As we have told you—and you have seen evidence
That what we say is true—this is not the only place
Where I have been commanded to create
A sanctuary. We still must travel to
Orchomenos, and at Phineos
Dedicate a holy place to Poseidon alone.
Now, what better place than such a pious site
To ask the independent tribes of Arcadia
To join with you and your kingdom?
And if they will not, what better place,
At the point where the two ranges merge,
To begin a campaign? Especially when
You could do so allied with us,
Two armies to defeat your enemies?"

Aepytus was startled by this proposition
And for a moment did not speak, but both
Odysseus and Orestes could see him weighing
Possibilities, his ambition stained
With his humiliation. Finally:

"The plan could work; there would be enough
To overcome each tribe, hard as it would be."

Then his eyes narrowed, looked at them cunningly.

"But what is in this for me?
It may add to my kingdom, but I am still
In thrall to you."

Odysseus nodded to Orestes, who seized the moment:

"You have sworn allegiance with us
And we with you. For me it means Arcadia
Is united with the Argolid, to both
Our mutual advantages. If in war,
We aid each other, our numbers stronger;
If in peace, we build prosperity between us,
And you prosper because you are not vexed
With raiding and independent tribes.
Is that not a worthy aim for you?"

Aepytus thought again, his swart face
Shifting in the roaring flames and then he nodded.

"That is true. Such an alliance could help us.
I am willing to consider it.
What, then, is your strategy?"

Orestes glanced at Odysseus, who then continued:

"We will take our combined forces to Phineos
To celebrate both the sanctification
And the alliance of the two nations.
In the meantime, tomorrow send messengers
To the commanders of the rest of your army,
And have them join us there, the night that
The ceremonies are completed. Then,
According to what happens with the tribes,
We will go to war or return to our homeland."

Aepytus, now much more relaxed with talk of conquest,
Agreed, and the feast later finished with him,
Drunk, carried to his tent, and the others,
Who had refrained from drinking much,
Remaining to talk quietly. Orestes
Sent for the commanders and guides
Who had led the greater army there,
And while they waited for them to arrive,
Orestes turned to grasp Odysseus's arm.

"My friend, all that you had suggested
Has come to pass—a brilliant stratagem!

Let us hear how they found our company."

When the commanders and the guides arrived,
Orestes requested that they tell him
Of their journey to Arcadia.
The chief commander, strong featured,
Mature and powerfully built, replied:

"My lord Odysseus, we did just as you ordered.
The night before you left, in darkness,
The bulk of the army quietly moved off south
In opposition to your northern route.
It was important, as you know, to be unseen,
And a small part of the force was left at the camp
To give the sense of the whole army for those
Who we knew spied on us from the mountains.
The initial journey south, much on more level ground,
Went easily and relatively swiftly,
For we had traversed this land before.
But then we turned west to wind along
A mountain's base, close to its river;
Here our guides proved their deep worth,
Helping our warriors along the narrow paths,
No light available, no moon seen
As had been planned. They took us around that
Mountain, across a valley, and then found
Us shelter in a deep forest at another mountain's
Base. We could not set up camp, had to conceal
Ourselves during the day from any view,
Nor could we start fires or attract attention.
Rations were slim—bread and cheese.
The next night was more difficult to start,
As we stumbled through a narrow pass
That led downward to a plain across which
We hurried as much as we could to reach
Our next destination on the thick-forested slopes
Of the final range. Again we rested, hidden,
For the day. That night found the greatest hardship
As we struggled across the winding passes,
Leading to cold heights, where at all times
We maintained utter silence, not knowing

Where observers might be stationed,
And finally, crossed over the high range
And found again a refuge in thick woods.
On the final night we fought both dark and time
As we hurried down the slopes on to the plain,
Then slipped past Tegea to reach at last
These present woods and here conceal ourselves
As you had directed, so that in the morning
We let by the Arcadian forces who did not see us
And then closed around them as you had directed.
And—the Gods be praised!—no men nor animals were lost."

All present applauded the heroes of this strange march,
And Orestes gave precious gifts to those who led them,
And to the clever guides who brought them there.
Then all dispersed to a well-deserved rest.

The next day, late in the morning, Aepytus,
His mood not helped by what he drank the last night,
Sent messengers to bring his army and supplies.
Orestes had done the same the previous day,
And for the next several days each awaited
The arrival of their reinforcements.
During this time Telemachus watched closely
For a moment to catch Halitherses alone;
And one day he went with him to see the progress
Of the planning for the sanctuary.
They climbed the slope toward the meadow,
Entering the thick-clustered forest dark
With trees. Little was said between them ·
For a while; then Telemachus softly said,
Making sure that no one could hear him,

"Honoured Halitherses, respected seer
And my friend from my youth to now, forgive
Me if I transgress in what I will say.
When the meadow yesterday was sanctified,
I saw you look at Aepytus and start,
Quickly recovering your composure.
May I ask you now what vision you had,
And if it will affect us, either for good or bad?"

The older man looked at him somberly.

"Telemachus, someday I will tell you
What I saw, but not for the present,
Not until we have left the campaign,
For reasons that then will be evident.
What I will say is this, and you must keep this
Close to your heart, not telling your father
Or anyone what I tell you now—your oath?"

And the intrigued young man made his vow.

"Apollo sent me one vision, clear and
Distinct; that is what I cannot tell you now.
But he also gave me a feeling, dark
And troubled, over what Aepytus will do
That will affect us all. What that is,
I do not know for now; but it will be clear
When it happens, and I feel that it will
Occur when we reach the next holy spot.
In the meantime, ask me no more, and as
I made you vow, tell no one else until
I release you from your word."

Telemachus agreed, and they entered
The meadow, where architects were busy
In working out the plans and dimensions
Of the future sanctuary. After consultation,
They returned through the forest and down
The slope. As they broke through the verge
They saw the great plain before them,
With the huge humps of the ranges brooding
On either side. Halitherses sighed.

"This will not be an easy campaign,
But rough and troublesome, with an ally
Not to be trusted and who lacks ability
To plan fully. He is cunning, not shrewd,
Relies on brute force more than diplomacy,
And must be watched always for treachery.
Keep your eyes open, be watchful at all times.
This you may mention to your father,

But choose your time well, when he is apart
From others—just as you have done at present."

And he smiled at Odysseus's son, showing that
He recognized his prudence and his tact.

Over the next several days Telemachus
Watched, quietly and keen-eyed, as the
Meetings took place to discuss strategy
And learn what they would face in the next range,
And where the tribes lived in that wild region.
Telemachus learned much as he watched there
And saw his father ask shrewd and searching questions
From Aepytus's commanders and his guides.
Aepytus himself sat back, letting his subordinates
Provide the necessary answers as he watched
Through sharp cunning eyes the tactics of the
Argives and the Ithacans. As before,
Odysseus pushed for diplomacy and guile
Before being forced to battle. Aepytus
Grunted his assent, but Telemachus
Saw that he was of a different mind,
And, worried, the son finally found a time
To speak to his busy father. At night
After the feasting and as they retired to
Their tents, he broached the matter in his mind.

"Father, may I speak to you of what I see?"

Odysseus looked carefully at his son.

"Of course, my prince, but away from the tents
And alert ears."

They strolled out beyond the boundaries
Of the camp. The moon was now in full bloom,
Casting its light on the harsh mountain peaks
And on the plain below, and they could see
Each other in the clear cold light. They
Chose to stop where they could see about them
Plainly in all directions, while they themselves
Squatted stilly, indistinguishable from
The small boulders and objects around them.

"Well? Tell me what you have seen when we meet."

Telemachus was thoughtful for a moment, then began.

"A few days ago I was in discussion
With Halitherses, who told me to watch closely
How Aepytus acted; he is troubled
By him and does not trust him—nor do I,
And I have seen in these meetings that he
Does little but let his subordinates
Speak and do the work, while he watches closely
And pays but lip service to what is said."

His father, experienced in war and guile,
Smiled.

"You are right in what you have seen of him—
But it is no more than what I expected
From what we had heard, and from what we saw
At our first meeting with him. We do not
Trust him. But he is useful to this campaign:
He wants to conquer his outlying regions,
And he knows he cannot do so without help.
The fact that we have given him the means—
And that for now he is clutched in our hands—
Will keep him with us until the armies win.
And he knows he cannot attack and win
Against the larger and more trained Argives
And ourselves. I am watching him as well,
And I think that we Ithacans are safe,
Until we leave the campaign as promised.
But you and Halitherses are right to watch,
And we must always be on our guard.
Keep me informed of what you learn as you watch."

Then they returned to their tents, Telemachus
Admiring of his father's acumen.

Both forces now started to arrive.
From the Argolid came both the soldiers
And the supplies, packed on mules and donkeys
To allow them to traverse the mountains

With their steep trails and dangerous passes.
Telemachus noticed that the Arcadians
Came as bands, rough and undisciplined,
More like pirates of the land than an army.
Orestes had given firm orders that
There should be no quarrels among his men
And these violent and uncouth forces,
And with only a minimum of fighting
They faithfully obeyed his stern commands.
Finally, all reinforcements had arrived,
And the great mass of men and horses,
Began the journey up the plain to
Orchomenos and Phineos.

The Argive King, yielding to the suggestion
Of the shrewd Odysseus, placed his cavalry
At both the front and rear, encompassing
Their Arcadian allies, and Aepytus
Was kept with the kings with only few
Of his commanders. Like a thick worm
That slowly winds and creeps over the loam,
Making its way with what seems blind purpose,
So the huge army crept down the broad plain,
Through its groves of olive trees, its grain fields,
And past small settlements from which emerged
Men and children, women and animals,
To stare without expression at the march.
The ranges narrowed, and high hills enclosed
The end of the plain. The army veered right
Through a valley to circumnavigate
The hump of the main hill, and in a large
Basin on a farther side camped that night.
The next day they followed a large pass
Past hills on either side and entered
The plain that led around the sharp-edged spine
Of a mountain to where a smaller peak
Supported on its sloping sides Phineos
And on the plain before it Orchomenos.
Here the force made secure its final camp.
The kings with their supporting bands climbed up

The slope high above the hill nestled by
The mountain and followed a trail that wound
Through the woods that clothed the steep incline.
Finally they reached a more open space
From which, through the trees, they could see the plain
Stretched out before them, and the mountains that
Surrounded it.

"Here the God has guided us to construct
His holy sanctuary,"
                    Odysseus said.

"Have the architects work out the best plan,
And set up an altar now for the sacrifice
Once the tribes have arrived for witness."

Before the forces had left the kings had sent
Messengers to the Arcadian tribes
To join them here for the sanctification.
The group now returned and entered Orchomenos.
Again Telemachus saw Halitherses
Glance and pale, but this time his gaze was fixed
On Orestes with a look both of dread
And compassion. This time the clever son
Of the Ithacan king knew not to ask
The seer of his vision until they were
Well away from Arcadia and safe.

The next day was set for the ceremony,
But when it dawned, only one tribe's ruler
Arrived, from the neighbouring valley.
He came with his delegation of four,
As rough in his way as Aepytus was.
Disappointed as the kings were, they still
Kept to the appointed date, and the group
Climbed to the sanctuary's site, where they
Found ready the altar and the beasts for
Sacrifice. Odysseus, as its true patron,
Stepped before the group and told again
How the Gods had ordered him to come here
To build Poseidon's temple and give praise
To him. His speech done, with the priests he cut

The victims' throats and made the dedication.
The ceremonies finished, they returned
To the plain and to the place for the feast.
The tribe's representatives were given
Places of honour, beside Aepytus and
The kings. As the feast progressed Odysseus
Looked for an appropriate time to speak
To the leader of the tribe; but before
He could start, Aepytus confronted them.

"You see our army's strength; will you now bend
To us and see me as your king?"

Odysseus and Orestes looked at him, appalled
That he would ruin their diplomacy
In this crude way. They winced when the leader
Glared at Aepytus, then spoke in a voice
Harsh and contemptuous.

"Why should we bow to your insulting demand?
We have been always independent, and
Will continue in this way. All your troops—
And I mean your Arcadian troops, not
Your Argive visitors, who have their own
Reason to be here, and are sensible
To bring forces that you cannot betray—
All your own troops could never overcome us
In our mountain fastness. Do not bring up
This stupid request again."

And he nodded to his colleagues; they rose
Together and left the feast. Aepytus
Sat frozen, his face purple, contorted
With rage. Then he also arose and left,
Taking with him one of his commanders.
Odysseus, Pylades, and Orestes
Themselves sat stunned by the raw incident.

Then Odysseus roused himself and said softly,

"The strategy for the campaign must now change.
We have succeeded up to now by use

Of diplomacy; but with this one only
War will work. It may turn out worse, when he
Responds to what just happens; we must watch
Carefully and try to salvage what we can.
But my advice is this: if—when—we must
Use force to conquer tribes, let his troops lead
The way, not ours; let them take the brunt
And save our forces' casualties until
We must join the fight. It is difficult."

The others nodded at his sage advice.
But before they could speak, beyond the feast
A great clamour arose, shouting erupted,
And the clash of swords. They hastily arose
And rushed out. A short distance away
The blaze of another fire showed two groups
In battle, one much smaller than the other.
Even as they arrived the smaller group fell,
Cut down by the larger group. Standing there,
Smiling in victory, Aepytus held
High his bloodied sword.

"No one can insult the Arcadian king!"
He shouted wildly, his eyes glaring bright
In the fire's flames.

"Let these bodies be dragged to their home
As a lesson for those who stand against us!"

The kings were aghast at this foul breach
Of hospitality; then Odysseus
Prayed to Athena to fill him with strength,
Strode to Aepytus and grasped his sword arm,
Forcing him with his great strength to release
The blade, which fell at their feet close to the
Corpse of the murdered tribesman. In fury
Aepytus strove to break the warrior's
Merciless grip but found himself helpless.
He glared at Odysseus, but could not speak
When his eyes met the other's and were caught
In a pitiless and terrifying stare.

He suddenly knew what the Trojans killed
By the fierce warrior had felt in each last moment,
As a bird first clutched in an eagle's talons,
Helpless to move, sees the eagle's harsh eye
Just before the beak strikes out its life.
He froze in terror, then heard words piercing
Through his head like physical cuts, to carve
Into his memory what he had done.

"Because you are a king and now our ally,
I will not kill you as you deserve for
What you've done. By all laws that govern
Hospitality, you have wrought great wrong.
Look at your work!"

And he bent the man down to see the corpse
That lay beside them, face to the ground.

"Not only did you attack a man whom
You invited for a holy dedication,
And sat beside at our mutual feast
In celebration of this event that
United nations in a common good,
But you gave him no chance for defence—
He had barely time to draw his sword
Before you plunged yours into his side,
Not even facing him directly.
Is this the way a king should act? Like a
Pirate or a bandit, cowardly and base?"

Aepytus wished to shout he was insulted,
That he had taken just revenge, but now
Odysseus dragged him upright again, and
Held his gaze again so that he could not speak.

"Hear now what you must do to propitiate
The Gods. These slain will be returned
To their home dressed in proper raiment,
And given full honours, complete with gifts
From you to acknowledge what has happened.
We will accompany you to make sure
That you do all these things properly, as

Befits a king—who wishes to expand
His territory. Now make your vow
Before all here that you will do what
The Gods through me have ordered."

Though Odysseus had not raised his voice
While he spoke, his words had carried clearly
Through the throngs about them, who stood frozen,
Stunned by the awesome power of the king.
Now Odysseus released his grip, so that
The arm of Aepytus fell nerveless to his side,
And he felt himself, in a quavering voice,
Make his vow to fulfill what had been ordained.
Then his men, without his orders, picked up
The bodies carefully and took them off
To be tended properly, and Aepytus
Himself was led, staggering and dazed,
To his own tent by his subordinates.
All watched him go; then Odysseus nodded
To Orestes, and the leaders followed
Him to the royal tent. There, around a
Small fire, they sat to consider what next
To do. All was silent as the warrior,
Like a panther motionless, in the fire
Studied the twisting flames and glowing logs.
The others waited patiently, disturbed
By the murders and what they portended.
Finally he roused himself to speak.

"Until now, King Orestes, we have been
Fortunate, forcing this alliance
And arriving here with no loss of men.
But the future looks much darker for us:
Only one tribe came for the dedication,
And its representatives have been slaughtered;
We will not encounter good will when we go there,
And there will be hard struggle in these mountains
To gain the ascendancy. As well,
We are burdened with this Arcadian king,
Who has shown he does not deserve his title."

All murmured deep-felt, angry agreement.

"We can hope that what we have made him vow
Will show to the aggrieved tribe that we act
Honourably, despite Arcadia."

Grunts of proud agreement from the group.

"But we must now be on our guard in two ways—
First, to avoid the ambushes that will be
A major strategy in the mountains;
And second, to keep a wary eye always
On Aepytus, who will act treacherously
When he is given any chance.
I have earned his deadliest enmity,
But he will be too cowardly to attack me
Openly, and I will give him no chance
Otherwise. From now on, then, we must plan
To keep our forces always at alert,
Not only guarding us in all directions,
But with our men drifting through Arcadian
Forces to make sure they do not turn on us.
Fortunately we have agreed that they
Will always be in the vanguard of the action.
Tomorrow we set out for the tribe's home.
Keep spies and guides always available."

Orestes agreed, grateful for this advice
And for the fruitful actions that the king
Had provided for him. All then retired;
But Odysseus lay open-eyed, thinking
Of what he must do to finish his task
For this campaign and leave Orestes
With his companions safely for Sparta.

The next day the armies struck camp and marched
To the north of Orchomenos to a plain
As large as the previous. Before them
The bodies were carried on litters rich
With cloths and carrying precious gifts.
They passed along the plain, skirting
The north side of the sanctuary's peak,

Another that gave to two valleys; down
The western one they travelled, then turned
South on an opening plain to reach a slope
Wedged between two mountains, where was built
The fortress of the tribe to which they went.
Orestes, Pylades, and Odysseus
Brought up to flank, Aepytus in the forefront,
And before the fort Medon as herald
Stepped forward to address those waiting
On the battlements.

"People of this well-favoured citadel,
We greet you, not in war but in sadness."

As Medon spoke on before those silent
On the walls, Odysseus studied the fort
And the terrain. Built high on the slope
It afforded a site both to observe
The plain and difficult to attack,
Situated on a narrow valley's side,
Built of heavy logs, its façade high, like
Some large dark growth that stands alone.
Behind it a forest reared higher, but
The sharp-eyed warrior saw a ledge jut
Out above those heavy evergreens, that
Behind the citadel were cut away
To allow no shelter to any siege.
His attention was brought abruptly
To where he sat on his horse as a cry
Rose from the wall as Medon gestured to
The bodies that were now carried forward
On the luxuriant litters. Without
A word two men removed from the wall;
Bowmen on the ramparts raised their weapons
At readiness; and the gates swung open.
Through them passed the men who had just quitted
The wall. They were dressed more like priests, their robes
Long but thick with fur. With them came a troop
Of warriors similar to the ones
That now lay lifeless and spread before them.
They acknowledged Medon with a curt nod;

Then warriors took the litters back through the gates.
The two men remained; Medon bowed and moved
Aside to let them speak directly to the kings,
Who then dismounted for the solemn parlay.
One of the men, taller than his fellows,
With a full mane and beard, his face weathered
And lined, his eyes with the sharpness of a hawk's,
Moved slightly forward to address them:

"We thank you, King Orestes of Argos,
And your fellow king of Ithaca, Odysseus,
Whom we know well as Arcadia's friend
When he fought at Troy with its former king,
The dauntless Agapenor"—

Here Aepytus scowled and would have spoken
But for Odysseus, who, close to him, gripped
Secretly his arm, reminding him of
The grip the previous night—

"For bringing us the bodies of our comrades
In this state, with gifts, and in observance
Of their deaths as should please the watchful Gods.
But we know that you had no hand in their deaths,
Having come to dedicate a holy place;
But that this one"—

He pointed to Aepytus, his look stern
And contemptuous—

"Treacherously butchered them, catching them
Unawares, having just left the banquet.
For him we have nothing but disdain—
Contempt, not honour, is his lot for us."

Aepytus ground his teeth in rage, helpless
To respond beside the grim Odysseus.

"As to his demand that we bow down to him,
We refuse, as did our slaughtered leaders.
We will remain independent, do what
He will. And you, King of Argos, with whom
We have no quarrel, know that we will owe

Allegiance to no ruler so long
As we can defend ourselves. You have brought
Forces more than you need for observance
Or to keep secure from this craven man,
But keep in mind that these high fastnesses
Are impregnable, or their defeat
Will prove a terrible cost to those who
Wish to conquer them. We ask you, then, to leave
Us with our dead and to return to your own land,
Knowing what consequences will occur
If you attempt more here."

In this way he ended, then bowed and with
His companion returned through the thick gate
Not allowing Orestes to speak one word.
Odysseus looked at Orestes, and they
Signalled their forces to move back along
The floor of the narrow gully.

When they had moved to where the gully
Opened up to greet the plain, a distance
Much longer than a bow shot, they set up
Camp on this late afternoon, and council
Was taken among the different allies.
Aepytus, now freed from his vexed constraint,
Now raged at the other kings.

"Why did you not attack when you had the chance?
The gate was open, the men unprotected!
Why did you not let me take revenge
On what he said? You heard him—they will not
Serve me nor you. We must conquer them,
Or none in these mountains will obey us!"

Odysseus, who had listened quietly
While the king had shouted at them, now spoke:

"Aepytus, would you have attacked then
And found yourself, like a dog that attacks
A hedgehog, peppered with quills? Those bowmen
Would have slain us all before we could act.
I for one do not see suicide the better choice.

But if you wish to attack the citadel
Tomorrow, it is your choice and your action.
We will be there as well, is that not right,
My lord Orestes?"

Orestes, surprised by his fellow king's
Mild words and quick acquiescence to these
Demands, muttered his agreement.

"Then, King Aepytus, check with your forces
To plan your attack, and we will support you."

The Arcadian king, now filled with pride
And exultation that he had won the day,
Swept out to find his followers. The rest
Remained on Odysseus's quiet gesture.

"Why did you agree to his wild demand?
Do we know enough to make such a strike?"

Odysseus, seeing his companion's alarm,
Smiled.

"No, we do not know what their defences are.
But we will know, once Aepytus begins.
We may support him, but not in that battle.
Let him waste his men in this attempt—
It will be a lesson cruelly learned.
I am interested in what may happen
Among those trees above the citadel.
But we will know more in the morning."

Then Odysseus's face grew grave, and he faced
Orestes directly, looking into his eyes.

"As we have promised, we have brought you
Successfully through this first phase of your campaign.
You must agree that we have come much farther
Than you may have hoped at first."

Orestes, seeing where the Ithacan
Was leading, reluctantly agreed.

"And I'm sure you will agree, conquering
This tribe is vital to the rest of the campaign,

For all the other settlements will see
Who will be victorious here, and when
It is seen that you, not Aepytus, has won,
Then they will conclude two things:
First, that it will be hard to fight you back;
And, second, that it is you who has won,
Not Aepytus, and they will be more willing
To concede, knowing that you are the strength
In the alliance."

Orestes, intrigued by this argument, agreed.

"Then I ask you to acknowledge that if I
Engineer the fall of this citadel
I have fulfilled the promise that I made,
And you will keep your promise to release
Me and my companions to journey on
To Sparta and the rest of my pilgrimage."

Orestes was torn at this request; he
Wished the hero to remain to help him
To finish the campaign, but he knew he
Must keep his own promise for his honour.
He glanced at Pylades, who had listened
Closely to all that had been said, and his friend
Gravely nodded to him to accede.
And the Argive king sighed and assented.

"I thank you, King of Argos. You have proved
Yourself a true son of Agamemnon.
Let us feast now and then retire early.
We will see more clearly what to do
After tomorrow's battle."

The conference finished, each left for the feast,
Harbouring his own thoughts about the future.

The next day Aepytus's army was ranged
Across the opening to the gulch in lines
Bristling with spears and shields, with strong bowmen
And fierce warriors. Behind came an engine
With a great ram to batter down the gates.
Aepytus and his commanders rode back

Of this army after he had incited
His men to march forward to victory.
The lines first marched together to the base
Of the slope on which the citadel
Was perched, then wheeled about to face its wall.
The first line started up the slope, slanted
Steeply. As they moved on, they came within
The range of the bowmen on the battlements.
Like a swarm of hornets who quickly reach
Their victim and, like a black cloud, obscure
The stings that they inflict so mortally,
So the defenders' arrows struck the line,
Whose soldiers had not realized how far
The arrows could hurtle down the sheer slope.
One caught a soldier through the throat—he fell,
Writhing, to trip the one behind him;
Another pierced a shoulder, others
Hit bodies, heads, legs, before the shields
Could be raised to fend them off. Behind,
Aepytus's own bowmen let forth a volley,
But they were too far below to reach home.
The line, shields raised to ward off further hits,
Staggered farther upward, followed by the rest.
The bowmen above disappeared; but then
Men on the palisade brought forth great stones,
Which they levered over the top; these rolled
And bounded down the slope, careering
Into the lines of men, who were crushed or killed
By the boulders striking with such dreadful
Force, or who scattered to escape the surge.
As soon as they did, from the forest
To their right new swarms of arrows
Cut down survivors, their flanks unprotected.
Aepytus immediately sent
Forces to attack those among the trees
But they were seen quickly retreating
To the rear of the citadel, and any
Who pursued them were picked off by the bowmen.
His forces, the lines broken and confused,
Now retreated back to their base, leaving

The dead and wounded, who were picked off
By the merciless bowmen.

Aepytus, raging in humiliation,
Stormed back to the other kings, who had watched
The battle carefully, their men in formation
But kept well back in safety.

"Why did you not assist me? Do you call
This your support? Are you cowards? Traitors?"

Odysseus strode up to him, causing him
To back up involuntarily.

"What could we have done, given the tactics
That you used? Do you think anyone could reach
The citadel up such a slope and against
Such a deadly defence? No, as you have
So clearly shown us."

Aepytus, still smarting from the defeat
And from the words of the wily veteran,
Then snarled,

"What will you do, then? What victory
Can you conjure up in this situation?"

Odysseus looked at him shrewdly, then said,

"If I win this place for you, will you make
A new vow? That you will promise
To acknowledge Orestes, not only
As an ally, but as your superior king,
To whom you will owe allegiance
While you keep your crown?"

Aepytus stared at him, astonished, then
Laughed and said,

"Since you cannot do what you boast you will,
I will make such a vow, but only on
The condition that you fulfill your
Vainglorious boast."

And there, in front of the kings and all the men,
He gave such a vow, chuckling as he did so.

"I thank you, King Aepytus, for your vow,
And tonight, after we have feasted well,
I will consult with you all what next to do."

And he did as he had said that night,
And all were amazed by his daring plan,
If not convinced that he could bring it off.

On the next fateful day, the armies assembled,
This time when Helios had galloped to
The apex of his journey in the sky.
Aepytus's men were still in the forefront,
But the other force was now massed behind,
So that at the base of the slope were found
A huge mass of men, many with their shields
Raised above their heads, obscuring them.
Again the lines advanced up the slope,
But then stopped just where the arrows could strike,
And there they waited silently, still.
Up on the parapets it was clear that
The defenders were puzzled by this action,
And their leader joined them to appraise
The situation. As he did so, he
Gasped and fell forward into the arms
Of his amazed companions, a long arrow
Protruding from his now lifeless body.
Even as they looked about to find the source,
Other arrows followed, each finding a prey.
In a panic, some fled the battlement;
Then someone called out and pointed upward.
There, silhouetted against the bright sky,
On the ledge high above them stood Odysseus
With his great bow, loosing more swift death
Even as they gaped at it. Quickly they
Sent men from the rear of the citadel,
But they were cut down as they neared the forest
By the wily veteran's warriors, who had
Climbed there during the night and had ambushed

The bowmen who had gone there when there seemed
To be an attack about to happen.
Bowmen on the battlements sent flights
Of arrows at the ledge, but it was too distant
And their arrows fluttered harmlessly down.
While all were concerned with the dread sniping
The army below had crept quietly
Up the slope to where they were now in range
For their bowmen to move through the soldiers.
Now their volleys caught the defenders
Off guard, their shields protecting them from the shafts
Hurtling from above; and men were cut down
Before they could adjust. Even as they
Were beset above and below, soldiers
Rushed to the base of the huge wooden wall,
Carrying branches and logs, tinder and brush,
Which they piled high against it despite
The desperate efforts of the defenders,
Who could use neither rocks nor arrows
Against the deadly barrage from the two
Places. Torches lit the piles; and soon flames
Licked up the wooden sides, smoke enveloped
The defenders, and the army brought
Its battering ram with which it hammered
At the gate, which, groaning under such blows,
Finally gave way. As when a high dam
Forms a crack that widens farther until
The structure cannot fight the pressure
And crumbles, huge segments crashing down,
And a great wall of water bursts forth,
A deluge sweeping all away before it,
So through the gap rushed the flood of soldiers,
Overwhelming the despairing forces
Before them. Racing through the breach with them
Came Telemachus with his comrades, who
Had been active in the forest and now
Joined with the main force. The men of the tribe
Fought with ferocity, but the numbers
Of the invaders were too great, and they
Were forced back through the narrow ways, dying

As they went. Telemachus himself drove
His sword through the leather armour of one,
Who doubled over in pain, but looked up
At him with hate-filled eyes even as he died.
As they fought along, some of the soldiers
Set buildings ablaze with torches; as those
Inside were forced out, the women were grabbed
And thrown to others to cluster them together;
Their children were torn from them, and before
Their eyes they saw, even as they screamed in horror,
Their sons and daughters hacked to pieces, babies
Dashed against the stones; inside the huts
Old men and women, and those weak with fever,
Were burned alive, their screams of agony
Adding to the crescendo of the cries
Of the victims, the victorious shouts
Of the victors, and the crackling noises
Of the blaze that now engulfed the citadel.

In the midst of this inferno, racing
Through the streets, Telemachus chanced upon
A strange sight: backed in a corner, wild-eyed,
A girl crouched, sword in hand, warding off four
Soldiers. Already one was lying prone
On the ground, his blood staining the street's stones.
The others, furious, were poised to strike
But still kept their distance warily—
One other had a cut across his arm.
Telemachus took in the situation,
And, without thinking, leaped to them and pushed
Them aside. They turned to strike; then seeing who
He was, turned away with an oath and ran
Down the burning street. The young warrior turned
Toward the girl, who flew to attack him.
He found that she knew sword play well—her thrust
He barely parried, and her own defence
Was skilled and strong. But she was exhausted
And soon her strokes and parries weakened,
Until finally Telemachus moved
Suddenly close to her and beat the sword

From her hand. Sobbing in anger and despair
She tried to claw him, but he caught her hands,
And she writhed in fury and frustration.
Catching his breath as he held the struggling
Girl, he spoke in her ear,

"It is no use—you cannot get free—and
You are better off in my hands than in theirs.
You have shown courage and fought well, as well
As any man, and you should have respect
For how you tried to defend yourself here.
But now it is over; your town is doomed;
And you must stay alive as my prisoner."

As he talked, the girl kept writhing in defiance.
But with his final words, she slumped, sobbing
Bitterly and uncontrollably. She
Let her hands be bound without more struggle,
And he led her hurriedly to the gates
As the burning buildings began to collapse
Around them. As they moved through the red streets,
They saw soldiers with women they had caught
Hurling them to the stones, ripping away
Their clothes, and taking turns, while others held
The terrified girls' arms, to rape them repeatedly.
The girl Telemachus led cried out
When she saw her friends, whom she had known
Throughout her life, so viciously abused,
And her cries blended with their sobs of pain
And shame. But Odysseus's strong son dragged her
With him past the gates and into the clear air
Beyond. Already the corral of women,
Many of whom showed the signs of rape
Or rough abuse, were being herded down
The slope, while behind them the plume of smoke
Marked the extinction of the doomed citadel.

Telemachus descended to the camp
With his captive in tow, to find his father
Returned, meeting with the other kings.
Aepytus, caught between the victory

And his own oath of allegiance
Proclaimed before all, stood with the others;
Then, catching sight of the valiant son,
Roared out, pointing at the pinioned girl,

"There is the daughter of the dead ruler—I
Demand her as the spoil of my kingdom!"

Telemachus, only half surprised
At the identity of his prisoner,
Stopped before them, his face dark with anger.

"I won her fairly in battle; by right
Of war she is mine to keep as I wish!"

Aepytus turned red with fury and snarled,
"I am the king here; I command you now
To hand her to me!"

He beckoned to some of his soldiers
To come forward to take the girl by force,
But before they could move, Odysseus quickly
Strode between them and his son, whose sword now
Had left its scabbard, and he said mildly,

"Aepytus, you may be king for this country,
But you forget your oath of allegiance
To Agamemnon's great son. You demand
A prisoner despite the known rules of war.
Let King Orestes decide this matter
For us."

He turned to the king, surprised as all were
By this twist, given that Telemachus
Was Odysseus's son, but made vulnerable
By this declaration.

"My lord, it is you who must now decide
Which of these two men is in the right."

Orestes frowned but knew that his judgment,
The first in his new reign, would determine
How he would be seen through this country and

His own. He was silent while all waited,
Then said,

"Both men can demonstrate a right—the king
By his rank, and the warrior by his action.
In this case, a trial by combat will be
The way to resolve this matter: who wins
Will be the one who gains this royal captive."

All saw the justice of this decision,
But they were aghast at what it meant
For Odysseus and his valiant son.
Odysseus frowned but said nothing; his son,
However, immediately agreed.

Aepytus, who had no intention
To fight the young warrior, said,

"I assent, but as king I have the right
To choose as champion in my place—and I
Choose this man to represent me."

He turned and beckoned to a soldier
Who strode forward. He was huge for his race,
Bulky, powerfully built, with the neck
Of a bull, a leathered face, coarse dark beard,
And he grinned contemptuously at his foe,
Who was almost as tall, but slighter than
His stocky opponent. A circle opened
For them, and they stepped into it to face
Each other, swords in hand. There was a pause;
Then the bigger man shambled forward
And unleashed a vicious blow; a quick duck
Made it harmless, and Telemachus swiftly
Struck back, slicing his opponent's arm.
He roared in anger, then swung his own blade
Back so hard that the parry stung the arm
Of Telemachus with its force, and he
Was forced to give way as the enraged brute
Hammered violently at him. Like two
Wolves circling one another, then leaping
For a throat or leg, so the two sustained

The same tactics for some time, the stronger
Lumbering after his opponent, who,
More agile, ducked and jumped away from each
Powerful swing. But to all it then appeared
That the young man was tiring, his parries
Less vigorous, his steps less quick. There came
A moment when he moved too slowly;
The sword missed him, but then the champion
Twisted and smashed his elbow into the ribs;
There was a crack clearly heard by those near,
And Telemachus, grimacing with pain,
Knelt on one knee, his sword trailing in the dust.
Triumphantly the burly veteran strode
Before him, a sadistic grin twisting his
Face, and raised his sword to cleave the man below.
But even as he raised his arms, holding
His sword with both hands, Telemachus
Suddenly raised his sword, and with all his might,
Thrust upward. The sword pierced the leather armour
Just below the rib cage and ripped through
The stomach and the heart. The man's grin turned
To a gape; his sword dropped backward from his
Nerveless hands; and as Telemachus,
In pain, yanked out his sword, the body
Swayed and fell to the ground, where his blood
Collected in a pool, staining the dusty ground.
A cheer arose from the victor's comrades;
And Telemachus painfully arose
And moved with all his will to Orestes.
In a low voice, with little breath because
Of his cracked rib, he said painfully,

"I claim by right of victory my prize."

Then he fainted at the Argive king's feet.

As when we, drowsy, find ourselves in thick fog
And feel our feet barely touch the soft earth,
What is above, below, or forward unknown,
And then the fog clears slightly, and we see,
But do not know for the moment where we are,

So Telemachus slowly awoke,
To see above him a tent and before
A girl and an older man who he then
Recognized as his father and the girl,
The one for whom he had fought valiantly.
He tried to raise himself, but pain shot through
His side so that he gasped and lay supine,
Keeping from the slightest movement, his breath
Slow and slight to avoid the pain in his
Tight bandaged side as he now discovered.
His father smiled and put his hand gently
On his son's brow.

"Keep still—your rib is cracked, not broken,
Apollo be praised. You will have to stay
Here for several days to recuperate.
And here is the prize that you won so well.
She is the one that must tend to your needs
For this time."

The girl said nothing, as she had done since
Her capture, but both men noticed her eyes
Betrayed for a moment grudging respect
Before her thoughts were again veiled from them.

Odysseus looked at his son again, then
Said quietly,

"I am proud of you, my son. You have shown
Courage and honour. I will talk to you
Later about our plans."

Then his father turned to the girl, whose gaze
Had studied them throughout this exchange.

"You would do well to consider his fight
For you, both against the soldiers"—

Both Telemachus and the girl were surprised
That the wily veteran knew of their combat
And the son was again struck by his father's
Astute command of fact and situation—

"And against the champion of this kingdom's
King. If he had lost in either case,
Your lot would have been dismal indeed
As slave to that brutal king or another
Lord, both raped and shamed to begin,
And abused and mistreated all your life.
But you have gained my son's deep respect—
And mine as well—for your courage and skill;
And as a high-born woman we will treat
You with more esteem than others we take.
Therefore I suggest that you watch over him
These next few days, both for his sake and yours,
So that he can ride well when we leave here."

Odysseus smiled at her; but she could see
That he meant what he said, and she shivered,
Remembering his figure, black against the sun,
High above the town, raining death upon them.
But she also kept deep in her mind
What he had just said. She saw the young warrior
Move his head slightly to see her.

"Come closer—I have never had a chance
Truly to look at you."

As she moved forward to his side, he saw
That she was now clean, dressed in a man's chiton,
In which she seemed not embarrassed but at home.
She was tall, almost as tall as himself,
Statuesque, with dark hair that had been clipped
To flow at the level of her shoulders.
Her face was tanned and clear; her character,
Strong and intelligent, shone through to make
Attractiveness irrelevant, although
He knew well how passionate she could be.
He looked her over carefully; her gaze
Did not waver; she showed no embarrassment
In his frank examination of her face
And body. He was impressed by what he saw;
And when he had finished, he looked in her eyes.
There he no longer saw hate but instead

An open look that took in but betrayed
Nothing; but deep in her he sensed great grief
And loss, terrible loss, and no means yet
To find her way back to a direction
For her life. Despite himself he was moved
By what he sensed; to cover his feelings
He asked,

"You have not uttered a word since we met.
Will you speak now?"

"If you wish."

Her voice, although quiet, was rich and low,
Matching her commanding presence.

"Do you know now who we are, my father
And myself?"

"I know only that you have destroyed my town
And my family, and that I am now
A slave with whom you can do as you please."

Despite her attempt at control,
Her bitterness burst forth, and she began
To shake as she relived the day's events.
Wincing with the pain of the movement,
Telemachus reached forth his hand for hers.
At first she refused it; then, grasping it,
She broke into rasping sobs, falling on her knees
And burying her head in his bedding.
He continued to hold her hand while she wept,
Letting her release her anguish and her grief.

Odysseus, when he left the tent, crossed
To where Orestes and the others sat
Before a blaze that overwhelmed the site
Which glowed up on the slope. Night spread darkly,
And the forces were all feasting, or those
That had finished and who had been assigned
Women as slaves were amusing themselves;
The women's soft cries could be heard over
The crackling of the flames. The Ithacan

Sat with the Argive and Arcadian kings,
Accepted the meat and wine proffered him,
Settled down comfortably, then said,

"The main work has been done for you, I think.
Tomorrow I suggest that you send heralds,
One from you, King Orestes, and one from
You, King Aepytus, who together can
Announce to the mountain tribes the alliance
Between you, the allegiance of the
Arcadian king, and the victory here
Which can serve as an example of what
Can occur to any of them who should
Deny allegiance to you. They will,
I'm sure, see the necessity to do so."

Orestes nodded in agreement, then looked
At Aepytus, who reluctantly agreed as well.

"Then let us feast and relax after this
Victory."

And he told stories of the Trojan War
For their entertainment. After some time
Aepytus excused himself—he had picked
One of the women with whom he intended
To enjoy himself.

                    After he had gone,
Odysseus turned to Orestes and said quietly,

"While Aepytus is not here, I wanted
To give you some final advice, if you
Wish to take it."

Orestes, surprised, agreed, and Pylades,
And he listened carefully to the subtle king,
Who first gestured to Halitherses
To join them. He did so, and Odysseus began:

"Within this week all of Arcadia should be yours.
But as you realize, you cannot trust the word
Of Aepytus. And so, I recommend

That you build a capitol here, here in
Arcadia."

The two kings were surprised at this; Pylades
Was the first to speak:

"But if we do so we will be risking
Further war here, will we not?"

Orestes nodded in agreement with him.

"I would have normally agreed with you,
But hear what Halitherses has to say."

Halitherses moved forward quietly to speak
To them:

"When we dedicated the ground that time
For the sanctuary for the two Gods,
I was watching Aepytus. Suddenly
I had a vision: I saw the temple
Completed and the priests installed; the ground
There was now fully holy, so that no one
Who was not a votary could enter
Its sacred precincts. But then I saw
Aepytus arrive with his cohorts,
Jealous of what you had dedicated
There; and he strode past the outraged priests
Into the sanctuary. Immediately
He cried aloud, struck blind on the threshold,
And I knew that he would not then live long."

Odysseus then spoke again:

"Halitherses has always told the truth;
His visions invariably come true.
If that is so, we know how much time we have.
The temple should be completed within
Three years. This should give you enough time
To plan where you wish to place such a
Capitol—central, I should suggest—and
What you wish it to look like. Even while
He travels to the temple, you can start

Your own journey with your architects
And builders to your site, so that when
A new king is enthroned, you will already be
In construction. Also, you should consider
Who that next king will be, and cultivate
Him, train him as your lesser king, so that
The transition will be smooth. This is my
Last suggestion to you. And now that I
Have fulfilled my obligations to you,
With your permission and, I hope, good will,
As soon as my son's rib is healed sufficiently
We will depart to continue on to Sparta."

The Argive king smiled, amply content
In what Odysseus had accomplished
For him. Pylades as well grinned at him
In good humour and friendliness.

"You have both my thanks and blessing, good friend.
Truly you have earned your worth as a wise
And valiant hero. However, you will not leave
Without receiving from me appropriate gifts—
And you may take that young band of Corinthians
With you, for I suspect that the present king
Of Arcadia is not happy with you or your son."

All chuckled at this; but all knew danger
Lay in the enmity of Aepytus.
Odysseus for his part made light of his enemy,
But he knew well what he could expect there,
And he thanked Orestes for his cohorts.

"We will leave quietly one morning,
Before Aepytus knows that we have gone.
But for these next few days, please let on
That we will continue with you."

Orestes agreed, and their conference
Ended with all pleased with its conclusion.

While Telemachus waited for his rib
To heal, sometimes his father, sometimes

Halitherses or Medon, or his
Corinthian friends conversed with him;
But much of the time he talked to the girl,
Whose name, he finally discovered,
Was Pelagia. She said little, and when
She did, it was to ask about himself,
His father, and his family. He told
Her their history—his father hero
Of the Trojan War and a comrade
Of King Agapenor and the warriors
He brought from the mountains of Arcadia.

"Agapenor—my father knew him
And respected him as a king. Not like
This present would-be king, Aepytus!"

And she spat at his name; then, in control
Again, listened further to his stories.
As he talked, a grudging admiration
Grew in her heart for this family,
Indomitable in war and in adversity,
And she looked with reluctant but growing
Favour on the young man who had treated her
With courtesy and as an equal,
Even though she now was no more than a slave,
Or at best, might be his concubine,
As she well realized. But he did not
Touch her, and since that first frank look had used
A modest gaze that left her more comfortable
In his presence. In return she did all
She could to alleviate his pain.
Telemachus himself found in these days
Of conversation a growing fascination
With this girl, whose presence was so strong,
And found it a pleasure to have her there
To talk to. But he did not ask her
About her family and her past; he
Knew that what had just occurred could not
Be discussed until she had overcome
Her loss, her grief, and her new condition.
And so the two grew accustomed to their

Continual proximity, and both
Felt a loss when not together.

But the young warrior healed swiftly, and when
Several days had passed, he was able
To become more active, and finally
Could exercise and ride his horse and train
With his sword and spear again. One night
Odysseus came to his tent and told him
Quietly to prepare secretly
To leave at dawn the next day. Pelagia
Helped him secure his possessions, and then
All was ready for tomorrow.
Just before dawn the troop silently crept
Away, leading their horses until far
From the camp. Then, as the blackness turned
To grey, and then the dim rays of the sun
Began to tinge the high mountain peaks
With a first pink stain, they mounted
And began their journey to their next
Destination: Sparta.

# Canto 4
# SPARTA

As they trotted on, the Corinthian
Cavalry looked dubiously at who
Rode before them, behind Telemachus:
The woman he had captured from the doomed town,
Who rode in a man's chiton, as a man,
And confidently rode, and well. The two
Rode just behind Odysseus, Medon, and
Halitherses, and the Corinthian commander.
No woman, other than an Amazon,
Rode like that, and never in men's company;
And they saw her as a slave at worst,
A concubine at best. But she showed herself
More like a queen than servant, rode erect,
Nodding as Telemachus spoke to her.
What surprised them more was that Odysseus
Himself accepted her in this higher state
And showed no discomfiture nor anger
Over this bizarre arrangement, nor that
His son treated her as if an equal.

The sun had now blazed upon the peaks
And they had rounded the blunted edges
Of the Ménalo range, past Orchomenos,
And were cutting through the winding passes
That led to the Arcadian highlands.
Both Odysseus and Telemachus
Had been surprised two days previous
When, as Telemachus had walked out
To see his horse, Pelagia, walking with him,
Suddenly sprang forward and mounted, lithe
And skillful, the horse next to his own mount.

When she saw how amazed he and his father were,
She smiled at them and said,

"I have ridden horses since a child."

Odysseus concealed his anger and walked
Back to his tent; there Halitherses spoke:

"Odysseus, do not let yourself rage
At this woman. I sense that she means much
To you and all of us. For what reason
I cannot fathom yet, but I know that
She must with courtesy be treated,
And though she cannot be a wife
And at best a concubine, yet she will
Bear a child to Telemachus to affect
You and your family significantly.
Therefore let her ride with us, however
Strange it may appear to others, and let
The relationship, yet somewhat distant,
Grow and blossom between the two."

Odysseus, who had listened carefully
And saw how seriously his seer spoke,
Looked more closely at the girl on the horse,
Proud and confident, her character strong,
Then turned to his confidant and agreed,
Although within his heart there was foreboding,
For he had killed her family and people.
He did not return himself, but ordered
Medon to speak to his son and Pelagia.

"Odysseus, wise king of Ithaca,
Wishes to congratulate you, so skilled
At horsemanship, and to decree that now
You will have the right to ride with his son
And us wherever we may travel
When we leave this place."

Both Telemachus and Pelagia
Were astonished at this news, especially

When they remembered how Odysseus
Had left them in anger concealed but little.
But Pelagia acknowledged this favour
With a regal nod of gratefulness
As Telemachus smiled at the herald
With a happiness that he was surprised
To feel so sharply.
Now the young couple rode together,
Telemachus chatting with animation
As they rode along a sinuous river,
The Oligirtos Mountains at their backs.
Pelagia said little, just enough to
Prompt her partner to continue on,
But she kept her gaze before her always,
Focused on the back, so broad, the shoulders,
So powerful, of the warrior,
And saw him, not as he rode now, but when
He stood, that black silhouette high up
On the ledge above the town, like a God
Raining his arrows of death upon
Her town and family, which he had destroyed;
And the black bile of bitterness welled up
In her; and deep in her thoughts flickered now
A tiny spark, hate blown, not yet ignited
To the blaze it would become, nor was she
Aware of what it signified; but she
Sensed it was there. And as they rode on,
Now riding easily down the highland
Plain, the lush heart of Arcadia,
She let herself be more aware of how
The young man next her, so vibrant and strong,
Began to stir her own emotions
In a new, different, sensual way.

While they rode, Odysseus gestured for his son
And his companion to ride with him;
The others fell back to ride behind them.

"Telemachus, you came to Sparta
When you searched for news of me; please recount
What happened to you there."

Telemachus was happy to oblige,
And told his father and Pelagia
Of his arrival there with the son of Nestor,
Clear-eyed Pisistratus; how they had been
Greeted hospitably by King Menelaos
And his queen, incomparable Helen;
How splendid was the palace and the feast
Which they enjoyed; how his own tears, falling
When Menelaos praised Odysseus,
Betrayed whom he was; how the next morning
Menelaos met with him privately
And told him the fates of those who returned
From the Trojan War, and of his own trials;
How he had sent him away with splendid gifts.
Through all this Odysseus listened closely,
And at the end he asked his son to say
Again what the king had said about himself.

"He said—and this moved me greatly, father,
Even as he wept for those who had been killed—
That he grieved for no man so much, even
That his sleep and food were hateful to him
As his friend's memories consumed him,
As you, who, he said, worked so hard, achieved
So much, only to have disappeared,
Your fate not known. When he knew who I was,
He exclaimed that you were his dearest friend,
One who had performed innumerable feats
In combat for him; and he said that he had sworn
That when you came he'd give you a hero's welcome,
That he'd have started an Argive city for you,
Built you a palace, brought you and all your people
And your wealth over to a city of his own
That he would empty for you, so that both
Peoples would mingle, and you could unite
With mutual love and joy, until death
Wrapped its dark clouds about you. The next day
I told him of the suitors and he was outraged."

After this Odysseus nodded and thanked his son;

Then they rode again behind him as he
Mused on what his son had related.

That day they traversed the length of the plain
And camped where the mountains enclosed it
In the south. The next day they worked their way
Through narrow passes and deep ravines
With swift-moving rivers, careful to keep
Their horses' footing on the narrow
Winding trails. The sun, shadowed by the peaks
That towered over them on either side,
Had made its majestic journey
To the afternoon when they at last
Broke out onto the Lacedaemon plain,
Rich with its ripe fields of bright wheat and oats,
Rich barley, and fields of clover
Undulating in the soft winds overhead.
Behind them they saw the lower slopes
Of Mount Ménalo, to the west those of
The towering Taïyetos, that huge giant
Slumbering as it lay stretched south down to
End at the peninsula of Taenaros;
All these slopes were thickly wooded, mixtures
Of plane-trees, mulberries, the dark green-leafed
Olive, Italian poplars, pomegranate,
Orange and citrus groves. Before them lay
In the distance, shining in the slanting rays,
The white marble of the Spartan city,
And King Menelaos's dazzling palace.

"Medon, ride forward now to the citadel,
And announce to the Lacedaemon king
That we will shortly be there."

The herald nodded and spurred his weary
Horse to make the final gallop through
The verdant fields.

When the company drew near the Spartan town,
Resting by the banks of the river Euratos,
They saw more clearly, above the lesser houses,

The high-towered palace, now gleaming golden
In the late rays of the declining sun;
Then toward them rode a princely delegation,
Bright with spears and banners, helmets with plumes
Flaring with colour. As it drew nearer
Odysseus saw Medon riding by a
Gilded chariot glowing in the light,
Drawn by proud horses of the purest white,
With rich golden trappings; and in it
The driver stood, in splendid armour,
His helmet with the highest plume blazing
Over all, the tall figure of the man
Odysseus knew so well, King Menelaos.
When the two processions met they stopped,
And Menelaos, his strong voice ascending,
Spoke so all could hear:

"Odysseus, greatest victor of the Ilion War,
Without whom all we strove to do would be in vain,
Saviour of the Lacedaemon host
And all Achaeans and our staunch allies,
My dearest friend, so long unknown, whose exploits
And sufferings now are legend, we greet you here
In gratitude, in joy for your return,
And in friendship more as brother than as a king.
Welcome, welcome, my friend above all other!"

And Menelaos stepped from his chariot,
And Odysseus dismounted from his horse,
And they embraced while time seemed to stop,
And tears coursed down their faces in a torrent,
While all stood by in wonder, moved by the sight.
Then, when their emotions had subsided,
Each separated and stepped back to look
Intently at the other. Finally
Menelaos looked away to see his friend's son
Mounted near him.

"And welcome again to you, son of your illustrious
Father! This time you return with happier tidings."

The glittering king laughed happily, then turned to see
The rest of the cortege. His eye paused briefly on
Pelagia, sitting erect on her horse,
And his brow raised slightly but then recovered
Quickly, and he raised his hand to them all.

"Welcome, all you fortunate to ride with this man,
And accompany us back to our palace,
Where you will not regret our hospitality!"

With that the two heroes mounted again,
And the two groups rode as one toward the town.
When they came to the outskirts, great horns blared
A welcome, and as they moved down the street
Crowds on each side roared their praise and blossoms
Fluttered before them; children raised up on
Fathers' shoulders gaped and pointed at the
Two kings, the chariot and the horse side by side.
Then the high marble walls of the palace
Loomed before them, and they stopped outside
The court and its pristine steps, up which they mounted,
To enter in while attendants, ordered,
As Telemachus remembered from before,
By the lord Eteoneus to take the horses
And chariots away to the royal stables
Where they were rubbed down, the white barley mixed
With the golden wheat tossed at their worn hooves,
And the chariots leaned again against
The walls glowing in the sun's fading rays.

Now the tired men were led through the halls,
Immaculate in their marbled surfaces,
Inundated with the sun's resplendent,
Dying light. They were brought to where women
Took their dusty clothes, led them to steaming
Baths in great bronze tubs, washed them, and oiled them,
Dressed them in fresh chitons and soft fleeces.
Pelagia, wondered at by the women,
Was taken to other quarters, again
To be washed, perfumed, and dressed in a gown,
Of the lightest wool, that enhanced her form,

Her hair brushed and arranged with ornaments
Artful and ingenious.
When all were ready they were led back through
Halls now torch lit, alive with warmth and shadow,
To the great high-ceilinged hall where waited
Atrides Menelaos and a huge feast.
Odysseus and his son sat at the king's side,
The others ranged close to them. As the previous time,
Telemachus saw water brought in its pitcher,
Golden and elegant, and tipped into
The basin of figured silver as they
Rinsed their hands in preparation. Tables
Were placed before them, wrought in gold and bronze,
And then the feast itself began.
Attendants brought plates of bread and tidbits
To whet their appetites, as Telemachus
Remembered from before; cups, golden and
Graceful, were filled from great pitchers, adorned
With figures that portrayed heroic deeds
From the Trojan War. Then, as was his custom,
As huge serving plates heaped with many meats
Were brought forward by his sweating servants,
King Menelaos greeted with affection
His guests and his close friend:

"Again welcome to you all, and to you
Especially, great hero of the Ilion War,
King of Ithaca, that now-famous island,
And, best of all, my dearest friend! Eat now,
And celebrate with us this joyful time,
When father, son, and friend are here united!"

With that he took the choicest morsel
From his own and placed it on Odysseus's
Plate, and all then partook of the great feast,
Eating and drinking their fill contentedly.
While they ate, Atrides Menelaos
Asked his friend to relate his adventures;
But before he could, into the hall came
Radiant Helen, who had beside her
Pelagia, now arrayed in her graceful clothes.

For all who sat there, the sight of the woman
Who had been captive, then had ridden with them,
Amazed them, for now she appeared almost like
The Goddess Athena, statuesque
And striking in her beauty; and none
Was more amazed than Telemachus,
Who had been impressed by her strength of mind
And character, but now saw her in a new light.
But before the group could reflect on what
They saw, Helen herself moved into the light,
And all gasped at her incomparable beauty.
Odysseus saw that the years had matured
Her well: her loveliness was now unearthly
In its attractiveness and power; and
Her eyes and face, even as she looked at them
As should a gracious hostess, revealed
A deeper depth than he had known before.
Behind her came her train of women,
Filling the hall with their perfumed scents,
And as Telemachus had seen in the past,
Adreste brought forward her figured chair,
Phylo put beside it another
For Pelagia, and Alcippe placed
Before them the soft deep-piled fleece carpet.
Telemachus now realized why he
Had been so enamoured of Hermione:
It was the remembrance of her mother
That had so strongly moved him then; and now
He realized the potency that Helen
Bore to all men; and only his youth
And her maturity allowed him
Some freedom from her charms. Before she sat,
Helen moved to Odysseus, who stood before her.

"Odysseus, precious friend of my husband
And myself, I must give you my welcome
With all my heart."

And she took and embraced him warmly,
Staying in his embrace, both moved, as time
Paused again. Then she held him at arm's length.

"I see how the last twelve years have affected you,
And all because of what I did; our lives,
Yours and mine, have been intertwined for most
Of our lives: your courtship of me when
My husband won me"—

She smiled at Menelaos, who nodded back—

"Your statesmanship that allowed us to wed
So that no strife broke out among my suitors;
Your diplomacy to try to get me back
When Paris took me off to Ilion;
And your stratagems that pulled down Troy
And brought us all to where we are tonight.
You of anyone are to be praised, praised
For your deeds for my husband and myself."

Then she left him and sat down, beckoning
To Pelagia to sit beside her, as
Food and drink were brought to them in plenty.
For a moment there was silence as all
Began to feast; and during the brief lull
The sharp-eyed Ithacan studied closely
The couple as they fed: the lovely Helen
Clad in the richest gown, for Olympus
Fit; and her husband, Atrides Menelaos,
Handsome and vivacious, his hair still
Tawny and luxuriant, his tall figure
Still powerful and graceful—although
Odysseus noted grey now crept stealthily
Into the hair, and fat had begun
To enclose the flesh and rippling muscle.
Now the king spoke again, his rich voice
Ringing through his tall-roofed, spacious hall:

"Odysseus, my good friend, we were delayed
In hearing your adventures by the entrance
Of these two lovely women. Would you now
Relate to us what happened after Troy,
Great exploits that we have heard from afar,
But now can truly hear from you in person."

Odysseus nodded to his gracious host,
And then began his story, his own voice
Filling the hall without effort, compelling
All to hear. Telemachus, knowing now
What his father would say, took the time
To study Helen and Pelagia
As they listened, caught up in the story.
Keen in observation as his father,
He saw that Helen took careful note
Of all that was said; but she studied deeply
The eloquent warrior, and her eyes
Revealed a curious look that the son
Could not decipher well. He also found
Himself filled with a strange sensation as
He watched the gorgeous queen; when he came
The last time, she had worked with her spindle
And the violet wool and yarn resting
In the heavy silver castored basket
Given her by the wife of King Polybus
Of Thebes in Egypt; this time she remained
Motionless, her whole attention on the man;
And Telemachus saw her as a statue,
With the same impenetrable spirit
Cloaked in the marble of such a sculpture.
When he turned to watch Pelagia, he saw
The same stillness; but the girl's dark eyes
Took in both man and story fully, and
Those dark eyes flashed, her breathing quickened,
As she relived in herself what was narrated.
Yet even as she was absorbed in the tales,
Her eyes grew darker when she watched the man,
With feelings that the son could not fathom.
Several times he felt her turn her look on him,
And he made sure she did not know he watched her;
But when he looked back just after such a look,
He found her in a mood of troubled appraisal.
When Odysseus finished his long account,
A collective sigh rose in the high hall,
And Menelaos laid his hand upon
The arm of the redoubtable warrior.

"Truly, my friend, you have suffered far more
Than the rest of our companions who fought
In that war. We thank the Gods that at last
You have returned to home and wife and child."

As the moved king said these words, Telemachus
Looked at Helen; and although she remained
Still as a statue, he saw tears now trickling
Down her lovely face which she did not deign
To wipe away. Pelagia's face he found
Betrayed emotions that struggled to win
An ascendancy; but as he watched her,
He saw that with enormous effort she
Suppressed what she so strongly felt, and sat
Again with face composed, as still as her hostess.
Odysseus now turned to his fellow king
And, placing his hand on the other's, asked:

"And now, Atrides Menelaos, please,
I beg you, tell us of your own journeys
Back to your great kingdom."

Menelaos showed his pleasure at this request,
And told his saga: how he had left Troy
Too hastily, without sufficient sacrifice
To the hungry Gods, despite his brother's
Warning; how his ships had blown to Egypt,
Where he was stranded but received with
Hospitality, and where Helen in that time
Learned the mysteries of herbs from Thon's wife,
Polydamna, bringing her lore from there
To Sparta. He told of how on an island
Not far from the shores of Egypt he trapped
Proteus and learned both of his own missteps
With the Gods and of the tragic fate
Of many of the heroes as they returned
From ill-fated Ilion; how he took
The advice of the old God, returned then
To Egypt and made copious sacrifice,
And how the Gods sent the winds that brought him
Home. During his account, Telemachus,

Who had heard the story on his previous
Visit, realized the difference between
The two men's way of telling: the Spartan
King retold his tale just as he had done
When Telemachus had heard it before;
No word was different, and it now seemed
To the sharp-eared son that the handsome king
Loved to relate it as a performance,
Showing off his rich voice and handsome face,
Gesturing gracefully or forcibly
As the need arose; and the young warrior
Noticed that Helen barely listened, eyes
Heavy lidded, and that she glanced between
The two kings, as if in appraisal.
But his father, the son noticed, used few gestures,
But with his compelling voice let the events
Unfold in such a way that all were caught
In the vision of the moment; and he
Also realized that the astute Ithacan
Varied what he said to affect the ones
Whom he wished to address, making sure
In the case of the Spartan king that nothing
He said would reflect unfavourably
On the reputation of his fellow king.
And, as he continued to observe closely,
He came to understand why the couple
Suited each other—a handsome couple,
Helen incomparably beautiful,
Menelaos magnificently handsome—
And that their relationship was in part
A consequence of that attractiveness—
That neither could have accepted someone
That could not complement their own splendour.
When he turned to glimpse Pelagia's response
To Atrides Menelaos and his story,
He was startled to see that, far from
Absorption in those adventures, instead
She observed him coolly, considering
Him and his wife, her face still composed;
And he wondered what took place behind those dark eyes.

When Menelaos finished, Odysseus
Nodded, then spoke gravely:

"My fellow king, we have both suffered over
These long years, both in war and in struggle
To return. The Gods have exacted much
From us—and from those who did journey back,
Dying on the way, or after they reached home.
Let us now drink to those, hosts in the war
Itself, on both sides, and on our departed friends."

And all raised their cups in solemn salutation,
Pouring out afterwards on the floor
The dregs to honour the harsh-dealing Gods.
The shades of night now shadowed all present,
The torches blazing in the great hall
Making its marble walls seemingly alive
In their continually changing blushes.
Helen had already sent her serving women
To prepare proper bedding for her guests,
Thick purple carpets, warm fleeces on top.
Odysseus and his son were led with torches
To a chamber; women led Pelagia
To their quarters near Helen; the others
Went to sleep under shelter in the forecourt
Outside the palace; and Menelaos
Took Helen by the hand; they went deep in
The palace to his chambers, the king
Eager to sleep with his wife, exquisite
In the torches' ever-changing radiance.

The next morning serving women brought
Pelagia to Helen in her lofty chambers,
First dressing her in new clothes and arranging
Her hair. Helen on her favourite chair
Sat working her spindle, the silver basket
At her side. She nodded and gestured
To the girl to sit beside her.

"We did not get a chance to speak with you
Last night, and so I thought we should know each other

Better. Tell me, who are you, and what brings
You here? In what royal family born?
Are you betrothed to King Odysseus's son?"

The girl looked at her, her mouth twisted,
Her eyes black.

"I am a captive, torn from my family
When the kings Orestes, Aepytus,
And Odysseus attacked our citadel
And destroyed it and my father, chieftain
There. Telemachus fought with me, driving
Other soldiers away, and conquered me."

Here she stopped for a moment and struggled
To control her deep passions. Finally
She spoke again:

"Why I ride with them I do not know—
I showed them I could ride a horse
Like any man; Odysseus left then
In anger, but shortly after sent word
To let me ride with them and to treat me
With all courtesy."

Then she burst out bitterly,

"I do not know why they do this—my lot
Must be at best a concubine, at worst
A slave, nor will I see any that I know
Again. You can now send me back to your
Serving women, if you like, because I
Am no better than they are in this state."

Helen listened carefully to what
The distraught girl said, showing nothing
Of what she felt, except that her eyes
Narrowed when she heard of the three kings
And their conquest. For a time silence spread
Around them. Then Helen looked at the girl
And said in an even tone,

"If Odysseus treats you thus, he must have
Strong reason to do so, and we can do
No less. Therefore be easy: you will
Stay by my side and be treated with all
Courtesy while you are my guest. Your pride
Shows you have a strong character; but it
Can lead you down wrong paths if you allow
It to control your acts. Remember: we
Are women, and as such have little power."

At this, the girl fiercely interrupted.

"You say that? You, who could choose whom you will?
You, who have conquered hearts wherever you are,
For whom Ilion was utterly destroyed?"

Helen looked at the impassioned girl, struck
Both by her audacity and by what she said.

"You say that I have had power? I have
Only one power, the power of my beauty,
And it has never, never been a good.
Yes, I could choose—but only because
I was forced to make a choice among
Suitors selected for me for reasons
Of politics: the binding of alliances
Through marriage. Two of the kings competing
For me you see here, and one of them
I chose, and over the long years I think
That it was the choice that I was right to make.
But as for Troy, I was abducted there,
And although treated as royalty,
I was more concubine than wife; Paris
Was more enamoured of my beauty
Than of myself, and when he died, I was
Fought over by his brothers, then given
To Deiphobos, a decision over which
I had no control, and a man with whom
I found no pleasure whatsoever."

Helen shuddered at the memory,
But then her eyes blazed as she continued.

"But when my husband broke into Troy,
He revenged me, taking my new so-called
Husband and making him die slowly
And in agony, one limb hacked off,
Then another, after his sexual organ
Had been severed and thrown into the dust.
And now I am back here, a dire legend,
Reviled by many; only when they see me
And come under the spell of my beauty,
Do they change their attitude—and, of course,
Only the men, never the women, never!"

Pelagia looked at her, wide-eyed, as she
Continued:

"Despite the horrors that you went through,
You yourself were not raped or killed, mutilated.
You have been privileged for some reason,
Perhaps divine or perhaps because his son
Desires you"—

At this a slight blush betrayed the girl's cheeks—

"Which, I see, you may not find disagreeable"—

She raised a hand to stop the indignant protest—

"But for whatever reason, choice is not yours,
And you must make the best of what the Gods
Decreed for you. I know what it is like
To be a concubine, even without
The name: not much different from a wife.
And you are not the first to suffer such a fate:
Think of staunch Hector's faithful wife, loving
Mother, Andromache, who lost her husband,
Then his son, hurled cruelly from a cliff,
Then was thrust into the hands of the son
Of Achilles, Neoptolemos, who
Had just come back from slitting the throat
Of lovely Polyxena on the grave
Of his father—into the hands still reeking
With the blood of the murdered woman.

She had to live with him as his concubine,
Bear his children, live with memory and shame.
You at least have not had to bear that burden,
And you may find Telemachus to be
More bearable than that brutal victor,
Who also took my daughter before
Orestes in an ambush took his life.
Live for what you can; use your womanhood
To persuade men to your wishes while your beauty
Lasts; after that we have just the feeble power
That comes with old age and must take what comes."

Then Helen, who all this time had worked her spindle,
Put it down, and laying her hand on the girl's arm,
Said:

"Remember these things I have told you; keep
Them tight within your heart to tell your daughters
If you have them. And now we must go
To meet the men."

And both women unconsciously touched
Their hair and arranged their loose-flowing gowns.

Early that morning, when Dawn's soft touch
Had left her tint upon the snowy peaks
Of Taïyetos, Atrides Menelaos
Took Odysseus, his son, and several
Of the Corinthian friends,
Up the mount's forest-laden slopes to hunt
Wild boar. As they rode from Sparta's plain
Onto the first wooded inclines, the king
Chatted with his distinguished visitor.

"Ah, my friend, does this not take you back
To those days in which we could hunt without care,
Concerned only with the chase and kill?"

Odysseus, smiling, nodded his agreement,
Telemachus listening, riding behind
The two veteran kings.

"Now, tell me, what brings you here, and by such
An odd route? I would have thought you to arrive
By ship, and come to me from the south,
Or from Pylos in the west, as did your son."

With this he glanced back at the young prince,
Giving him a dazzling smile. Odysseus
Then told him of the prophecy, his quest
That had brought him first to Corinth, and then
To Mycenae and Orestes. Upon
The mention of the Argive king's name,
Menelaos's face tightened slightly,
Leaving as a mask his expression
Of hospitality and friendliness.

"And how is my son-in-law, present king
Of Argos? As you know, we have not seen
Much of him since he went mad after
The murder of his mother, Helen's sister,
And after he killed Neoptolemos
And married our daughter, then wife
Of the late son of Achilles."

Telemachus then remembered that when
He had come there last the king had begun
The celebrations of the wedding of his son,
Slave-born Megapenthes, to Alector's daughter,
And the departure of Hermione, Helen's
Only child, north to the Myrmidons
To be wedded with Achilles's hardy son.
He saw that Atrides Menelaos
Was troubled by the Argive king,
Whose gory deeds had caused more grief
To the doom-laden family. He
Now listened carefully to what his sire,
Crafty in thought and word, would say.

"He shows the same spirit as his father,
Your brother and great general
Of the Achaeans on our quest for you,
So shamefully murdered when he returned."

Your daughter—whom, I understand, had first
Been betrothed to him"—

A flicker of annoyance, quickly suppressed,
Crossed Menelaos's face, who said nothing
But listened as his guest continued—

"Is happy in her union with him,
As is his sister with his close friend Pylades.
He has become a good Argive king,
Building roads to increase prosperity.
And when I had a prophetic dream
To build two sacred sanctuaries
In Arcadia as part expiation
For my transgressions against Poseidon,
He agreed to accompany me,
And in Arcadia we met with Aepytus,
Not Agapenor, former king of the land,
Formidable warrior and loyal ally
To us in the War with Ilion,
Who was sent by the Gods to rule in Cyprus.
The new king vowed allegiance to Orestes,
And together they have united
Arcadia under one rule. Once
I had set up the shrines and witnessed this,
I continued on my pilgrimage
To visit here with you."

The Spartan king was shaken by this news,
So close to his own borders, but for now
He delayed further talk, for they had reached
The mountain's spacious lap clothed with forests,
And they dismounted with spears and swords
On the ready as they began their search
For the boars who terrorized these slopes.
In silence they moved forward through dense brush;
The trees were now dark pines and firs; below
The ground was carpeted thickly with their needles;
All that could be heard was not birdsong,
But the rasp of ravens that soared above them,
Gliding without effort among the limbs
And branches of the thick-bunched evergreens.

Now the undergrowth became more bushy
And entangled. As they crept through this brush,
Suddenly, without warning, a huge boar
Burst forth from beside them, and before
Any could respond, his sharp tusk ripped at
The calf of Menelaos. The first
To act was quick-moving Telemachus,
Who before the boar could strike again,
Drove his spear through the shaggy body.
Squealing with pain and anger, the boar
Turned to attack the man who had struck him,
But even as he tensed his muscles
To rush toward his tormentor, down
On his neck came the sharp sword of mighty
Odysseus. Muscles, bone, and sinews
Were sliced through in one fierce blow; and the head,
The vast tusked jaws gaping, fell to the ground,
Now flooded with the slain beast's blood.
All sprang to help the wounded king, now lain
Upon the ground. Odysseus quickly staunched
The blood, using his cloak to tie up the wound;
Then four men carried the stricken man down
The slope, others bringing the carcass of the boar,
And carefully he was ridden home,
All about him anxious to keep him
From further harm.

The sun had now reached its zenith as they
Rode into Sparta and to the palace;
Helen and Pelagia were now awaiting them.
When the stunning queen saw her wounded husband,
She swiftly had attendants take him
To their quarters. Letting Pelagia come
To watch, she then mixed herbs as a poultice,
Which she applied to the wound, then bandaged
The leg itself. When the king had been made
Comfortable, she turned to the girl, who
Had watched everything she had done
With deep concentration. Helen noted
The interest the girl showed, and said,

"Did you take note of what I have done?"

Pelagia nodded gravely.

"Would you like to learn the lore of herbs
As I learned it from my instruction in Egypt?"

Again the girl nodded.

"Then while you are here I will work with you,
Once I have talked to King Odysseus."

For a moment the girl's face fell, but she
Quickly recovered her composure.

"Now let us join the others while the king rests."

And they went to the great hall where
They found the Ithacan king and the others,
Waiting for news of the king's condition.
Helen addressed them all:

"Although the wound is deep, the king rests
And is in no danger; you may speak
To him later when he feels more fit."

Courteous Odysseus moved to the queen
And, saluting her, said,

"Gracious Helen, incomparable queen,
It is evident that the skills you learned
In Egypt have been put to good use here.
Your husband is blessed by the Gods to have
So gifted and so beautiful a wife."

Helen, gracing him with a dazzling smile, replied,

"King Odysseus, you always know the words
That most suit the occasion. But now, please
Use your words to tell me of how this wound
Came to be."

Odysseus described the hunt, the sudden
Charge of the wild boar, the deep gore he made,
And the quickness of his son with his spear

To save the King of Sparta's life;
But he did not mention his own action,
And Telemachus burst out,

"I may have stopped the boar from further harm,
But it was my father who in one stroke
Took off the huge beast's head. It was he
Who saved us both."

Helen smiled at the son's earnest interjection.

"I thank, then, both of you—the son for his
Quickness and bravery, the father
For his strength and skill. My husband owes both
Of you his life—and yet a further debt
To you, matchless Odysseus."

The doughty veteran acknowledged her praise
With dignity; but before he could reply,
Helen said,

"And now, great king, I wish you to grant me
A private audience. Telemachus,
I'm sure, will not be unhappy to stay
With Pelagia and entertain her
With the others."

And before the startled son could respond,
She swept from the hall with Odysseus
By the arm.

"Come see our gardens, while we have the chance."

She led him into an enclosed walled garden.
In its centre spouts from a fierce triton
Gushed into a small tranquil pond where fish
Of all varieties and colours
Languidly swam. Olive trees, pomegranate,
Orange, and lemon trees were scattered
By paths and shady bowers; flowers
Exploded their colours in beds throughout
The small park; and in one corner, divided
From the rest, Helen brought Odysseus

To a herb garden profuse with pungent
Plants, both plain and exotic, many which
Odysseus had never seen before.
Not only the hedge separated it
From the rest of the park: the familiar
Scents of the trees and flowers, grass and shrubs,
Were changed to strange new aromas: some sweet
And cloying, which, if smelled too long, left him
Dizzy and thick-headed; others with sharp
Or stinging smells that made his head jerk back
In avoidance. Plants of all shapes and sizes,
Of all shades of green or yellow, dark red
And lavender; or with blossoms of one shade
Or blossoms speckled in ways that to him
Appeared sinister; all carefully laid
In distinct plots, with small paths between.

"Here is my kingdom, and these my subjects
That I learned to rule when I was in Egypt."

She gave him an inscrutable smile,
Then led him to a stone bench well sheltered
By thick-clustered branches overhead,
And by curved trellises of roses
Whose scent enveloped the fertile space.
They sat down, Helen gracefully arraying
Her thin loose-flowing gown about her.
Odysseus, who had known this exquisite woman
From a time when she had newly entered
Womanhood, and had wooed her fruitlessly,
Found now the mature queen irresistible
In this cloistered place, its scents overwhelming,
And in such close proximity to him.
But he had not lived with the divine nymph
Calypso, who had kept him in erotic thrall
For seven years, or the sorceress Circe,
From whom he had rescued his men and escaped,
Without becoming wary of the power
Of a woman's attraction; and he saw
Now how familiar all three were:

How their divine beauty was unearthly,
Beyond the normal bounds of flesh and blood;
That they were works of art, erotic
But even in consummation unapproachable.
And so he let himself show to Helen
The undeniable strength of her attraction
But kept, within, his mind alert and watchful.

"Now, my old friend, we can have that long talk
That we have never had the chance to have.
Tell me now, as you have, I'm sure, told
My husband, but which I wish to hear
From your own lips"—

Odysseus found the way she said "lips"
Was like a kiss itself, and he responded
As he was sure she wished—

"How you have come to be here at present,
Only two years after you finally reached home.
Why have you left your kingdom, as we heard,
Just as you have completed making peace
Among your island's subjects? And what of
Penelope, who waited twenty long years
To see you again? What strong reason
Could you have in these circumstances?"

Odysseus stared out at the lush garden
Spread before him, then turned to speak to her.

"Fairest of women, I make this journey
From necessity and not desire,
Though to meet you and my dear friend, your husband,
Should be wish enough."

Then he told her of the prophecy,
The journey to Delphi and then his trek
Through the Peloponnesos and whom
He had met and what he had done.

"A hard quest for you to do now, after
So many years of travel, and such grief.

But, tell me, who is this girl Pelagia,
And how is it that she travels with you?"

Odysseus gave her a wry smile, then said,

"For her you have Telemachus to thank—
When we sacked the town in Arcadia
He fought with her and took her captive.
She now rides with us like a man
For two reasons: first, she rides very well,
And, second, my seer Halitherses
Has warned me that he has divined she
Will have some significance to us.
What that will be, neither he nor I can tell,
But even though she can be no more
Than a concubine, we must treat her
With courtesy—as well, she appears
To be the daughter of the slain chieftain,
And therefore high born. And, as you have seen,
She is strong in character."

God-descended Helen listened closely,
Then said to him in affirmation,

"She is indeed as you say, as I find
In my conversations with her. Your son,
I think, will come to be closer to her.
As for him, he has become a man
Since last he came here, and shows
The better parts of Penelope and you."

At this they both chuckled, Odysseus pleased
That his son had matured so well and that
He was now recognized for himself.
Helen now laid her hand on his;
He was surprised not by its warmth and softness,
But also by the strength that he felt in
Those slender fingers.

"Ah, Odysseus, we have known each other—
How long?"

"Over half my lifetime—
And you are now more beautiful than ever."

She playfully slapped his hand in mock
Remonstration, then became serious.

"When you came to woo me, I was a girl,
Barely into womanhood, forced to choose
My husband from among you princes
And kings. You knew I would not choose you,
I am sure"—

Odysseus acknowledged her insight
With another wry smile and a shrug
Of his powerful shoulders—

"But you showed your wisdom in your skill
In winning Penelope with the pact
That saved us from Achaean civil war.
Is it not strange that each act that you made
Has led to tragic consequences?"

Odysseus looked at her gravely.

"I had no way to know that Ilion
Would catch us up, and that so many
Direful outcomes would result. And yet
You also must bear a burden in this—
Your beauty provoked Paris to carry
You away; and you did not betray me
When I stole the statue from the city
So that it became more vulnerable.
But tell me, when the giant horse was brought
Within the gates, why did you go about it,
Calling in the voices of the wives
Of us who were inside it? Did you know
That I, enclosed there, had to hold Anticlus,
Clasp his mouth to keep him from shouting out,
So desperate was he when he heard the voice
Of she whom he thought his wife, his desire
For her so strong that it deranged his senses,
And in that way he lost his breath and died?"

At this Helen looked toward him, and in her face
He saw what she had never let him
Or others see before: grief and anger
Mixed in terrible proportions, as she cried out,

"Why did I help you and then seem to betray you?
What was I to do? So many killed on both sides
Because of me? Whoever was the victor,
Terrible disaster would befall the other.
In my torment I tested both of you—
Troy lost its divine protection through me;
And I made you in the horse pay in full
For the ghastly slaughter you stayed to do.
I was an instrument without will,
A cause without intention, helpless."

And as she spoke, her fingers strained at his,
Hand gripped tight as the passions pulsed
Through her in her agony. He let her
Hold his hand thus for some time, and neither
Spoke; in the silence their senses sharpened
In the shock of this moment; the garden
Around them seemed alive with sounds; the leaves
Rustled slightly in the quiet breeze
Which they felt caress their skin; birds chirped;
The tiny scamper of small animals
Was heard on the luxuriant grass,
Among the thick-branched shrubs, upon the limbs
Of the fruit-bearing trees; the scents of flowers
Twining on the bower lay thick
Within their nostrils.
Finally her grip relaxed, her breathing
Steadied, and in control again:

"You spoke of Orestes—how is his wife,
My daughter Hermione?"

"She is well and happy with her husband.
They make a good match, as do Pylades
And Electra. You have no worries there."

A sigh came involuntarily.

"He was our first choice until the dreadful
Murders and his later madness. Is he
A good king?"

"He will be the greatest of us who are left.
He has made his Argive lands prosperous,
And now has secured Arcadia
Under his sway. It would be politic
For Menelaos to reach out to him."

Helen nodded but said nothing; but he
Knew that the Spartan king would find it hard
To seek reconciliation with the young king,
Not only for the family's tragic fate,
But also that again his brother's family
Proved to be the stronger rulers;
Nonetheless, both Odysseus and Helen
Knew that for a secure future he must
Suppress his pride and envy and embrace
His triumphant son-in-law and fellow king.
Now, as the shadows stretched out around them,
They talked together of inconsequential things.
At last Helen smiled and said to him,

"One other matter that I've just thought of.
Since Pelagia will be with your family
From now on, what would you think about her
Learning the lore of herbs from me? Such skill
Could be useful for injury or illness,
As you have seen here."

Odysseus looked at her thoughtfully, then:

"Gracious Helen, I should be pleased that you did so.
The problem that I see is that she harbours
Bitterness and hatred toward me."

Helen nodded, looking speculative.

"I have noted that, which is natural,
Considering that you destroyed her town
And her family. But I may be of help

To quiet her mind and make her more
Receptive. Leave it to me, if you will."

The crafty veteran, remembering
The power Circe possessed, reflected
For a moment, then gave his consent.
Helen gave him her most radiant smile.

"My Odysseus, this is the longest
Conversation we have had, and the most
Open. We may never have another such,
But I thank you for this close moment
Between two who have known each other
For so long. My grateful thanks, good friend,
For your wise words, as always. And we will,
I'm sure, keep what we have said in our hearts,
For each other and for no one else."

The wily king knew fully what she meant,
And he nodded his agreement. Then they
Arose and Helen led him from her park
And sanctuary to the outside world
Of the palace and its machinations.

During this time Telemachus had been
With Pelagia; they had attendants bring
Horses, and they rode out along the banks
Of the Euratos, letting their mounts
Canter easily in the bright sunshine.
They let themselves indulge in the soft breezes
That played across the plain, saw around them
The majestic peaks and mountain ranges,
Still snow-tipped, riven with ragged gashes
Or descending first to dark-forested slopes,
Then to laps of verdant groves, particoloured
As seen afar by the two keen-eyed riders.
While they continued beside the swift current,
In silence, clear-eyed Telemachus saw
That the girl had relaxed more, free with horse
And open air, and that she was deep in thought,
Troubled still, but less so than before.

Several times he tried to speak with her,
To start a conversation, but each time
She glanced at him and shook her head, still caught
In her own inner struggles. And so
He let her be and let himself indulge
In the journey and the view, not least
Of which was the girl herself, erect
Upon her horse, her chiton shifting
In the movement of the breezes and the horse.
Thus they continued for a while; and then,
Her eyes challenging, the girl turned her horse
And galloped wildly back to the palace.
Telemachus did so as well, but she
Stayed ahead of them as they raced up to
The gate and the outer court, where surprised
Attendants took away the lathered horses.
Together they crossed to the inner court
And up the marble stairs, now dazzling
In the bright sun's rays, and into the shade
Of the high-roofed hall, still bound in silence,
Where they met Odysseus and Helen,
Newly returned themselves from the garden.
Helen at once took the girl off to her chambers,
While the warrior remained with his tall son.
The older two soon found that few words
Had passed between the younger couple, and
Odysseus wondered wryly what Helen
Would do to change the situation.

That night a bull was sacrificed to aid
The healing of the wounded king,
And at the feast that followed, the women
Came as before, and Pelagia sat with
The lovely queen. The large golden bowl arrived,
But the crafty Helen had placed in it
Earlier a potion that she had used
Before, when she had eased the pain of those
Who remembered, when Telemachus
Had visited before, the Trojan War
And those who had been lost in battle,

Perished on the wave-wracked voyage home,
Or murdered treacherously when they crossed
The threshold of their homes. This sweet potion
Now worked its heady way on those placed there,
Who, relaxing at the feast itself,
Then laid down their heads in restful, pleasant
Oblivion, Odysseus not haunted
By the turmoil he had instigated;
Telemachus not restless from concern
With his captive; Pelagia no longer
Visited by the nightmare of her home's
Destruction. Only Helen, who had not
Quaffed from the infused bowl, lay restless,
Her mind filled with antic thoughts provoked
By her words with the Ithacan king:
The memories of her girlhood, courtship
And marriage; abduction to Ilion;
Her usage there; the pitiless war fought
Over her; her long return and present state.
And so the mares of night passed over most,
But galloped away, all through the dark,
Exquisite Helen hapless on their backs.

After Dawn had spread her blush over
The shining marble of the palace
And Helios's horses now trod the sky,
Atrides Menelaos, now well enough
To sit, though his leg still complained against
The deep gash it had endured, called his friend
To an audience. Odysseus found him
In a golden chair well stocked with cushions,
His wounded leg resting, well padded,
On a small stool. They were in the great hall,
Now empty but for the king's minister
And closest confidant. The island king
Noted as he entered that the lions
Of the Atrides hung above them,
Golden and dazzling in the morning sun.
When he saw him, Menelaos exclaimed
Jovially as he invited him to sit,

"Well, my old friend, again you have saved me,
Both you and your agile son. At this rate
I will owe you my whole kingdom!"

Odysseus smiled broadly.

"You would have done the same for me, if luck
Had fallen from me in such a moment."

The Spartan king laughed heartily at this,
Then let his face become more serious.

"But now we should continue our talk
That was so rudely interrupted."

Odysseus chuckled politely, alert.

"You say that Orestes has gained power
Over Arcadia?"

"An alliance—but Aepytus has vowed
Allegiance to the Argive king as well."

Menelaos shifted uneasily,
Wincing as his leg adjusted.

"What do you think his intentions are
With regard to Sparta?"

Odysseus made a gesture of dismissal.

"He has his hands full in Arcadia
And Argos. In his own country he must
Construct roads and make secure all the towns
Under his rule. In wild Arcadia
He must deal with a shifty king, whose rule
Is rough and unsteady; and so he must
Build a city there for himself, so that
He can make stronger his influence there.
Also, you are well protected here,
Surrounded as you are with high mountains
And their narrow passes, as we ourselves
Have witnessed."

Menelaos nodded, but he was not
Satisfied fully, as Odysseus saw.
The veteran leaned closer to his friend
And said,

"Besides, all of this land is in your hands,
Since it is your family that rules all here.
You are uncle to Orestes, and
His wife is your daughter; after you have joined
The shade of your brother, it will be
His progeny that will govern most
Of Peloponnesian territory,
And so the house of Atrides will live on
Well into the future."

The sharp-eyed Ithacan saw that his words
Had struck home, distasteful as they seemed;
And he then pursued his theme:

"Therefore, my good friend, forget the horrors
Of the past and embrace your son-in-law,
Both for the sake of the house of Atrides,
And for the happiness of your two families.
Let this reconciliation be your gift
To me, the payment of any debt
That you feel in obligation to me."

Menelaos, startled by this offer,
Looked troubled, then said:

"My dear friend, I know the debt I owe you
Is deep and richly deserved—but there is
Another problem. I have two strong sons
Borne to me by a slave, Megapenthes
And his younger brother, Nicostratos.
Both of them will want to rule when I die."

Odysseus looked at him thoughtfully, and
At his councillor, uncomfortable
At the thought of the two sons of the king.

"All the more reason to make friends with him.
Both of us know that they are not destined

To rule because they are illegitimate.
Lacedaemonians will accept
Only a true-born heir of Atrides—
And Orestes is the one true heir
For both the families. They may try
To rule, but they will not stay on the throne.
You, my good friend, know that as well as I."

Menelaos glowered at this, but when
He saw his own councillor nod agreement,
He knew that wise Odysseus was right.
Sighing, he said,

"As usual you speak truth, Odysseus,
However difficult it may be.
I will make overtures; Hermione,
I hope, will help to sway Orestes
To me. In the meantime, I must ask you
Not to make mention of what has been said
Here; my two sons return in the next day
Or so, and I would not see strife among us
While you are here."

Odysseus smiled.

"No word of this will come from me, my friend,
I promise you. And now may I feel relieved
That I do not have to uproot my kingdom
And bring it here, as you promised to my son?"

Atrides Menelaos looked at him,
Astonished. Then, remembering what he said
To Telemachus when last he came here,
He roared with laughter, joined by his fellow king,
And Odysseus left him, still in some pain,
But chortling further at the joke between them.
But even as he left, the Ithacan also
Remembered what the Spartan king had said
To his son: how outraged he was to hear
About the suitors, but how he did not raise
A finger to help the powerless boy,
And a grim smile formed on his lips.

That day as well, Helen brought Pelagia
With her to the herb garden and began
Her training in herbs and potions. As they passed
Through the grounds, the colours and the vivid scents
Exotic and strange, bewildered her senses.
The queen led her down the fragrant byways
To a high-hedged corner, overhung
With thick-leaved boughs from surrounding, graceful trees;
There, hidden away in the cooling shade,
They came to a small building nestled against
The garden walls, its shining surfaces
Shadow-mottled, with openings high, beneath
The well-crafted roof, to gain access
To light and breeze. Helen knocked on the door,
Fashioned of sturdy oak and reinforced
With bands of gleaming copper, and shortly it swung open heavily.
For a moment inside, Pelagia
Could not see in the interior gloom
And her senses were overcome by pungent
Fumes, sweet and acrid, heavy, unnerving.
Helen gave a short command, and a still shadowed
Figure silently swung shut the thick door.
As in a morning just before the dawn
All around is but palpable black shape
That in the first faint rays then resolves
Into lightly penciled outlines of things,
So Pelagia began to see the space
Define itself, the streaks of bright sunlight
Braiding the walls with their protruding shelves,
Below which on the right ran a long counter
On which sat many bowls and instruments
And other objects which she did not know.
The wall found to her left bristled with shelves
Laden with containers, and below them
The stone floor carried the weight of amphora,
Large and bulging with strange flowers and herbs,
And other substances unknown to her.
Facing her was a wall bifurcated
By another door, on either side of which
Were many cupboards, their contents concealed

By their doors. Helen motioned her forward,
And as she did so, the queen spoke again,
And Pelagia recognized the voice
Of a mistress to a slave.

               "Amunet,
Come here."

          The figure bowed and came before them.

"Amunet, this is Pelagia, one
In the company of King Odysseus
And his son, Prince Telemachus. You will
See to her needs in our workshop here and
Assist her in her study of our craft."

A nod to the queen, and a bow to the girl.
By now Pelagia's eyes had adjusted
To the room's light, shaded but fully clear,
And she looked carefully at the woman
She saw before her: shorter than herself,
Wearing white linen wrapped tightly around
Her slim form, with a corner over a shoulder
And down to pin the cloth above one breast
And to leave the other exposed, with arms
Clear. But it was her face that intrigued
Pelagia most—a skin dark like that
Of the herdsmen of her ravaged town,
High cheekbones from which the face narrowed
To the chin, past a straight nose and firm lips—
And the eyes, dark and large, their size increased
By the thick graceful outline around them
(Made of kohl, as she discovered later),
Eyes that for a moment sharply appraised
Her before glancing in subservience
Downward.

          "Amunet was given to me
By the woman with whom I studied herbs
In Egypt; she has proven excellent
In assisting me, and she will train you well,
Although I will be with you when I can."

Pelagia glanced quickly at Amunet
And saw that she remained expressionless.
Then Helen showed her the workings of the room,
And they immersed themselves in the techniques
Of the craft—the use of the mortar and pestle,
And how potions were concocted, and as
They surveyed and Pelagia attempted these,
Amunet was always there, noiselessly
Helping discreetly. The hours passed in a blur
For Pelagia; but Helen soon found
The girl eager to learn, and adept; and
By the evening she had progressed farther
Than Helen had thought possible.

Menelaos could attend the evening feast;
And again Helen slipped her powerful
Infusion into their wine; and again
The palace slept in peace and happy stupor.

The next day went as the last, the women
Busy with their ingredients and lore;
And still Pelagia absorbed all Helen
Demonstrated and kept it in her mind
And deeply in her heart. Helen observed
As well that little had grown between her
And Telemachus; and that night she slipped
A different mixture into the young
Couple's wine, but for the others the same
Drug as before. When the women retired
To their quarters, Helen closely observed
The girl: she saw that she was flushed, restless,
Her breathing unsteady. Helen began
To talk about Telemachus, asking
Pelagia if she did not think him handsome,
How strong he was, how manly and graceful.
Pelagia began reluctantly
To agree, but as Helen spoke further
Of him, she saw that his image flooded
The girl's mind, and that she was confused
By the new, strange stirrings within her.
Then Helen whispered, close to her ear,

"I have placed Telemachus in a room
Which no one else inhabits: go there now."

And her attendant led the dazed girl
To where he was. While Helen worked on the girl,
Telemachus had also found himself
Stirred deeply with desire, the image
Of Pelagia flaming in his mind.
An attendant found him and took him,
Unresisting, to the appointed room.
A few moments later the girl, breathless,
Arrived. The moon from a window above
Let her cold rays caress the two bodies,
Standing for the moment motionless
In the room dark but for that clear night light.
Each saw the other newly born in that
Unearthly radiance, whose shafts let shadows linger
To enhance a curve or muscle draped in
The graceful cloth, or gave new definition
To the young strong faces as they stared entranced.
Pelagia now saw him fully as a man,
And in her heightened sense she saw him see
Her a woman, and his gaze, that took in first
Her face, then fastened, rapt, upon her body,
Made her skin alive both to the air that
Gently touched it and to her gown,
That as it clung or hung from her, combined
With her own uneven breathing, caused her
To sense each curve of her limbs and her body,
To form them anew as objects of desire,
And she found herself with new intense feelings.
The two seemed to drift helplessly toward
Each other; for a moment, their breaths
Intermingled, they stood absorbed in
The other's face, their lips slightly parted;
And then Telemachus found his lips
On hers, and their bodies strained together
As they freed their passions in that first kiss.
Time slipped from them while they embraced in that
First urge of desire; then, trembling, they

Released to see faces flushed with such strong need;
And the man let slip the gown from the
Moon-white shoulders, and the woman let fall
His garment; and now, the two white-stained bodies
Stood for a moment as the couple studied
Greedily the exposed body of the other.
Then Telemachus took Pelagia
By the hand and led her to soft shaggy fleeces
Where they lay down and new exploration
Began. Pelagia now first felt a man's hands
Touch and move over her skin and body,
Which she gave over to him without thought,
And each part began to madden her
With pleasure and desire—his hand at nape
And shoulder, tracing lines of fiery shock;
His hands sliding down her back and sides
And hips; the first thrill of her breasts cupped
And fondled, and her nipples traced, and how
Unexpected the force of these new
Caresses were; and as his hands and lips
Continued to explore her feet and legs
And thighs, she found herself loosening,
Wet with craving; and then she let her thighs
Spread open, and she felt him at her mound,
And then he entered her, and there was
A sharp quick pain, and then all was given up
To the frenzy of the movement in her
And a final explosion of something
She had never dreamed could be; and then,
In quietness together, he still inside her,
A feeling of lush peacefulness; and then
He pulled gently from her, and they lay there,
Their bodies close, limbs entangled, feeling
Each other's breathing and heartbeat.
Under the cool white observance of the moon,
Throughout the night their ardour reignited
And their intimate ritual played many times.
Dawn replaced the moon's cool rays with her own
Warm touches as she found the two asleep,
Locked in each other's arms.

An attendant tactfully awoke them with a cough;
The first thing each saw was the other's eyes,
And they slowly separated, each now
For a reason that they could not explain,
A little shy; then each went a different way,
Pelagia to Helen, Telemachus
To the men. No one knew yet what had happened—
And so no one joked with Odysseus's son,
And Helen said nothing to the girl
As she continued with her instruction.
That night Helen again used her potion in the drink;
And again the young couple met to make
Ecstatic love. And when they awoke
The next day all could see in their eyes
What they felt for each other, and Helen
Knew her work was done.

At this time the two sons of Menelaos,
The older, Megapenthes, and his brother
Nicostratos, returned from the south, where
They had been visiting their mother,
Who was living on an estate near the sea.
Their chariots clattered through the streets
And raced to a stop before the outer court,
Where the two young men gave them to the charge
Of their attendants, for they had been
Their own charioteers. Through the inner court
They strode, and into the lofty hall, where
Atrides Menelaos now sat, his leg
Now healed enough for him to stump about,
Cursing his disability; only
Odysseus, who was his companion frequently,
Kept him in good humour through his quick-witted
Conversation. The two, dusty still from
Their long ride, brusquely saluted their father,
Then looked curiously at Odysseus,
Who mildly saluted them himself.

"My sons, this is my old friend, Odysseus,
King of Ithaca and greatest hero

Of the Ilion War. Do him all honour
And reverence."

As the two did as they were told, their faces
Showing some disbelief between the legend
And the shorter man with broad chest and shoulders
That stood before them, the perceptive Ithacan
Quickly studied them. Megapenthes
Showed the more brutal aspects of the Atrides,
Tall, with a physique more like his uncle's
Than his father's, burly rather than
Proportioned, with a face that showed in its
Lineaments little of his handsome father,
But much of his ego and his love of power.
Nicostratos had inherited
The handsome features of his father,
But was slim and lithe, more crafty in wit
Than his warrior brother. In both of them
The veteran sensed traces of a mother
With a strong will and, if the younger man
Was evidence, a beauty which had seduced
The king when the lovelier Helen
Had been abducted—or earlier,
He abruptly thought, given their ages,
And the whole legend of Helen twisted
In his mind with this conclusion.

"And how is your mother—well, I hope?"

In their response to their father's formal
Question, Odysseus saw fleeting looks
Of resentment, and he realized that
They were well aware of their situation
But were drawn irresistibly
To the power of the throne and rule
And their own illegitimacy to them,
And he knew without further thought that strife
Would break out when the throne was relinquished
On Menelaos's death.

"She continues well, but misses the life
Here at court."

It was Nicostratos who uttered this,
With what Odysseus felt was malicious
Courtesy. Menelaos felt the gibe,
But out of respect for his guest chose
To ignore it.

"I'm glad to hear that she is healthy. Now,
Go, refresh yourselves and change to meet
All our guests, who include my friend's son
Telemachus, whom you may remember
When he came during your wedding, my son."

It was evident that both remembered
Nothing of that meeting, but they nodded
Courteously.                          ·

"There is also a troop from Corinth who
Accompanied them. They bring much news
That you will find of great interest,
I'm sure."

The sons were curious, but held their tongues
From further questions and quickly withdrew.

When they had gone, Menelaos turned
To his old friend.

"You see my problem, wise Odysseus.
What can I do?"

The sage Ithacan pondered for a second,
Then replied gravely,

"There is little you can do here; but
To preserve the pure line of Atrides,
You must strive more fully for friendship with
Orestes. He is the only one
Of your family that has the influence
To perpetuate a proper reign here
In Sparta. Do so as soon as the moment
Is right, old friend and companion."

Menelaos smiled wryly, but he took
The advice to rest within his heart.

They then took leave, each of the other,
And Odysseus quickly sought out his son,
Whom he found with his companions, but
Distracted and with his mind elsewhere.
Odysseus knew what had happened between
His son and the Arcadian girl, and
He suspected that Helen had had a hand
In the sudden fruition of the relationship.
However, he put this aside to speak
To his son.

"Telemachus, the two sons of the king
Have returned. You need to know important
Things about them: first, that they were born
Of a slave, not Helen, and therefore not
Eligible to rule in Sparta.
But I have just seen that they have that wish
And that there will be trouble here in Sparta.
Therefore I ask you, your fellow Ithacans,
And your Corinthian companions
To treat them with all courtesy. Do not
Mention the circumstances of their birth,
Talk of matters congenial to you all,
Hunting, our adventures coming here,
And the pilgrimage itself, and be mild
In your responses to them, however
They may provoke you, either by accident
Or intentionally. Do this for me,
Not only because the king is my friend,
But also to keep peace within his realm."

Telemachus was startled by what he heard,
But he promised his father he would
Obey him in this, and he went off to
Inform the others.

In the late afternoon they all met
At a great feast that Menelaos
Had ordained. Telemachus was seated
Between the two brothers, close to the two kings.
The meats were carved and distributed

In plenty, as were baskets of bread
And other good things. Abundant wine
Was poured from the golden bowl into
The splendid goblets; and as they dined well
Both Menelaos's bard and Medon vied
In singing of the exploits of the Atrides
And their allies in the Trojan War,
And the adventures of the Ithacans
And their Corinthian companions
In the Arcadian expedition;
And tumblers showed their gymnastic prowess
And dancers gracefully performed dances
Of beauty and agility, fair to see.
The visitors were courteous to the sons,
Who in their turn joined willingly in bright
Revelry. Only near the conclusion
Of the entertainment did Helen,
Pelagia, and the other women join
The men, now flushed with feasting and drink.
Alector's daughter, wife to Megapenthes,
Was not present, although invited.
When Helen entered, the attentive son
Of Odysseus noted that the brothers
Stiffened and their eyes narrowed; but she took
No notice, and he quickly forgot all else
When he saw Pelagia enter, glowing
With health and gladness as she glanced at him.
They were acknowledged by the two kings
And sat slightly apart, Helen as usual
In her golden chair, and food and drink
Were brought to them. Nicostratos was struck
By the dark beauty of Pelagia,
And asked Telemachus who she was.

"She is from Arcadia, the daughter
Of a chieftain, whose town we captured."

"Ah, a slave then,"
Exclaimed Menelaos's son,
"May I ask her as a gift from you?"

Telemachus frowned at this, furious
That his loved one was so casually treated,
But he kept his temper and replied,

"Any other I should gladly give you,
But she still has royal blood, and I
Cannot consider giving her up."

Nicostratos, who had already drunk
Too much, grinned maliciously and said loudly,

"Oh, I see, you want her for yourself
And won't be generous enough to share
Her around with others."

Telemachus, who had also drunk too much,
Now replied with intense anger,

"She is mine and mine alone and will be
Treated well."

The hall had become quiet on this loud
Exchange; Menelaos and Odysseus
Watched carefully their sons.
Nicostratos laughed scornfully, saying,

"You make a great deal of a lowly slave."

Before he thought of what he said, in rage
Telemachus said sharply,

"You of all men should be sensitive
To slaves, since you are born of one!"

A shocked hush fell upon the feasting hall
At this interchange; then, with a roar,
Megapenthes rose with his brother
To face Telemachus, who rose as well,
His ribs now well healed but still sore.
The two kings had looked at each other
In concern as the argument had grown,
And when the elder brother lunged at his son,
Odysseus, swifter than any had thought possible,
Interposed between them; the younger man

Was over a head taller than the king,
But when he raised his fist to strike the son,
Odysseus grasped his arm and with great strength
Forced it to his side, to the amazement
Of Megapenthes and all those present.
At the same time Menelaos grasped
His younger son in a grip that could not
Be loosed by the struggling youth. It was then
That those present truly realized
The strength of the two veterans, who still
Retained, so many years flown by, the prowess
That had served them well in Ilion.
Telemachus, seeing this, came more
To his senses, and to the raging,
Impotent youths before him he said,

"I have transgressed in what I said in anger;
May the Gods bear witness that I here
Apologize to you and to your mighty father
And the mother who bore such stalwart sons."

All who listened were impressed by this speech
And the nobility of the man who spoke it,
But the brothers, who stopped struggling, still
Showed in their bitter glances that they were
Not mollified; and the two kings knew that
There could be trouble in the future.
During this time Helen and Pelagia
Had listened, appalled, to what had been shouted.
Helen, who had no love for her stepsons,
Nor for their mother, her husband's paramour,
Saw them again as a danger to the throne
In their unbridled actions, and she knew
That if they came to rule she would be
In mortal danger. But she also was concerned
About the girl beside her, at whom
She glanced surreptitiously. Pelagia
Was in turmoil—she admired her lover's
Description of her and his staunch defence,
But in the coarse way in which the other
Treated her she understood, far more

Than before, what her true status was;
And anger flooded her—if she had had
Means to a sword, she would have attacked
The brothers without hesitation.
But mixed with her new rage came something else—
Humiliation, and a sense of shame
That she was the cause of such uproar
At a feast of high-born kings and guests.
When the two brothers had been pinioned
And Telemachus had apologized,
Helen rose, and taking the girl with her,
Began to leave. Nicostratos, still drunk,
Saw her do so, and shouted bitterly
To his father who restrained him,

"Our mother may be a slave, but there goes
Your whore!"

A gasp whispered through the lofty hall;
Helen stopped, turned, and looked at her step-son,
Who froze when he saw her deadly glance;
Then she nodded to her husband
And the Ithacans and left gracefully
With Pelagia. Menelaos, enraged,
Hurled his son to the floor.

"You have said enough in your drunken state!
Back, back to your mother now, and stay there
Until I say that you may return here!"

He motioned to his attendants, who brought in
Armed soldiers; and the two brothers, sobered
By this decree, were escorted out.
Menelaos then turned to his startled
Guests, and in his most gracious manner, said,

"My friends, I grieve that this affair took place
Here. Forgive us, and let us leave in peace."

The wise Ithacan king moved to his friend
And put his arm on his companion's shoulder.

"My good friend, we have seen before what drink
Can do to warriors, have we not?
Remember at our camp before Troy,
Before the ships left for home, how all men
In their joy and hope drank too much wine,
And how skirmishes broke out between
The two halves of our army? These boys
Of ours continue what the fathers did,
Do they not? We all have said harsh sharp things
That we regretted in the pitiless light of day."

Menelaos could not suppress a smile
As he remembered the days passed in folly,
And he relaxed under the friendly grip.

"True indeed, old friend, as always with you.
And let us drink to that, shall we not?"

Both laughed and drank from the golden bowls,
Alone, as the assembly had left
At the Spartan king's command. For a time
They stayed silent, each lost in memories
Of that distant war and decade. Then,
Turning to the Spartan veteran,
Odysseus said, with a smile,

"We must be stern with our children—I will
Attend to mine this night—but we must keep
In our minds and hearts that they are our flesh,
They are the ones here when we have become shades,
And therefore we must finally forgive them.
Your two sons are built as heroes, I see well—
Make sure that they can return within
A convenient time, and try to effect
A reconciliation between them and Helen."

Menelaos sighed, looking into his bowl.

"I promise to do the first as you suggest,
But the second is more difficult.
Their mother lives well near the coast, but she

Cannot be here, for Helen is at odds
With her, not only for the sons that
My wife has not had, but also that I
Had them even before she was abducted;
They are a reminder every day to her
Of these two unpalatable facts.
But I will try again to soothe them all,
Or at least as king force them to live
In peace in Sparta."

Odysseus nodded sympathetically;
But he wondered to himself what would be
The situation when a new king
Came to power, and what would then happen
To Helen in a world so hostile to her.
Then he skillfully changed the subject,
With stories of the past and of themselves,
And the two kings sat there as the clear moon
Explored with its cool shafts the marble walls
And floor of the spacious hall, and they talked
Until the moon crept away before
Fair Dawn revealed her glorious presence.

When the sun blazed, majestic in the sky,
Telemachus awoke, dry in his mouth
And sore in his head. Pelagia was not there;
She had not come to him in that night.
He groaned slightly, then arose to prepare
For the day, which he hoped would relieve
The state in which he now found himself.
Relief, however, was not to help him,
For an attendant came to him to say
That his father ordered him to come before him.
The young man, now abashed, remembered what
Had befell at the feast, and he went
With trepidation to see his stern sire.
When he came to Odysseus, he found him
Sitting on a marble bench, slightly in shade,
So that his features could not easily
Be seen.

"You realize what you accomplished last night."

"Yes, father."

"You managed to quarrel in rage with sons
Of your host, a breach in the friendship
Of a feast."

"Yes, father."

"In so doing, you have gained the enmity
Of those who may be in power later,
And who could cause our family harm."

"Yes, father."

"Not only that, you have torn the bonds
Among the Atrides themselves, so that
The queen may be in peril if the king
Dies and they come to power."

No reply to this.

"I should send you home immediately,
In disgrace, so that you cannot cause
Further grief to us."

The stricken young man bowed his head.
Then the terrible voice softened somewhat.

"But …"

The head began to rise, then stopped.

"You did the one thing that can save you."

The head lifted fully, but the eyes
Could not make out the face in shadow.

"You made amends with your apology,
Which all found noble and appropriate."

Telemachus said nothing, straining
With all his being to hear his father
As he continued.

"And your quarrel was not without merits.
Pelagia is no longer high born
As the captive that she is"—

His son made to protest, but a gesture
Silenced him

—"but you have not made her a slave either."

The son relaxed slightly, but remained alert.

"She may be—she is now, I know—
Your concubine, and as such has a place
In our family, but she will never be a queen.
However, your defence of her in this
Present situation was right and proper.
Yet, my son, the skill is not to quarrel,
But to find the means to deflect such moments."

"But father, what other could I have done
In this present case, when he was too drunk
To give up his desire and words?"

The son heard his father chuckle in the shade.

"Sometimes drunk men can be distracted
With a joke, a change of attention
Such as saluting them with drink; but here
I think you did not have many options,
And you acted only as you could have
When he could not be swayed in what he wanted.
But use this lesson to help you in the future.
And know that Menelaos and I
Are still good friends despite the spoiling
Of his feast. Now go and prepare for the day."

And Telemachus stumbled off, amazed
At his father's authority and wisdom.

Later that morning a chariot
Rushed in, its horses foaming and dusty,
And stopped at the steps of the inner court.
A messenger quickly stepped from it
And raced up the steps to confront a guard.

"Take me to your king—I have important news!"

The guard told him to stay there and brought out
The able aide-in-arms Eteoneus,
Who saw that the messenger was high born,
And courteously asked him his business.

"I have dark news from Pylos for the King
Of Sparta."

Eteoneus, seeing that there was
Serious matter here, beckoned to him,
And they swiftly crossed through to the hall,
Where Atrides Menelaos conversed
With his friend Odysseus. Both kings looked up
As the two men saluted them.

"Sire, here is a messenger from Pylos."

Menelaos, surprised, addressed the man
Courteously.

"What is so important that you have rushed
Here from that distant place?"

The messenger rose and said with dignity,

"Great King of Sparta, the news I bring
Is black, both for us of Pylos and for
All Achaeans, but especially you.
Our king, Nestor, beloved of everyone,
Hero of the War with Ilion
And of many more, veteran of decades,
Sire of many sons and daughters,
Nestor, King of Pylos, is dead."

Both the kings who heard him gasped; both knew
His great age, but both thought him ageless,
And his death now sundered a link from
A distant past that few of them had known.

"When did this dire thing happen?"

"Two days ago, my lord. Since then, myself
And others have been sent through Achaea

To proclaim his death to all, and to
Invite kings and veterans who knew him
To his immolation. If you wish
To attend, please hasten to Pylos
As soon as you can, I beseech you."

The weary messenger finished, close to tears.
Menelaos had Eteoneus
Lead him away to rest and refresh himself;
Then he turned to Odysseus, who stood
Thoughtfully considering what he had heard.

"I had never thought that this could happen—
The most respected and beloved of us all.
I must make ready—will you go as well?"

Odysseus nodded, still in thought.
Menelaos gave brisk orders to prepare,
As attendants scurried round about him.

"Only a small number should go, and all in
Chariots,"

He commanded. Odysseus returned
To where Telemachus was with his companions.

"We must leave for Pylos at once—find Medon
And Halitherses, and representatives
From our Ithacans and the Corinthians."

Telemachus hurried away to do so,
And the palace rang with the frenzied noise
Of men dressing, chariots wheeled out
And horses harnessed, and all the business
Necessary for such a trip. Helen
And Pelagia interrupted their work
To see what had happened. When the queen
Heard the news, she was clearly shaken,
More than anyone had ever seen her,
Now or in the past.

"He was loved by all, Achaean or Trojan.
His great age shows us mortality
Will always come among us in its own time."

She quickly went to Menelaos,
And Pelagia sought out Telemachus.
When she saw him, she exclaimed,

"I never thanked you for defending me!"

And then she flung herself into his arms
And wept uncontrollably. Her lover
Held her awkwardly, startled by her passion,
Then held her more closely to let her
Purge herself from all that she was feeling.

Soon all was ready, and men leapt unto the chariots,
Resplendent in their armour and their
Plumed helmets. Menelaos stood astride
In his dazzling golden chariot;
On either side in other brilliant
Vehicles stood Odysseus and his son;
And behind the three were found ranks
Of horses and chariots, warriors
In blazing armour, their plumes foresting
The streets. Then Atrides Menelaos
Gave the signal; the horses reared and started,
And the procession, glittering, formidable,
Roared into motion in huge waves of sound.
Helen and Pelagia mounted up the walls
Of the palace and stood there, watching
The procession clatter through the streets,
Then gallop through the fields, clouds of dust
Rising, toward the great range towering
Over the plain and city. Gradually
The movement and the dust grew smaller
And dwindled into the shimmering fields.
Then the two women left the lofty wall,
And returned in silence to the waiting garden.

# Canto 5
# PYLOS

Through the long ravine of the mighty range
The chariots thundered, their rattling din
Startling the ravens and the crows, who rose
In sable clouds from the dark-forested slopes.
Little could be said as the grim charioteers
Lashed onward their foam-flecked steeds.
Once past the towering peak the twisting trail
Straightened through a long valley huddled within
More frowning slopes of a new range.
As Helios's chargers swept their way past
These high sentinels to the sky, dusk settled
Swiftly, and the pace slowed in the encroaching dark,
Until they came in the clear night upon
The high halls of Diocles, son of the son
Of the River Alpheus, Ortilochos,
A place familiar to Telemachus,
Who had stayed there on his way to Sparta.
But this time no smiling host guided him
To where he slept; instead, the courteous Diocles
Welcomed the host with somber and with anxious face.
A feast had been prepared; and once the necessary sacrifices
Were accomplished and the wine spilled dutifully,
Attendants hewed the fragrant roasted thighs
And courteously served the hungry men.
The host sat with the two kings, Telemachus,
And the chosen Ithacans and Corinthians
On one side, Lacedaemonians on the other.
Sharp-eyed Odysseus, aware of his host's
Unease, gently probed to confirm the cause.

"A sad time for us all, the death of a dear friend."

All nodded and murmured in assent.

"But doubly hard for the house of Nestor
And for Pylos and for you, Diocles."

His host nodded sadly but said nothing—
And the keen-eyed king noted the involuntary glance
Made by Diocles toward the red-haired king
Menelaos.

"I assume that his son Thrasymedes,
A comrade and brave fighter in the War,
Will become King of Pylos?"

Diocles smiled wryly.

"We hope that such will be the case,
For no man would be worthier than he
To lead the kingdom. But …"

"But?"

"There are rumours that Elis to the north
Desires to invade us as they did before,
Now that the bulwark of King Nestor
Is removed. And we know nothing out of
Arcadia or the Argoliwwd."

Odysseus looked sympathetic but stopped
His fellow king from speaking as he said,

"I'm sure such problems can be resolved
With the help of my fellow king and hero
Of the Peloponnesos, Menelaos."

That king, who had been about to speak,
Was startled by this unexpected offer
Of his help, but he saw Odysseus's look
And continued to keep silent.

"You will, of course, attend the funeral rites?"

"Of course."

"Why, then, not ride with us? We would enjoy
Your company as we have your gracious hospitality."

Diocles looked surprised and pleased by this
Unexpected invitation, and quickly
Acquiesced. The feast now finished, and
All prepared to go to their sleeping quarters,
When Odysseus said to Menelaos,

"The night is clear and bright, and I feel the need
To walk to clear my head and exercise.
Will you join me?"

Menelaos saw that his friend wished to talk,
As, indeed, did he, and quickly agreed.
The two walked from the halls and into the valley.
The night was bright, moon and stars vying
For brilliance. For a time they walked in silence,
Then Odysseus turned to the king, whose hair
Showed black in the cold white light.

"Forgive me for using your name in vain,
But such opportunities do not present
Themselves so readily."

His fellow king looked at him, perplexed.

"Opportunity?"

"This whole area is unsteady
And ripe for change with this death.
Not only Elis, but other kingdoms can covet
This land, such as Arcadia. And we cannot
Forget the Heraclides, who wait
Impatiently to make their claim."

Menelaos frowned as he took in the situation.

"But there is a way to solve the problem."

"How?"

"Let us persuade Orestes to make an alliance
With Pylos and yourself. In that way

Your house will have influence across all
The Argolid, from one coast to the other,
Something never done before."

In the clear star-strewn night the Spartan king
Suddenly saw the vision that his friend
Had shone before him, and the whole pattern
That Odysseus patiently had woven
Blazed clear and bright in its meaning.
He turned to his friend, his eyes gleaming.

"My great companion, truly you are
Wiser than even Nestor was.
I will owe you much if this marvel
Comes to pass."

"Then be led by me in the discussions,
And do not question me until we are alone."

"I will do so, I swear by Zeus and all
The Olympian Gods!"

"Zeus will be quite enough,"

Odysseus replied, amused.

"Now let us return and get much needed rest
Before our journey in the morning."

And the two walked quietly back
As the moon laced their shadows on the ground,
And separated, each to his own bed and thoughts.

Early the next morning, before Dawn touched
The highest peaks with her soft fingers,
The chariots were harnessed and away.
Down the valleys they sped, then out on to the highlands,
Where in the distance the first gleams of ocean
Could be glimpsed. Finally, as dusk descended once again,
The host wheeled to ascend the slope to Nestor's palace
And found already groups from nearby countries
Encamped upon the land that spread below.
At the propylon the kings' chariots swept to a stop;

And Telemachus, not far behind, spied
Waiting for them in the light of many torches
Nestor's youngest son, Pisistratus,
With whom he had become friends on the last journey.
The solemn-faced prince courteously greeted
The two kings as they dismounted, their chariots
And armour gleaming in the torch light,
But he brightened as Telemachus
Leapt from his chariot to embrace him
Vigorously.

"I had heard that you and your illustrious father
Were in the Peloponnesos,
But I did not expect you here so swiftly."

Attendants quickly led away the horses
To be rubbed down and fed rich oats in the stable
As the procession moved to Nestor's great hall,
Now filled with those leaders previously arrived,
Their many shadows flickering in the torches' flames.
Thrasymedes, talking with one group,
Spied them as they entered, and, having excused himself,
Hurried over to them. All three embraced
Without a word, Nestor's son, Odysseus,
And Menelaos. The hall's din died down
As the rest saw and recognized the veterans
Clasped thus. Finally, still moved, the trio
Broke to look at one another. Thrasymedes,
As host, first broke the silence.

"It has been too long, too long, that we
Have not met, and hard that we do so
Only after my father's death. But you,
Odysseus, I am doubly glad to see,
First, because of your survival
After ten long years of struggle to get home,
And then, because with you is your son
Telemachus, who nobly searched for you
In those final years, and who came to us
In that quest. And you, great Menelaos,
Have been absent from us far too long—

My father often spoke in admiration of you
And wished to see and talk with you again."

The red-haired king showed his regret, open
And unaffected, but could find no words to speak.
But Odysseus, who had now recovered
From that first encounter, placed his hand
On the shoulder of his son, who with his friend
Pisistratus had hung slightly back, stunned
By the deep feeling of the veterans' meeting,
Then gravely addressed Thrasymedes:

"I wish as well we had met earlier
To see your wise and noble father once again
And talk with him of all we did together
And of his exploits in the distant past,
But it was not to be. I am glad
My son met such a man and king, and that
He made such noble friends in Pylos here."

Thrasymedes and Pisistratus smiled
And acknowledged the compliment; then
The senior prince stepped forward to address the throng:

"Good friend and noble princes all, let us
Now attend the sacrifice and feast
That awaits us at a distance from the palace."

All then followed as he led the way
Out beyond the portico to a large field
At whose centre sacred bulls awaited them
And with them Nestor's other sons,
Echephron and Stratius, Perseus and Aretos.
Vast fires in pits lit the faces of the throngs
Who enclosed the field, the leaders found
As the inner circle, their followers
Massed behind. The six sons raised huge axes;
The milling beasts, bewildered, were first stunned
By blows, then their necks severed as hymns
Rose in the smoke to the Gods. Attendants
Swiftly dressed and dismembered the carcasses,
And soon the smell of roasting flesh
Drifted among the hungry men. Women

Now brought among them breads and delicacies
To touch their appetites, and after wine
Was ceremoniously spilled and mixed
With water, goblets and cups were distributed
And all quenched their thirst in the smoky wines
Of the western coast. After a time
The roasts and other pieces were sliced
And the choice bits sent to the honoured guests.
Each prince sat with a different group.
Thrasymedes stayed with the two kings,
And Pisistratus with Telemachus
And Diocles; Halitherses and Medon
Ate just behind their Ithacan king;
The Corinthians with Telemachus.
The veterans ate and drank with gusto,
Reminiscing at length of the Trojan War,
Their battles, whom they killed, their wounds,
And as they talked, stories accumulated
About Nestor in the war, his wisdom,
His courage and diplomacy. A pause
Broke the conversation for a moment
As each reflected back on the old
Warrior they had known; then Thrasymedes
Turned to Odysseus.

"Renowned King of Ithaca, you were the one
Who knew my father best, who with him
Was the wisest of all Achaeans,
And in strategy was unsurpassed.
I crave from you, then, on behalf of all
Of his descendants, that you will honour us
By delivering the oration
At his funeral—no man, no God,
Could do so better. Grant us this, we ask you."

For once the astute Ithacan was nonplussed
And speechless, as well as deeply moved
By the earnest request. Menelaos
Placed his hand on his arm to urge his consent;
And after a moment of thoughtful silence,
Odysseus responded.

"Thrasymedes, you know that in battle
I am afraid of no man; but now you
Have sent fear I have not felt before.
How can I speak in such a way to show
Worthily the greatness of my dear friend?"

The others made to expostulate, but
Odysseus gestured them to silence.

"At the same time, this may be the only
And the greatest gift that I can give him.
With humility, then, I grant your wish."

The others shouted their joy, startling
The other groups in the field; but again
Odysseus silenced them.

"But on one condition: that your herald
Sing to us now how the death of Nestor
Came to be."

Thrasymedes face grew drawn at this request,
But summoning up his will, he called for quiet,
Then ordered that the death of his famed sire be sung.
The man assigned to this task was famous
Along the coast for his eloquence,
And all were hushed as he stepped forward,
Lyre in hand. By this time the fires had died down,
And in their glow he strummed a first few notes,
Low and resonant, that, quiet as they were,
Still pulsed and lingered in the night air.

"I sing of the great Pylian hero,
Nestor, son of Neleus and his wife Chloris.
It was through the family of his mother
That he lived to so great an age. Her house
Blasphemed against the Gods, comparing
Themselves to the immortal ones, and
Leto's sweet son Apollo, in revenge,
Killed all but one child, to the remorse
And grief of their mother, Niobe.
That one married noble Neleus, and

Nestor was his son. Apollo, relenting,
Gave to the boy all the years that he
Had torn from his aunts and uncles,
To the extent that Neleus's son would live
The span of three human generations.
I will not list the great deeds done by Nestor
In the course of his great life—it is fitting
That these first be told at the oration—
But I will describe only the events
That led to the end of his illustrious life.
By this time, our king had lived well into
The span of a third generation,
And yet he continued strong and able,
If not for so long a time as earlier.
As the world knows, he was renowned
As a charioteer and horseman, and throughout
His life he loved to hold the reins and drive
His horses to their limits. On this day,
The last he lived upon the earth,
As Helios appeared in his blazing
Chariot, our king had his own brought forth,
And with a cry he was off across the land
Which he knew and loved so much. His hands
Guided his horses surely; and they, who
Knew his touch, responded fully with speed
And power. Across the plain they flew,
Seeming to race the Sun God himself overhead.
The old man was at his happiest, the wind
In his face whipping past him, for he wore
No helmet. As they sped thus, he did not see
A deep hole hidden in the grass, and as
The horses galloped at full speed by,
One of the wheels caught in it, and at once
The chariot lurched and tilted over.
Nestor was thrown from it; and the great speed
Of the vehicle caused him to land with
Such force that his neck was broken; he died
Instantly. And so it has come to pass
That Apollo's gift of time had run out

In this third generation. But he died
Well, as he would have liked, doing what he
Loved; and he died quickly, without pain,
An end all might wish for from the Moirae,
Our threads of life spun by Clotho, their length
Allotted and cut, by Lachesis, then by Atropos."

The singer's final words drifted over
The hushed field, sibilant as a snake,
And a few low vibrant notes from the lyre
Gave them a quiet and inevitable support.
Silence slunk through the space as every man
Thought deeply of the ancient king and his fate.
Then Odysseus stood, tears in his eyes,
And addressed the singer:

"A more eloquent song could not be asked for,
And I thank you for what you have related
And for your way of doing so."

And he gave the singer his own dagger,
Engraved in gold, with its gleaming blade.
For a time the feast continued, the wine
Flowing; then the Pylian princes bade
Goodnight to all, and each group drifted away
To its own camp or quarters. Odysseus
And Thrasymedes, however, stayed behind,
The Ithacan king questioning the prince
About his father and the long life he had.
The embers were near to cold, the night lit
Only by the stars and the waning moon,
When he was satisfied with what he learned;
And then he moved slightly closer to
The dark figure by his side to say quietly:

"Beyond the grief you feel for your father's loss,
This must be a time fraught with problems."

The shape did not move and was silent for a time;
Then:

"I do not need to tell you, wise Odysseus,
How fragile is our kingdom at this moment.

Elis once more eyes us with avarice;
And others also watch us hungrily.
You, I know, have no designs on us, and
Therefore I now speak plainly to you
And ask your advice. Although we are strong
We do not wish to battle first one kingdom,
Then another. What do you think we should do
To solve this situation?"

Odysseus stared at the embers for a moment.

"You have heard what happened in the Argolid?"

"We have heard rumours but nothing specific."

"Then let me tell you, for I have been there
And active up to the time I came to Sparta.
Orestes has become a good ruler;
Argos is in order and is flourishing,
With new roads and commerce; and with me
He has forged allegiance with Aepytus
And extended sway over all Arcadia.
This means that between him and Menelaos
The east and centre of the Peloponnesos
Is controlled by one family. With them
Forge an alliance; together no one
Will dare to invade you, and you will reap
The rewards of peace from sea to sea."

There was silence as the still dark shape
Beside him thought of what he had said.

"But would Orestes not annex our land,
If, as you say, he has extended rule
Beyond his borders and up to ours?"

The night concealed Odysseus's smile.

"That is why alliance must be made with both,
So that one will be checked in ambition
By the other. The two are not friendly
With each other despite the ties of kindred
And of marriage. But, if you will let me,

I will see if this can be arranged
To benefit you and your people."

Again silence in the star-strewn night.

"I will discuss what you have said with
My brothers and my family. Tomorrow
You will know our answer."

"I can ask for no more. And now let us
Get some rest before more visitors arrive
And you are engulfed with the funeral."

Each rose; then Thrasymedes placed his hand
On the veteran's shoulder.

"I thank you, famous Odysseus. In peace
As in war, you have always been the wisest,
Wiser even than my father.
My family will always be grateful
For the help and aid you give us."

The two dark figures embraced for a moment;
Then they moved toward the palace, where torches
Dimly lit their way, and there the veteran
Found his way to quarters and to sleep.

Dawn had already tinted all the land
As Odysseus walked from the palace
To see the sea and beach far off, where ships,
Black prowed or coloured, ranged along the shore,
With others in the far, far distance, sailing
To join the ones already there.

*Many ships, and a reminder of a*
*Different time and beach; but there they crowded*
*On the beach as far as one could see,*
*A thousand landed, and the many camps*
*Before them. So must the Trojans have seen*
*Our encampments from their towers. And now?*
*So few among those thousand who returned,*
*And here still fewer who have sailed afar*
*To honour this old man for what he was.*

He smiled grimly, then breathed in the morning air,
And went to find his host and Menelaos.
They were at the propylon, preparing
To mount chariots to drive down to
The distant beach to meet arrivals.

"Will you join us, my friend?"

Called out Menelaos jovially
As attendants brought his shining chariot
To the entrance.

"The new ships are still some distance off.
Why don't we see those that we did not hail
Last night? An hour or two should see
The others land."

His fellow king looked slightly disappointed,
Having prepared to enjoy the run to the beach
And to display his magnificence; but
He thought a moment, then laughed.

"As always you are right, you wily Ithacan!
Let us walk together to the camps."

Odysseus grinned, and the three set out
Down the slope to where camps had been set up.
At the first tents they found three Elisians
Whom they knew well from Troy, sitting before
The tent of Thalpios. Menelaos called out,

"Thalpios and Polyxeimos, old comrades,
At last we meet again! And you, noble
Automedon, we are honoured that you came.
But where is your father, mighty Diorês?"

The Elisian's face grew sombre.

"My father is no longer with us. We
Both suffered grievous wounds at Ilion
But his have proven over time to be
Fatal to him, strong as he had been."

Odysseus quickly spoke:

"We are all saddened to hear this news.
At least his house continues with a worthy
Son."

Automedon acknowledged this response,
And all nodded to each other. But
Sharp-eyed Odysseus noted that, courteous
As Thrasymedes was to his Elisian guests,
Warriors he had known at Troy, he still
Remained guarded, even as they showed
The same distance to him. Odysseus
Also saw the changes that twelve years
Had wrought on these men, whom he had known
As chieftains in their late twenties when he
And they had gone to battle on those
Distant beaches. Thalpios was the smallest
Of the three, but still a big man; his
Former litheness now seemed to have slowed,
And there was in his eyes, as in the others,
A weariness and emptiness, as if
Something vital to his being had been lost.
Polyxeimos, so well built before, now
Betrayed muscles turning to fat, and
A habitual look of avariciousness.
Only massive Automedon, who towered
Above them all, almost a match for
Peerless Ajax, showed not only strength
But intelligence and courage, just
As he had at Troy.

*He is still as formidable as ever.*
*I must be careful with him.*

Menelaos had not bothered to study them,
But started in immediately to reminisce,
And soon they were caught up in the old days
And battles and the incidents in which
They all had taken part. Menelaos
Turned to the huge Elisian:

"Automedon, who will forget your prowess
As Achilles's charioteer, and that

Terrible time when Patroclus, wearing
Achilles's armour, had you drive the chariot
Into the thickest of the battle, where
He was slain by Hector, and you had
To drive the chariot out of the fray
To console the desolate horses.
And then when you finally got your own
Driver, Alcimidon, how you returned
To wreak havoc on the Trojan forces,
Repelling Chromios, Aeneas, and then
Hector himself—and then, to kill Aretos
And take his armour! How fine you were!"

Odysseus noticed that Automedon
Did not swell with pride at the mention
Of his exploits; instead, pain filled his eyes
At the memories of that dreadful day, when
The fate of both Hector and Achilles
Was sealed by Patroclus's blood.
Instead, he gazed down at the beach and said,

"The latest ships have landed."

Menelaos turned to look, then shouted,

"We must go down there at once. Have them bring
The chariots quickly!"

While they waited, Odysseus said quietly
To the Elisian hero,

"That day was the turning point for all of us,
And you played a valiant part in it."

Automedon smiled grimly at him in agreement.
In a short time the drivers brought the chariots
To them, and they sped down the slope and onto
The flat land before the beach.
Megos Phyeides, of Dulichion
And holy Echinol, the islands
Across the waters from Buprasion
And Elis, had beached his sharp-prowed ship
And now stood before them as they swept

Onto the beach. This time the greetings
Were warm and friendly; no danger from him
And his people, and rich memories of
The past. Thrasymedes conferred with him
About where he may encamp, and he was
Guided with his men to the location
By a courteous attendant. Farther on
Two larger ships had landed, their prows
Brightly painted, and the three princes
Found awaiting them the Boeotian chief
Leitos from Scoinos, and Ialmenos,
Arês's son, from Minyeian Orchomenos.

*Only two ships from Boeotia?*
*Only Leitos, and he comes afflicted*
*Still with the wounds given him by Hector.*
*How slowly he moves. Each motion sends pain*
*Throughout his body. Gone are Peneleos,*
*Leader of that huge expedition,*
*And Arcesilaos, Clonios,*
*Prothoënor. But Leitos still came.*
*And Ialmenos, formidable*
*And dangerous. He has not changed much*
*Since the war, although his hair begins*
*To grey.*

The veterans greeted each other
With that familiar affection
That comes with years of absence that smooth away
The differences that rankled in the stress
Of combat and the grinding lulls between.
As they spoke, giving their histories
To bring them up to date, and lamenting
The death of Nestor, which provoked more rich
Anecdotes about the legendary king,
A distance down the beach two more sleek ships
Slid onto the sand. One was dazzling white,
With a graceful, brightly coloured prow;
The other, black as Acheron, its prow
Carved with a grotesque monster gaping wide

At the beach. From the former stepped, clad in
White and shining gold, Merionês of the
Hundred-citied Crete, still lean, with sharp face,
Still the image of the famous slayer
That he was, rightly called the peer of Arês,
The man-slaughtering God. Odysseus glimpsed
The haughty Cretan down the beach and pointed
To the others where he was; but even
As he did so, the other ship disgorged
Its crew, and all gasped. For from it came,
With lithe panther-like motion, the long hair
Sweeping behind their swarthy faces,
The men of sacred Euboea, fierce
And proud, the famed and feared Abantês,
Who had been led by their chieftain, dark
Elephenor Calchodontidês,
Who with his warriors had ravaged those
Of Troy until he himself fell in the thick
Of battle. With their arrival, all knew
The strength of Nestor's popularity
And fame, and Thrasymedes took heart
At this demonstration of respect.
The whole group met with courtesy these new
Arrivals, and with the sun now high in the sky,
They were led to set up their encampments.

While all these arrivals were dealt with,
Telemachus and his Corinthian comrades
Remained in the company of Pisistratus,
Who was eager to hear all their news
Even as he had to attend to other
Duties of the now frantic household.
While they were chatting, the Pylian prince
Said suddenly,

"Have you yet seen my sister, Polycaste?"

Telemachus admitted he had not.

"Then you'll see her now—but be warned, she's not
The youngster that you met last time!"

Telemachus remembered the scrawny
Girl who had served him at his bath, oiling
His body and dressing him in clean clothes,
Only fourteen at the time, he guessed, but he
Politely averred that he would like to meet her,
And they went off to wait in the inner
Courtyard while Pisistratus went to get
His sister. While he was gone, Ithacan
Telemachus talked casually
With his comrades, telling of his last
Encounter. Facing them and away from
Where the Pylian prince had gone, he
Was startled when they gazed past him, enthralled.
Turning, he saw Pisistratus leading
A girl whose doe-eyed beauty held all
In thrall. Shyly she approached them, her
Brother making her move forward. Stepping
In front of the stunned Telemachus,
He said, tongue in cheek,

"Son of Odysseus, here is the servant
Of your bath."

His sister blushed at this introduction,
Which seemed to accent her loveliness more,
And inclined her head to Telemachus.

"Noble prince, I am glad to see you again,
Even in the sorrow of this time;
As you have found a father, I have lost mine."

Telemachus noted her low voice,
Melodious, and her appropriate speech,
And he replied,

"Gracious lady, I am grateful also
For this opportunity again to see you,
And I grieve with you for the loss
Of your great father, whom I feel honoured
And fortunate to have met, if only once."

Again she blushed and lowered her head
In acknowledgement, but the sharp-eyed prince

Had seen her look closely at him as he spoke,
And realized she was comparing him
Today as she had seen him three years ago
Rising from the bath, and he tingled at the thought.

"Well, I'm glad that's done,"

Broke in her brother mischievously,

"She's done nothing but talk of you since you left."

Polycaste shot her brother an angry look,
But when she turned back she looked straight into
The prince's eyes, and in her violet eyes
With their lush lashes, he saw that what she
Had seen before was now confirmed, and her
Heart locked in its choice. He was nonplussed;
Here was a girl exquisite in form
And feature, whose character appeared
To match her physical beauty, and
Utterly desirable; but in his mind
He saw Pelagia, and the memory
Of her, combined with the erotic presence
Of this girl, sent a rush of longing through
His body. Before he could respond,
Pisistratus said to the others,

"Come with me and I will point out the
Various camps while these two get reacquainted."

And before the couple could reply,
He led the others off through the courtyard,
The group laughing as they went. For a moment
The man and girl stood silent; then he said,

"Shall we also walk out to see what is
Happening?"

She gave a lovely smile, then said,

"Let us get a better view from the walls
Above."

He assented, and she led him to a stairway
Which led to the balustrade above.

There they saw laid out before them the hills
And plains, covered with olive and citrus
Trees, and among them the camps now set up,
And farther on, the sandy beach on which
The many ships lay scattered like a thick forest.
For a time they looked out, taking in the
Activity as camps continued to be set up,
Silent, but acutely aware of the nearness
Of the other. Finally, she broke
The silence.

"Can you see your father from here?"

"No. I know that he has gone to the beach
To greet the newcomers, and it is
Too far to pick out anyone, but I will
Introduce you to him when he returns."

She glanced sideways at him, then to the view.

"I should like that very much.
There have been stories of what happened
When he finally returned. Are they true?"

Telemachus reminded her of the suitors
For his mother, and that his father, with his help,
Had massacred them all, and then won
The civil war that had ensued. Throughout
She had turned to watch him closely,
Then questioned him on how they came here.
He told her of the prophecy, their trip
To Delphi, and their journey now through
The Argolid, Arcadia, Sparta,
And now here upon word of Nestor's death.
Although he did mention the fortress sacked
By Orestes and Aepytus, he made
No mention of his rescue of Pelagia,
Or of the girl herself.
As he talked, Polycaste began
To flush slightly, and the high colour
Made her even more enticing, so that
Telemachus found it difficult to

Concentrate on what he said. Finally
He finished, and then asked her about
Her own life.

"There is not much to tell. I was born
Near the end of the war"—

Telemachus was surprised—

"My father's wife had died before he left
And he took a new one from the high-born
Captured in the raids on neighbouring towns."

He looked at her, again in surprise.

"He did marry her—he would not keep
A slave or concubine—so that I am
A true member of this family."

The way she said it, with a slight defiance,
Told him that she was sensitive about it
And how it might affect her own prospects
For marriage.

"I could not think someone so lovely
As yourself could be otherwise—the king
Could not have sired a finer last child."

The look she gave him was so honest and so
Naked, showing her gratitude for his assurance
And at the same time the desire for him
That now consumed her being, melted what
Was left of Telemachus's caution and reserve,
And without thinking he leaned toward her,
So conveniently close, her body
Almost touching his, and kissed her soft
Compliant lips; immediately she
Melted to him, her body pressed to his,
And the kiss grew in intensity.
For some time they stayed locked together,
Her desire, total, unrestrained, provoking
His, until at last, Telemachus
Realized what had happened and gently

Separated them despite her ravening need
For him. They stood there, gazing, and then,
Trembling, her eyes still glazed with her desire,
She spoke huskily, the words rushing forth.
She told him that she had been attracted
To him from the moment that she bathed him
And had to oil his body—here she swayed
And would have pressed against him again
But for his hands holding her slightly away.
She told him that over the three years
Her love and need for him had matured
As had her body and her character,
And, although she had tried to forget him,
Thinking that she would never see him again,
When he did return and she saw him now,
She was helpless to stop the passion
That now overcame her. When she had said
This, she broke into racking sobs, looking
So helpless and forlorn that he embraced
Her gently and let her cry against his chest.
He now found himself in a situation
That he had never dreamed of. To hear this
Confession from one so young and lovely,
Was startling enough, and in another place
He may have dealt with it and left her
And her adolescent feelings; but
She was a princess from a famous family,
The daughter of a good friend of his father,
Only recently deceased. Not only that,
But he suddenly became aware
Of where he was, on a parapet
Above the courtyard and in full view
Of those both in the palace and without,
And any action that he made would be construed
In the light of this passionate embrace
First, and then this present comforting.
And even as he considered this,
He remembered Pelagia and their union,
And how deeply each had loved the other,
And he shivered even as he held

The lovely girl now sobbing passionately
On his breast. For the moment he remained
Frozen, uncertain what to do, then he
Decided to let her purge herself of
What she had now to release. Some minutes
Went by until her crying started to die down,
And she finally rested against him,
Exhausted by what she had just undergone.
Finally he raised her head and brushed away
The tears lingering on her long lashes.

"We must go back inside,"

He said quietly,

"And you must return to your room to prepare
To help your family with your visitors."

She looked at him fearfully, clinging to him.

"I will see you again?"

"Of course. I told you that you would meet
My father on his return. But you must
Calm yourself first and get ready."

She looked relieved and moved slightly away,
Then turned and said innocently,

"My mother told me that you would like me,
And I know my father thought well of you."

Then Telemachus understood what had happened.
Nestor and his wife had seen him as an
Ideal match for their daughter, and they used
These three years to work on her initial
But immature feelings for him. Although
Nestor had died, the prince's arrival
Had provided the opportunity
To cement the match and force his father's
Hand. He felt he had been tricked into this
Compromising moment; and yet, as he
Looked at the young girl before him, now
Glowing in her happiness and love,

He could not blame her for her innocence,
And her beauty had affected him as well.
As they walked in, he made up his mind
To find his father and warn him of what
Had happened, and to ask his advice.

Odysseus had now left Thrasymedes
And Menelaos at the beach and driven
Back up to the palace. As he came to
The outer gate and left the chariot
With attendants there, he saw his son
Waiting for him.

"Father, would you walk with me?"

Odysseus saw his expression and knew
That something serious had occurred,
And so he nodded, and they strode forth
Among a grove of olive trees. Neither
Said anything for a time, the father
Waiting for his son to speak first, and then
Finally Telemachus told him all
That had occurred, leaving nothing out, for
He knew his father would need to know all
That had happened. When his son had finished,
Odysseus walked with him, deep in thought.

"I remember well when Nestor returned
From a raid near Troy that netted him both
Booty and a high-born woman, whose
Beauty in some ways rivalled that of Helen.
And the girl is right—he did not keep her
As a slave, but married her with all proper
Rites, so that she became a lawful member
Of his house. I did not know her much then—
He kept her well within his camp—but I
Would like to see her again, and this girl,
Before we commit ourselves more."

Again he thought deeply as they strode along.

"Nestor was wise—a union between our
Kingdoms would be advantageous, and keep

Some of the greedy kings away from war
With Pylos. But what do you feel about
This girl? Could she be your wife?"

Telemachus was both moved and flattered
That his father would concern himself
With his own choices, and he answered thus:

"As you will see with your own eyes, she is
Of women one of the most beautiful
Who has been seen in Hellas. But she is
Young, and though she loves me with a passion
That both stirs and disturbs me, yet she needs
More time to mature."

His father looked at him, admiring his
Wisdom and discretion. Then he said,

"But you have a further hesitation,
Have you not? What of your captive woman,
Pelagia? You are involved with her too,
Are you not?"

His son nodded, and Odysseus saw that
His feelings for the Arcadian girl
Ran deep.

"Let me think on this as we walk back."

"We may have to come to a decision
Quickly, father. I promised, as I said,
To introduce you to her when you came back,
And I'm sure her family also will be there."

Odysseus smiled.

"I will have thought it through by that time.
Just let me handle what occurs, I ask you."

They turned and walked slowly back in silence,
As the king pondered what he would now do.

When they reached the inner courtyard, the prince
Saw he had been right: there waiting for them

Was Polycaste, and with her, her brother
Echephron, who, although the eldest,
Had forgone the station of the king, for
He found himself much more at home in
Stewardship of the household—all brothers
Had, in fact, ceded the title to
Thrasymedes as the one most worthy
To succeed his illustrious father.
Another woman stood there as well, whose
Beauty matched her daughter's—more, in fact,
Because of her maturity, although
Telemachus noted that she could be
Only in her mid-thirties at the most;
And he came to know with a start that she
Must have been near the same age as her
Daughter when Nestor had destroyed her town
And taken her as wife, she in her teens,
He in his seventies; and with that thought
An avalanche of others cascaded
Through his mind: the mother had devoted
Her life to making sure her daughter would
Make a true high-born marriage, not forced through
War into a captive choice; that Pelagia,
Not more than a year or two older than
Polycaste, had been subjected
To the same dark fate, without recourse;
And that if he did marry the one girl
And keep the other as a concubine,
The situation would be much like that
Of Menelaos and his two sons
By a concubine in conflict with
His wife. Then he remembered that Helen
Had born a daughter, and that Polycaste
Could bear him more children, and he felt
More comforted. By this time they were
Before the family. Odysseus made
The first move.

"It is a pleasure for me to see you
Once again, Aristomachê, beloved

Wife of Nestor. Your beauty has grown
Even more wondrous since last we met."

Aristomachê coloured slightly
And smiled in acknowledgement of both
The recognition of her status
As true wife and the compliment over
Her appearance. Odysseus continued,

"And this is your daughter, whom my son
Has told me so much about. Truly she
Is more beautiful than he could tell me."

Polycaste, who had watched him with
Enormous eyes, blushed more than her mother,
And lowered her head in modesty.
The family visibly relaxed with Odysseus's
Words, but still listened anxiously
To hear what further he would say. The king,
Now in complete charge of the situation,
Continued.

"I hear that these two have shown some feeling
For each other. Do you find this to be true?"

Polycaste raised her head and looked adoringly
At Telemachus, who smiled back, and
Aristomachê and Echephron both nodded—
Betraying to both son and father that
The meeting of the couple had been
Arranged. Odysseus now nodded and said,

"A marriage between the two houses
Would be helpful to both, would you not say,
Echephron?"

Echephron nodded, hardly crediting
What he had hoped for; Aristomachê's face lit
Triumphantly, and Polycaste almost
Fainted with the possibility.

"I am happy with such a union"—

Telemachus was startled by so strong

An assertion, but dutifully said nothing—

"And we could announce their betrothal, once
I have consulted with my seer"—

The family looked startled and concerned—

"But I am sure that there will be no problem."

The family relaxed uncertainly.

"We should know what he says within the hour,
For I will consult with him now. But
I ask that in the meantime you talk
With my son further on the matter."

And with that he acknowledged them and strode
Off to find Halitherses. For a moment
All stood astonished at the abruptness
Of his leaving; but then Aristomachê
Moved forward and embraced her future
Son-in-law, saying how happy she was
In this hopeful betrothal; then Echephron
Clasped his arm and welcomed him; and
Finally Polycaste rushed forward
And flung herself into his arms. Her
Mother mildly remonstrated with her, but
Made no attempt to part them. Telemachus
Was dizzy with the speed of these events,
But he held Polycaste with him as they
Moved into the palace hall.

Within the hour Odysseus returned with
Halitherses, who announced to the family
That such a union was propitious.

"All portents seem propitious."

Polycaste was beside herself, and clung
Closely to Telemachus.

"But one thing only must be fulfilled
Before the nuptials can take place: the King
Of Ithaca must complete his pilgrimage

So that Poseidon is appeased and
King Odysseus can attend the wedding
Purified."

Consternation broke out in the family.
Echephron looked nonplussed; Aristomachê's
Lovely eyes grew dark with rage; and her
Daughter burst into tears and clung again
To Telemachus. Odysseus watched patiently,
Then said,

"Nothing untoward has happened. I will
Return within the year, as will my son.
And a year will let Polycaste mature
Even more. Besides, we can announce
Immediately the betrothal,
So that the marriage will be fixed during
This time."

It took a moment for Nestor's family
To digest what Odysseus had said,
And then they relaxed once more, confident
That the union would take place—except for
Polycaste, who showed plainly that she wished
The consummation of their marriage
Could be at this very moment. But then
Odysseus came over to her and kissed
Her gently, and with his strong authority
She relaxed, and with Telemachus's strong arm
Around her, the negotiations finished.

Even as Helios lashed his chargers
On the last stage of their journey,
So did the charioteer bring his team,
Lathered and foam-flecked, racing up the slope,
To stop abruptly before the palace.
Then from the chariot, dust-blown but in
His still gleaming armour, magnificent,
Stepped down the King of Argos, Orestes.
His coming had been noted, and before
Him there stood Thrasymedes as the host,
And beside him Menelaos and Odysseus.

"Welcome, great Orestes, ruler of the
Argolid. You honour us by coming
To commemorate the death of my father,
Gerentian Nestor."

Orestes acknowledged his host's address,
And smiled at Odysseus; but when he saw
His uncle, his smile stiffened, and he gave
Him a courteous but curt nod. The king
Was irritated by the gesture, but
Acknowledged him in turn. Odysseus saw
The awkwardness of the situation,
And quickly spoke.

"We also welcome you, Orestes,
And I know all veterans of the War,
Led by your illustrious father,
Will appreciate your coming, given
The affairs that now consume you—
And especially your father's brother
And your uncle, Atrides Menelaos,
Who owes so much to your father
And your house."

Both Orestes and his uncle were
Surprised by Odysseus's smooth statement,
But after the diplomatic Ithacan
Gave him a significant glance,
The red-haired king responded.

"It is true, Orestes, I do owe your house
Much, and I have grieved the death of my brother,
Murdered as he was. You took vengeance,
And the Gods adjudged you just in doing so,
But you paid a terrible price for a long time,
Until your sanity was healed.
I am sorry for any wrongs you feel
That I have done you, and I hope that you
And my daughter will become reconciled
To myself and to her mother."

Orestes was taken aback by this submission,
But he gave no response except a nod.

"I thank you, uncle; we will speak further of this."

Thrasymedes interrupted quickly,

"My attendants will show your entourage
Where to encamp. You will, of course, stay here
In the palace."

Orestes nodded, relieved that this encounter
Was now finished, and he went off with his host
To make the arrangements, leaving the kings
Alone. Odysseus saw that his fellow king
Was truly angry.

"Did I not offer him a welcome
And make offer of reconciliation?
All rejected! Did you see how cold he was,
How distant? What can I do now?
Or why should I even think of seeing him again?"

Odysseus took his arm.

"Come walk with me and work off your anger."

They strode off, the red-haired king still fuming.
Odysseus let them walk in silence for a time;
Then he said,

"You are right to feel hurt at his rebuff—
What you said was good and a start to this.
But keep in mind that he has been through much,
And that you gave your daughter to Achilles's son
When you had first promised her to him."

"I know!"

Expostulated the annoyed and frustrated king,

"But you were not here when we saw the shape
He was in after he had killed his mother
And her lover—mad, violently mad.
How were we to give our daughter to a madman?
The only thing we could do was to marry her
To Neoptolemos, whom we had spoken to before,
To protect her from what we thought would be

A catastrophic marriage. And then
The next thing we know he has been acquitted,
Regained his senses, killed Achilles's son,
And married Hermione anyway!"

Odysseus let them walk farther on in
Silence for a time so that his companion
Could finish the release of his anger;
Then:

"All that has now passed for some time; for you
And for the house of Atrides, as we
Have agreed, this reconciliation
Must be made. I will do my best to bring
Him to this possibility. Meanwhile,
Be patient."

Menelaos looked at him and nodded;
Then he stopped and cried out,

"With what ills my house has suffered! My wife,
The most beautiful woman alive,
Abducted; the terrible war, slaying
So many, and the destruction of a great city;
The sacrifice of my niece to start
The war; the murder of my brother after,
And the slaying of my wife's sister,
And the wounds which followed. When does it end?"

And he stared out at the distant sea
And beach, stricken. Odysseus placed his hand
On the grieving king's shoulder, and, with a prayer
To Athena, spoke in that voice which forced
Men to be swayed by what he said,

"The House of Atrides has indeed suffered;
But there is new hope: your own kingdom
Is prosperous and peaceful; Orestes
Has made his land flourish and brought under
His sway Arcadia; and the two of you,
When together, can wield influence over
All the Peloponnesos, as we have agreed.
Therefore, you are right to grieve for past ills;

But do not give up on what the future
Promises."

His words struck deeply in Atrides
Menelaos's heart, and he relaxed and
Turned to his fellow king.

"Again, my old friend and advisor,
You persuade me with the power of your words.
I will do my best again to undo
The errors of the past and gain once more
The friendship of my nephew and the love
Of my estranged daughter."

Odysseus smiled and warmly pressed his arm; then
The two kings walked back to the palace.

Later, as dusk's mantle settled gently
On the land and sea, sacrifices were
Made again, and feasts prepared, this time
With the kings and chieftains in the great hall
And the others feasting in the camps, each
Brother hosting separately the visitors.
In the hall Thrasymedes sat with Orestes
On one side, Telemachus beside him,
And on the other Odysseus and Menelaos;
Close to them were proud Meriones
Of Crete, the three Elisians, Megos
Phyeides, Ialmenos, and
Crippled Leitos, Phocian Epistrophos,
And the swarthy leader from Euboea
Of the Abantês—he particularly
Odysseus watched, for he was unknown
To them all. But Thrasymedes proved
An able host, as he kept Orestes
And Telemachus in conversation
While the veterans reminisced about
The war. While they were talking, Odysseus
Called across to the Euboean leader,

"Your late leader, great Elephenor
Calchodontidês, was one of

The finest warriors in the War
With Ilion—there were no fiercer
In battle than he and his Abantês,
All feared by the Trojans, and he fell
In the thickest of the frays against
Numbers that could not be dealt with but by
The Gods."

All of the veterans present gave voice
To their assent of what the Ithacan
Had said, and the swarthy long-haired chief
Gave a wolfish grin in pleased acceptance
Of the compliment. Orestes could not
But hear this conversation, and he stopped
Talking to hear the stories now passed
Among the warriors, noting as well
Their scars, and particularly the crippled
Leitos.

"Your father has been given great respect
By these men in coming,"

He said to Thrasymedes, who nodded proudly.

At this point the topic changed to Nestor,
And as the wine flowed the anecdotes passed
Among them, and both laughter and respect
Arose in the group. Finally the stories
Waned and it grew quieter. At this point
Odysseus saw his opportunity
And arose; all hushed when they saw him stand.

"My old friends, and those new to our tales,
This time, although sad because of death,
Is still precious to us, for we do homage
To a man we all loved dearly, and here
He brings us once more together."

All murmured assent to these good words,
And a glow of companionship warmed
The hall.

"Let us thank Thrasymedes, our host
And long companion, for his labour,

And that of his family, in showing
Us such hospitality."

A roar of approval rang through the hall.

"No one here has been unaffected by
The conflict with Ilion—whether
From wounds, the loss of friends or dear ones,
Or, as we have heard, betrayal at home."

All became silent at these words, each
Struck in his heart by what had pained him most.

"But now, for twelve years—and as you know,
For ten I had to struggle home—there has been peace,
And each of our lands has prospered again.
With Nestor's passing the last of a distant
Generation now has gone; new generations
Must now arise to take over from each of us"—

The hall now was silent, each wondering
Where the eloquent king was going
In his thought—

"And I must act, as must we all, to make
This happen. Therefore, my friends, I announce
Before you all that this day my son
Telemachus is betrothed to Nestor's daughter,
The lovely Polycaste."

There was shock, then general applause
At this revelation, but Telemachus
Noted that the Elisians were not
Happy with this union, and that Orestes,
First startled, then looked thoughtful. Thrasymedes
Was proud, happy, and relieved, and turned
To congratulate the prince. Odysseus
Then went on, inwardly invoking
His patron Goddess for authority:

"The link between our houses bodes well
For all us Achaean peoples. For here
We link this Gerentian house with ours
From far across the land and sea. And here

I invoke the Gods to favour such
A union as a sign of how our countries
Through adversity have now found peace."

The power of his utterance had its effect,
Even upon those who did not wish
This union, and a great roar reverberated
Through Nestor's hall. Odysseus sat down,
Noting carefully how each had responded
To his words. Thrasymedes then stood
To thank the Ithacan king and say
How proud and happy his house was with
This union; then thanked all for coming,
And told them of the funeral ceremonies
That would begin at dawn tomorrow.
Everyone then began to leave, most
Congratulating the two families
Before they left. When most had gone, Odysseus
Turned to Orestes.

"Perhaps a walk in the night air would clear
Our minds?"

Orestes nodded, and they took leave of the others.
Outside the night sky was clear; only stars
Lit the heavens, the moon now shrouded in
Her sable robes. The two men walked quietly
Along the slope, the groves of trees blacker
Than the star-speckled dark. They looked down
Over the hills and plain to where the curved line
Of the beach with its white sand could just
Be seen. Orestes, aware of Odysseus
Waiting for him to speak first, began:

"It is the first time that I have seen
Veterans of the war together
In such numbers. I am surprised that
They show such comradeship."

The other shape chuckled.

"When you must rely on everyone
In battle, you soon grow close to them,

Regardless of their country or their
Temperament. But do not be deceived—
They still have their own interests close
To their hearts, despite their respect
For their fellow warriors' reputations."

The black form stayed silent; then:

"I must congratulate your son and you
On his betrothal; Polycaste
Has been compared in beauty to my wife
And her mother, I hear.
She is indeed exquisite, but still very young.
It was evidently a surprise
To everyone, including me."

Odysseus laughed easily and said,

"It was a surprise to us as well;
Apparently after Nestor saw my son
Three years ago he made up his mind
That his daughter should become my son's bride.
We became aware of this when we arrived;
And when the girl showed great affection for him,
And he was not adverse to her as well,
We made up the match."

In the dark Orestes's thoughts on this
Could not be seen; then he said,

"Some in the hall did not seem pleased
By your announcement."

"The Elisians, you mean? They had
Their own plans for Pylos with Nestor gone.
But now the fate of this kingdom
Will concern me much, needless to say."

A pause as the two dark figures looked
Across to the distant sea. Finally:

"What do you really mean by this match,
Cunning Odysseus?"

His fellow king laughed heartily.

"I do not have plans hidden long before
This betrothal came to pass; only when
We got here did this affair spring up,
As I just told you."

Then he became more serious.

"But since the match occurred—only today—
I have been thinking, as you know
I usually do"—

Both chuckled wryly—

"And it has led me to you and to your house."

Orestes said nothing, waiting for more.

"Listen carefully, King Orestes,
To what I propose to you. You now
Control the Argolid and Arcadia;
Here is an opportunity for you
To reach an alliance that would stretch
Your reach across the Peloponnesos.
As someone with concern now vested in
This kingdom, I would find this arrangement
Desirable, as you may suspect,
For it would keep Elis from invading
And would give you influence as far as
Ithaca. I can be instrumental
In effecting this, if you are willing."

Orestes was silent for a long moment,
Then said thoughtfully,

"As always, you see through to the best plan,
Wise Odysseus. I can see how this
Can work to the benefit of all.
Persuade the Pylians, and I will agree."

Odysseus chuckled again.

"I do not think it will be difficult
To have them accept this proposition."

He paused briefly, then spoke again,
This time far more seriously.

"But, noble Orestes, we should think
Further on what other things you might do.
Today you met your uncle face to face
For the first time since the dreadful times
Which had afflicted you"—

The dark figure stiffened at this mention—

"And you heard with your own ears his concern
Over what has occurred with your wife and you
And his own apology for the wrongs
He did you."

Orestes snorted contemptuously.

"But, even though you still are bitter
Over what he did and do not wish
To speak with him or see him, as a king
You must consider these things as well:
He is a fellow king and still popular—
You saw that at the feast today—
And you cannot help but have business
With him in the future. As well, your house
Is his house, the House of the Atrides,
And we all fought a war for this house.
To see it now in disarray makes
A mockery of all the men who died
For it, the great city that was destroyed
For it, and your father, who led it
For his brother, and himself was murdered
On his return. As a king, and as
An Atrides, you must lay enmity
Aside and reconcile with him.
If—and when—you do, then more than this
Will happen. Suppose he joins in this alliance:
Most of the Peloponnesos would be
Under the sway or influence of
The House of Atrides. Has there been
Such an empire in Hellas before?

Would you lose such a chance to gain such fame?
I have seen what you can do as king,
And I know that your reign can be great
For all the lands you rule or influence.
There will never be such an opportunity
Again—seize it and prosper."

The dark form beside Odysseus was still;
The sound of the night breeze could be heard,
And the distant noises of the camps.
Then Orestes spoke huskily,

"No one but yourself could have devised
Such a plan, King of Ithaca. No one
But yourself could persuade me to join
My uncle in such an alliance.
I will do as you suggest. Tomorrow,
Once the funeral rites are done, bring us
Together and build this alliance,
As I know you will. Now, let us go back."

The two turned and started back. As they walked,
Odysseus asked,

"King Pylades stays with Aepytus
While you are here?"

They both chuckled and continued on.
Then in turn Orestes asked,

"And what will happen to the Arcadian girl
That your son championed?"

"She will sail home with him when we go."

"And how will that affect his young bride?"

Odysseus chuckled again.

"We have determined that they will not wed
Until I have been purified and returned.
As that should take at least a year, the one
Will be established in Ithaca,
And the other hopefully will have matured."

Both laughed at the situation; then,
Having reached the palace, they separated,
Each happy over what they had decided.

The next day, Dawn spread her delicate fingers
Over the sea and shore, plain, hill and range,
As to the beaches poured all Pylians,
Prepared for the momentous day. With them
Came the visitors, and Telemachus
Remembered the time before, when his ship
Had swiftly cut through the waves to the beach
Where he had seen the people in their groups,
Five hundred strong in each, each sacrificing
Nine bulls as they made their prayers to
The earth-shaking God Poseidon. This time
They were joined by a thousand more, so that
The shore was thick with their numbers and with
The smoke from the fires prepared for the
Innumerable sacred bulls ready
For the slaughter. The first prayers sent forth
Were to their patron God,

"Ποσειδάωνα θεόν,
Mighty deity, mover of both earth
And the bleak sea, monarch of the depths.
To you, Lord of the quaking earth, the Gods
Appointed two distinct offices:
The breaker of horses; the saviour of ships.
Hail, hail, blue-haired Cradler of the Earth,
O blessed Poseidon, be favourable to us:
Support those in their journeys on the sea!"

Then from the lowing, milling herd the bulls
Were ritually stunned and their throats cut,
And a hymn to Zeus rose from the voices
Of the thousands there.

"Ζῆνα θεων τόν ἄριστον ἀείσομαι ἠδέ μέγιστον
I sing!"
          the crowd roared,
                    "I sing of Zeus,
Zeus above all Gods, supreme, supreme,

Far-seeing lord, ruler of fulfillment,
In intimate conversation with reclining Justice
As she inclines toward him.
Be gracious, oh be gracious, noblest,
Greatest, far-seeing son of Cronos!"

Then, to the sweet and deadly son of Zeus,
A hymn soared up in thanks for the gift
Of the many years he had granted Nestor.

"Είς Ἀπόλλωνα!
Phoebus, Phoebus Apollo, even the swan's song
Can sing beautifully of you, as his wings stroke
And he berths upon the bank of Peneus,
River of eddies. Minstrels with their golden voices
And their melodious lyres in every song
Begin and end in honour of you.
Hail, Apollo, God of the silver bow and the arching shot,
Most glorious son of Zeus and Leto!"

And as the hymns soared forth, on a great litter
Richly adorned with carpets and cloths
Of gold and silver, borne by all his sons,
The body of Nestor was brought to lie
In state, while all the women of his house,
Dressed in black, wailed, cried out, and rent their clothes,
Their hair, even their faces in their grief,
Their nails clawing at their flesh.
When the solemn rites had been performed,
Odysseus stood on a platform behind
The place where Nestor had been displayed
On high to let all see his body in its glory,
And he said quietly a prayer to
Pallas Athena to let his words be heard
By all the thousands that packed the beach
And plain. Then, as he raised his arms to
Silence crowd and family, he spoke,
And his voice was heard clearly over all:

"People of Pylos and of the House of Neleus,
Achaeans and all those who come this day
To give respect to, and to venerate,

As I do, this hero, Gerentian Nestor,
Let me here offer up what words I can
To remind us of whom he was amongst us.
The Gods blessed him, especially
Zeus's dear son Apollo, who balanced
Life and death even with the Moirae,
When he apportioned to Chloris's son
The years that he had torn from her
Brothers and sisters who had defamed him,
And so he has lived through more than most men
Are allotted, three generations.
In that time he has proven his worth
Many times over. As a youth, without
Experience, he yet fought and killed
Two worthy men, Elean Itymoneus,
Son of Hypeirochos, and Mulius,
The son-in-law of King Augeas;
And in another battle, this time
Against the Arcadians, he slew
Their champion Euruthalion,
Despite the armour given by Arês
To King Lycurgus that he wore;
And he fought with the Lapiths in their
Famed war with the centaurs, beside
The legendary Theseus and Peleus.
And when he came, now aged, to assist
Achaeans in the dread War with Ilion,
He still showed his strength and courage
In the ill-fated battle when Zeus forced
Our side to quit the field and he remained,
His horse shot dead by Paris, attacked
By Hector, until assisted by Diomedes,
And continued until a lightning bolt
Before their chariot convinced him
To leave the field. But he is not known
Only as a warrior. He was the wisest
Of the Achaean rulers, striving
Through diplomacy and persuasive words
To keep us all from war with Troy, and they
With us, and when that effort failed

Through no fault of his own, he did his best
To keep us all together. When
Achilles quarrelled with King Agamemnon
Over Briseias, he was the one who
Tried to mediate between them;
When he rescued the wounded Machaon,
Son of Asclepius, from the battle,
He was the one who persuaded Patroclus
To convince Achilles to fight again,
Or at least let his friend do so. Patroclus
Himself went to battle and was killed
By Hector, thereby provoking Achilles's
Grief and wrath; and it was therefore
Nestor's doing, honourable as it was,
That brought the turning point to the war.
He was blessed, and blessed others, in further ways.
He is one of the few of us who returned home
Straightway from the war—one of the few,
Indeed, who survived at all. And he
Has shown himself in Pylos to be
A wise and honourable ruler who
Has helped his kingdom grow and prosper.
His family knows his goodness too,
Over its own generations, for he
Continued to sire children into the years
Of the third generation, and all knew
Him good and loving"—

An agonized cry arose again from the women—

"For myself, throughout the years I found him
A true friend and the wisest man I know,
And most knowledgeable. I learned much
From him and regret the years in which
I could not see him and talk with him again,
As we used to in the war, sitting outside
His tent as he sipped wine from his golden bowl
And we talked of all things that mortal man
Can ponder on. He always surprised me
With what he said—and he left his best

Surprise for now, when I discovered that
He wished my son to wed his beloved child
And youngest of his daughters, Polycaste,
Most beautiful in the eyes of Gods and men,
And I have with joy agreed to his request."

Telemachus saw the girl and her mother
Weeping as his father told of the betrothal.

"What more can be said? The Gods loved this man,
As did we all; and no mortal man will
Ever live such a long and full life again
As he has done. All honour be to him."

He finished, tears streaming from his eyes,
And a silence lay on all who heard him.
Then a full-throated roar was heard from
The gigantic throng that reverberated
Across the hills and plains and out to sea.
Then, to the long sounds of horns and wails,
The sons bore up the body and, leaving
All behind, carried their father alone
To his tholos, into which he was lowered,
His sword gleaming at his side and his
Golden dagger placed beneath his arm.
While these solemn rites were practised,
The beach now gave way to feasting as
Attendants carved the great roasts and
Distributed the succulent innards,
The appropriate portions left for the Gods.
Telemachus and Odysseus now
Ate with the family, Polycaste,
Her hair, clothes, and face dishevelled
By her mourning, but looking even
More attractive in that state, sitting
Closely by her betrothed and watching him
Adoringly. Pisistratus again
Teased the couple, but Telemachus
Grinned and threw a bone at him.
Throughout the afternoon the feast continued;
Then Odysseus sought out Thrasymedes.

"All are in agreement for the alliance;
Get a scribe to note it while I find the others."

Thrasymedes looked at him in amazement,
But did as he was bade. Then Odysseus
Found Menelaos and told him of Orestes's
Change of heart. The Spartan king was overjoyed,
And they went together to find Orestes.
The king of the Argolid, sitting with
Stratius, son of Nestor, saw them coming
And arose, saying,

"I greet you again, Atrides Menelaos.
Odysseus has done both of us a service,
And himself as well, with this betrothal."

Orestes's manner was reserved, but he
Did greet his uncle in a manner
That heartened the red-haired king, who returned
His welcome heartily. Then the three kings
Were joined by Thrasymedes with his scribe,
And together they formed the alliance
That knit their kingdoms together.

# Canto 6
# SPARTA

In Sparta the incomparable Helen
Continued to instruct Pelagia
In the mysteries of herbs and their use,
And always Amunet was there with them,
Bringing from their storage those substances
That Helen had commanded, making sure
That all was put away and the place clean.
But always she remained silent throughout.
Before the men had left for Pylos
Helen had already shown the girl those plants
Which helped to keep wounds and cuts from festering:
Courageous Thyme, lavender-flowered,
Aromatic, cleansing tables before food,
Applied to outside wounds or swallowed;
Euphoriaceae, the glad flower
Appropriate to Euphrosyne
Of the Graces, astringent, a lotion
For the eyes; the military Yarrow,
Achilles's treatment to staunch his soldiers'
Wounds but not, alas, his own; succulent
Dill, boiled in wine to cleanse the mouth;
Red-flowering Centaury that honoured
Chiron, exiled to Saggitarius
By troubled Zeus; and then, brought out from
Its secret place, red-brown, precious Myrrh.

"Use this sparingly, given its expense—
Use it in liniments, in healing salves
On abrasions and lesser skin ailments."

Then she showed her in the garden the many
Plants used for digestive purposes:

Fennel, held in reverence, because
Prometheus brought fire to man in its hollow stem,
With its feathery bright yellow flowers,
A stomachic, a carminative,
Its pleasant flavour useful in formulae
With many bitter herbs used as cholagogues;
The hairy Chamaedrys, with labiate flowers
Of rose, a tonic, stimulant, diaphoretic,
Diuretic, aperient, bitter,
Odorous; the warm, pungent Juniper,
Bearing small purplish blue gabuli;
Manna; white-flowered Caraway;
Marsh-dwelling Cyperus, warmth-giving,
Anti-emetic; and the herb of the dead,
Committed to Persephone and sprung
From the blood of Archemorus, Parsley.
Cosmetics for the skin were now displayed:
Balanos oil, Egypt's finest unguent,
Derived from the fruit of a thorny tree;
Behen oil, from the nuts of the Maringa;
Sweet Almond oil; the yellow-flowered Aloe,
Succulent and spiky, of many uses,
But here to keep skin beautiful
And healthy. Then Helen showed her student
Fenugreek, smiling as she did so.

"I will show you how to make oil from this,
Which has many uses and is blessed
Of the Gods: as a poultice of pulverized seeds
It treats wounds, sores, skin irritations,
Swollen glands; as a tea from seeds it can
Increase a mother's milk; as a wash it
Stimulates breast growth—something neither
Of us is concerned about"—

Both chuckled as they considered their shapely forms—

"And it is a remedy for infections
Of the lungs. But for me, as well as its
Power as an aphrodisiac—
And for you later, as for most women—

Its oil can transform an old man into
A younger, important as my husband
Becomes older."

She smiled, and Pelagia saw in her eyes
A flash of raw hunger and desire
That shocked and disconcerted her.
Helen took no notice but went on.

"There are more plants that can increase
Our appetite for men, and they for us."

She gave a throaty laugh before she
Showed what plants these were.
"Loose-threaded Saffron has other uses,
But used in a warm bath it can provoke
More pleasant love-making. The Cucumber
You can use to be more fertile—and you
Would do well to consider its use soon.
The Parsnip can arouse; and the great sign
Of death, sex, and fertility, the
Loranthacae, must never be forgotten."

By this time the men had left for Pylos,
And Helen led Pelagia into a study
Of the darker purposes for plants.

"This plant is imbued with magical powers
That can alleviate nervous disorders,
And even insanity. The resin
Of the root of this one, Asafoetida,
Is antispasmodic, calms hysteria
And a woman's emotions after her time.
Here, the resin of Hemp is intoxicating;
To strengthen the memory here is
Mnemosyne's plant, Rosemary;
And the great nepenthe, Borage, to drink
Steeped in wine after battle to bring about
Almost complete forgetfulness; or this,
Zizyphus-letaes, which causes those
Who drink it to sink into lassitude
And a dreamy contentment—do not

Forget these drugs, for they will prove useful
To you in later times."

Now she turned to a bed of Poppies,
And her eyes grew heavy-lidded as she spoke.

"The sacred flower of Demeter,
The Goddess teacher of womankind,
And also a plant linked with Thanatos,
Lord of the Dead and of eternal sleep.
A many-sided plant, a great sedative,
A killer of pain, but also potent
As an aphrodisiac and herald
Of our dreams as Hypnos, God of Sleep,
Brings us prophetic thoughts."

And Helen picked the scarlet flower
And showed Pelagia how to obtain
Its sap, cutting round the star while careful
Not to penetrate the inside of the capsule,
And making straight incisions down the sides.
Then she used her finger to wipe the droplet
Into a shell, leaving it to thicken
For the next day. Helen now turned to
The most dangerous plants:
Black Helebore, toxic but medicinal;
The pale pink Cyclamen, a risky
Purgative; the poisonous Aconite,
Invention of Hecate, which made
The user seem to fly, but was also
A diuretic and diaphoretic;
Henbane, narcotic; and the beautiful
Blue flower, Amaryllidaceae,
The deadly shade of self-smitten Narcissus.
Finally she turned to the deadly nightshade
Atropa Belladonna, the plant of
Atropos, the Fate who cuts the thread of life.
But then she showed an antidote to these:
Rue, plant of many uses. Now
The training was intensified, Helen
Leaving her at times with Amunet
To learn by the slave's example the skill:

Other plants and drugs she showed her; but while
She did so she also instructed her
In preparations—infusions and decoctions,
Poultices and herbal creams and ointments,
Extractions for essential oils, unguents,
Powdered herbs and tablets. In all that
She was taught, Pelagia proved adept,
And Helen approved. One day, when all three
Were kneading seeds and pods of Fenugreek
Into a dough before boiling in a clean pot,
Pelagia turned to her instructor.

"Why are you, a great queen, spending time
In teaching me, no more now than a slave
Or concubine, so much?"

Amunet glanced swiftly at her, a flash
In her dark eyes, but she still said nothing.

Helen kept them working as she replied,

"You've seen the sons of my husband's concubine.
She has no value, no authority,
And she has been tucked away, far away
From Sparta. Her sons are disaffected,
Knowing that they cannot rule the land,
And the three breed discontent among them.
You are the daughter of a chieftain,
And as the last of your family must
Survive with some form of worth. You will find
That Penelope, mother of Telemachus,
Will not put up with a useless slave,
Good only for his sexual desires.
But if you can arrive with these herbs and skills,
And can show your worth, then you will be
Accepted, although your children will not
Reign after Telemachus. Keep in mind
That he must marry sometime and have
Legitimate children, however he
May love you; you must be prepared for
That moment, whatever hurt it does you."

The girl looked at her, her face grim.

"All this is true, and your advice wise—
But you have not truly answered my question."

Helen was silent for a moment
As they worked; then she gestured at a bed
Of wild yellow flowers, tall-stalked and large.

"You see those flowers?"

Pelagia nodded.

"Those are Elecampane. I had a
Large armful of them when Paris stole me
From here. Was I then more than you are now?
Yes, I was high-born in another land,
But still a chattel, still an object
Desired and fought over, without my will
Involved in any of the actions that
Killed so many and destroyed a city."

She stopped kneading and exclaimed in despair,

"We have no power, none, as women.
We bear children, we raise them, we persuade,
But our actions are not our own from
Our childhoods. I was courted by many
At too young an age, and I had no choice
But to choose one. I chose one I liked
And grew to love, but I was too young,
Too young. And the choice led to barter—
Penelope became Odysseus's wife
Because he negotiated for her.
She had no say in it. And the bargain
Struck led again to the War with Ilion.
So when I saw you brought here, a captive,
Your family and citadel all
Annihilated, I felt that I must
Do something that would help you, however
Slight. And here we are. So learn, learn all you can,
Before they return and take you away
Across the land and sea to Ithaca."

The three went back to work without a word,
For Amunet had also paused during

The queen's outburst, but she now was thoughtful
As she worked, covertly watching the other two;
And deep inside Pelagia's heart a seed,
Dark and insidious, began to germinate.

That night Helen brought the girl to her own
Quarters, "as a reward for your good work
As a student." They were served by Helen's
Attendants, who then left them with goblets
For their wine. Before they drank, however,
Helen lit candles through the space, dousing
The torches on the walls. Pelagia
Was used to candles that sputtered and stank,
But these burned pure and clear, and from them
Came exotic smells, heavy but pleasing
To the senses, which drifted through the room,
And made her slightly dizzy. She thought
She could recognize the scent of drugs
She had worked with in the garden, but
She found it difficult to concentrate
And gave herself up to the pleasure
Of the scents and Helen's talk. The queen
Now poured wine into a single bowl, which
She then proffered to her, smiling.

"Let us drink from the same bowl."

And each in turn sipped from the shining gold.
Again Pelagia thought she detected
A drug in the wine's exotic flavour,
But she did not care to examine what it was.

"Tonight will be our last lesson,"

Smiled the queen, and the girl as she quaffed
The potent liquid felt its warmth seep
Through her body, and while she found her limbs
Relaxing, she also felt her senses sharpen
And new sensations work within her.

"Say nothing; do what I do from now on."

And so saying, she led her to beside
The royal bed, and while the girl swayed there,

Now rapt with each move, Helen reached forward
And unpinned Pelagia's gown, which slipped
To her feet, leaving her naked; the air
Shocked her skin but seemed to caress her
In a way that began to spark her desire.
Helen nodded to her, and Pelagia
Undid her gown as well. In the flickering
Glow of the candles the girl gazed
In wonder at the perfect body
Before her, the skin lustrous; emotion
That she never dreamed a woman's body
Could provoke surged through her; but still she stood
Until the queen slowly laid her on the bed,
Then lay beside her, their bodies warm and close.
Then began an amorous encounter
That burned itself into the girl's memory:
Lips and mouths seeking each other hungrily;
Mirrored touches and caresses that
Explored limbs and body more than she thought
Possible, and in the touching of the
Other woman's body as she touched hers,
An awareness of herself as a woman
That she never knew before; arousal
Grew more and more; she abandoned herself
Totally, and they both reached a climax
Together that exploded, limitless
In its power. Exhausted, both lay there
And slept, their bodies glistening in the
Guttering light.

# Canto 7
# PYLOS

The morning light shone on the final rites
At the brilliant beach which lay a distance from
The palace. Once again the nine ranks of
The people of Pylos; again the ranks
Of the far-ranging visitors; again
The hymns to Zeus, Apollo, and Poseidon;
The wild tearing of hair and face by the
Grieving women; the stunning and the
Throats cut of the lowing sacred cattle;
And finally the feast. It was then,
While all ate and drank, that the kings announced
Their alliance. A roar burst forth from those
Who were their subjects; but the Elisians' faces
Grew black with fury and frustration.
As the feast ended, gifts were given to
The important guests. Thrasymedes,
After distributing precious objects
To Orestes and to Menelaos,
Then turned to Odysseus and his son.

"Great King of Ithaca, and you, my friend
And future brother-in-law"—

Polycaste, who was now allowed to
Sit with Telemachus, looked at him
With pride; despite the rituals of grief
She still looked lovelier than ever—

"You have done more than anyone
To assuage our grief at Nestor's loss,
Not only with this betrothal, so dear
To my late father's heart, but also
With the creation of this alliance

That will sustain the peace and prosperity
Of all our lands. To you, Telemachus,
We give with joy Nestor's own chariot,
As the one who most worthily will use it
In this country; and to you, dear comrade,
We give an object smaller but more
Precious in our eyes. What lies with Nestor
Are his ceremonial arms; here we
Hand you his true dagger, one that you knew
In Troy and admired greatly."

And he put into the hand of the
War-scarred veteran the dagger of gold
And bronze, worn with use but splendid
In design, and with its blade still sharp,
And all well balanced. Odysseus, holding it,
Was deeply moved, remembering well
The times that he had seen the old warrior
Use the blade, both for feasting and for battle.

"I will keep this with me through my pilgrimage,"
He promised.

        Soon the feast was concluded,
And the visitors returned to their encampments
To prepare for their departures. The Elisians
Left early, thundering across the plains
In their chariots; the others smiled
At each other as they went. While the group
From Sparta swarmed around as they packed,
Telemachus had gone to the palace
With Polycaste and her family.
Again he stood with her on the balustrade,
Watching the activity below them
On the hills, the plains, and beach,
As if ant hills had been uprooted
And the ants milled about, a scampering
Black mass covering the ground. Neither said
Much but stood together, eyes on the sight
Before them. Then Polycaste turned to him.

"Do not forget me during this long year.
Come back, please come back for me."

He looked at her, the breeze rippling
Her rich hair, her face upturned to his,
Betraying her grief at his departure,
Her longing for him, and her fear
That he may not return for her,
And he marvelled at her beauty
And her innocence.

"I have given my word, and I will return
The moment that my father finishes
His quest. Watch for my ship as it sails
To your beach."

She swiftly moved into his arms, and
Their embrace and kiss was long and passionate.
Pisistratus suddenly called to them
From below.

"Telemachus, your father and the others
Wait for you at the gate!"

Without a word the prince led his betrothed
Down from the balustrade to where her
Mother and her family were assembled.

"We wait anxiously for your return,"

Aristomachê said to him, her eyes shadowed
With worry, and he smiled and reassured her.
The brothers made their farewells to him
And he went through the gate, mounted
The chariot, and the large troop rattled
Off, even as the sharp-prowed ships slid
From the sand to sail past the horizon.

# Canto 8
# SPARTA AND CORINTH

A call from a watchtower alerted
Helen that the chariots' dust could be seen.
She left the garden where she had been working
With Pelagia, and together they climbed
To a balustrade to watch as the cloud
Drew nearer. Soon the noise of chariots
And horses could be heard, and then,
In the setting sun, the horsemen arrived
At the palace. The women met them
As the chariots were led away by
The attendants, and Menelaos
And his guests entered the great hall.
During the two days of travel,
Telemachus had found himself confused:
The image of the exquisite Polycaste
Never left him; yet he still was deeply
Involved with Pelagia and could not
Forget their nights together; nor could he
Think what to say to her, now that he was
Betrothed to another and she confirmed
As his concubine. But when he entered
The hall and saw the two women together,
He was struck by how much the girl had changed—
More mature, more poised, and far more mysterious
Than he remembered from before. They
Greeted the men warmly and courteously,
But all felt something that could not be defined,
Something between the two that had not been
Before. However, in the confusion
Of the arrival and of finding quarters,
This feeling soon was forgotten; and when
Pelagia bathed him, the water warm

And with a pleasant smell, then oiled him,
Letting her fingers massage his skin
In such a way that he found himself aroused,
Telemachus forgot completely what
He had felt, forgot the image of his bride,
And thought of nothing but their tryst after
The feast. Soon all met in the hall, and
The rites and sacrifices done, all ate
With gusto, hungry from the trip. Later
In the feast, Helen and Pelagia entered,
Each dazzling in a gown that showed her off
To great perfection; and Helen sat in
Her golden chair, Pelagia close beside her,
And all the men marvelled at their beauty.
For the feast, those of importance who
Had not made the journey to Pylos
Came to join them; and after they had
Feasted awhile, Menelaos rose to speak.

"Spartans and my good friends who feast with us
Here, I bid you welcome and bring you news.
As you know, this has been a time of sadness
For Pylos and for us all with the death
Of the great hero, Gerentian Nestor.
But we have brought back happier news
As well. Know then, that an alliance
Has been formed among our lands: the House
Of Atrides, both Spartan and Argolian,
Have joined with Pylos and with Ithaca
For mutual aid and profit."

All those in the room who had not gone
Murmured in surprise at his statement;
And Helen became alert when she heard
That Argos had joined the alliance; but
All were astonished at his next words:

"This loose union of our lands makes us
Rule across the Peloponnesos, for
King Orestes now holds sway over
Arcadia as well; and all this
Has come to be because of my old friend

The King of Ithaca, whose house has joined us
Through the wish of Nestor that his beauteous
Daughter Polycaste should be betrothed
To Odysseus's son, Telemachus.
When the king has returned from his quest,
The wedding will take place. Let us therefore
Congratulate them and do them honour."

And Menelaos raised his golden goblet
To honour the Ithacan king and his son.
None were more shocked by this news than
Helen and Pelagia; and for an instant
Their eyes darkened, then met as if some thought
Sped between them; but they immediately
Assumed an expression of well-mannered
Approval. As the news sunk in, talk grew
More animated and enthusiastic,
And attendants were busy filling bowls
With wine; Helen and Pelagia personally
Attended to Menelaos and Telemachus,
Carefully pouring wine from their own pitcher.
Soon Menelaos grew restless and his eyes
Continually found his lovely wife.
Telemachus as well found himself aroused
And glancing to see Pelagia, who
Returned his gaze from lowered lashes,
Modest but enticing. At last, to the two men's
Relief, the feast was finished, and after
Each had made his courtesy of exit,
They hurried to their quarters. Telemachus
Now had a room of his own close to
The women's quarters; and there he waited
In an agony of expectation
Until Pelagia entered quietly.
Before he could speak she put a finger
To his lip; then slowly she undressed him,
And had him do the same to her.
They lay down; and Telemachus was drowned
In lovemaking that he had never
Experienced, both lost in an abandonment
That her caresses and guidance

Brought them to. For the whole night they continued,
Each time the ecstasy intensifying,
Until both slept in each other's arms,
Exhausted and drenched.

During the next few days, preparations
Were made to leave for Corinth; Helen
Informed the two kings that Pelagia
Had been an apt student and was now
Conversant in the use of plants and drugs;

"However, she still has much to practise
And to learn; therefore, until such time
As you return for the wedding, good King,
I will lend you my Egyptian slave
Who can assist her and instruct her further."

Pelagia, who had been present while
Helen spoke, was thunderstruck by this news,
But Odysseus smiled and nodded.

                              "You show us
Once more that you are as wise as lovely,
And we accept this loan with gratitude."

Turning to the astounded girl he said,
"I am sure you will make good use of her."

And Pelagia in confusion bowed her head.

Helen soon led her to the garden, where
They were admitted by the noiseless slave.

"Amunet, for the next year or more
You will live with this woman in the land
Of Ithaca."

                    For an instant the eyes
Betrayed but the face remained expressionless.

"Continue to train her well in all ways."

Then Helen, her hand on her slave's shoulder,
Addressed Pelagia before them.

"Amunet is a good teacher, as I
Myself found in Egypt."

                    Pelagia
Was startled by this admission; the slave
Bowed her head.

                    "She will instruct and assist
You in preparing for the journey."

Then the queen smiled and left the two alone.

As two cats, lithe and graceful, might meet
Suddenly by surprise, and for a long
Instant each eye the other carefully,
So the two women stood before each other,
And silence sat heavily upon them
As Amunet waited patiently for
Her new mistress to speak. In this moment
Pelagia, who had wrestled with how
She should treat her in their new circumstance,
Found her answer and with firm quietness
Addressed the figure, still, before her.

"Amunet, although you are the queen's slave,
For us both to succeed you must for me
Be more the teacher, less the servant;
We both will find ourselves in a new land,
Foreign to the two of us, and uncertain
Where the Fates will lead us. I know that I
Have much to learn, starting at this moment
With what we must take to far Ithaca.
Will you work with me in this fashion?"

After Amunet had studied her briefly,
Her look penetrating Pelagia
To her very core, she nodded and then
Spoke for the first time, her voice
Dark as her skin, and low.

                    "I will do so."

Her accent washed the language in liquid
Syllables, exotic but understood.

Then before Pelagia could respond
The figure before her in authority
Grew stronger, and Pelagia saw now
That the woman was at least older by
Ten years.

      "Now, let us begin, so that we
Will be ready in time."

         And she led her
To the stores, and in a torrent of words
Told her what they must take and how to bring
It in suitable condition aboard.

As a consequence, they had seeds, shoots,
And sprouts packed carefully for the journey.
During the next few nights, Telemachus
Could not be without his concubine,
And all thoughts of his young betrothed
Were lost in the passions that were unleashed.
Finally the time came when the company
Was ready to leave. The two kings had their
Last meeting; Menelaos, moved by
The departure of his old comrade, gave
Him as a parting gift an oar made
Exquisitely of the finest woods,
And inlayed with signs and images
In praise of Poseidon.

"If you have to make a gift to the God,
At least make it a good one!"

He joked, but Odysseus knew what he meant
By the gift, and he was moved in turn.
Helen spoke briefly and quietly to Pelagia,
Who smiled and nodded; then they embraced,
Lingering a moment longer than was
Necessary if anyone had cared
To notice. Then all the company
Mounted their horses—Telemachus
Had left his chariot in Pylos
As token of his return—and in a

Cloud of dust they galloped off; and Helen
Climbed to stand at the wall and watch the cloud
Disappear toward the mountains, then turned
And went down to meet her husband.

For three days the group made its way quietly
To Corinth, taking time to make sure the wagons
Packed with Pelagia's precious objects
Were secure, as Amunet sat among them,
Alert. Pelagia felt free again
As she rode, with Telemachus always
At her side. His father noted how they
Related to each other, and he privately
Prayed that the year would help to make
The future marriage viable; but
For the present he did and showed nothing.
Through the long ravines and valleys
Of Arcadia they progressed, and over
The great ranges' passes until they reached
The familiar hills that reached to Corinth;
And finally they wound up the twisting
Highway to the huge citadel perched
Like an eagle on its precipice.
Again the sun was setting, throwing its
Long shadows across the space before
The gate; and there Escalios was seen,
Waiting for their return. Inside all
Had been made ready for the sacrifice
And feast; and when they had been warmly met
And found quarters and been bathed and oiled,
All gave thanks to the Gods for their return
And sacrificed the bulls and spilt the wine
And feasted. Then, as was fitting,
The eloquent Odysseus told of their exploits
In the Argolid and in Arcadia,
In Sparta and in Pylos. Escalios
And the Corinthians who had not gone
Sat entranced by his account; and they saw
As well that a woman was given place
Among them, against their custom, and this

Too caused them wonder. When Odysseus
Had finished, Escalios laughed and said,

"Truly you are not called cunning in vain,
My good old friend. Who else but you could
Have wrought such wonders? I am proud that you
Are my friend—and overjoyed at this
Alliance. What now will you do? What more
Can you do?"

Odysseus sat for a moment; then he said,

"My journey changes at my next landing.
Until now I have been among friends
And old comrades, or men that were connected
To men I knew; and all things that have come
To pass were implicit in the stars; all
I had to do was unlock the secrets,
Untangle the confusing web to
Bring forth what should be. This could happen
Among men. But now I must go a
Solitary way; now truly begins
My search, which I must make alone, in
Isolated lands and places, until
The God's will is revealed in the sign
That will come only when it will come.
Who knows what this path will offer?
Yet I must walk it, come what may.
I thank you all for what you so far
Have done for me. Soon you can leave me,
And my son and she whom he has found
Can return to Ithaca. May I join them soon."

He sat down; and all were silent, awed
By what he had done, both in the past
And now, and the new quest he must begin.

When the early light of dawn sent long shafts
Of light through the citadel, Odysseus
Stood on a height in the fortress to look
Out over the land that in the last few weeks
He had travelled and had changed; for some time

He gazed at it thoughtfully, scanning plains
And hills and mountains; then he turned to look
At the sea and the land opposite.
At last he sighed and went back in to talk
With his old friend for the last time.
Telemachus as well, although besotted
With Pelagia, spent time with his comrades
Among the Corinthians before
The departure. During the day the ship
Was loaded with what had journeyed with them
And with its regular supplies. As her
Precious cargo was transferred, Pelagia
Insisted on supervising its
Installation, to the anger and distress
Of the crew, but Odysseus ordered them
To obey her as the one who knew
What was necessary to be done,
And with gritted teeth and muttering
They obeyed him, casting dark looks at her
And the dark shadow always by her side,

And soon all was done. A last feast was held
That night, at which all that was left
To be said was said. Pelagia herself
Was apprehensive, never having sailed
Before, and leaving the mainland for
An island that would be her home while
She lived the rest of her life; and she
Began to think of what would happen
When the mother of Telemachus
Would see her and soon after hear of
Her son's betrothal. But with the dawn
All was finally made ready; and
Corinthians and Ithacans alike
Stood by the altar at the dock and made
Their prayers to mighty Poseidon
To keep their voyage secure and swift.
Then farewells were completed; all embarked,
And the slim vessel slipped out of the dock
And sailed out onto the dark gleaming sea.

# Canto 9
## CALYDON

Bright the day and dark the sea as the prow,
Sharp-edged, cleaved the reluctant waves.
But a brisk west wind forced the straining steersman
To tack often, lacing his trail across the Gulf of Corinth.
As the lean ship deviously thrust on, Pelagia,
Telemachus at her side, was absorbed
In checking all her fragile bales were fixed fast
In the uneven movements that betrayed her feet
In this new world of the restless sea.
Throughout this work Amunet, who was now
Shrouded in a sleek cloak of strange design,
Quietly showed her how to test the lashings
And the knots. Telemachus was intrigued
By the exotic woman and her strength
Of authority, unobtrusive as
She seemed; yet the crew remained uneasy,
Casting shaded looks at both women, but
Particularly the Egyptian, strange
And mysterious, as the women worked on.
As they were thus engrossed, Odysseus
Called to his son to join him,
And Telemachus left the distracted girl
To join his father and their seer in the prow,
As far away from others as they could find.

"My son, Halitherses has something of note
For our ears alone."

The seer huddled with them, heads close
To hear against the breeze's chatter.

"My lord Telemachus, you asked me some time ago
What vision I had seen that struck so deep.

I could not tell you or King Odysseus then,
For it was not wise to speak where those concerned
Might hear. But now, because of separation
So soon to be, I must tell you both.
Know, then, that as I watched Orestes
In the plans for his Arcadian city,
Apollo vouchsafed me two deep insights:
First, that the Argolian king would not build
A new city, but instead develop one already founded—
Oresthasium, named for its builder, Orestheus.
Now, Orestheus was the son of the impious Lycaon,
And as such, with no cleansing of the father's stain,
The city is itself tainted, and that taint still lies upon it,
Even with its name changed to Orestium.
And the second revelation is that the stain
Will be scrubbed clean only with the death of its owner.
And so Apollo has decreed that sometime in the future,
When Orestes stands at his city's threshold
A snake will strike him and he will die.
What I saw was this act, and I saw
An Orestes no longer young, and I sensed a king
With most of the Peloponnesos under his sway."

Horrified, Telemachus interrupted in concern:

"Should we not warn him now, and so forestall
Such an end?"

Both other men looked at him sadly and shook their heads.

"What is ordained must be: we cannot change the fates."

Then Odysseus said to his son,

"Two things as well for you to learn from this.
You must tell no one of what you just heard,
For your safety, and not to defy the Gods.
And so you may prepare for this event,
For by its appointed time you will be King of Ithaca,
And will have to deal with Nestor's land
With which you will be closely linked
Through Polycaste."

Telemachus thought for a moment,
Then realized the wisdom of the two beside him.

"I thank you both for what today you teach me.
No word of this will fall from my mouth.
And I will study carefully the situation—
As I have the most skillful in this art
As my model, and before me."

Odysseus smiled at this compliment
And was proud of his son's fast-growing wisdom.
Then, glancing at the girl still occupied
With her precious store, he said,

"Now we must talk of Pelagia and what will occur
When you reach Ithaca. You, I am sure,
Have wondered why I have allowed her so much freedom
In what she does, both in company and in her skill,
Despite her position."

His son, surprised by this new topic, nodded.

"I have done so because of Halitherses, to whose words
I have always harkened with respect, profound seer
That he is."

Halitherses bowed his acknowledgement.

"He has told me that Pelagia will be significant
In our family—in what way, and for good or ill,
He cannot say."

A solemn nod in agreement.

"I have therefore given her free reign
And encouraged Helen's suggestion that she learn her lore
Of herbs and drugs. This skill will be useful to us,
Not only for our health but to give her
A position of worth that your mother can accept.
For without Penelope's approval"—

Here he cut short his son's expostulation—

"There will be no happiness nor peace at home.
As a concubine alone, Pelagia would have little place,

Even with children—she will need to earn respect.
And there is little time to accomplish this,
For in another year you will have a young wife
Who will not take kindly to another woman in your bed."

His son, dismayed, burst out,

"I did not know of Halitherses's divination,
But I can see the rest without foreknowledge.
What, then, should I do when we get to Ithaca?"

His father let the breeze sweep his face,
Then after a long moment he replied.

"When you reach Ithaca, let our seer be the first
To disembark and to your mother speak
Before you appear. Then you must meet her
With warm words and embrace—and only then
Bring forth Pelagia. Let Halitherses meet with Mentor
To find a place for her to work her art.
When all is in place and she has earned respect,
Only then let Halitherses talk of the marriage
To your mother. I cannot be there to aid you,
But he has my trust and confidence—and as
The wedding cannot occur until my return,
I will deal with that situation when I get back.
For this moment, I wish to speak with Pelagia privately."

The son saw his father brooked no argument,
And so he nodded, went to Pelagia and returned with her,
And all left them alone at the spray-drenched prow.
As a wrestler meets his opponent and for a time does not act
But watches the face and eyes to betray a sudden lunge,
So Pelagia stood before the king, her hair wet with spray,
Her chiton tugged at by the wind and water.
She said nothing, but waited for the interview.
Odysseus studied her fully and carefully,
Making no move to hide his frank appraisal.
All that she sensed were the wind, the spray,
The prow's rise and fall, and his cool eyes
Upon her. Finally he spoke.

"Pelagia, this is the first—and perhaps last—time
That we may speak frankly to each other, from our hearts."

She looked at him steadily, lashes beaded with the spray.

"You hate me for your family and your city's death."

Eyes darkened, but her face remained impassive.
Odysseus wondered at the growth of her maturity.
As in a rifted landscape its surface,
Refulgent with trees and bushes and rocks
Sleeps peacefully in the bird-chirping air,
Yet beneath in caverns dark and huge
A river's currents thunder and roil,
Unseen above, so the weathered king,
Experienced beyond most in searching out
The thoughts and feelings of those he watched,
Sensed the deep stirrings in the girl before him,
And what he found there chilled his heart
Yet he continued.

"I cannot take that from you,
Nor would I wish otherwise—it does you honour
To hold in reverence what you have lost."

She had not expected to hear him speak thus;
He noted the flicker of surprise, quickly suppressed.

"You have been told, and you yourself know well,
What your lot should be—a slave, a concubine,
Your past value lost, nothing but servitude and shame
To expect. But your life will be different from this.
How, I do not know, but you are fated to be linked
To our family. My son feels deeply for you—
He has risked his life in your defence—
But for him you can be no more than a concubine,
Your children never to be lawful heirs."

Her impassive face set tighter, now a pure mask.

"Yet it seems your moira to mean more than this:
Helen has embraced you, brought out your talent

For the art of herbs and drugs, and you have learned
In this short time, in the midst of grief and rage
And a new passion"—

Despite control, a blush betrayed her feeling—

"Much that she could teach you."

The blush continued, but for a reason
That he could not fathom.

"In Ithaca your art, and what you bring here,
Will command respect and your state increase.
But for this to happen, you will first have
To win over someone who could be your most important friend
Or your worst enemy—Penelope, my beloved wife.
She has been loyal to me over the long years
Of the war and after"—

Here he paused for a moment, moved—

"She has not had to deal with another woman
As my concubine, and will find it hard
To accept one for her son. You must therefore
Earn her confidence. I cannot be there to help you,
But Halitherses will do his best to assist you
With her. With Penelope on your side—
As least as far as she can be—your next task
Will be less difficult. As you know, my son
Is now betrothed to Polycaste, Nestor's daughter."

He chose not to tell her that the girl's mother
Had also been a captive but made legitimate
By Nestor's marriage to her. But as he spoke
He saw her eyes flash briefly, and he knew
There could be much trouble.

"She is younger than you, and incomparably beautiful
And she is passionately in love with my son.
As well, the union is important for peace
Throughout the country. Fortunately, as you know,
The wedding cannot take place before my return,

Which hopefully will give her more time to mature.
You have this year to gain your place, no more,
Before she comes to Ithaca. But heed this"—

He moved closer to her, their eyes locked together—

"Do not tell Penelope of Polycaste. Halitherses,
Then Telemachus, will prepare the ground.
Your building must be built block by block."

He ceased; and for a long while there was silence
Between them. Only the wind, the prow's surge,
And the creaking of the thrusting ship was heard.
Then, her eyes still on his, she replied.

"You are right, King Odysseus. We have not so frankly talked,
Nor for so long, and for this I am grateful,
And give you thanks. All that you say is true:
I cannot help but hate you, and in my dreams
I still see you high above, black against the sun,
Raining your deadly flights of arrows upon our men,
The death of my father, and later my family."

Here her breath caught, and she took an instant
To compose herself, then continued.

"And in my dreams I see my friends, their families
Slaughtered, themselves raped and abused,
Now nothing but playthings for the tyrant Aepytus
And his soldiers—at best, slaughtered when
They have satisfied their lust; at worst,
Made lowly slaves for the rest of a miserable life."

Odysseus said nothing for a moment,
Letting her, breathing hard, her passion
Now burst forth, return from her dread memories
To the salt breeze and bright sky.
Then he said quietly, in her ear,

"All you say is true, and you cannot escape these dreams
Nor deny them. Hopefully, as time moves on,
They will recur less frequently and you find greater peace.
But did you not also have slaves?"

She stared at him, startled, then slowly nodded.

"Have you not thought of where they came from?
Even those who grew up with you, where their parents
Came from to be slaves?"

She looked at him again, eyes wide, then reluctantly
She shook her head.

"Our world is based on this fact:
Those who today are masters, may tomorrow
Be another's slave. And you are not the only one
To have such dreams."

Now she looked at him intently, fully caught up
In what he said, and she caught the haunted look
In his own eye.

"Your citadel was precious to you, as it should be.
But I have seen many towns so destroyed,
And I have seen a great city levelled to the ground
And its citizens massacred or taken slave.
It is the way we men live and die,
And women have our burdens to carry with them.
And we sometimes try to do other than this way.
I tried to keep Troy from its mistake and war,
And when I could not I kept my word
And was an agent for its terrible destruction.
With your town also I tried to act to save it
But could not keep Aepytus from his barbaric ways
And again kept my word and acted as you know.
Acts bring their consequences, for good or ill."

Again silence spread between them, and no sound
Could they hear around them of sea or wind
Or bird or ship as each considered what he had said.
Then Odysseus roused himself and held her shoulders
In his strong grip.

"Now, despite your misfortune and your hate,
You must here promise me these things:
That you will practise your new art for good, not ill,
As succor for us all, with harm to none;

Do you promise this?"

And she, shaken by his fierce determination, replied,
"I promise."

"And will you, who I believe truly loves my son,
Assist and comfort him and bear what children
You may have despite their condition, and
Be loyal to him whatever happens,
Despite his marriage, and keep peace with his young wife,
However hard you find it?"

This time, her eyes filled with tears, her struggle
Open to him, she finally whispered,
"I promise."

"And will you obey and keep peace
With my wife Penelope, whatever may occur,
And make no mention of Polycaste and the marriage
Until you hear it from her own lips?"

Shuddering,
"I promise."

Like a tree caught in a raging storm,
Its trunk bent almost to the ground,
Its limbs thrashing and its leaves stretched taut,
That when the gusts subside and moderate
Returns to stand erect and undestroyed,
So the girl almost broke into sobs,
But then, with an indomitable will,
Pushed her feelings down, deep down,
Presented to Odysseus a calm exterior
And looked him fully in his eyes.
He marvelled at her strength of will
And realized that no more would he,
Sharp-eyed as he was, have ways to read
Her thoughts, emotions, and her plans.
He released her shoulders, and without a word
She left him to return to her work
And to Telemachus, who had watched anxiously
The interview unfold.

As the Sun God drove his fiery steeds over the horizon
The ship against the wind had reached no more
Than part way to her destination;
But now the breezes softened, then slipped away,
And for a while the crew rowed the vessel
Until darkness mantled them and they ate and slept.
With Dawn's blushes a new wind swept in,
But this time from the south and east;
Their sail filled, and like a filly set free
In an open place, who gallops with delight,
Mane flying in her rush, so the ship
Sped forward eagerly, and in late afternoon
Attained the coast that they were searching for.
That night they kept at sea, not wishing to land
On the uncertain shore before them,
No knowing of what dangers might be there.
Before they slept, Odysseus brought them together.

"Tomorrow we will reach our destination, Calydon.
Our reception there, I think, will be a welcome one,
For King Thoas and I know each other well.
But I must warn you not to talk of my quest
To those you meet, nor wonder at the way
In which I tell it to him. Promise me
That you will do what I request."

And all promised, wondering at his words.

At dawn they unshipped their oars, and,
Finding the wide opening of deep Evenus,
They rowed up the waters of its winding way.
On either side they saw plains on which rested
Fertile fields, now ripening for rich harvest,
But no people were seen among them.
Onward they rowed around the river's curves,
At times aware of salt-pans found beside it.
The current they found strong but steady,
And by noon they could see ahead and to the west
The outline of the mountains; and soon after
The fields lay on rolling hills; and at last
They came to a landing place where they secured

The ship, for Calydon was in the hills above it;
Before, Mount Zygos towered over all,
The sentinel to the rugged peaks that ranged behind it.
As they attended to the docking of the ship,
A lookout shouted,

"Take care! A chariot and a troop of soldiers
Come this way!"

When they looked up, they saw, not far away,
The chariot and the dust of the soldiers,
Their spears glittering in the sun.
Odysseus quickly ordered his men in ranks,
But with their weapons still seen to be undrawn,
And then he and his retinue stood before them.
As the chariot thundered into sight
Odysseus grinned and stepped well in front
Of all the others. Telemachus was alarmed,
As were the rest, but the Ithacan king stood his ground.
The chariot, of sumptuous gold, with its black horses
Snorting in their effort, now drew near enough
For its occupant to be seen. He had no driver
But himself held the reins—a massive man,
With plumes that waved high above his helmet,
Which was richly embossed, as was his armour,
But of a deadly shape. He slowed his horses
As he saw the man in front; and then, with a yell,
He drove directly at him, stopping but a few feet
In front. Then he stepped from the chariot,
Ripped off his helmet, revealing his shaggy head
And beard, his dark wolfish face, leaped toward
The Ithacan king, who stood there, not only unconcerned
But now laughing, and swept him into his huge arms.

"Odysseus, my dear friend and fellow warrior,
What a delight and a surprise to see you here!
Our lookout saw the ship approaching from afar,
And we marched out to receive it, ready for greeting
Or for war. At this time it is hard to know friend from foe,
For now the border raids increase, both from them
And, of course, from us."

He laughed heartily at this, still holding the half-suffocated king,
And then released him to look at the others.

"But tell me, why have you come here, and with such
A ship and retinue?  But wait"—

Said he, releasing the still chuckling king, if somewhat
Out of breath, and looking at the others—

"First introductions, and then up to my citadel,
And at a feast you can tell me all."

Odysseus, now with recovered breath, laughed heartily,
And in his turn embraced the one before him.

"Thoas you old bear, you are the same as you always were.
Here now, meet my people, and then off we go!"

Odysseus brought forward Medon and Halitherses
And introduced them to the Aetolian king,
Who quickly studied them with searching glance
And greeted them with gusto. Then the king
Brought forward Telemachus.

"And here is my son, who as you know was but a child
When we were at Troy. But he has now proved himself
A man."

King Thoas looked at the young man long and hard,
Then grinned and nodded.

"I see you there, Odysseus—and Penelope as well.
If he is like his father, he will be much feared
And admired. Welcome, Telemachus, son
Of such a hero."

And he embraced the startled youth, then stood back again.
Odysseus then showed him his company.

"These are all good Ithacans and good warriors,
King Thoas, and they have well proved themselves."

Behind them, still on the ship, stood Pelagia, watching
As these greetings took place. Thoas saw her there,
And turned to Odysseus.

"And that woman there? Why is she on your ship?"

Odysseus gestured for Pelagia to join them,
And she walked toward them as the company
Parted ranks for her. Thoas was struck by her
Authority and dignity, particularly in one so young.

"This, King Thoas, is Pelagia, now a member of my household,
Close to my son, and important to us
As one skilled in the arts of herb and drug."

The Aetolian king found this description odd,
But he said nothing and greeted her politely.
Then he sent a soldier with his chariot to bring
Chariots and horses from the citadel.
As they waited for them to arrive,
Sharp-eyed Telemachus observed their host closely:
A giant of a man who, though his father's age,
Was still powerfully muscled, despite his mass,
And quick on his feet. But it was his face
That most captured the young man's attention,
For Thoas had powerful features that seemed
To be the sum of many animals—his eyes fierce
And sharp as an eagle's; his nose aquiline;
His mouth curved much into a wolfish grin;
And his thick beard, with just a fleck of grey,
Like the pelt of a great bear. Even his movement
Seemed sometimes like that of a great cat
Whose body can relax completely, no muscle
Under strain and then can be in an instant
Alert and coiled to spring. Telemachus
Could sense the intelligence of this king
And could imagine in his savage state
That he would be a fearsome warrior.

While they waited, King Thoas talked further
Of his kingdom and the skirmishes at its borders.

"As you know, my old friend, we Aetolians
Are independent peoples who don't believe much
In alliances, but forage for ourselves—as you do

When you are not running around waging wars
Or giving and taking gifts."

He gave a feral smile, and Odysseus grinned back,
Knowing well from Troy the Aetolian predilections.

"Well, our neighbours on either side are like ourselves,
And so there is always some raid going on
At the borders. But lately I have grown tired
Of all their raids and am preparing, on the east
At least, to take over that country.
If I could bring forty Aetolian ships to Troy,
I think I can have enough to work for our own
Mutual interests here."

And he threw back his head and laughed heartily;
But Odysseus knew that if Thoas wished to do
What he intended, bloody as it would be,
It would be successful; and the Ithacan king
Was thankful that his fellow king was preoccupied
And not considering raids farther west.
Thoas also described his kingdom, pointing out
The mountain ranges, Calydon that could be seen
Up the long slope, Pleuron, Chalcis, and other towns
Under his domain.

"I rule a rugged country. You have seen the plain
With its fields and orchards. There is one other,
Smaller, surrounding Lake Trichinas,
But otherwise we have harsh mountain ranges
And narrow valleys, with not much to sustain
Each village. And each of them is a law
Unto themselves, difficult to attack,
Easy to defend. And so I am a king
Of those regions which I reach, and leave
The others to themselves so long as they
Do not pillage in my territory."

Soon the chariots and horses came, and like
A great insect slowly crawling upward,
Deliberate and intent, so the groups wound
Their way along the slopes. To their left they

Could see the great plain and Evenus winding
Its way across it; before them a secondary hill
Appeared, and as they passed by, Halitherses gasped,

"Is this not the Laphrion, famed Aetolian sanctuary
Dedicated to Artemis Laphria and Apollo Laphrios?"

Thoas replied gravely,

"It is as you say. They are the two to whom we sacrifice most—
Artemis the Hunter and Apollo the Destroyer."

Pale, Halitherses turned to Odysseus.

"Before we go our respective ways tomorrow,
You must sacrifice here, for I expect a sign for you."

Odysseus frowned and turned to Thoas.

"Of course. We will arrange for a sacrifice in the morn."

And the Ithacans gazed at the sanctuary's exterior,
Resplendent in its marble slabs.

Now on the second slope, steeper than the first,
The citadel of Calydon towered over them,
Its massive walls standing ominously against the sky.
As they reached them, huge bronze gates
Grated open to admit them, and through the gaping mouth
They passed, Ithacan and Aetolian together.
They passed down a way, and then the visitors gasped,
For ahead of them an agora was spread,
Filled with buildings of dazzling marble,
And across from them they could see the palace,
Which in the sun glittered and shone
With marble and gold decoration.
Thoas led them there, and together they entered,
To find an interior more resplendent than any they had seen.
Between marble columns great tapestries woven of gold were hung,
Depicting famous scenes from Calydon's past:
Oeneus, once king, who was seen sacrificing to the Gods
But neglecting Artemis, who, raging, sent a great boar
To ravage men and prevent crops being sown;
The Calydonian hunters, great heroes including

Castor and Pollux, famed twin sons of Tyndareus, King of Sparta,
Renowned Theseus of Athens, and Jason, leader of the Argonauts,
And Atalante, daughter of the king of Arcadia, and many others,
Were called together by Meleagrus, son of Oeneus.
Then was depicted the killing of the boar—
Atalante hit it with the first arrow,
Then Amphiaraus, King of Argos,
Struck it in the eye with his own barb,
And finally Meleagrus himself
Killed it with his knife, earning the spoils, which he gave
To Atalante. Then another tapestry
Noted the consequences of his act,
Fatal to those concerned, with his uncles claiming
That as they were his closest relatives
He should give them as their due the spoils
If he did not want them; in this argument
Meleagrus slaughtered every one of them.
Then his mother Althea, their sister, who saved a brand
From a fireplace when he was seven years old, warned
By the Fates that he would die as soon as the brand burned out,
Now removed it from its coffer and threw it in the fire;
Meleagrus died; when she realized what she had done,
She hanged herself, as did Cleopatra, Meleagrus's wife.
Another tapestry depicted the centaur
Nessus in his ill-thought attempt to rape
Heracles's wife, the Princess Deianeira,
In the midst of the river Evenus
Across which he was supposed to transport her;
She was seen with her clothes ripped, terrified,
Calling for her husband, who aimed an arrow
At the impassioned centaur. All there knew
The dreadful outcome of this act, with the death of Nessus,
His tricking the princess into saving his blood to smear
On Heracles's chiton to save their love if he strayed,
And the agonizing outcome for Heracles trapped
In the garment stained with blood which contained
The deadly poison of the Hydra he had slain,
And whose blood he smeared on his own arrows.
After this ornate passageway they came
To the central room, and opposite them they saw

Thoas's throne. When he saw it, Odysseus was shocked,
For the throne, gilded in gold and bronze, upon which
Rich fleeces rested, he recognized: the very throne
Of the last king of Troy, the venerable Priam.
Thoas saw his look and laughed.

"We Aetolians are noted for our looting—and
As Apollo is our patron God, and favourable
To Troy, he let us take this prize to keep
A remembrance of that fated city."

Odysseus nodded and said nothing; but he let
His thoughts wait for later, when he could consider
More deeply what he had seen and heard.
Rooms were then appointed for the visitors,
And the main company given space in the foyer;
Attendants guided them to where steaming baths
Awaited them, and slaves washed and oiled their bodies.
Finally the time came for the banquet.
All assembled in the large hall; the bull was sacrificed
To Artemis and Apollo; they sat; and slaves
Brought in choice tidbits and served them drink,
Giving them goblets and pouring the wine from golden jugs.
Again Odysseus and his companions were startled
At the luxury surrounding them: all the dishes,
All the goblets were of gold, adorned with carvings
Of scenes of war and heroes. Odysseus, as he looked
At the sumptuous articles, began to recognize
Some of them—and realized, with a start, that he himself
Had drunk from the cup that he now held, had drunk
From it a libation for the Gods with Hector and Priam.
Many were from Troy, as he could tell from their decoration;
But others he saw came from many places,
And he realized that his host had been busy elsewhere
From Troy. As he waited for a female slave
To fill his cup, inadvertently he raised his eyes to hers;
Looking into large violet eyes that widened as he stared,
For he had seen those eyes before and marvelled at them—
She had been a Trojan gentlewoman renowned for her beauty,
Married to one of the great warriors of that ill-fated city;
Now she was reduced to a slave, and he could see how

The twelve years of slavery had left her drawn,
Although her beauty still showed despite her slave's demeanour.
She gasped slightly and almost spilled the wine she poured,
But quickly recovered, looking fearfully toward Thoas,
And again wore, if strained, the mask of submission.

Thoas, who had been watching closely their encounter,
Bared a feral smile.

"I see you remember her, my fellow king.
Another of the prizes from that fallen city.
Perhaps you would like her tonight, for old time's sake?"

And he chuckled at the thought. Odysseus demurred politely.

"The only woman that I favour now, my fellow warrior,
Is my wife, from whom I was away so long."

Thoas grew more thoughtful, then said,

"Perhaps you are right, old friend. As for me,
My wife is no longer here; the Gods have taken her."

Then he shifted yet again, his eyes on the woman.

"And so I have no compunction as you have.
You, see me in my quarters later on."

For a moment the woman's eyes filled with fear and pain;
Then she bowed gracefully and returned to her task.
The libation done, Thoas signalled to a servant,
And into the hall came Pelagia, dressed in a rich dress
Almost transparent, that showed her striking beauty
To advantage; and beside her, followed by her slaves,
Came another woman, slightly older, whose hair was black,
Her complexion almost swarthy, but whose face
And body were voluptuous and showed to advantage
By the gown of vivid colours that she wore.

"Ah, here comes your lady Pelagia, and with her
My daughter, Artemisia."

Odysseus could see some of Thoas's lineaments
In his daughter, but it was evident that her mother
Must have been herself a woman of unparalleled beauty,

And Artemisia had inherited the best qualities
Of each of them. Both women acknowledged their recognition,
And they were seated together and beside the kings.
Now the best slices of the meat were brought by attendants
To Thoas and Odysseus, and then the others were duly served.
As they began to eat, Thoas turned to his fellow king.

"And now, destroyer of Ilium, tell me what took you so long
To return home, and why you now have come here."

Odysseus nodded, but then said,

"Before my story, please allow me to tell yours. My son
And my Ithacans have not heard fully of your prowess,
And I would be honoured here to tell them."

Thoas, pleased, nodded his approval, and Odysseus began.

"Know then, that the power to rule this kingdom
Was bestowed upon King Thoas when the dynasty
Before him perished—we have seen in the golden tapestries
The story of Meleagrus, the last of that line,
And of his family's tragic end.
The warrior before us was very young,
As many of us were, and was with me and others
A suitor for the hand of the enchanting Helen,
And, like us, bound by his oath to assist whoever
Won her if the need arose. With her abduction
He kept his word, and to the Trojan War brought forty ships,
One of the larger fleets. He proved himself formidable
In battle, with many Trojans dying at his hand,
And showed his courage when he volunteered
Among eight others to fight Hector in single combat.
When the lots were drawn, he lost to Telamonian Aias,
But he might on his own have shortened that war.
Later, he proved his wisdom and knowledge of war
When he advised our forces, when Hector had broken through
To the ships and was pressing hard on us, to retreat,
Not out of cowardice, but to prevent
Further disorder among us. As a result,
Many escaped who would otherwise have perished
In the Trojan attack. Later he was in the giant horse

With me and those warriors who brought about the fall
Of the city and Ilium. I have fought by his side
And know him one of the ablest and fiercest fighters
In all Achaean lands, and one of the most important
In the war, even at his young age. I therefore here
Salute you, Thoas, king of Aetolia, and greatest hero
Of your country. Thoas!"

He raised his cup, and all others did as well,
Roaring their salute and drinking to the smiling king.
When the uproar had died down, Thoas turned again
To Odysseus.

"Thank you, my old friend and fellow warrior—
As usual you speak as from the Gods.
As for you, no one here does not know of your exploits
At Troy, and all know that it was you, and you alone,
Who caused with your stratagems that great city's fall.
Of course, we all thought that you had been lost
For ten long years, before you returned to Ithaca
And reclaimed your family and your throne.
But here we get few hints of what befell you—
And why you now appear before us.
Now, please tell us fully what occurred."

Odysseus acknowledged his friend's request
And began. Again Telemachus heard the story
Of that ten-year ordeal: how, following the war,
He first had travelled to the land of the Ciconians
In Thrace, where he pillaged Ismarus, sparing only
Apollo's priest (here Thoas quietly made a prayer
To his patron God); how he sailed on to the shores
Of the Lotus-eaters, losing some crew there
As they succumbed to its sweet forgetful fruit;
His capture by the Cyclops and escape in blinding
The huge creature, but the curse laid on him by
That son of Poseidon; how he came to the Aeolian Isles
And befriended there the keeper of the winds,
Who gave him winds bound in a bag;
How the crew, thinking the bag contained gold,
Greedily opened it while he was asleep so that
The winds escaped and they were blown back

To the isles and Odysseus punished with adverse winds;
How his ship arrived at the island of Aeaea,
Where the witch Circe transformed his men to animals
Until he forced her to release them and tell him
The way to Hades; how there, after a blood offering
He met with the shade of the seer Tiresias,
Who warned him of the wrath of Poseidon
And not to harm the cattle of Helios in Thrinacia;
How he had bound himself to the mast to hear the Sirens,
Who then died according to the ancient prophecy;
How when they passed the cliff of Scylla she gobbled up
Some of his men before they escaped; how on the island
Of Thrinacia his men slaughtered the sacred cattle
And Zeus punished them by destroying the ship
And causing them to drown, with only Odysseus saved
By clinging to the broken mast; even then he was almost
Killed in the whirlpool of Charybdis; how then he drifted
To the island of Calypso, who, loving him, kept him there
For seven years and offered him immortality, which he refused,
Wishing instead to return home to his wife Penelope; how
Hermes ordered the nymph to release him; how he drifted
On a raft until washed up, naked, on the shore of the Phaeacians,
Who returned him to Ithaca in their magic ship; his slaughter
Of the suitors to his wife with his son Telemachus
(who nodded in acknowledgement, his mind full of the memories
Of that cruel time); and, finally, of the need to fulfill
The prophecy of Tiresias, that to appease Poseidon
He must travel to many cities and must find
A land that knew no salt and there make sacrifice
(Telemachus, sharp-eared, noted that his father
Made no mention of the oar, and thought to ask him
When they were in private why he did so).

"And so, my good friend, I have made this voyage.
So far I have travelled through the Peloponnesos
To visit King Orestes, his friend and fellow king Pylades,
Arcadia, and Menelaus in Sparta, with whom we went
To honour the death and funeral of Nestor."

Thoas, who had listened closely, absorbed in everything
That Odysseus related, suddenly exclaimed,

"Nestor? He has died? When was this?"

"But a week ago. His family sent out messengers
Hastily. Did one not arrive here?"

"No. But given the skirmishes here, it is unlikely
That one could have reached us safely.
Tell me what happened, and the funeral."

And so Odysseus related how Nestor had died,
And the great funeral for him, attended by so many
Veterans of the Trojan War from other countries.
Thoas was intent as he heard the tale, and so was Pelagia,
Who noted that no mention was made of the betrothal.
When Odysseus had finished, Thoas sighed.

"It is good to hear that Nestor was recognized for
His long and glorious life; I am sorry that I could not attend,
For I would have longed to honour him, to see his homeland,
And to see our old companions once more.
And truly you yourself have lived a remarkable life,
As well as showing, as always, your subtle gift of speech.
But what makes you think that my land has no salt?
You have seen the salt pans on your journey up the river."

Odysseus nodded.

"I did not think that I would find my destination here,
Close to you. But the vast Pindos range looms nearby,
And there are many valleys shut off from the sea,
Rivers, and the world that can be searched east and north
Of your kingdom."

Thoas replied dubiously,

"There may indeed be such as you describe,
But I would myself not venture into them—
They are inhabited by tribes that cherish their freedom,
And"—

He smiled wryly—

"Are even more addicted to pillage than we Aetolians.
Any troop that invaded their areas would not escape

Slaughter or slavery. I would hate your countrymen here
And you to suffer such a fate."

"None will accompany me. I do this quest alone."

Thoas looked at him, astonished.

"You could find no better way to die
Or be made a slave. Please, reconsider
What you so rashly propose here."

"I have no choice. It is ordained by the Gods
That I do so or both I and my kingdom will suffer."

Thoas frowned and growled,

"You always were stubborn and took chances,
As I know personally"—

Odysseus shrugged, and each smiled at the other knowingly—

"But if you wish to pursue this mad scheme,
Then I will advise you as best I can.
Tomorrow, I know, you will visit the Laphrion,
Where Apollo is sure to give you guidance,
But as well I suggest that you travel
To the north-west region of my kingdom,
Where the mountains range thickly,
And from thence follow them north to Doloaia,
Keeping away from the great Pindos barrier
On one side, and the slopes facing the sea
On the other. That way you will be as far away
As you can be from the Thessalian plains
Or the sea, both of which are well acquainted
With the salt that you wish not to find.
Other than this advice I cannot give you,
Except to stay alive and free."

Odysseus smiled and took the king's arm.

"Thank you, my fellow king and brother;
As usual, you show your wisdom in this matter,
As you do in most others. But now, let us
Talk of happier things. Tell us of your daughter,

Who I see is most beautiful, as must have been
Your late wife."

Hearing this, Artemisia nodded in acknowledgement
Of his compliment, but both Odysseus and his son
Noted that although she acted with some dignity
She did not blush but knew her own attractiveness.

As a wolf looks at his she-cub with pride,
Standing with it to show his parentage,
So Thoas reached to touch his daughter proudly,
And she did not flinch at his touch.

"She is indeed beautiful as her mother,
Whom she never knew,
For my wife died at her birth.
She had become my wife when we fought at Troy,
And left me with the baby; both I had concealed
From you and from the others, and I sent her back
To Aetolia to be with nurses here;
But I had dedicated her to the Goddess Artemis,
And while I was away she began to learn the Goddess's arts
Of hunting and riding, as well as those things
Women in Aetolia must know. And when I returned,
We worked together,
And she can do all that a man can do.
She will make a fine match for a warrior."

Artemisia smiled and laid a hand comfortably
On that of her father. During the banquet
She had been enthralled by Odysseus's tale
Of his adventures, and she also had watched covertly
His son, examining him both for his appearance
And his manner, and both left her pleased.
Pelagia also had been fascinated, finding
The Ithacan hero more complex than she could have
Imagined, although her feeling against him
Was no less strong. As she listened to Thoas
And saw his close relationship to his daughter,
She could not stop the memories of her own father,
Who had also taught her in like fashion,

And she looked at the striking girl beside her
With new eyes.

Then Thoas continued,

"And what about your son Telemachus?
Is he now ready for an appropriate marriage?"

Father and son looked at each other quickly.
It was a delicate moment, for it was evident
That both Thoas and his daughter favoured
Telemachus, and the revelation
That he was not available would not go down well
With these fierce people. Pelagia also was
Interested in how the situation would be resolved.

"Thoas, my old friend and companion, such a match
Between our children would be fortunate for Ithaca
And for my son, for who could resist your daughter's
Splendid beauty and her well-accomplished education?"

Both Thoas and his daughter smiled.

"But the Gods have not ordained such a desirable union."

Father and daughter were startled by this statement,
Delivered by Odysseus with affecting sorrow.

"When we were at Nestor's funeral, we soon discovered
That he intended his own daughter for my son
And that she herself desired it with all her heart.
As a result, Telemachus is now betrothed to Polycaste,
The young and lovely daughter of that great hero."

The Aetolian ruler was stunned by this revelation;
His daughter's breath caught as she realized
That Telemachus was beyond her reach;
And the young man himself suddenly understood
The politics of princely marriage and its significance
Among these lands. For a moment
Thoas reddened in anger and frustration,
And Odysseus and his followers watched him
Guardedly. Then he relaxed and placed his hand
On his old friend's arm.

"I cannot say that I am not disappointed—
As you say, a match would have been good
For both of us. But the Gods thought otherwise;
And for the sake of Nestor, whom we all revere,
This betrothal would seem best for both your houses.
I should like to come to such an august celebration.
When will it be?"

Odysseus answered smoothly,

"We will send to you when preparations have been made."

His son noted the vagueness of the answer
And was relieved when Thoas did not pursue the matter
Further. The two veterans now talked about the war
And relived their experiences together
As the shadows darkened and the figures
In the tapestries seemed to move in the flickering
Of the torches. Telemachus engaged in conversation
With Aetolians seated with him, but from the corner
Of his eye he could see that Pelagia had begun to talk
To Artemisia, drawing out the disappointed girl.

Finally the feast drew to a close, and attendants led them
To their quarters, their torches lighting up each gleaming column.
Pelagia went with Artemisia to her quarters,
And they lay together, talking now with animation
About those things in which they had a common interest—
Riding, hunting, skill with a sword. Neither had had
A confidante with the same ability and skills,
And both found themselves, strong-willed and passionate
As they were, talking to an equal they had not thought
To find. Pelagia asked her new-found friend to tell
Her of her country, and Artemisia responded eagerly,
Telling of her father's prowess, the raids and counter-raids
At each border, and the booty that he brought back.
As well, she talked of galloping on the plains and hills,
And climbing the mountains that loomed over them,
Exploring valleys, and hunting the wild boars with the men
On the slopes above them.

"You are a true follower of Artemis, your patron Goddess."

"Yes, I worship her, make sacrifice to her daily, and
Try to be like her in any way I can."

"Does that include the way she treats her would-be lovers?"

Both girls giggled at the thought. Then Artemisia
Grew more solemn.

"Do you have a suitor or lover?"

Pelagia answered carefully,
"I had many suitors at home, but no lovers there."

"Where is your home?"

"It was in Arcadia, but now I will live in Ithaca."

"Why?"

In the darkness of the bed, Pelagia thought for a moment.
"I cannot tell you, except to say that I will be useful there."

Intrigued, Artemisia wanted to pursue the matter further,
But she soon realized that Pelagia would say nothing,
And so she returned to her original theme.

"What do you think of Telemachus?"

"He seems to be a true son of the King of Ithaca.
He can ride well—of course, not as well as us."

They both laughed.

"He is a strong swordsman and is courageous—
I have heard"—

She added hastily.
"Nestor's daughter, Polycaste, must be a lucky woman."

"Yes, I'm sure she is."

"I had hoped to find someone like him;
Now my father will have to arrange something else.
He had hoped greatly for this match,
And I would not have been unhappy with it."

"Yes, it could have been a very good match."

"My father will now have to go far afield,
For there are no men in this area who would be worthy."

She sighed.

"I do not look forward to a happy outcome.
I am much happier with my freedom now.
My father treats me more as a son than a daughter,
For which I am grateful."

"Yes, I would imagine so."

"Did your father treat you in the same way?"

"Yes. He had no sons and trained me as if I were one."

"Why did you leave, then?"

"Someday I may tell you, but I cannot now."

"Are you a priestess?"

Pelagia answered wryly,
"No, nor will be one."

And then she diverted the conversation to ask
About Artemisia's friends and more about the country.
The conversation continued for a while,
And then both women turned to sleep;
But for a long time Pelagia lay awake, considering
Her own life against that of the girl gently breathing by her.

Distant from their room, Odysseus slept.

*The noise*
*The roar of buzzing*
*Flies*
*Flies again*
*Clouds of flies*
*Enveloping me*
*Their bulging faceted eyes*
*The terrible snarl of their wings*
*Through them the white face*
*Of Apollo*

*Unearthly   beautiful   deadly*

"At my sanctuary this next day
Heed what I say"

*The flies crowd at me*
*His face lost behind them*
*A hurricane of flies*
*Then gone*

*Thoas*
*A natural killer*
*But crafty*
*His young body at Troy*
*Swift and strong as a bear*
*The Aetolians his followers*
*Because of his own prowess*
*Little discipline among them*
*But respected fighters*
*Their use of the javelin*
*Thrown as a huge flock against the sky*
*Always finding a body to pierce*

*A suitor of Helen*
*With the rest of us*
*No chance of course*
*He kept the accord*
*Came with his ships*
*Forty ships*
*One of the larger numbers*

*No knowledge in the camp*
*Of his marriage there*
*Or of the birth of his daughter*
*The death of his wife*
*Good at keeping secrets*

*In the horse with us*
*Like a panther released*
*When we roped down*
*From its belly*
*Slaughtered the drunken guards*

*Opened the gates*
*Started the massacre*
*They must have plundered much*
*And their ships returned*
*Unscathed*
*Apollo's men*

*The Trojan slave*
*My mission to Troy*
*At the court*
*She was there*
*A lovely blossom*
*In that rich garden*
*Gay    laughing*
*Eyes unconcerned*
*Oblivious*
*Witty with the other women*
*Attractive to the men*
*Her slaves attending her*
*Now*
*She has learned what to do*
*In the last twelve years*
*As a slave*
*Still traces of her beauty*
*Habitual grace*
*But broken*
*Part of the pillage*

*Faint noise of buzzing*
*Will not stop*

Nor did it for the rest of the night.

The next morning Dawn rose from her lover's bed
And her blushes tipped the mountains and slopes.
When all had assembled, Thoas led the way
Down the slope to the Laphrion sanctuary.
There they were met by the priests and priestesses
And their acolytes in their white robes and ranks.
The high marble pillars glowed in the early morning light
As they progressed into the enclosure, where at each end

Huge statues of Artemis Laphria and Apollo Laphrios
Faced each other across a sacrificial area.
The area was stepped down toward the centre,
Where an altar stood, surrounded by pure white sand.
The assembly stood on the upper steps while
The priests were ranked to protect a wide passageway
To the entrance; their leader stood by the altar, while
A pure white bull with gilded horns was led
To the centre, where the main priest with skill
Stunned and cut its throat, and while the beast
Was dragged to be carved and offerings made to the Gods
While the white robes now encircled the altar,
The priest poured its blood from a bowl into the sand
As the others raised their voices in a hymn.

"We celebrate Apollo and Artemis,
Bright children of Zeus and Leto,
Far-reaching deadly archers.
Hail to you, Artemis Laphria,
Tall to behold,
Glorious in your beauty,
Who delights in the arrows of your hunt.
Hail to you, her splendid brother,
Apollo Laphrios, God of the silver bow,
Radiant, striding high with gleaming steps,
Feared destroyer, beloved healer,
Lord of prophecy and divination,
For whom the swan himself can sing
With harmonious cries, beating his wings
And settling on the swirling Peneus's banks.
Hail to you, all-glorious children of Zeus!"

Outside the sanctuary wood had been stacked high,
And with roaring flames the smoke of the offerings
Drifted high into the bright blue sky.
Within the sanctuary, the main priest brought forward
A young priestess, supported on either side
As she staggered to the altar.

"Now ask our lord what you need to know."

Odysseus made to step forward,
But Halitherses put his arm upon him,
Then stepped forward himself.

"I ask the great lord Apollo for my king
Where he should travel to fulfill his quest."

The priest beckoned him to move closer
To the entranced priestess; he did so,
And with glazed eyes she viewed him.
Then, with no word spoken, she touched his face.
He cried out, his face shining, and dropped to his knees,
Unable to stand. The priestess was escorted,
Half-carried, away from the altar,
And two other priests raised the dazed Halitherses
And returned him to the Ithacan king.
As though a swirling wind suddenly arises
With strange quickness from a tranquil sky,
So all were struck by the mystery of what had happened.
A paean arose from the priests; drums and horns sounded,
And while they chanted and sang, with rhythmic sways and steps,
The main priest now led the assembly out of the sanctuary,
Where there was now provision for a feast,
As attendants carved slices from the roasted carcass
Of the sacred bull, and Thoas and his guests arranged themselves.
By now Halitherses had regained his senses,
Although his face remained pale and haunted.
Thoas wondered at what had happened,
But despite his curiosity he remained at a discreet distance
As the seer and his king discussed quietly
What had been revealed to Halitherses
By the prophetic God.

"His voice ... his voice unutterably distant but clear,
Like a trumpet far away and heard at dawn."

Odysseus waited patiently for the white-faced man
To recover and continue.

"Three things he ruled that you must bear:
First, that a twisted trail must be travelled patiently;

Next, that what was won by you
Was lost by others who now must change;
And finally, once you may win your quest,
The oak and doves will tell you what to do."

Odysseus thought for a while, then shook his head.

"I can see little clearly in these divinations.
Can you interpret them more clearly to me."

"I will try.
Your attempt to find the place for your redemption
Will be difficult, both in the exploration
And in the suffering that you may bear.
As for the second, I do not know what it means,
But you will discover this for yourself.
As for the third, it is ambiguous—
The possibility exists that you may not succeed,
But if you do, you must travel to Dodona,
Where again he will speak to you, for there
His sanctuary is more wild than here."

"I thank you, faithful Halitherses;
Now relax and enjoy this feast."

The Ithacan returned to sit with his fellow king.

Like a badger that first sniffs the air
As he prepares to leave his den,
So Thoas spoke tentatively to his guest.

"Can we be privileged to know anything
Of what Apollo Laphrios has divined
For you?"

Odysseus smiled wearily.

"I cannot tell, good friend—to do so
Would be to break faith with the God."

Thoas nodded somberly and said nothing more
About the matter. Instead, he poured out wine
Onto the sand in the libation to the Gods,

And the feast began. Together, Artemisia and Pelagia
Continued in animated conversation,
As if their night discussions had not ended,
And both kings and Telemachus noted
Their closeness and their happy chatter.
Thoas and Odysseus now talked of his daughter.

"Well, hero of Troy, you have disappointed me
With the news of your son's betrothal, as you know."

Odysseus laughed heartily.

"I could not have guessed how you felt,
My fellow king. But I know that it is difficult
For you to find a suitable mate for her,
Desirable as she is."

Thoas grunted.

"Let me suggest some possibilities, then."

Like a wolf that pricks up its ears at sounds nearby,
Thoas looked at him, alert again.

"In Corinth there are young men of princely blood
Who I know from my adventures
Are strong, good fighters, excellent at horsemanship,
And worthy to wed with your admirable daughter."

Thoas looked at him dubiously.

"I am tied to my kingdom for some time
With these skirmishes and counter-raids.
How would I see them?"

"Send a messenger with gifts, asking those who wish
To visit you and contest among each other
For the privilege of marrying your daughter.
You might also send such a messenger to Pylos,
For some of Nestor's sons are still unmarried,
And with such a marriage we would also have some bond.
But in both cases warn all that you will have the final say
If the victor will win your daughter."

Thoas thought for a moment, then laughed delightedly.

"You have not lost your cunning, my subtle Ithacan.
A splendid plan, and one that I will set on
With great diligence."

"And you may use my name with both groups—
I think it will be good currency for them."

For this suggestion Odysseus received a huge slap
On his back from the rugged king
And the others looked at him, startled.
Thoas rose to his full height, then roared to the banqueters,

"We have made a libation to the Gods, as is right.
Now let us do the same for glorious Odysseus,
Hero of the Trojan War, greatest of adventurers,
And dear fellow king, warrior and friend."

And like a wave that can be seen afar
Only as one crest among many, then races
Toward a beach, towering above the others before it breaks
With a crashing roar onto the unresisting beach,
So all raised themselves from where they sat,
Lifted high their cups and shouted with one voice,

"Odysseus, King of Ithaca, Conqueror of Troy!"

When all had resumed feasting, with Ithacan and Aetolian
In animated discussion each with the other,
Thoas turned to his daughter, who sat with Pelagia
Not far from him, and told her of his plan.
Wide eyed, she listened to him and then was enveloped
In his spontaneous and bear-like embrace.
She thanked Odysseus for his consideration of her,
Then moved back to Pelagia to tell her of this
Unexpected possibility, so soon put forward
Just on the subject the two women had discussed,
And then asked her if she knew the men
Who had been identified as suitors.
Pelagia answered, subdued, for the Corinthians
Had helped to destroy her home.

"The Corinthians he speaks of are indeed strong warriors,
And they have seemed to me worthy of consideration
For a high marriage. As for the those of Pylos,
I have not knowledge, never having met them,
But as sons of Nestor they must be worthy."

As a magpie that sights a bright object and chatters
To his fellow birds of his acquisition,
Now Artemisia, excited, peppered Pelagia with questions
About each Corinthian—what was he like? How tall?
How strong? Which one would she choose? Why?
Which would she think suitable for her? Who might
Win in the contest her father had proposed?
Pelagia, showered with these questions, answered them
As best she could; but even as she did
The memories of their expedition together
Returned her to the downfall of her citadel,
And finally she made an excuse that she had had
Too much wine, and left the feast for a while
To brood as she looked over the plains below the slope.
She saw the fields now ripening in rich variety,
With shifting shades of green from grain and orchard—
Vivid emerald fought with somber sage and olive,
And the yellowish tinges of pea and chartreuse
Vied with blue-green and teal, and the fickle jade
Purloined all their tinctures and their shades.
Through this sweet cacophony, punctuated
By the orchards with their boughs heavy
With fruit and olive, ran the winding Evenus,
Dark waters clashing with the salt flats
That stained its banks at different intervals.
Turning from the lush pattern spread below her,
She looked north, where she saw the huge peaks
In all their harsh ranges sitting sentinel
To where she knew Odysseus would venture,
And she sighed, both for the daring of his trek
And for the feelings that still stained her soul.
She sat staring for a time at the two worlds around her;
Then, looking down toward the feast nearing its conclusion,

She rose and returned, more calm and in control.
Both Artemisia and Telemachus greeted her,
Each concerned about her health; but she calmed
Them as the feast began to break up.
But Artemisia had noted Telemachus's concern
And realized that there was more between the two
Than had been publicly discussed; and she felt
A twinge of jealousy at their intimacy
And yet also knew that he was betrothed,
So that Pelagia could have no standing in Ithaca
Except as slave or concubine. She had seen
How her father treated the Trojan gentlewoman
As both concubine and slave, but the relationship
She saw between Pelagia and the Ithacans bore
No resemblance to her father's conduct; in fact,
She saw the respect with which the girl was held
By Telemachus and the others; and so for her
The mystery and puzzle of Pelagia and her part
In this expedition deepened. However, with
The bustle of the feast ending, she had no time
To follow what her instincts had told her,
And instead talked to Pelagia as they left the feast,
And as a falcon will soar in wide circles,
Wings spread to catch the supporting air in silence
Before plunging to grasp in its fierce claws
Its unsuspecting victim, so the young woman
Chatted as if unconcerned about Pelagia's horsemanship,
How she knew the valour of the Corinthian men,
And how she came to know Telemachus and his father.
To all of these Pelagia gave but slight answers
Which only fed the girl's curiosity; but no matter
How she tried, no further information could she capture
To give light to Pelagia and her journey.

Now at the palace the group prepared for the return
To the ship and its departure. Helios lashed
His charges halfway along their fiery journey
As the group on horses and in chariots made their way
Down the long slope. Artemisia rode on one side of Pelagia,

Telemachus on the other, and the two kings rode chariots
Side by side. Despite the thunder and the noise of chariot
And horse, Thoas shouted across to his fellow king,

"As I have told you, it is dangerous to travel here
On your own. I ask you again, let me accompany you
With my forces, at least for the first while,
Until you come to my border farther north."

"I thank you for your concern and for your offer,
But from now on I must make my quest alone.
Do not worry if you cannot find me, nor hear news
Of my whereabouts—as you know, for ten years
No one except the Gods knew where I was."

Thoas shrugged and rolled his eyes upward.

"You have not changed one bit—remember
That nocturnal expedition that Diomedes and you
Made, killing a whole troop as they slept?"

Odysseus grinned at him in reply.

"This is in the same mould, I can see. Well,
I will not press you farther on the matter.
Nor will I give you a gift, since you have no means
Of taking it with you."

Odysseus laughed and nodded, his hair blowing in the wind.

Soon the assembly had thundered down to the ship,
And all got ready to take their leave.
Artemisia and Pelagia embraced; and close to the other's ear
Pelagia quietly said,

"I promised you, and I will fulfill my word,
That one day you will know my story.
Be patient—and may the Gods allow you
A worthy husband."

Then she broke from her and ascended to the ship.
The kings made their farewells, and the Ithacans
Trooped back onto their ship, Odysseus among them.

"Do you go with them?"
Thoas called.

Odysseus shouted back,
"I must confer with them regarding their return.
Please leave now with my gratitude and thanks."

And he waved to his old friend, then disappeared
Among the others. Thoas, disconcerted, shrugged,
And his troop thundered back up the slope
To the rugged citadel.

Within the sharp-prowed vessel, Odysseus gave
His last instructions.

"I will leave shortly, but you must not tell how
Or in what manner I go. When you return
To Ithaca, which should not take long as you know,
Tell Penelope, Mentor, and my father the long tale
Of what has occurred on our adventures since we left.
Halitherses, we have discussed what is to be done
About the other matters."

The seer nodded gravely.

"Telemachus, this time you will have no need
To search for me as you did before.
If I do not return within the year"—

He stopped his son's protestation with a gesture—

"Two things you must do.
First, you must consider that I am dead"—

All gasped in horror at this thought—

"And you must take on the kingship.
Then you must leave with your entourage
For the anticipated marriage.
However"—

Again stilling protests, this time from most there—

"You must know that I fully intend to return
And to live as has been foretold, and so
Do not be disappointed when you see me."

All smiled at this and felt more at ease,
Calmed by his confidence and faith.

"And now, let your trip home begin."

The sleek ship moved from the dock,
Its rowers pushing it into the current,
Where it swiftly turned to begin its descent
Of the flowing river. Odysseus then
Spoke quietly to the steersman.

"A short distance down the river you will come
To a bend at which a grove of trees is found;
When the ship has rounded to a place
Where the citadel cannot see it, there
Let me off."

The oarsman nodded, and Odysseus moved
To a bundle that he had kept close with him.
There he removed his rich clothing, and from
The things now displayed before him,
He found a ragged chiton and cloak
And a large floppy hat. These he put on,
And as well he sheathed the oar given him
By Menelaos as a gift, and from each end
He tied a small bundle containing such
Food and utensils that a poor traveller
May have; his dagger he carefully hid on his person
Where it could not be seen but could be
Retrieved in an instant. During all this time
He made sure that he could not be seen
Either from the bank or from the citadel.
Then he dirtied his face, made his farewells
To the others, embracing his son and looking
Pelagia in the eye. As the ship swept around the bend,
The steersman directed it to pause for a moment
At the bank, and Odysseus leapt out and

Quickly disappeared among the trees, and
The ship continued on its way in the swift current.

Dusk finally came, and with it Odysseus left
The grove to begin his quest.

"Pallas Athena, as you have done before,
Keep my disguise effective, and grant me
A safe journey."

And with that fervent prayer, he turned north
To travel first to Lake Trichonis.

# Canto 10
## AETOLIA

As a shadow shifts among the patterns of the leaves
Stirred by the wind, so that it joins, then moves apart
From all the rest in ways that make it indistinguishable,
So in the gathering darkness the wily Ithacan moved on,
Ready at any moment to merge his shadow with the others
At the trail's edge. Silently he moved along the river bank,
Following its course to the forbidding north.
Soon the banks deepened on either side
As the river wound through the mountains lowering
Menacingly above it. At times the river bed broadened,
Leaving a clearer and more navigable path
In the dark now black about him.
A clear sky let stars suggest his way
But, cloudless, it breathed a chill that cut through his cape,
Despite his onerous trek. At other times
The ground rose steeply, and he was forced to climb
And feel out what narrow trails he could in the icy night.
For many hours he struggled thus, as around each bend
More shadows towered huge above him.
All this time he heard the sound only of the river
As its current rumbled along the path
It had cut through the roots of the resistant mountains.
Finally, as Dawn threatened her appearance,
He found a clump of bushes, and there he hid
In such a way that none could see him without effort.
During the day he heard boats move up the river,
Their rowers straining against the powerful stream,
And from what he overheard he learned that Thoas
Had sent men to look for him as he suspected.
That night his trek continued as the land
Beside the river grew more wild and difficult;

And again as the first grey light appeared
He found a place to shelter undisturbed.
On the third night in the early hours
The sky began to cloud, and he realized
That no more could he travel as he had.
He then rested briefly; and when the sky
Turned to grey under its cloudy cover
He started his journey once more;
But now he climbed higher, above the thin faint trails
By the river's banks. His way was more treacherous here,
And he began to doubt the wisdom of his strategy.
Then a valley opened to the left of the river's winding way
And as he came around a spur he saw above
Vast flocks of birds flying down it, intent
To find a destination beyond sight.

*Where but the lake?*

And he hastened along the new route,
Careful to keep high up on the range's flanks.
At the valley's end the mountains twisted to the right
And he followed a narrow pass up to its height.
Suddenly he crossed over a ridge, and before him
He saw a huge plain, in the midst of which
A lake stretched into the far distance.

*Trichonis.*

He paused, then sat to ponder his situation
And to eat from his now diminished supplies.

*It will be impossible for me to traverse the plain and lake*
*At night, with so many farms and their dogs alert to intruders.*
*Besides, I need new provisions and knowledge of the valleys*
*Which I must explore.*

He looked up and across the plain, to where he saw
The largest mountains yet, snow covered and in saw-toothed ranges.
He sighed, then having finished his sparse meal,
He rose and started down the slope to the valley below.
Slowly the trek-worn Ithacan descended the steep incline
Until he came to a trail carved in its side;

This he followed as it wound down toward the plain,
Where he found a dusty road that led toward the lake
In what appeared an aimless fashion.
For some time his ragged boots, his koila upodémata,
Shuffled forward in the dust,
And still he saw the lake distant and yet unattainable.
Now parched to his extremity, he sought for some farm
That might have a well or water.
Finally, through an olive grove he spied a house
And moved haltingly toward it.
As he approached, a dog barked fiercely,
Tethered at the entrance. The house, he noted,
Was not large, with walls of stones collected, it appeared,
From the mountain slopes he had descended.
An older man, in rough clothes, opened the door
As Odysseus came nearer but stayed clear of the dog,
Who, snarling viciously, strained against his cord.
The man looked suspiciously at the ragged beggar before him,
And the sharp-eyed king saw that his hand stayed close
To a knife tucked into his belt.
As a beggar he spoke to the now-scowling host:

"I greet you in peace and mean no harm.
All I request is but a drink of water from your well.
If you grant me this, may the Gods smile upon you."

Odysseus kept the manner of a beggar,
But his voice had not lost its persuasive power.
The man still scowled and said nothing,
But he curtly nodded and gestured to the side of the house,
Where Odysseus glimpsed the corner of a well.

"Thank you, gracious sir, and may the Gods
Reward you well for this kindness."

The man did not reply, nor did he move
But watched closely as Odysseus shuffled to the well,
Where he carefully drank cool drafts of water
And filled the goatskin bladder that he carried with him,
Then returned to the man and the still-snarling dog.

"I thank you again; and if I may ask,

Can you tell me the best route across this plain
To the north?"

"Around here we don't talk to strangers."

And with that brusque remark he moved back
And abruptly shut the door.
Odysseus shook his head at the ungracious incident
And then returned to the road, tired but refreshed.
Soon, however, with the sun now midway in its fiery journey,
He found some shade beneath a nearby olive tree
And lay down to rest, careful to choose a spot
As unobtrusive as he could find.
On his back, his head resting on one of his bags,
He saw through the restless leaves
A sky in which flocks of different birds winged overhead,
Their calls faintly reaching him as he saw them
Heading toward the still-distant lake.
Then his eyelids closed as sleep gently brushed them.
As Helios drove far across the sky,
The sound of voices wakened the tired warrior,
Who did not move but listened carefully
To determine the number who approached.
Two old men drew nearer, and he could hear them
Grumbling in the way that farmers do
About their crops, their groves, and the tribute made to Thoas.
After they had passed by, the cautious Ithacan
Arose with his sheathed oar and packs,
Then stepped out onto the road and, shuffling forward,
Called out to them. Startled, they turned toward him,
Pulling knives from their belts. When they saw him
Shuffling toward them, both hands occupied with his burden,
And that he did not appear to be a threat,
They put away their weapons;
But as a group in a strange place they do not trust
Will see a stranger near to them and will not show
A hostile movement but will still be alert to whether
Such a man is dangerous to them,
So these farmers watched warily the beggar now near.
Odysseus stayed a discreet distance from them,
And then he addressed them:

"Good sirs, as you can see, I wish you no harm,
Nor could I do so if I wanted.
Because I am a stranger and do not know this land,
And am alone, I worry that I may be robbed or worse
As I walk this road. Please, I ask you,
Let me walk with you for company; you know the way
And I am sure will not be molested by any here."

Again Athena intensified his persuasive power,
And soon the three walked together.
As they moved on, Odysseus studied them covertly.
He saw that they were younger than they seemed,
That they had toiled hard and were weathered
From the time that they had spent in a climate
That could be harsh in all seasons.
One he saw was taller, with a long lined face
With eyes that retained a permanent squint
From his hours below the tasking sun
And whose mouth was now almost a slit;
But the king saw intelligence in those chary eyes
And knew he would need to speak carefully to him.
The other was stockier, his back bent from time spent
In working close to the soil or in other labour;
His face was flatter, his eyes deep set,
Hard to see in the shadow of his brow,
And his mouth beneath a corpulent nose
Seemed pursed quizzically, whatever occurred.
Each carried a rough staff that Odysseus thought
They could handle capably if the need arose.
For some distance they walked on in silence,
And then the wise Ithacan gradually drew them
Into conversation. He learned that they were on their way
To a small town some distance toward the lake.
As they began to talk, they heard noise behind them,
And turning, they saw approaching several chariots
With armed soldiers. They moved to the side of the road
To let them pass, but instead they stopped,
And an officer spoke brusquely to them.

"You there, have you seen a stranger richly dressed
Pass down this road?"

All three looked at him and shook their heads.
The officer scowled and said,

"If you do see such a man, please report to us at once.
We will be in the plain for several days more
In search of him. King Thoas is eager to find
Him, who is his friend and fellow king."

Then he gave a curt order and the chariots swept off,
Leaving the three in their choking dust.
Odysseus turned to the others with a look of wonder.

"What would such a king do on this road alone?
Why would he not be with his friend, King Thoas?"

The two looked at each other, then chuckled in a way
That confirmed his suspicion about his fellow king.
Then the taller one turned to him.

. "Rulers in these mountains rarely have friends—
At least not ones who stay long alive.
Most of the time they fight, not make alliance.
It was only when the Trojan War was fought
That Thoas brought some together, and that
With great difficulty and not a little force.
But now they all battle each other or anyone
To gain more land or spoil."

The stooped one nodded.

"That king was lucky to escape, but why
He would come by here puzzles me.
There is no way that he will not find
Towns deep in these mountains who will steal
What he has, possessions or his life."

The other agreed.

"We have, at least, King Thoas, who protects us
From those who are much worse."

And both nodded in agreement over this.

Then the rangy one turned again to him.
"And what about yourself, who appear

From nowhere and more a beggar than one
With wealth."

Odysseus knew that he would be asked such a question,
And he replied,

"Mine is a sad story, but know first
That I come here as a pilgrim, ordered by the Gods
To travel north through this region
To Dodona, where at Apollo's shrine I must submit."

The others looked at him, clearly amazed,
But not yet accepting what he said.

"Know then, that I come from an island
Far off in the east. It was there that I
Angered the Gods, although I did so in ignorance,
Trespassing on a shrine that I knew nothing of.
When the oracles had spoken, I was banished
From the island, set on a ship for the mainland.
Pirates attacked us, and I became their chattel,
And would have become a slave but that
In a storm their ship was sunk, and I escaped,
Clinging to the wreckage until swept onto a beach.
There I was fortunate to meet a man who befriended me,
For whom I laboured until I had amassed
A modest amount to make this pilgrimage.
I managed, the Gods know how, to travel
Through Aetolia without incident,
Which you suggest to me is wondrous in itself.
And now I must make my way north,
Passing over these forbidding ranges to find
My way to the shrine at Dodona.
This poor staff"—

He shrugged his shoulders at the sheathed oar
Resting there—

"I must bring there as token of my ordeal
And my submission. As you see,
I have little with me now, and must beg
For food and water wherever I might go."

The others listened, fascinated by his tale,
And again his persuasive voice lured them
Into accepting what he said.
Now, as they walked along, their own tongues loosened,
And the stooped one spoke:

"You will not have an easy time of it in this land.
Strangers are not welcome, or if they are,
They find themselves stripped of their possessions."

"Not that such would happen to you,"
The other said, chuckling,

"For there is little that you have that any want.
But they do not give to beggars either.
And keep away from any soldiers such as those
A short time ago we met. They are like wolves,
And though we come under their protection,
It is not good to encounter them,
Especially if you are a stranger."

The rangy man nodded at what his friend said.

"What should I do, then, if all are so inhospitable?"

A look between the two. Then the tall one spoke.

"We are on our way to see a friend.
You may come with us for this day at least.
Then you must strike out on your own."

"Which way should I go?"

The stooped one pointed north.

"It is best to pass by Thermon on your way
To the farther mountains."

The long-faced one interjected,

"But for your own sake, do not enter it.
It is the fortress guarding this plain,
And strangers are not welcome in it,
As the soldiers there would quickly prove."

His companion nodded.

"You must pass by it, preferably at night.
Do not light a fire until you are out of sight,
So a patrol will not be sent to search for you."

By now the sun was ripe to touch the mountain tops
As they came to an olive grove not too far
From the cliffs overlooking the long lake.
A larger house than the one he had seen before
Odysseus now saw; and he saw as well that
It was a prosperous farm, with animals and grain
As well as the olive trees through which they now passed.
As they approached the mud-bricked house,
Dogs began to bark, and a man came out
To see who had come. When he recognized his friends
He settled his snarling beasts and hailed them.

"Welcome, my good friends! You have arrived
In time for a meal, of course, as is your habit."

The two laughed at his ribaldry and retorted themselves.
Then he turned to Odysseus, frowning to see the stranger.

"Who is this you have brought with you?
I had not expected others."

"He is a pilgrim that we met on the road,"
Said the tall one.

"We suggested that he come with us,"
Added his bent companion,
"So that you might be entertained by his tale."

Their friend looked dubious, but he accepted all three,
And they entered into a room dark and dirt-floored,
With little furniture, but kept neatly.
After an initial conversation, with the Ithacan
At his most charming, a slave brought them
Wine for the libation, and then bread in a wicker basket,
And finally meat for them all as they sat
On stools and benches about a wooden table.
All objects were rough-fashioned but serviceable,

And Odysseus enjoyed his first full meal
Since he had left Thoas's palace. All this time
He regaled the wondering men with tales
Of his supposed adventures, at which they gaped
In astonishment, their skepticism held in check
Both by his voice and the quantities of wine
That they consumed. Finally, as the night deepened,
All prepared to sleep, the three men bedding down
On the same room's floor, a fire in its midst
Smoky but warm, and Odysseus slept in comfort
After his nights upon the mountains.
But before he fell asleep he could hear
From the lake the wailing songs of the thick-kneed plovers
As they foraged for their nocturnal meals.

As Dawn left her palace in the morning
To light the tips of the surrounding mountains,
They all ate again. Then, with much thanks,
Odysseus left them, but not before his host
Gave him a glowing brand to use that night.
He moved to walk along the edge of the cliff
That stood against the water's edge.
As he strode forward, huge flocks of birds wheeled
Over his head, their graceful wings of all shades—
Ducks and widgeons, with their twanging cries
And high pitched "whew-whew-whew, fi-ew-whew, kaow-kaow"—
Curlews, slender-billed, streaked and spotted ("cour-lee, ai-ee"),
Pochards in bright colours, triangular heads,
Red-orange–billed oystercatchers
("whee-whee-tee-tee-tee, kak kea"),
Long-legged, long curved-bill avocets,
Caspian terns, with slow graceful flight,
Calling to each other through the sky
("ra-ra-ra ratschrau, ra-ra-re raeu ra"),
Kestrels swooping for prey, chittering and whining,
Cormorants wading, long-legged, with deep guttural calls,
Beside them ibises, wading or in flight,
Glossy bronze, clattering and grunting in their flocks
With their harsh rasping "graa-graa-graa."
Never had Odysseus seen so many flocks of birds

Congregated as these were now, and even from the cliff
The cacophony of their multitudinous calls
Deafened him. With the flurry of the winged thousands,
The long lake on one side and the plain on the other,
And surrounding all, the towering mountain ranges,
The bewildered Ithacan felt himself in another world,
And for hours he strode on in this dream-like state,
Still keeping sharp lookout for any persons
That he might see approaching or might see him.
None appeared as he continued on the edge of the cliff;
And in the afternoon he found himself nearing
The steep slopes that led to the north.
A small valley seemed to lead to a pass
And he followed it, to find that it soon narrowed
And became much steeper. Dusk was now falling,
And he searched for a place where he could make a fire
And camp unobserved. Behind a rocky outgrowth
He found such a place, gathered what wood he could find,
And spent the night beside the hidden flames.

The next day, removing traces of his camp
And carefully preserving a glowing brand,
He started out again. The way now was more difficult,
With deep ravines that showed little evidence
Of human travel. As he moved around the roots
Of mountains, he found himself climbing upward,
Until, by late afternoon, he crested a ridge
And saw in the distance the fortress of Thermon.
That night he made his fire on the side of the ridge
Away from that citadel. The next day he crossed
A small plain to enter a ravine that put a hill
Between him and Thermon's precincts.
During all this time he saw no one
Through the dark trees that clung to the precipitous slopes.
Now his way led into the heart of the great ranges,
The more forbidding for their bare stony sides,
Bereft of all but a few stubborn trees
Even in the rugged land that he trudged through.
The immensity of the gigantic slopes on each side

Began to press on him; as well, although he found
Water in the thin creeks along which he moved,
His provisions were now almost exhausted,
And he found himself taking time to stalk
Whatever animals unfortunate enough to stray by.
The land had been rising even from the roots,
And he could see the snowline of the peaks
Descend against the cold and mists and rain
That now seemed interminable. He also found
Himself more alone than ever he had been before,
Even during those ten long years of return from Troy.
His hearing became more acute; he could hear
The movement of animals and hear the echoing caws
Of the crows and croaks of the ravens that inhabited
This wilderness. Several days went by in this fashion,
And with the winds and turns of the twisting ravines,
With no sight of the sun hidden by the heavy clouds,
He began to lose his sense of direction—where north was,
The most important—but he kept moving forward,
Making sure that in the morning he had left a sign
Of what direction he should follow.

Then one dawn the mists cleared, the sun broke through
The now-retreating clouds, and the worn warrior,
Cold but refreshed, could now look about him clearly.
The cold gray walls still towered over him on either side,
Iced with snow high up; but where he stood
There were more trees along the murmuring creek
And the sounds of more animals and birds.
As a bear first leaves its lair in the spring
And, sniffing the new-born air, breaks into a run
For the sheer pleasure of it, so Odysseus,
Heartened by these changes, broke his camp
And moved on with new energy, taking in
The scents and sights and sounds around him.
The ravine he trekked, even as it twisted in the roots,
Began to open up, and he found himself
In a narrow valley which revealed more vegetation.
As the sun reached its zenith, he stopped to drink

From the crystal water and to eat and briefly rest.
Then he moved on again, exhilarated
By the life surrounding him and lost in thought.

*Athena, you have been kind to me so far—*
*Meeting the two farmers was a stroke of luck*
*When those soldiers passed by, and also for their help*
*And hospitality. And I was not discovered*
*While I still remained in Aetolia.*
*Soon I should take the oar from its sheath,*
*For in this wilderness there must be a tribe*
*That has not yet discovered salt.*

While he strode along, thinking thus, he suddenly
Was aware of a change about him. Puzzled,
He looked about, but saw nothing different
From before. Shaking his head at his own foolishness,
He started forward again; but even as he did so,
He realized what had changed—no sounds
Of animal or bird could be heard.
Then, as he became alert, but before he could respond,
He heard a swishing sound, and felt a sharp pain
In his shoulder. Looking down, he saw
A javelin protruding; and then, as if in a dream,
He sensed himself falling and then knew no more.

# Canto 11

# ITHACA

Telemachus watched his father disappear
Into the bushes on the bank as the ship
Veered back into the centre of the river
And moved swiftly downstream in the strong current;
The oarsmen rested then, letting the helmsman
Keep the ship trim. As the land slipped by
On either side, the prince, musing, took stock.
This was the first time since the voyage began
That his father was not here; and for a moment
He remembered his previous journey
When he had searched for the missing king,
And the old feeling of loss and danger
Overcame him, his eyes staring without focus
At the shifting landscape. Then, without warning,
The image of his father's great bow flashed
Clear and bright: the first time he had seen it
In the storeroom, its sheath high on a peg,
When he went to bring it to his father;
The wonder of its strength, with no one
But Odysseus himself capable of stringing it;
The wonder of his father's skill, targeting the axes
Then and the later triumph before Orestes;
And his deadly aim, first among the frantic suitors,
And then against the mountain fortress.
As he thought of that encounter, he remembered
His father's vow to use the bow only in Ithaca—
That Iphitus had given it to him as Apollo's instrument;
That he had slain the suitors on Apollo's day,
The deadly archer of the Gods;
That it had stayed in storage, undisturbed,
The length of the Trojan War and beyond.

Yet, without a word, he had brought it with him
On this journey, and he had used it
Two significant times. But now he had gone on
Without it, leaving it sheathed again
In his son's care on this sharp-prowed ship.
Abruptly his reverie was broken by a shout.
Now alert, he saw on the far bank
At the curve in the river, a band of men
With javelins poised to strike at them.
Quickly he and his companions raised their shields
And the rowers strained to quicken the pace.
As the sleek vessel surged under their stroke,
At the curve a thicket of spears flew to meet them
When the ship swung round, the helmsman sheltered
By the prince's shield, with brute strength
Steadying the rudder. The javelins sped true,
But thudded into the shields, or glanced off them.
No one was hurt except the prince, whose knee
Was grazed by one spear that remained, shuddering,
In the deck. A second set of javelins were poised,
But the swift ship by then had careered past them
And now sped out of danger. For some time
The oarsmen rowed mightily; and when at last
No danger could be seen on either side,
They raised their oars and, exhausted, rested,
With the current moving the ship at a good pace.
They made the estuary before nightfall,
And that night slept beneath the stars while
Another helmsman took the nocturnal watch.
And the sail-shrouded ship slipped silently
Along the black quiet sea.

The remainder of the voyage was uneventful
Except when they reached choppy water on the open sea
And Pelagia found the true horror of sea-sickness,
While Amunet herself appeared immune
To the wayward shudders of the ship,
And gave her mistress herbs to sooth her distress.
All the men now looked at Pelagia with new respect,
For when the attack took place she seized a shield

And stood dauntless with them—and this fearless act,
More than her arts with plants and drugs,
Gained their acceptance and their favour.
Thus when the black-prowed ship slid home in Ithaca,
All on it disembarked as a true company
In their hard-won identity together.
By this time Pelagia had recovered;
She watched closely as the rocky island
Rose on the horizon; she saw its steep hills
And its mountains, how sparse and bare it was,
And for a moment her heart leapt as the thought
Sprung forth of her old home, with its forests
And the plain spread before it; then she forced
The memory down and looked at her new home,
Fast approaching, with clear eyes; until a voice
Near her said,

"I must ask you for the time being, Pelagia,
To remain with your cargo here, unseen,
Until I request you to join us on the landing."

She turned, saw Halitherses standing kindly by her,
Knew what he intended, and with a slight twisted smile
She nodded and went to where her bales were secured
And Amunet sat motionless.

In the palace the watchman's shout brought
Penelope to her chamber window, where she saw
The first fleet glimpse of the familiar sail.
Hastily she called her women to her
To adorn her hair, add graces to her face,
Help her adjust her best chiton and hymation
Dyed in rich hues, to show her lovely form
To full advantage, and all this time
In her excitement she kept up a stream of chatter—
How near now was the ship? A girl was sent
To report back several times. Could anyone
Be seen? Too far yet to determine.
Were her hair and dress arranged well?
A polished metal held before her let
Her make a few inconsequential adjustments.

Now the girl returned to tell her that she
Had seen Prince Telemachus standing in the prow—

"And King Odysseus?"

On the negative reply her face fell, but now
She swiftly composed herself and, leaving
Her lofty well-lit chamber, descended
The steep stairs and came to the long hall,
Where Mentor and attendants waited for her.
All left the high-standing palace to descend
The slope that led to where the ship would dock,
And there they stood while the graceful ship slipped home.

On board, Pelagia had also occupied herself
In preparing for the arrival, combing
And arranging her hair as best she could
After the days of travel, and tidying her clothes
With some help from Amunet, whose own clothes,
With her cloak, still seemed immaculate.
As the ship came in the harbour, Telemachus,
Standing at the prow, saw the delegation,
His mother in the front with Mentor,
Awaiting them. For a moment he wished
To point her out to Pelagia, but
She was nowhere to be seen, and Halitherses
Had warned him of the tactic that Odysseus
Recommended. Then, as the ship hove to,
He leapt from it, raced to his mother,
And swept her up into his arms. She hugged
Him back, both with relief and love; no word
Was spoken for a long moment; and then
They separated.

"Your father?"

                "He was fine the last time
We saw him. He made us leave him back in
Aetolia so that he could begin
His final pilgrimage."

Penelope turned pale.

"Aetolia?"

"Don't worry, my dear mother, I will tell you
All. But let us first finish what we need to here."

And he turned to greet Mentor, who had waited
With the others patiently. All then made
Happy greetings, Halitherses and Medon
And the others surrounded by their friends and families.
As they did so, Penelope noticed that her son's knee
Was neatly bandaged, and she exclaimed,

"My son, what happened to you? Are you well?
What is your injury? Is it serious?
How did it happen to you?"

Laughing, Telemachus quieted his mother.

"It's nothing serious, mother, and I will tell
You all about it later."

But, looking more closely, she saw how neatly
It had been treated.

"How did you come to have such a neat bandage?
I know of no one among you capable
Of treating a wound so well."

Uncertain what to say, her son exchanged
A look with Halitherses, who had overheard
Their conversation and now interjected,

"My queen, we have been fortunate to obtain
One gifted in the arts of medicine and plants
Who will remain here, live with us, provide
For our healthful states as may be needed."

And he brought Pelagia from the ship
To present her to the queen, while Amunet
Remained behind unseen. The striking girl,
Whom the crew applauded as she came ashore,
Made a graceful, if slight, obeisance to the queen,
Who, startled, acknowledged her by habit,

And then each woman eyed the other closely.
Pelagia saw a woman on the cusp of age
Still attractive in both face and body,
But no match for the peerless Helen.
Yet she showed in her stance and feature
Signs of great character, one who had suffered
And bore the burden of it with strength.
She was dignified at this present moment,
But the girl had seen the passion with which
She had embraced her son, and she knew then
Why the king was so steadfast in his love.
The way in which she now inspected her
Pelagia found honest and without guile,
And she realized here was a woman
That she would wish to be a friend and fear
To be an enemy. From her perspective,
Penelope saw a young woman not yet
In her twenties, with attractive and distinctive
Features, though not truly beautiful, who
Possessed a voluptuous but athletic body
Revealed in her stance and in her firm arms.
But what intrigued her most was what might lurk
Behind those clear dark eyes that looked so directly
At her, for the queen could sense currents deep
Within this girl that both fascinated
And frightened her. She found her unlike any
Other woman she had met and was curious
To learn more of her, especially as the seer
Had proclaimed her skills in the art of medicine,
And she was also surprised by the respect
The crew had so openly awarded her.

"My queen, may I present Pelagia,
A native of Arcadia and trained
By Helen herself in all skills dealing
With plants and drugs. And, Pelagia,
Great Penelope, Queen of Ithaca,
And beloved spouse of King Odysseus."

"Welcome, Pelagia of Arcadia,
I am sure your skills will prove useful here,

And I look forward to talking with you
On these and other matters."

Pelagia acknowledged gracefully
The queen's words with a nod of her head,
But Penelope noted that the girl
Treated her as an equal, which she found
Disconcerting but intriguing as well;
But even as she thought this, from the corner
Of her eye she caught Telemachus's look
As he watched Pelagia, and the mother knew
With shocking clarity the two were intimate.
For a moment she stiffened, then regained
Her composure, but in that instant
Pelagia knew the queen had realized
Her relationship with her beloved son;
And in the next instant both women knew
The other's insight. Yet what shook the queen
More was that Pelagia still held her gaze
And showed clearly that what the queen had felt
Was true but that Pelagia felt
No fear nor shame for her feelings for the prince.
For a moment neither spoke; then Halitherses,
Sensing what had occurred between the two,
Spoke again:

"If you would excuse Pelagia, my queen,
It is important that she supervise
The unloading and disposal of her
Precious supplies."

                    With this the queen
Nodded and released Pelagia, who
Returned to the ship, but not without
Letting a look pass between the prince and her.
Before the queen could respond, Halitherses
Hastily said,

"We must meet soon, Queen Penelope, for
I have much to tell you on this matter."

"I'm sure you do, Halitherses, and I
Look forward to this conversation
In my chamber shortly after we return
To the palace."

And the queen swept away with her entourage,
And her son in tow. Pelagia was now occupied
With the unloading of her bales and boxes,
Making sure no bale was harmed on the voyage
And cautioning the attendants to move them carefully.
Amunet worked with the men silently,
Gesturing as to how each object should be handled,
And though she made no sound nor seemed too bold,
Pelagia was struck by her quiet authority
And her ability to have the men do her bidding.
Because for the present time the cargo
Was to be secured in the palace courtyard,
Pelagia and Amunet walked with them
As they laboured up the slope. As when a visitor
To a strange land sees for the first time its buildings
With eyes still fresh that take in all the features
That glow in newness for them, so Pelagia,
As she progressed up the slope, saw before her
The palace, and, surrounding it on three sides,
The town huddled by its strong walls, its stones,
Mammoth and impregnable, thrusting upward
To the ramparts; and behind these giant walls
High as they were, could just be seen the upper storeys
Of the palace itself, with its sturdy roof.
All of this made her heartsick, for her home
Had been constructed much the same, although
Perched much higher on its mountain fastness,
And its walls were built fatally of wood.
They now reached the gates, which reared above
And in front of them; these were not wood but
Beaten bronze reinforced with huge iron bands
And were hung on giant hinges. Presently
The gates were open for them, and she passed
Into the large courtyard, where the loads were placed
Under the porch, sheltered in case rain should fall.

The two women spent some time in arranging these supplies,
Now precious to them, so that they could be used
Efficiently when needed.

Penelope had swept up the slope saying little;
Her son at her side was nonplussed, but he suspected
That she had guessed Pelagia's relationship to him.
As one walking along a narrow path, on either side
Of which bend stinging nettles perilously close,
So he carefully refrained from speaking of the girl
But instead filled the silence with chatter of the trip
And of his father's exploits. Penelope
Was eager to hear of Odysseus, but
Still in her mind was the question of her son
And Pelagia. When they crossed the threshold
Of the palace, she suggested that he supervise
The placing of his personal effects in his room,
Then nodded to Halitherses and Medon
To go with her to her spacious chamber.
When they had climbed the steep stairs to it,
Penelope had her women bring them chairs
Covered in purple and soft thick fleece,
And when they were comfortably seated, she began.

"Well, you two, how does this girl come to be here?
And what relation has she to my son, the prince?"

Both men knew from her tone her deep concern
And that she was upset, particularly for the royal house.
Medon nodded to Halitherses, who carefully
Laid out the pieces of the complicated tale:
How Odysseus was obliged to aid Orestes
In his plan to acquire Arcadia;
How in that campaign when diplomacy failed
Because of the brutish actions of the Arcadian king
Odysseus had, single-handedly, to make the siege
Of an Arcadian town a success; how Pelagia
Was the daughter of the ruler of that doomed
Citadel; how the prince had rescued her
When she was defending herself against
Three warriors; how he had later been her champion

To save her from the Arcadian king;
And when he had killed the king's champion,
How from a serious injury incurred
In that combat—Penelope caught her breath
At this comment—she had nursed him back to health;
How in Sparta Helen recognized her talent
And trained her in her healing arts; how there
She became the prince's concubine.

At this point the queen exclaimed vehemently,

"But how could Odysseus permit this?
She may be the daughter of the chieftain
Of some small insignificant town
Yet by all the rules of war she deserves to be
A slave and nothing more. And Helen, who
I would have thought had more sense, takes her
Under her wing and trains her as if
She were an equal! And I saw myself
The respect given her by all of you
At the ship. What madman has infected
All of you?"

The queen would have raged on in disbelief,
But Halitherses raised his hand for silence,
And as Penelope saw the aura of the seer
Descend upon him, she abruptly stopped,
Awed by the strange power she sensed in him.

"We do not willfully act thus. I have felt—
Still feel—that her destiny is tied
To your family in some vital way.
What that may be has not been revealed to me,
But I know she must be treated with respect
And occupy a suitable position here.
So I told the king, your husband, and in
His wisdom he acknowledged what I said
And has acted accordingly. Helen knew
Something of this by our respect and learned
The true talent of the girl, who I must say
Has shown herself remarkable—adept

As a man at horsemanship and martial arts;
Courageous and intelligent. There is
Every reason for your son to fall in love
With her—he championed her and saved her life;
She has nursed him well. Her position is clear
To her that she can be no more than a concubine,
But also that she can hold a position of
Importance in her skill in the healing arts."

Penelope listened in amazement to
This extraordinary revelation,
And for a long moment sat in thought.
Finally she sighed.

"What, then, is your advice now?
As a healer I can see her importance—
But never in this household has there been
A woman intimate other than a wife!"

She spoke passionately, and the two men
Knew that she remembered well the twenty years
When she had been without her husband,
Always faithful. Medon then spoke with sympathy.

"Dear queen, we understand how you feel—
And you are right to feel so, and honourable
That you do. But we cannot tell what the Gods
Intend for us, nor should we dare to thwart them.
This, then, is my advice: give her a fine house
Not far from the palace, with a garden
Protected there; let her practise her skills there;
And when the prince chooses, let him visit her"—

At this Penelope flinched, but Medon continued—

"And let her become, so far as possible,
A member of your household, sharing meals
And, I suggest, becoming your friend;
For you will find, I think, that she will prove
Interesting and a good companion"—

At the queen's look he quickly added—

"And in that way you may forestall any
Problems that can occur from misunderstandings.
I tell you this, dear queen, as the best way
To proceed in this unknown journey."

Penelope sighed again, then nodded.

"Find her a place as soon as possible
So that her garden can be planted before
Winter comes. In the meantime, have
My women prepare a room for her
Here in the palace and make sure she knows
Of it and that she will feast with us.
And ask the prince to come to me here."

They bowed and left her there, sitting still
And musing. Restless, she rose and paced the room,
Stopping before the large bed that Odysseus
Built himself, fashioning it from the olive tree
That grew there to its maturity, and she
Stroked the inlays of ivory, the fittings
Of gold and silver that he himself made;
Glanced across the room that he constructed,
Stone on stone, and the high sturdy roof, and
The tight, well-hung doors, all done by him;
Remembered the conception, then the birth
Of her son in this room; thought of the time
When Odysseus feigned madness to keep from
Going to the War, but could not destroy
His baby boy placed in the path of his plough;
Saw him leave in those ships that never came back;
And with him gone, the years passing without
The chance for more children, with all her hopes
Resting in one child; and she sank to the
Magnificent bed with harsh wrenching sobs
Until, exhausted, she lay there staring
At the high ceiling, with time dissolved around her.

Pelagia had almost finished with
Her stores, when an old woman greeted her,
Glancing with curiosity and apprehension
At the slight figure of the Egyptian,

Who nodded to Pelagia to leave the rest to her.
The two moved away from the noisy space
And Pelagia received the invitation
To the feast and where she was to stay from
The old woman, who, as she spoke, made a
Close inspection of her. Pelagia,
Disconcerted at such frank appraisal,
Nonetheless did not lose her temper
But replied civilly and was led in
To the palace over its great stone threshold.

"You've come from far away, I hear,"

The ancient servant said as she bustled
Down a long hall.

"Yes, from Arcadia."

                    "What brings you here?"

"I will practise the healing arts in this place."

Eurycleia—for it was the old nurse herself—
Although surprised, queried the girl further.

"Did you accompany your husband here?"

"I have no husband."

The nurse's lips pressed firmly together at this news.
Pelagia could sense that the other
Was concerned about a young attractive
Woman, unattended and with what appeared
Some status, living in the palace,
But as yet she could not see the reason
For her concern, and she was intrigued by
The apparent authority she seemed to have.
They had by now reached the room where the girl
Was to reside, and the servant let her in.

"I will return with appropriate clothes
And will supervise your bath myself."

Then she left the surprised girl on her own.

As a garden, glowing with the petals
Of its flowers in their luxuriant beds,
Is suddenly beset by a thunderstorm
Whose winds whip against the swaying buds
Pelted by rain, with petals driven to the ground,
Yet, when the storm passes, appears again
In its vivacious colours, the bruised ruins
Hidden in the glistening foliage,
So Penelope, her passion now spent,
Repaired her ravaged person and composed
Herself to meet her son. When he arrived
She embraced him warmly and sat him down
Next to her. For a moment she studied him.
She confirmed what she had seen at the ship—
That he had now matured and held himself
With a natural authority.

"And now, my dear son, tell me of your father—
But only the outline, for I'm sure all
Will wish to hear your tale at tonight's feast."

He quickly sketched in Odysseus's exploits
And how he had left them, wearing his disguise,
In Aetolia. When he had finished,
His mother asked,

"And you, Telemachus? What did you do?"

Her son knew that Halitherses had told
Of Pelagia, and he decided truth was best.

"Mother, you know by now about Pelagia—
Let me tell you the whole story, omitting nothing."

He told her much of what she had heard
From Halitherses, but he also made
Her understand his own feelings: how he
Had been struck by the courage and prowess
Of the girl when she fought off the warriors;
How he became her champion against Aepytus;
The battle in which he was the victor
And bore a wound (his mother forced him

To tell more of his injury); how when
She nursed him back to health they became
Closer; but that it was not until Sparta
That their feelings for each other blossomed;
And that she was now his concubine, but
With her new skills deserved respect, adding
The importance Halitherses felt she had
For their family.

        "I have told you all,
Mother. I sincerely love and respect her;
And although she can be no more than a
Concubine, she will always be constant
In my heart."

        His mother looked at him, moved,
And stroked lovingly his cheek with her
Graceful fingertips.

        "I see how deep
Your love is for this girl, and may the Gods
Allow you happiness and peace in your union.
But keep in mind that any children
She has cannot be true heirs; that some day
You must marry one suitable to bear
Your legitimate offspring, and that you
Must honour such a wife so that no strife
Breaks out within the family."

Telemachus coloured: he knew that he
Must not yet let her know of his betrothal
To Nestor's lovely daughter Polycaste,
And so he hung his head and said nothing.
Mistaking his blush and reticence for
Confusion and embarrassment over
Such possibilities, his mother laughed
And took his hand.

        "Do not fear, my manly
Son. I will try to keep your domestic
Affairs smooth and peaceful."

                    And with that
She kissed him and sent him off, for the time
Was not far off for the banquet to begin.

Eurycleia led Pelagia to
A bath of bronze fitted snugly into
The nesting stones. Serving women filled it
With water hot and scented sweetly.
The old nurse watched as Pelagia was stripped,
Bathed by the women, and massaged with
Perfumed unguents. She saw, with grudging
Admiration, the girl's splendid body;
It reminded her of a panther's, smooth
And sleek, but capable of moving
With strength and dangerous grace; with this sight
Her worry increased, and even more so
When the stunning girl's hair was arranged
And her chiton and hymation adjusted,
For she wore them superbly, each drape
Gracing her body, all showing her full beauty.
While Pelagia was being prepared,
In the courtyard below priests brought before
Zeus's altar a young bull garlanded
For the occasion, and a hymn arose
In praise of the dread ruler of the Gods.
Then the bull was sacrificed, and its parts
Roasted in the fires for the purpose.
Pelagia, now ready, waited with attendants
In the long hall outside the handsome door
Of the queen's chamber. At last Penelope
Swept out to join her; but for a moment
Each regarded the other with wonder,
For the queen also seemed transformed, radiant
In her mature beauty. Both then acknowledged
Their respective comeliness, and they descended
To enter the palace hall. Pelagia
First saw the large double doors, snugly fitted,
Shining and impressive in their smooth-planed
Oaken doorsill. Stepping onto the stone
Threshold inside the spacious hall, she saw

The thick timbered columns that towered up
To support the sturdy roof, with its fine
Crossbeams and rafters cut from good pinewood,
Its central beam smoked black. Along the walls
Below the high-placed smoke ducts were hung
The martial accoutrements of the family—
Bronze armour, helmets with vivid plumes, shields
Massive and studded, embossed with the deeds
Of their heroic owners, and spears, long,
With deadly sharp brazen heads. The floor she
Saw was of packed earth pressed smooth;
Light flared from braziers set along the walls,
Heaped with seasoned chips and new-cut kindling that
Gave both flame and the pleasant scent of seasoned wood.
In the centre of the hall a large fire
Blazed comfortably; and surrounding it
Were placed tables, chairs, and stools occupied
By those from the ship, the palace, and the town.

Like two gorgeous orchids suddenly discovered
In some unexpected barren place,
The two women entered the hall. All there
Gasped in admiration at their loveliness;
And as they moved to the queen's table
The proximity of Pelagia
Increased her erotic power over them,
For the cunning girl had made good use
Of her new skills and had applied such scents
As would arouse those men about her.
Her women drew the queen's favorite chair
To her table; Pelagia saw the beauty
Of its exquisite workmanship, with its
Inlaid rings of ivory and silver.
She herself was seated in a chair
Polished and spread with a soft fleece.
Libations were made and more wine poured;
Bread was offered them in handsome wicker baskets;
And then succulent slices were carved for them.
At Penelope's table also sat the prince,
Who looked with pleasure at both

His mother and Pelagia. Mentor
Sat with them as well; and at a table close by
Were found Medon and Halitherses
With Laertes, Odysseus's ancient father.
Pelagia saw Telemachus rise
And greet his grandfather, embracing him;
But the sharp-eyed girl saw that he did so
Gingerly, with the old man responding
Brusquely. Looking at him more closely,
She saw him dressed in rich clothes that he wore
Uncomfortably, his skin tanned dark, seamed
By the sun, his body, despite age, strong,
Thick-torsoed like an ancient oak,
And when she made quick sharp glances at him
Over time, she saw that he spoke little
To the others but watched all through his deep-set eyes.
Penelope kept the conversation
At her table moving as a stream slips
Over rocks and pebbles to make a sweet
Refreshing sound. Telemachus, eager
To discover what had occurred in Ithaca
While he had been away, plied Mentor with
Questions which he in good humour answered; and
Pelagia listened closely, curious
About her new country. Penelope
Sat quietly, speaking only to nudge
The conversation on, but studying
Attentively her son and his lover.
She noted how Odysseus had helped his son—
His questions now were deeper and more pointed,
And he took time to listen and to think through
What he had heard. Pelagia she
Found listened with close attention, weighing
Carefully what she heard, and asking
Mentor questions that built on what had been said.
The queen also saw that the girl looked
Directly and openly at whomever
She talked to; and she saw, not without a pang,
That the looks that passed between the girl
And her son revealed without a hint

Of shame or guile the deep and intimate
Feeling between them.

               The moment arrived
For the story to be sung of the trip
And its exploits. The queen rose and bade
Medon to begin. He sang in detail
Of all that had occurred, but carefully
Omitted any mention of Polycaste
Or the relationship between Pelagia
And Telemachus, although the circumstances
Hinted at this. Then he turned to the queen.

"Then great Odysseus, destroyer of Troy,
Unparalleled warrior and conciliator,
Having resolved the problems of the Argolid
And of Arcadia and Sparta and Nestor's land,
Renewed his friendship with King Thoas,
Fierce ruler of Aetolia, then departed
From the cities and the lands that he knew
To disappear into the northern wilderness
To fulfill his pilgrimage to the God
Poseidon, dread Lord of Sea and Sky.
To our heroic king sing praise, and raise up
Prayers to all the Gods to keep him safe
On his perilous journey."

All were moved by his fine recital;
The queen and her son covered their faces
While they wept softly, and then the prince rose.

"Medon, your skill increases each day.
We thank you, both for this magnificent song
And for your value as our herald on the journey."

And he gave Medon a purse of gold
And had a choice morsel carved for him
And himself served him his wine. The queen
Rose again.

           "Medon has sung incomparably
And I also thank him for it. But he,
In honour to our king, told his story only.

Yet I am happy that you hear another tale,
And I ask Halitherses to tell it."

Then the seer arose and told them all
Pelagia's story, from her capture
As the daughter of the chieftain of the doomed town
(She could not keep dammed her tears when she heard this),
Through his own revelation of her importance
To Ithaca (murmurs of surprise and wonder),
To the prince's championship of her against
Aepytus, despite danger to his own life
(Murmurs again, this time of admiration),
Her training and adeptness in the arts
Of drugs and plants at the hand of Helen
(More murmurs, of astonishment, for none
Had known of Helen's skill in these arts),
And of her courage shown on the ship
(Shouts of agreement from the crew), and her
New position in Ithaca as healer.
When he had finished, the queen looked at her son
And nodded. He smiled and arose.

"From the moment I saw Pelagia
I was struck by her courage and ability.
Then she showed skills equal to a man in
Swordsmanship and horsemanship"—
(Murmurs, some less approving, from older men)
"Now, skills in arts essential to us all.
But, as important to me, I have come
To know her as a woman whom I love
And honour; and today I tell you all
That she will share my bed and life with me
As befits one so beautiful and fine."

Then he sat down. For a moment there was silence,
For all knew that she could not be his wife
And that he had named her truly as his concubine;
Then the members of the crew stood to cheer,
And those near the family, Medon and Mentor
And Halitherses, did so as well. Then
Laertes, Odysseus's old father, rose
And embraced first his grandson and then Pelagia

("May you prosper in your chosen art,
And may your union with my grandson
Be propitious,"

>                    he muttered in her ear),

Who had been astonished at what she just heard,
And was now moved more than she could have thought,
Even more so when the queen herself
Embraced her as well.

The meal continued for some time in great
Festivity. Then, finally, all began
To leave, first making their way to the fire
And the royal table to congratulate
The prince and Pelagia herself.
At last, the queen arose to go, kissing
The still marvelling Pelagia,
And departed with her attendants,
Leaving the young couple to themselves.
Pelagia led Telemachus to
Her chamber, and that night they lay passionately
Together for the first time since the ship
Had sailed from Corinth. When they at last
Rested from their love-making, their slick
Bodies nestled together, Pelagia
Murmured,

"I still wonder at the honour done to me
Tonight by the queen and by you yourself.
Never did I believe that you would make known
Our relationship in such a public way."

The prince nuzzled her fragrant hair.

"You may thank my mother for allowing
This. It shows that she feels from my own words,
Halitherses's avowal, and the showing
Of our love each for the other, that she
Is willing to trust you more than I had thought."

She yawned, stretching her body close to his.
"What happens now? Where will I be?"

"My mother has ordered that you be given
A house near the palace, and that your garden
Be there as well, protected as you would have it."

"Tomorrow I must thank her for all this."

"A good thought."

And he moved against her, and all thought left them.

The next morning, when she had been dressed again,
Pelagia went to see Penelope. This time the queen
Was in the hall, where the servants had cleaned
The tables, wet and polished the dirt floor,
And built up the fire, for the weather had
Turned, and a cold wind swept rain upon
The island and the palace. The queen sat
Close to the flames in her favourite chair
And another was brought so that Pelagia
Could sit next her and the warm fire. Penelope
Leaned forward and kissed the girl lightly on
The cheek.

"Queen Penelope, please accept my gratitude
For accepting me as you have."

The queen smiled, looking into the flames.

"If you can command so much respect from
Those who have met you, and can win my son's
Love, what else could I do?"

                    Pelagia
Leaned forward in her chair, and when Penelope
Turned to her, the girl looked deeply in her eyes.

"Nothing can be hidden between us, I
Feel. Know then that what I shall say is hard,
Both for the telling and the hearing, but
Only then can you determine if your decision
Is the right one, or whether you should take
Some other course."

The queen looked back in the other's eyes,
For some reason unsurprised at this outburst,
And waited for what the girl had to tell.

"When your son rescued me at the sack of my home,
He did not tell you that I fought him then,
And would have either killed him or myself,
For I had no wish to live a slave,
My family and friends slaughtered or worse.
But he conquered me, and later, when
The Arcadian king wanted me for his pleasure"—

She shuddered at this prospect—

"And Telemachus championed me as you heard,
And Odysseus forced me to nurse him—yes,
Forced me, because I still grieved and hated
All who had destroyed my home—I had to
Push those thoughts aside and tend to him,
And it was then I learned what he was truly like.
But, as you have heard at least twice now,
It was in Sparta that our love blossomed
And that new opportunities arose for me
With the generous help of Queen Helen.
And I do love your son, with all my being"—

This said with passion, and the queen saw in
The girl's eyes the intensity of what she felt—

"But I know well what my state will be, both
From others telling me, and my own sight.
I cannot marry; I must be his concubine;
I will have children that are his but not
Legitimate; and someday I must watch
Him marry someone else, and then wait for
Brief but precious moments stolen with him.
None of this can I change, nor can I help
Loving him just as I do."

Penelope
Thought that the girl would break down and cry now,
But instead she held the queen's eye to continue:

"On the ship King Odysseus, your husband,
Talked deeply to me. He knows that I saw
Him with his deadly bow break our defences
And cause our destruction; and he knows that
My hatred for him over that cannot
Be subdued"—

                 Penelope shifted uneasily,
But Pelagia still held her gaze—

"But he is wiser than I could imagine,
And he made me see things I had not thought of.
And he made me vow that I would never
Harm Telemachus or you or any of your family,
Nor do harm to Ithaca in any way,
And I will keep my vow, as I have kept
Any vow I made. Now you know all, and
My life is in your hands to do with as you wish."

Through all this Penelope could see the hard
Truth in the depths of the girl's dark eyes;
She was shaken Pelagia could be so honest
And so knowing of the situation.
When Pelagia had finished, she dropped her gaze
And sat back in her chair, awaiting the queen's
Pleasure, who sat for a moment, thoughtful,
Then said,

           "It is seldom that I have heard
One so truthful as you have been, hard as
It must be to face such truths. I understand
What you have been through and why you feel
The way you do. It seems the Gods give you
Few options—you must love, and you have no
Power in loving. But they also favour you—
You were saved from destruction; you have gained
The love of a prince; and you have acquired skills
That will bring you respect in this country."

Then the queen smiled grimly.

                "Women are not
Given much choice in this life. You were, in fact,

Fortunate to fall in love with a man who
Fell in love with you. If your life had continued
At home without incident, you would have
Had little say in who would marry you.
I myself was given to Odysseus
Through negotiation when he courted
Helen. I learned to love him deeply, and
He has been steadfast to me in turn.
But circumstances can make our lives a trial,
As the war did in our case. I had to
Struggle to keep my honour and my home here
For twenty years, and those years meant one child
Only. My son is precious to me—I
Pray you will keep him happy and protected
As much as you can do. Your place is now
Here; and may the Gods help you to make it
A place of peace."

Then she turned again to the fire, and Pelagia
Realized that she had now finished with her.
Moved by what she had heard, and now comforted
By the queen's attitude toward her, she
Left quietly and returned to her room.

As soon as the weather cleared, architects
Were sent to choose the appropriate place
For the house and garden, and soon the work
Began. Pelagia was there every day,
Concerned with every detail—her work space
In the house close to the garden, where
Her plants and herbs could be stored properly,
How the garden should be laid out, all done
In deep consultation with Amunet,
Who showed the full extent of her wisdom
And knowledge in all these areas.
Before the fall finished and winter began,
The house had been completed and the garden
Planted, and with a sigh of pleasure
Pelagia moved from the palace to her own place,
In which a room close to the workshop
Had been constructed for Amunet,

So that she was always available
To her mistress and continued to teach
Her further in their arts. But she remained
Secluded; and only once, when the queen
Visited the completed complex for
The first time, did she catch a glimpse of her,
Startling the queen. Only when both Pelagia
And Telemachus told her of the Egyptian's
Purpose, and that Helen had lent her to
Complete Pelagia's training, did she
Relax. But they did not tell her that when
The wedding took place she would be returned.
Besides those that she planted, the prudent girl
Had stores of drugs that she could use at once,
And when she was in her house, she began
To see patients and others who stopped by—
Some with internal complaints, which she could
Sooth; others with wounds or sores that she cured
With ointments and unguents; and, quietly,
Potions for women and girls to help them
With their husbands or their suitors, or with
Infertility or its opposite.
Throughout these appointments Amunet,
Not seen by the others, advised her.
Her reputation grew, and Penelope's
Respect for her was strengthened and her place
Secured in the family.

One day Halitherses, Medon, and Mentor
Met in discussion; and shortly after
They brought Telemachus to join them.
Mentor came shortly to the point of the meeting.

"Prince Telemachus, in discussion here
I have heard of your betrothal to great
Nestor's daughter, Polycaste. We think,
Now that Pelagia has shown her usefulness,
That the queen should be told. Would you agree
That we do so together?"

The prince had feared this moment, and the thought
Of facing his mother alone with this news

Dismayed him. He agreed, although he wished
That this moment could be delayed longer.
Accordingly they all went to meet the queen
In the long hall. She was surprised at their request
For a meeting, and had arranged herself
In her chair with others set out around her.
They bowed to her; Telemachus kissed her
On her cheek; and then they all sat down.
The queen looked at them, sitting there, serious
And uncomfortable, and was intrigued.

"For what reason have you asked to see me?
You all look as though the kingdom is about
To fall!"

Mentor cleared his throat and then spoke first.

"Queen Penelope, wife of the great Odysseus,
We come on the orders of your husband
Given before he went alone on his quest."

He then turned to look at Telemachus,
Who realized that he would have to tell
What had happened.

"Mother, you have heard that we did honour
To Nestor at his funeral—in fact,
It was my father who gave the splendid
Oration at the ceremony.
What you may not know is that Nestor had
Married quietly during the Trojan War
Aristomachê, daughter of a defeated chieftain."

"Yes?"
        Said the queen, uncertain where this
Was leading.

"She had a daughter, Polycaste,
Whom I met first when I came to the
Gerentian king looking for father.
She was then fourteen and had the task
Of bathing and oiling me."

His mother
Frowned, beginning to worry where this
Was leading.

"It turned out that Nestor found me a good
Choice for a son-in-law, both as a person
And for the two countries. We did not know
This to begin with, but after I met her
It became clear, both to father and myself."

The queen's frown deepened.

"After much thought,
Father thought such a match would benefit
Both that land and ours."

"And he agreed to this?"
His mother now exclaimed in agitation.

"Could he not have consulted me, delayed
Any conclusion until we could have come
To a mutual decision?"

Medon
Hastily came to the abashed prince's aid.

"The time had to be then, Queen Penelope,
Or there could have been strife between Nestor's
Land and the one adjoining it. The match
Is a good one for all concerned, we vow it!"

And the two advisors nodded gravely.
Penelope, distraught, turned to her son,

"And what do you think of this match? Do you
Feel forced to take this girl in marriage?"

Telemachus turned red, and then replied.

"I understand what father feels about
The union between our two peoples.
But as for the girl—mother, she compares
In beauty to Helen herself, and I
Would be happy to have her as a wife."

"Would you, now? What was she when you first met her?
Fourteen? And now sixteen? Still a child?
What can she bring you at this age, young as she is?"

Halitherses now spoke.
                                    "We all recognize
Her youth. For this reason, although he agreed
To the betrothal, Odysseus made sure
That no marriage would take place till his return.
He has told them that his pilgrimage will last
At least a year, giving the girl time to mature."

"So that she will be but one year younger
Than was your concubine when you became
Lovers?"
                    Penelope shot back.

Angered, her son retorted,
                                    "No older than were you
When father took you as his wife."

His mother turned white with rage, and the two
Stood face to face in angry confrontation.
Mentor felt it best to interpose between them.

"And that match was one made by the Gods,
As you both show the proof. Please, I beg you
Both, consider what this means for our land."

The queen forced herself to become more calm;
But then she said, more quietly,

"This girl's mother, then, is the daughter of
A chieftain slain? What makes her different
From Pelagia, whose fate is similar?"

Medon spoke gently.

"The difference, Queen Penelope, is that
Nestor chose to make her his wife in his
Late age, and thus she has been given
Legitimacy. Pelagia has no such advantage."

"Indeed she doesn't,"
                                    said the queen grimly.

Then, turning to her son again,
"And how will you reconcile the two women?
Does this girl love you?"

        "She adores him,"
Said Medon for the prince.

"So what will you do?"

        "I don't know,"
Said Telemachus abjectly; and his mother
Saw that he was truly torn between the
Two women.

      She softened, then sighed.

"You men complicate our lives more than you
Resolve them. It is evident that I
Have little say in this matter. Does
Pelagia, your concubine, know of this betrothal?"

Her son spoke so quietly he could
Scarcely be heard.
        "Yes, she knows all."

Penelope was surprised at this
Revelation, and that Pelagia
Had kept silent over it, and the queen
Realized that Pelagia was stronger
Than any of them knew.

        "Very well.
I assume that nothing need be announced
Until Odysseus returns—if he returns?"

The three, startled by her last comment, nodded.
Then she sent them off so that she could muse
On what would happen in the family.

While the builders had swarmed over her house,
Making sure that rock married with rock,
The wooden lintels and frames planed and fit smooth,
So that the house could stand trim and proud,
Pelagia, when she had time, rode her horse,

Sometimes accompanied by Telemachus as they galloped,
Their hair free in the breeze,
And sometimes on her own, when she let her horse trot quietly
As she explored the rocky island.
On one of these solitary journeys,
As she ranged remote from the palace,
She came across a fine farm, large,
With a vineyard in neat well-tended rows,
And an ample orchard bristling with trees
Of all sorts, pears and apples, olives and figs.
On the edge of the vineyard, beside a new stone retaining wall,
She saw a small group harvesting the grapes,
Now lush and bursting with their sweet juices.
In their midst she saw an ancient man, their master,
Dressed in good but modest working clothes,
With a strong woven shirt, leggings of fresh oxhide
Strapped to his legs to defend him
From the scratch or scrape from vines
And supple gloves to combat the aggressive thorns.
Looking more closely, Pelagia realized with a shock
That he was Odysseus's father, the former King Laertes.
She had met him only once before, at a palace feast,
When he had been dressed richly for that occasion
And she had been introduced to him by his grandson,
Who treated him with guarded affection,
As did Penelope.
Because he had not appeared since and no one spoke of him
He had faded into the shadows of her memory;
Only now did she start to consider his continued absence.
Intrigued, she guided her horse to the group,
Who were surprised that a rider approached them
And more surprised that it was a woman.
She dismounted lightly and turned her horse
Over to a workman, who, astonished,
Took it to graze beside one of the heavy laden trees.
The group parted to let her approach the old man,
Who stood there stooped but alert.

"Greetings to you, King Laertes, noble father of Odysseus,"
Pelagia said as she made graceful obeisance to him.

He squinted at her in the bright sunlight,
Then recognized her and made a brusque acknowledgement.

"Go and make sure drink is ready for us at the lodge,"

He ordered one of his field hands, who, agape, backed away
And ran toward a building that Pelagia could see
A distance beyond the orchard.

"Walk back with me,"
                    Laertes said,
And they began to walk slowly through the orchard,
The trees lined on each side of them
Their green-leaved branches bowing over them
To refresh them with their shade.

"Is this your farm?"

Pelagia politely asked,
Then bit her tongue for asking the obvious.

But Laertes did not seem to mind.
                       "My very own,"
He muttered, and for a brief time
All was silent save for the leaves' quiet rustle
And the occasional cry of a bird in distant branches.
Then he stopped to look around,
His wrinkled and leathery face looking with pride
About him.

        "I made this farm myself,
Spading the plot and planting these trees,
And placing the vines here"
                —gesturing behind him—
"And on the slopes farther on"—

              and Pelagia saw
That the vineyard was larger than she thought,
With the lines of vines extending up the steep incline
A distance on.

       As a man may carry tight-lipped within him
Some private thought not to be breathed into the air,
So Telemachus had said little of his grandfather,

Nor had she been told of the old man's past,
Although she knew that he once had been the king.
She now wondered at this great farm,
Her curiosity unleashed.

          "You made this farm?"

"With my own hands. Each of these trees
I gave a home and named."

          And he
Pointed at each tree as they started off again,
And said its name.

          "This section here I gave
To my son when he was little—thirteen pear,
Ten apple, forty fig—and you can see
How many more there are now. And fifty
Vine rows I promised him then, and look
At their extent now."

          Pelagia gazed,
Open-mouthed for once, but she could not speak,
So many questions crowding her mind,
And they walked again in silence
Until they came to the verge of the orchard.
There before them was King Laertes's lodge,
Well-timbered and capacious, around which
Were clustered a row of sheds, some for his bondsmen,
Some for the pigs and other animals found in
Fields stoutly enclosed. They crossed to the lodge's entrance.
Pelagia found herself in a sparse room of rock and wood,
With its dirt floor and planed chairs and stools
And table, all contributing to the heady mixture
Of smells of animals and fruit and humans.
A woman almost as old as Laertes himself
Was pouring cool wine and water into plain goblets
When she saw them. She had heard of the girl
From the field hand and could not help but stare at her
In disapproval. But while the old man sat
And caught his breath, Pelagia noticed
Branches of herbs on shelves, and soon she was having

An animated conversation with the pleased woman
About their properties. During this time
The old man sat quietly sipping, his gaze on Pelagia
Like an owl intently watching its prey.
Finally he spoke.

        "What they say of you I see is true.
You do have knowledge of the plants."

She smiled
And nodded as he gestured to her to sit opposite,
Where the old woman gave her a goblet.

Silence as both sipped for a time. Then Pelagia,
Inquisitive, asked,
        "I have not heard much
About you, Lord Laertes. May I know your story?"

Like an old lion suddenly alert to some new motion,
Laertes looked sharply at the young woman before him;
Then, seeing from her open and frank gaze
Her sincere wish to know, he sighed, then grimly smiled.

"This land we occupy here I won with
My Cephallonians, conquering Ithaca
When I was young and a mighty warrior.
In those glorious days I extended
My kingdom among these harsh islands.
The city of Nericus I besieged and sacked,
Formidable fortress that it was judged,
Supposedly secure in its isolation
On a cape projecting far out to sea.
Thus I proved myself the worthy son of Arcesius,
The son of mighty Zeus."

        For a moment
His deep shrouded eyes blazed, and Pelagia
Could see the warrior the old man had been;
She saw now where his son's prowess began,
And she shuddered with the memory of his acts.
But then a furrow crept into her brow.

"How do I find you, then, working here,

Upon this farm, which you told me in the orchard
That you had started long ago, before your son
Was born?"

        Old King Laertes sighed, and
A long moment passed in silence as his eyes
Focused far away on distant memories.
Then he let his gaze fall once more on her.

"After I had extended my kingdom with Ithaca
And brought back riches from my mainland raids,
I wooed and won the daughter of Autolycus,
Beautiful and worthy Anticleia,
Whom I adored and who loved me in return,
Giving me the best gift I could ever have,
My son Odysseus."

        Here again he stopped,
Moved to tears, and Pelagia waited patiently
For his passion to subside. Finally he went on.

"After we had wed, I showed her around
My kingdom, with its mountains
Up thrust on these islands. I would have had
Us live on Cephalonia, with its pure beaches
And its lush vegetation. Instead, she
Brought me back here and pointed to the place
Where we find ourselves.
'You have shown your worth as warrior and king,'
She said, 'Now prove yourself more strong
By creating in this barren place, with your own hands,
Life in all its abundance, with fruit and olive trees,
And a rich vineyard, and animals,
Even as you rule your kingdom.'
In my abiding love for her I did as she bade,
And also built her the palace that you know
And which Odysseus with his own hands
Added to and changed. During this time
I continued to rule, with Anticleia at my side.
When Odysseus was a little boy, as I
Have told you, I showed him what I had done here
And what I promised him."

                    Again he stopped
And sipped, brooding on what he had said,
And once more Pelagia waited patiently.
He spoke again, but this time his voice betrayed
That he was deep in his memories, living there.

"Odysseus was never tall, but always strong,
And quick-witted like his mother and more,
His wily grandfather, Autolycus.
As he grew older, we could see his talents,          .
Both in his warrior's skills and even more
In his sagacity, his clear thought that cut through
To the true substance of each problem.
In this he was helped by his mother,
Who honed his wits as I honed his other skills,
And who had always been my chief and wisest council."

Yet again he paused as he remembered
His beloved wife, his eyes glistening,
And he took moments for his breathing to subside.
Pelagia was astonished by what she had heard,
For although her father had treated her
More like a son, he did not consult with
Her mother, for women were not considered
Capable of matters other than house and children.
But her wonder grew at what next he said.

"Because I had married my wife at an older age,
By the time my son was approaching maturity
I was about to pass from an age in which
Strength and agility were essential for a ruler
To lead against dissension both outside
And within the kingdom, and my labours
As ruler and on the farm began to weigh
Heavily upon me. For several months
Anticleia pondered the situation.
Then she persuaded me on what we must do:
Odysseus as prince would be introduced
To the duties of ruling. I acted on her advice,
And Odysseus, still approaching manhood,
Began to take over much that I did,

And showed such brilliance in his actions,
Resolve and diplomacy that within a year
I was confident that he could rule on his own,
Ceded the kingship to him, and returned here
To work on this farm, which had gained my devotion.
Barely eighteen, he fulfilled the promise
That his mother and I had seen and became
A superb ruler, quelling discontent
Within our islands and gaining a reputation
For his daring raids."

                    Another pause while
The old woman refilled their cups.

"Then came the contest for Helen's hand;
His winning of Penelope and her arrival here,
Where we were won over by her charm
And character; his renovation with his own hands
Of the palace, and the happy birth of my grandson.
All seemed happy; but then the abduction of Helen
Led, despite his efforts to act mad, to his involvement
In the incident, first diplomatically,
And then, when all else failed, in terrible war.
Away he sailed, with the ships carrying
Our best warriors, and leaving me to rule
Once again."

                    He sighed and drank deeply
As if to drown his memories in the draft,
Pelagia thought. His face appeared older now,
The creases in his forehead and his lined cheeks
Seeming to deepen. Then, gathering his strength again,
He went on.

"For the next ten years we laboured on,
Supported by Anticleia and our able lords.
It was a hard time for us, with fears growing
Like a crawling blight from rumours
And infrequent messages which told of the death
Of many of our able young men.
Finally, word came of Achaean victory,
And we all rejoiced, waiting with eagerness

For the arrival of a triumphant Odysseus.
But no word came, no news about him found,
Only catastrophic news of the murder
Of Agamemnon and the fatal shipwrecks
That took their toll in many kingdoms.
And we waited as the days and months and years
Inexorably ground on without knowledge of our son.
Anticleia, even more than myself
And Penelope, occupied in the raising of Telemachus,
Felt passionately the suspected loss of her son,
And she slowly declined in despair, until one night,
As I held her hand and she could no longer weep,
She covered her face and died, that hand, which
Had held mine so firmly and warmly over the years,
Slipping lightly from me."

                He paused only briefly,
Still caught up in the grief of his loss, the lines
On his face rivulets of tears, the old woman
Behind him, her hands on his slumped shoulders,
Glaring across at the young woman
Who had reopened ancient wounds.

"With her death I could not contain my grief and despair,
Turned over the kingdom to Penelope and the lords,
And came to live here, alone except
For those who faithfully have served me."

He put up his hand to hold that of the old woman,
Who herself began silently to cry.
Then he straightened slightly, aware
Of the observant woman opposite him.

"And here I have remained over ten years,
Awakening from my anguish with the return,
Unexpected but joyous, of my son"—

He straightened up, and his eyes blazed;
Pelagia caught a moment of his fierceness
As a warrior, and her pulse quickened
Despite herself—

"And our defeat of the families of the slain suitors."

Then, grimly,
             "And now he has sailed away again,
And again we must wait, with no word, no hope."

He shook fiercely, as if to cleanse himself
From the grimness of his story, as a bear
Will shake the water from its fur, and then
He rose.
             "We must return to work."

                                    A nod
To the old woman, who made obeisance to him,
And then he strode from the lodge, Pelagia
Matching him step for step. Reaching the orchard,
She thanked him and he nodded, then turned back
To return to the grape gathering
As she galloped back to his former palace.

# Canto 12
# THE UNKNOWN NORTH

*Buzzing*
*Flies buzzing*
*Droning    droning*

As one asleep hears in the dark strange voices
And thinks them in a dream, but then half-awake
Hears them more clearly, and yet cannot waken,
Half in sleep, half conscious, and in this state
Feels terror unrestrained without the means
To conquer it, so Odysseus tried to swim awake;
But now understanding that the voices
That had sounded far away were clearer now,
Made no motion nor his eyes opened, but
Took careful stock of his own person.
Pain he first felt; harsh pain through his shoulder;
Then the heat of fever through his body,
Which ached from the onslaught. Vaguely
He heard voices of women and a man, and
Then sank back into unconsciousness,
The buzz of flies first loud, then fading far away.

*Flies again*
*Flies still*
*Weapons clashing*
*Screams   of men   women   children*
*A citadel*
*Fire raging over the roofs*
*Licking high into the air*
*Smoke through the streets*
*From the buildings*
*Over the town*
*I hack before me*

*Men groan as I cut them down*
*Women terrified as I cut their defenseless throats*
*Children screaming   cowering   stabbed to silence*
*Nothing around me but flames and destruction*
*Flames and destruction*
*Now ruins   ashes   no living thing*
*Except the flies*
*The flies and the smoke*

The smoke pushed him to consciousness.
Again the pain and the fever, and smoke
And voices somewhere around him, but he
Kept his eyes shut still and listened to try
To understand what was said, who said it,
But again the flies grew louder and then
They faded away and away and away ...

*Buzz*
*Flies*
*Always flies*
*Alone*
*Alone*
*A black current*
*Nothing but black to the thin horizon*
*Nothing but darkness in the sky*
*Hard to tell the black water from it*
*Nowhere to go*
*Movement neither forward nor back nor sideways*
*Drifting*
*Alone*
*No sound from the water*
*Only the buzzing drone*
*On and on*
*Then a great cloud of smoke*
*Covering the sky*
*Obliterating any sense of place*
*The smell of the smoke*

Once more the smoke awoke him, and he lay there,
Eyes still closed, sensing his body's state
And listening for voices once again.

*No longer feverish*
*The pain is now just an ache*
*Unless I try to move that shoulder*
*Not a good idea*
*I'm naked*
*Naked under furs and on them as well*

He opened his eyes to just a slit
To see where he was. Between his lashes
He saw a fire in the middle of a hut,
And beyond that a hide draped across
An entrance; a dirt floor, unswept, unkempt;
And to the left of the flames an old dame,
Dressed in furs, crouched close to the fire.
Then a great thirst afflicted him, and he had to
Cry for water. The old woman heard him
And quickly went outside, where he could hear
Her telling someone that he was awake.
The man grunted and went off as she returned
And brought a vessel to him from which
He drank huge drafts. He tried to raise himself,
But the pain and his own weakness forced him
Down. The old woman stayed with him, watching
Carefully to see what he would do. Then
The hide was lifted, and a burly man,
Swarthy, with a heavy face, a large beard
And beetling brow, stepped in and crossed to
The supine man, standing to look down at him
With a twisted grin.

       "You've managed to live,
I see. Well, what you brought us is not worth
Much, except for the knife—we have no need
Of an oar, and your clothes and bags are useless.
You must have been a thief to find such things,
But also crazy to carry round an oar
In these mountains."

       And he gave a booming
And harsh laugh.

"But once your wound heals, given
Your physique, you should make a useful slave.
You will find it better to obey all
Commands here than otherwise."

And he gave
Odysseus a kick in the ribs that made him
Gasp with pain. Already he could not keep
Conscious; and as he slipped back into darkness
He heard the man say,

"Make sure he recovers,
And tell me when he is fit again."

And
As the old woman grovelled, he strode from
The hut and Odysseus fainted once again.

The next time Odysseus awoke, he made
No pretence of sleeping but opened his eyes
At once. He still felt very weak, but the
Fever was now gone. The old woman saw that
He was healing well, and she brought him gruel
And water, helping him to eat and drink
Because his wound was still in the early
Stages of recovery. Days then slipped by
As he grew stronger, and as this time passed
The crafty Ithacan drew out from her
Where he was. He was in a high mountain
Fastness, where he had been brought after the ambush.
Strangers seldom passed by, and when they did
They were robbed and killed or made slaves, as he would be.
The man he had seen was confirmed as the
Chieftain of the citadel, and all there
Feared him for his brutality and strength.
His dagger and his oar, he had her reveal,
Were now displayed in the chieftain's house
As booty; trophies had no value here.
In turn he volunteered his story, for
He knew she would tell it to her master:
He had, he said, been a soldier in the war,
And when he had returned found his home gone,

His wife taken by another man.
In revenge he had killed him and been exiled
From the country. He had wandered far and wide,
Until at last an oracle had said
That he could propitiate the Gods
Only by travelling through these wild mountains,
Their valleys and their passes, carrying
His last two possessions, his oar and dagger,
Until he came to a shrine where the Gods
Would finally relieve him of his burden.
The old woman was impressed by his tale
And hastened to tell it to the chieftain.
During this time Odysseus grew stronger,
But always he feigned a greater weakness
Than he had. But at night he was still haunted.

*Towns burning in the distance*
*Women*
*Now slaves*
*Stumbling    herded to the beaches*
*Weeping*
*Now his slaves*
*The Trojan woman    slave to Thoas*
*Now his slave*
*The look in her eyes*

*Penelope's women who betrayed her*
*In the courtyard*
*Terrified*
*Hung in a line together*
*Straining for a breath*
*As they dangled and twitched*
*As they slowly strangled*
*For what*
*For what*
*And the flies buzz*

Now he was well enough to rise and move
Around; but his feet were pinioned so that
He could shuffle only, and his arms
Were bound as well. Despite this, he moved

Continually, letting his muscles work,
And in the hut at night, released from his bonds,
When he saw the old servant asleep,
Silently he exercised as best he could.

There came a day when he was brought forth
To the chieftain in a clearing before
The town.

      "You have lazed about enough; now
You can be put to work and become useful
To us. But to help you to remember
Always to obey me, you will have this."

And he had the Ithacan bound to a post
And whipped him with a lash until his back
Was raw and bloody; then he was helped back
To the hut. But the next day, while he still
Suffered from the scars of the lash, he was
Brought out, unpinioned, to start his work.
He had to fell trees, lop off their branches,
And chop them into wood and kindling for
The fire. While he did this heavy work,
Two men, with weapons, guarded him at all times
And then he was returned to the hut and pinioned again.
By now in this mountain place winter had
Gripped the citadel, and he was dressed in
Furs, body and foot, to keep from freezing.
In the first days of his travail, he still
Had not regained his strength, and several times
Was beaten when he was too exhausted
To cut more; but as time went on his muscles
Regained their previous strength, although he
Still pretended to be weaker than he was.
As the weeks wearily crept on, Odysseus
Now experienced to the full a slave's life.
Like a beetle toiling without pause
To remove a mote from its ordained path
Or the ceaseless ant or bee, he laboured,
Blows his one reward, eating a luxury,
Waking one long misery, his nocturnal sleep

The only escape; and all these indignities
He nurtured in his mind for revenge.
He was fed little, so that hunger was
His companion constantly, but he said
Nothing and endured. Months went by, and all
This time he studied carefully the town
And where all was located in it; the nature
Of the stockade and the gates; and outside it,
The valley and the mountains round about.
He learned from the guards that some distance north
There was a sacred cave which none dared enter;
That sometime before men had gone in and
Never returned on more than one occasion.
He made note of where they said it was
And what the route would be. Winter aged;
The snow began to turn rotten; and the streams
Swelled and torrents rushed down the mountain sides.
Still he did not act, for with the weakened snow
There were sudden avalanches that he saw,
Carrying all before them. Finally, spring
Blossomed, with meadow flowers and the few
Trees that showed their shy green leaves. Now as he
Worked he memorized the paths of the forest
And, unseen by his guards, walked with his eyes
Shut so that he could move easily in blind night.
In the town he did the same and noted carefully
The bar on the gate and those who guarded it,
As well as those who stood guard at the house
Of the chieftain himself. He had over the months
Learned to remove his bindings at night
So that he could exercise in those early times,
And he could replace them exactly so that
No one knew he could do it. At last
He was ready. That night he freed himself
And carefully arranged his furs so that
If the old woman looked across to him when
She waked, she would think him still there.
During the winter no guard had been left
Outside the hut in the frigid weather,
And none had been assigned, for he appeared

To be docile and his bonds sufficient.
Silently he crept through the pitch-black streets
Until he reached the chieftain's house. No guards
Had yet been assigned here as well after
The winter months—he thanked the Gods for his luck—
And he found a way to enter without sound.
In the chieftain's small hall, the fire now embers,
He found his dagger hung on a peg, and
The oar, without its sheath, leaning against the wall.
He retrieved the weapon, then crept up
The steep stairs noiselessly. He could tell
By the snores where the chieftain lay, apart
From his women. Like a shadow he moved
To the slumbering man, then swiftly from
The back swung his arm around his neck, his
Other hand clapped over the startled man's mouth.
Strong as the man was, he was helpless in
The veteran warrior's implacable grip,
Thrash how he may. Close to his ear, he breathed,

"Know in your last moments that it is
Odysseus, hero of Troy, that you dishonoured,
And die as you should, a brute without shame
Or value."

   And his powerful arms strained
Until the struggling man's neck cracked and broke,
And the body slumped back onto the bed.
Odysseus then slipped back down the stairs,
The women still fast asleep, unknowing,
Grasped his oar, and left the house. As a black
Panther creeps through the darkness of the night,
Invisible to its prey until too late,
So Odysseus moved through the murky streets
Until he reached the gates. There he saw two guards
Warming themselves at a fire near the entrance
And murmuring grumpily to each other
As they squatted there sleepily. In
The flickering shadows born of the flames
He crept behind them, and with a leap slashed
Their throats before they could make a sound.

Then he strained to lift the large bar from
The brackets in which it rested. For
One moment he thought that he could not pry it loose,
And he redoubled his efforts, his muscles bulging,
And then it moved, and he used all his strength
And agility to keep it from any noise
As he brought it to the ground. He slowly
Opened slightly one of the gates, making sure
That it did not rasp against its base, then
He returned to the fire, picked up a blazing stick
For a torch, and retrieving his oar, left the town.
He sped along the path that he had memorized,
Letting the torch help him for a while, and
Took no time to rest, for though he had part
Of the night left, he knew that soon he would
Come to where he would not know the route well
And would be compelled to slow and use the torch.
It was thus he travelled through the night, and
When the first grey signs of the impending dawn
Made clearer where he was, he knew that
In the town the bodies would be discovered
And the chase begin. Now he found himself
At the end of the valley, the mountains
Closing off all ways from it; and he climbed
The long steep slope. Once he looked back and saw
The town in the far distance and below;
And from it he now saw issuing a band
Of men who picked up his trail and began
Running after it. Still he hurried on,
And some distance from him, he saw above
The entrance of the cave for which he searched.

As he approached, the cave's entrance felt like
The mouth of some huge beast whose maw
Would devour him; but grim Odysseus
Thrust his torch before him and moved forward,
Then grunted and jerked back.
Like a demented mob skulls gaped at him
From all around, and piles of bones heaped the floor
Throughout the charnel of the large cavern.

In the wavering torchlight the shadows
Flicked in and out of the hollow sockets
And the lipless grins shifted as he turned.

*Their burial site.*

He moved carefully among the grisly mounds
To where he found the rock descending
To form the back of this crude crypt
And there he found rough furs that hung
From a wooden rail supported by thick posts
He pushed through them and in the flickering light
He saw a treasure horde—bracelets and ornaments,
Goblets and vases, armour and weaponry,
Of gold and silver, bronze and clay
Were heaped in profusion in this second cave.
Odysseus, now concerned that he not be trapped,
Moved past these rich glittering hills
To the rear, which to his dismay he found
To be only the rocky end of the dark space.
For a moment he felt panic and despair,
Without a means of escape from the mob
Who soon would reach this place;
But then he turned back to look more closely
At this rough wall and trace it with his finger.
As he did so, he discovered that a thin line
That curved about it revealed a rock
That sealed this wall shut.

*Athena, my patron Goddess,*
*Aid me now in this dire moment*
*And give me the strength I need*
*To move this rock!*

And he laid down torch and oar,
And, his back to the rough surface
Pushed with all his powers,
His mighty thighs and legs strained to the utmost.
Nothing happened for a moment;
Then he felt, almost imperceptibly, a shift,
A tiny shudder of the rock, and he again
Bent his full strength against it.

Again it moved slightly, and again he strove;
Then, finally, the rock moved farther,
And he continued until it had moved enough
For him to slide through the slight opening.
His torch revealed a rough passageway that disappeared
Ahead into the darkness.
He returned to the second cavern,
Then quickly sped outside to pick up several sticks
To renew the torch when it would die.
He heard, more clearly now, the men of the village
Now much closer; he ducked back in the cave
And hurried to the second cavern, where he stopped
Only to arm himself with a sword of bronze,
Its hilt ornate with silver and its sheath covered in ivory,
Then took his torch and sticks and oar and bundle,
Slipped through the narrow crevice,
And with great effort pushed the rock
Back to its previous niche.
Now he moved cautiously along,
The air old and musty.
The natural tunnel, for that is what
It now appeared to be, seemed to stretch
Far before him as he pursued his way.
For some time it continued level,
And then it slanted slightly down,
Just enough to confuse his senses
With the incline. Time seemed to slow and stop
As he moved ever forward, only the flames
Granting him a little space to see both front and back.
Three torches burned through in this journey;
He lit the final one and prayed that it would last
Until some other light would guide him.
But finally it too flickered out, and he was forced
To move on in utter darkness,
Each unseen step taken with care and caution.
Now he had no way of knowing what he did
Except for his touch and step; darker now
Than in that Stygian murk when he journeyed to Hades.
As he went thus, his inner sight forced him to see
What he had endured for the past several months—

The pain and hunger, rage and submission of his captivity,
The true feeling of what a slave's life must be,
And all the harsh existence of those without hope.
For what seemed an eternity, or no time at all,
He crept this way; then, far off,
He heard the whisper of a sound,
And as he progressed farther he recognized it
As the sound of rushing water;
And soon the air was damper and where he trod
Began to be less secure and more slippery.
Each step he now took with great care,
Keeping one hand upon the rocky side,
That arm extended before him
As he felt the rock slip by.
The noise of the torrent grew louder;
Then, suddenly, his hand reached to nothing
And he stopped abruptly.
The roar was now close to him;
And as he stood there, he realized
That he could see faintly before him,
A light so dim it barely penetrated
To where he was. But he now made out
That he had stopped at an abrupt edge;
And sinking to his knees to keep from falling
From this vertiginous ledge, he looked carefully
To see as much as he could within this murk
Of mist and water. He found himself at the side
Of a cataract that plunged from high above
Through a crevice which admitted what light there was
And descended to subterranean rapids a distance below him.
Water fiercely sprayed upon him, so that he had to
Squint. He saw the falls, like a quick thick oily snake,
Rushing pell-mell down the rocky cliff,
And when he looked down, he discovered below him
Rubble piled high on either side of the roiling pool
Where the plummeting water crashed,
And when he looked immediately below him
As he crouched on hand and knee
He saw the rocks crept close to where he perched.
But all was slick with the water's spray and mist,

And he would have the length of two tall men
Before he could gain sufficient footing,
Perilous as it may be, to reach the rapids below.
He took care to inspect, as well he could,
The rock face between him and that place,
Examining any footholds he might find
Among the cracks and rocks that jutted out.
Finally, with a fervent prayer to his patron Goddess,
He strapped his oar and bundle to his back,
Using strips that he tore fiercely from his cloak,
Then gingerly, with slow and cautious movement,
He lowered himself over the edge.
A toe touched a rock; he tested its stability,
Then searched with one hand for a crack
By which to hold his weight. His fingers touched one;
He searched it carefully, then reached his fingers into it,
And tested whether they would slip or hold him.
Satisfied, he let his foot rest on the rock,
His hand in the crack, and let go of the ledge.
As his hand strained to hold him close to the face,
He searched with the other foot for the next hold,
And his free hand as well. Thus he continued down,
Creeping painfully and uncertainly, at a pace
That seemed an eternity to his overburdened muscles,
Like an ant scouting down the side of a rough wooden wall,
Wary of anything that might obstruct it or take its life.
At last he reached the rubble and carefully stepped
On its chaotic surface. As he let go of his final handhold,
The slippery rocks beneath his foot gave way,
And he plunged headlong into the foaming pool below.
From deep within it he finally swam up to reach its surface,
Gasping for precious air, only to find himself
Carried inexorably along by the fierce current
Of the rapids. All he could see, as he was pulled under
Then up as he sped along, were the rocky shores
From which he swam desperately to avoid being dashed
Against them. Gasping in the racing water, he was
Bounced from side to side; then, even as he strove more,
The light disappeared and he was again in darkness,
With no way of knowing where were the banks,

But was swept on helplessly, fighting for precious air,
Until suddenly the water rushed through a cleft
Into open air; he felt himself falling;
He plunged into another pool, and before he could respond,
He was carried swiftly on; his head glanced off a boulder
And true darkness overtook him.

# Canto 13
## ITHACA

From her spacious house, so recently built,
Pelagia looked out one way toward the palace,
Against which her own structure was nestled,
With a walk that linked them comfortably,
And another way out beyond the hill and town and harbour
To the sea itself. She never tired of watching it
In all its changing moods, both from the sun
Unadorned, which blazed down, making the waters black,
And from the scudding clouds that turned it grey,
Or when the mists and fog lay upon it
As a thick fleece can lie upon a floor.
This late fall day a cold wind blew under a dark sky,
Whipping the waves into a sullen froth,
And she moved her chair, with its graceful arms,
Inlaid with silver, as were its legs,
Closer to her glowing hearth,
Wrapping her woollen cloak around her for greater warmth.
The signs were now definite, she knew;
The sudden nausea in the morning,
And she had mixed and drunk potions
To alleviate how she felt; but now, as she sat here,
She smiled to herself, knowing that what she had planned
Had come to fruition, whether through what she had taken
To aid, or by natural means: she was pregnant,
And she knew that the child would arrive
Sometime before the marriage of Telemachus and Polycaste.
She had another month or so before she told him
And before Penelope would suspect her condition.
The thought of her lover sent a shiver through her,
And she wrapped the cloak around her still more tightly,
For each night he came to her and the flames leapt up again,

Each time just as fiercely as before.
Restless as she thought of him, she rose
And moved to her workroom,
Where she now had mortars and pestles,
Vases of all sizes and all shapes,
Vials and funnels, and other instruments
That she kept neatly in their places.
A fire in the centre of the room
Struggled against the chill as its smoke rose
Up, drifting toward the opening above.
Amunet was quietly at work, grinding
Herbs to a fine powder; she looked up, saw
Pelagia, studied her shrewdly, then
Smiled at her knowingly, and returned
To her work. Pelagia had smiled back.
She knew that Amunet understood
Her condition, for the Egyptian
Had suggested some of the remedies
To her; and she also was confident
That Amunet would keep her secret.
She paused for a moment, then moved through the room
To where she gained access to her garden behind,
High-walled and sheltered from the winds,
Where her plants were now secured in their ordered beds
And where young trees were carefully arranged
According to the need for shade as well as for variety.
Wrapping her cloak again around her body and her hair,
She walked along the paths gravelled in fine stone,
Intently looking to make sure plants had survived
And were now sleeping through the colder months.
Having made her rounds, she returned, satisfied, to the house
And again nestled at the warm heart of her hearth.
She enjoyed this early time of day, when she was alone,
No clients arriving hopeful of her skills to cure them
Or to help them in other ways.
The weather was too chill and wet to ride,
Which she dearly loved, nor could she at this time
Continue her practice with the sword and other weapons.
Then, as she thought of these activities,
Which the court frowned upon but which she did

Despite disapproval, but with Telemachus's protection,
She realized that soon she would have to stop both
To make sure nothing would harm the baby in her womb.
The thought startled her and made her aware
Of the new feelings now growing with the child inside her,
Feelings that forced her to understand how utterly
Her life had, and would, change with the new deep bond
Forged by this tiny babe, and the need to nurture
And protect this new life. Suddenly she, who had been strong,
Became vulnerable; her breath caught in her chest;
Tears began to well; she panicked
At the sweet turbulence within her;
And for a time she could not think
But sat overwhelmed with the emotions surging through her;
Then, spent from this tempest, she sat quietly,
Staring into the fire before her.
A servant entered to tell her that her first visitor had come.
With a new effort of will she roused herself
And stood to begin her day.

That night, after she had feasted with Penelope
And talked with Telemachus, now showing his new maturity
As a man and leader, she lay with him
And they made love; but even as she gave herself to him
She found that in her new state her love was more complex,
For he now was both her lover and the joint creator
Of what she harboured in her body,
And a new tenderness entered into their embrace
That surprised him but to which he could respond as well,
And their relationship began to grow in new ways.

Near to the end of the year,
Even as the weather seemed to shift continually,
From the cruel rains and winds to days
When Helios drove his chariot unobstructed
Across a blue and serene sky,
Pelagia inspected herself closely and concluded
That the time had come to inform the prince
And then his mother.
She sent a servant to ask the prince to see her.
Soon Telemachus trod in, concern in his eyes.

"Is something wrong?"

"Let us walk in the garden, my good prince."

The sun was now rising high in the sky,
Cloudless, an unexpected balmy day.
They walked among the paths, silent for the moment,
Side by sensed side, the keen-eyed Ithacan aware
That this woman, while not speaking, stayed close to him.
Finally she turned to him, her eyes downcast.

"You know that I love you beyond all else."

Touched, he replied,
                              "And I you."

She gave him a quick loving smile,
Then became more serious.

"We do not have much longer
Until your father returns and all of you go
For the marriage in Pylos."

Both moved and troubled, he embraced her closely.

"Whatever my marriage brings, I will still love you,
See you, and protect you throughout our lives!"

She raised her eyes to his,
And with a look so direct and vulnerable
That his heart almost stopped,
In a voice barely more than a breath, she said,

"And what of our child?"

For a moment Telemachus stood, his arms still about her,
Not comprehending what she had said;
Then with a sudden rush of understanding
He gasped; taking her by the shoulders,
He looked straight into her fearful eyes
And said without hesitation,

"Any child we have is our own and will be
Known as such, and loved by me."

With a cry of relief and love and happiness,
She melted into his arms, and they kissed tenderly
While time tiptoed away and left them there.

When it returned, they began to walk the paths again,
His arm around her waist.

"When is the birth expected?"

She remained silent for a moment,
Then, without looking at him, she replied,

"In early summer, shortly before your father
May return."

        "And before my marriage?"

"Yes."

They walked on again without words.
Then she turned again to him.

"We must tell your mother, the Queen,
Today, I hope."

        Surprised, he looked at her.
"Today? Why so soon?"

She smiled at his innocence and stroked her belly.
"I cannot now conceal that I am pregnant.
It is better that she know from our own lips
Than suspect that we wish to hide it from her."

Telemachus immediately understood
The truth of what she said, and he promised
Her that he would arrange such a meeting
For the afternoon. Then they continued to walk,
Murmuring about what the child may be like,
Already starting the slow growth of parenthood.

That afternoon they met Queen Penelope
Where she sat in her favourite chair
Thick white fleece like pure snow over it
Beside the hearth in the great hall,
With the gold and silver gleaming

As she spun her wool fine and soft.
As they approached, she spoke, her attention
Still on the spindle in her slender practised fingers.

"You asked to see me?"

"Yes, my queen and mother.
We have something to tell you."

The fingers continued their swift accomplished work.

"Yes?"

Telemachus, for once at a loss for words,
Turned to Pelagia, who stepped forward.

"My gracious Queen Penelope, Hera has blessed me
With the gift of a child in my womb."

For a barely perceptible moment the fingers paused,
Then carried on, the queen still intent on her work.

"Yes? And when does she propose you bear it?"

The couple looked at each other, slightly taken aback
By the queen's response.

"In the early summer, gracious Queen Penelope."

Only the sound of the working of the wool could be heard.

"I see. Before the expected return of King Odysseus?"

"Yes, mother,"
                    interjected Telemachus, concerned
That he had left Pelagia to bear the brunt of the interview.

"And before your marriage?"

"Yes."

The queen still did not look up, intent upon her spinning.

"You understand, of course, that, as has been said before,
This child will have no true royal status."

"Yes, we both understand."

"You also understand that this child appears
At the most awkward time,
For your bride will arrive to find both concubine and baby."

Pelagia flinched at the name, and Telemachus scowled,
But both knew the truth of what the queen had said.

"I think that for the good of all of us
Pelagia should move to some farther location
On the island until she has borne the child
And for some months following the marriage
While the bride settles here."

Telemachus was about to protest,
But his mother implacably continued.

"After that time, Pelagia may return.
In the meantime,"
                                    she said, forestalling Pelagia,

"We will make sure that your garden will be tended
And that a new one planted where you will live,
So that you may continue with the work
That we all have found so valuable.
And you both have, of course, my blessing
And good wishes for this child.
Now my son, please leave Pelagia
And myself together; I will speak to you later."

Nonplussed, Telemachus bowed and left the hall;
Glancing back, he saw his mother still spinning
While Pelagia stood waiting before her.

When he had gone, the queen stopped her spinning,
Laid her spindle in the basket, and looked at
The girl before her, who now stood impassively,
Awaiting what might come.

"Come closer."

Pelagia moved to the queen, who with her fingers
Carefully traced the shape of the girl's belly.

"Yes, it is true. You are blessed by Hera.
Why did you not tell us before?"

"I did not know if you would believe me
Until my state was more apparent."

The queen nodded.

"Of course. You continue to be prudent.
And of course you steal a march
On my son's bride with a child
Before she can have one.
It is unfortunate that you are so fertile
So soon in this relationship."

And she looked into Pelagia's eyes,
Who knew that the queen understood her plan.
But the girl said nothing and looked straight back
Into the queen's eyes without guile.
Penelope felt a sudden chill;
She knew Pelagia was intelligent
And unusual in many ways; but she had not thought
She would also prove so adept at strategy,
For Penelope was certain that although
The girl was young and healthy,
Well capable of conceiving at her age,
She had also helped herself with her knowledge
Of herbs and drugs that could provide assistance.

"Let us be clear with each other.
You hold a special place in this kingdom
For reasons yet to be understood but still respected,
And your skill and lore have made you beneficial
To the court and to the people,
And I respect you for it.
But for yourself and for your children,
There can be no legitimate place in this family.
My son loves you and you love him;
But his marriage will also be important,
Both to this country and to others,
And to his bride and to himself.
Do not come between them, I warn you;
Remember what you promised my husband,
Noble King Odysseus. I like you and enjoy

Your company; but I will note how you act
From now on. Please do not fail me."

She nodded then, and Pelagia,
Realizing the audience was at an end,
Gave her obeisance and left without a word.

That night Penelope had a long and troubling talk
With her disturbed son, and the next day
The arrangements began for Pelagia's move
To a far shore of the island.

# Canto 14
# THE VALLEY

Brightness pressed, insistent, on his eyelids
As strife-worn Odysseus came to himself,
But when he opened them he was blinded
And shut them tight, for he had not seen such light
Since he had entered the forbidden cave.
Then a shadow fell over his eyes, and he tried again,
This time more cautiously, squinting in care.

"You seem, good Odysseus, to arrive to us
In the same well-watered way,"

Said the figure above him, for he found himself
On a pallet laid, his oar, bundle, and sword removed
From his person and placed by him.
He could not yet make out the person before him,
For he was silhouetted by the sun,
But the voice seemed somewhat familiar,
Though he could not place it as yet.
He tried to raise himself up, but found his body
Too weak and bruised, and he fell back.

"You must rest for now," said the man,
"And we will send one to tend you
That has done so before."

Odysseus tried to speak, but dizziness overcame him,
And he fell back into a sleep.
He was roused by slender hands that bathed his face.
This time when he opened his eyes he could see better,
For the sun was now just sinking below the peaks,
And when he looked up he gasped in wonder,
For the woman tending him was Nausicaa,
The lovely daughter of King Alcinous,

The God-like king of the Phaeacians.
She smiled at his wonderment, even as she continued
With her ministrations, winding a bandage around his head
Where he had been cut when the rock hit him.

"Is this a dream, or am I back in Phaeacia?"

He croaked, then realized that he was unused to speaking
And that it had been some time since he had drunk or eaten.
Nausicaa's smile wavered, and her eyes darkened,
But then she recovered herself as she lifted his head
To drink greedily from a goblet held to his lips.

"My father will tell you all when you are better.
Now rest again."

                And her slender fingers stroked
His brow and temples, and her light caresses carried him
Back to sleep. This time when he awoke
He found himself in a tent lying on furs,
Fleeces warming and comforting his aching body,
But beside him sat the princess still, watching him with care.

"Noble Odysseus, do you feel you now can stand?"

He nodded; she helped him to his feet, supporting him
As he stood unsteadily at first, her young body
Close to him, her arms around his. He realized
As he regained his stability that he was now dressed
In clean clothes; and when she saw that he could stand alone,
She brought him a fine wool cloak, for he felt
The air chill with the sun now past the peaks.

"If you feel well enough, my lord, my father
Invites you to this evening's feast."

"I thank you, gracious and beautiful Nausicaa;
I believe I can accept his invitation."

She smiled and nodded; and seeing that he could stand alone,
She released him, saying,

"I am pleased that you can come. My brother,
The Lord Laodamas will come for you shortly."

And with a graceful nod of her head she left the tent.

For a moment Odysseus stood there, musing;
Then, finding that he could move freely,
Although his whole body ached, he moved out of the tent.
It was now dusk, with darkness quickly settling in;
He could see that he was in a valley,
With huge peaks towering on either side,
And he could hear a river rushing by not far off.
He saw other tents close to where he was, with small fires
Close to them, but he could not see farther on.

He pulled his cloak around him, the chill descending
With the sun and darkness enveloping the sky.
While he stood thus, a figure moved toward him,
And the voice that he had first heard spoke to him.

"Well, King Odysseus, have you now recovered enough
To join us for the banquet?"

"Indeed I have, Lord Laodamas."

For it was the elder son of King Alcinous
Who was the first to speak to him
In that brief moment when he was conscious
After his turbulent arrival. Odysseus recognized him
And also that he was ravenous after so long a time
Without food. They both clasped hands,
And then the prince led him along past the tents.
As they reached a rise, Odysseus could see the valley
Filled with lights from tents and their fires,
And he realized that a huge number were camping here.
But Laodamas said nothing, leading him on
Until they came to a huge fire blazing,
Surrounded by rich tables and fine chairs,
And there he was led to where Alcinous sat
With his wife, Queen Arête, fair daughter
Of his brother Rhexenor, as Odysseus
Had discovered when they previously had met.

"Welcome, King Odysseus,"
                              the Phaeacian king said,
And grasped his arms warmly. The sharp-eyed Ithacan

Looked closely at him, and despite the flickering light
Of the huge fire, saw that lines of care had etched themselves
Deeply in his fellow king's face.

"You have returned to us again, and again by water."

"It appears so, my gracious king, and whom I take to be
My saviour. Can you tell me what happened?"

Noble Alcinous smiled.

"That can wait until we sup. Now sit by my queen
And myself and begin to eat."

Odysseus sat between them; he noticed
That Laodamas and his brothers sat near them,
But that Nausicaa sat with Alcaios,
The burly warrior who had taunted him,
Then saw his worth in sports and, ordered, gave him
A fine sword, atonement for his graceless words;
But the observant king also noted that Nausicaa
Kept her eyes on him throughout.
Then the banquet began, with breads and choice cuts
From the sacrifices and wine served by attendants
On the rich service which Odysseus recognized
From his previous visit to the king. For a time
He ate hungrily, answering the queen's questions
About his return to Ithaca and about his wife.
Then Alcinous asked him,

"Before we relate our own story, great Odysseus,
Please tell us how you came to be here."

Then the travel-worn Ithacan related how
He had had to make a new quest to placate Poseidon;
How he had travelled through the peninsula,
Of his adventures with King Orestes,
Then with Menelaos and at Pylos,
And how he had then travelled alone in his pilgrimage
Through Aetolia; how he had been captured by a tribe;
How he had escaped; and how he had traversed the tunnel,
Finally to be caught up in the rapids.

"Now, my gracious host, I beg you to tell me
How I came to be here, and where this is,
And why I should find you here."

King Alcinous smiled grimly.

"You shall know all. First, we found you, unconscious,
Floating on the rapids, from which we rescued you.
How you got there, and from whence you came,
We have not understood till now,
But we knew that you would come, and by water,
As you had previously. How we knew this"—

The king raised his hand to silence Odysseus,
Who had been about to speak—

"You shall know now, and why you find us here.
Pontonous"—

          and Odysseus recognized the loyal herald
To the king, who now stepped to his side,

"Bring forth Demodocus."

The herald bowed and retreated
From the blaze of the fire. Odysseus remembered
Demodocus as the inspired blind bard
And master of the lyre who had enchanted him
When at the feast in Phaeacia
He had sung eloquently of the Trojan War.
Soon Pontonous led forth the bard, who held firm
To his lyre, and placed him before the king
And by the fire. While he was being found,
Alcinous told Odysseus why the bard would relate
Their tale.

"Demodocus, as you know, is a great bard."

Odysseus nodded in agreement.

"It is he through whom the Gods spoke,
And particularly Apollo, that great lord of song,
To tell us what we must do—for, as you will hear,
We also have a pilgrimage to make."

Now Demodocus grasped his lyre, and his face
Suddenly was entranced, as if Apollo sang through him.

"I sing of the Phaeacians and of their destiny,
Children of Poseidon the direful God
And subject to his judgment and his will.
In times long past, Eurymedon, flint-willed king
Of the Giants, had as his youngest daughter, Periboea,
Whose beauty and loveliness no other woman could match.
The young girl's surpassing beauty caught the eye
Of the dread God of sea and sky, mighty Poseidon,
Who lay with the wonder-stricken girl,
Whose loins brought forth their son, worthy Nausithous.
Eurymedon became arrogant and audacious,
And he led his Giants in a war against the Gods,
Leading to their ruin and his own suicide.
But Nausithous became king of the Phaeacians,
Who lived in Hyperia, a land renowned for dance.
But too close to them lived other of Poseidon's progeny,
The brutal Cyclops, who afflicted them ruthlessly.
Nausithous, lion-hearted and God-like, then led his people
In a migration, all of them, to settle in Scheria,
An island far from other peoples, where they could live in peace,
Without fear of strife or invasion from those near.
Here their noble king ruled them in peace and prosperity;
Here they built well their sleek and swift black ships,
Favoured by Poseidon, with their own powers
To skim the seas to any port or place
Whatever weather may chance upon them.
And with these ships the fine Phaeacians sailors
Escorted and helped all ships that man had built.
But Nausithous learned that his father Poseidon
Was annoyed that the Phaeacian ships
Kept those ships they escorted from grief
When the God could have shown his might
In destroying some of them through gales
Or giant waves or by his own mighty hand.
The God then warned that on a fateful day,
As one of our graceful ships returned from its convoy
Across the heaving and the mist-ridden sea,

His hand would crush it, sinking it deep into the ocean's ooze,
And then pile around our port huge rocks to form
An impenetrable mountain. But the God's son
Ignored these warnings as an old wives' tale.
In time King Nausithous had two noble sons,
Rhexenor, much the elder, and the younger,
Our present king, Alcinous.
Rhexenor in his appearance and in his prowess
Seemed much a God, and he had a daughter
Who received his gifts as well. But the great lord
Apollo became angry that a mortal should seem
So God-like and with his deadly bow slew the hapless prince.
Alcinous, who loved his brother, was entranced
By the beauty of the daughter and married her;
And here she sits by the king, the beautiful Arête.
When his father died, Alcinous succeeded to the throne
And rules to this day, and both king and queen
Are much beloved by their people.
Now, the Phaeacians continued to escort the ships
Of other countries, and their fame and wealth increased.
But then a stranger arrived, cast destitute
Upon the shore, and as always the hospitality
And generosity of Phaeacia
Were extended to him, and precious gifts were given him,
And he was returned to his own land by a sleek black ship
Manned by fine Phaeacian sailors. But Poseidon
Was outraged, for the stranger was Odysseus,
Who had blinded his cyclopean son.
The wrathful God went to Zeus, who, uninterested in the fate
Of the sons of his fellow God, gave him leave
To wreak vengeance on them as he saw fit.
Accordingly, as the swift ship came in sight
Of the Phaeacian harbour, with all watching its return,
He turned it to stone and with his huge hand
Slammed it into the ooze of the ocean before the island.
All were appalled by this act; and the king Alcinous
Ordered all ships to return and desist from escort.
But all knew that the prophecy had yet to be completed;
That Poseidon intended to pile huge mountains about the harbour
So that no more could the Phaeacian ships sail the oceans.

But as Poseidon raised his hand to do so,
Apollo, the wise and dreaded God, spoke to him:

'My lord Poseidon, why punish your own children
In such an obvious and final way?
Why not extend their vicissitude and combine it
With your punishment of him whom you have condemned
To a hard pilgrimage, Odysseus?'

"The God of earth and sea paused to hear what the other
Would suggest.

'Command that they must migrate to a remote valley
In the harsh land of Aetolia, there to learn the skills
Of horsemanship and combat, the latter through
The instruction of Odysseus, who will come upon them
In his quest. Then let them take their black ships
For the last time and sail them far away,
To the westernmost isles, where they must battle
With a dreadful race for mastery of the island,
Where they must live without the use of their magic ships.
And there they will lose their identity as Phaeacians
And be called another name, yet to be revealed.'

"Poseidon considered what his fellow God suggested,
And then agreed, asking that Apollo himself
Give the order and the prophecy to Phaeacia.
Accordingly the great archer God and lord of song
Came to Phaeacia and chose me, blind Demodocus,
His faithful servant, who receives his inspiration
From the divine God, to reveal the judgment of
Our father, dread Poseidon. Accordingly
I took my lyre and sang what you have heard
To our king and queen and to our people.
In horror they received the dictates;
But then King Alcinous gave orders that
The God's commandments must be fulfilled;
And for a full half the year new ships were built,
Tents made, and provision for our treasures
And our household things.
Finally, all was in readiness, and the people,
Weeping, again prepared for their next migration.

The sleek black ships were crammed with effects;
Men, women, and children came aboard,
Looking back with longing and with sadness
At their homes and fields; then the innumerable ships
Slipped from the shore and sailed out of the harbour.
Just as the last ship left, a terrible roar was heard,
And while all those on the ships watched,
Again with horror, a fierce earthquake shook the island,
The great palace, with its bronze-clad walls and
Lapis-blue frieze, its golden doors and silver doorposts
And lintels, crumbled before their eyes, as did their city,
And the island itself, riven through, sank beneath the waves.
This was Poseidon's own signature to his children's punishment.
Dazed, we all looked at the empty sea where once had stood
So proudly the fertile island and the rich buildings;
Then the black ships sped of their own accord
Across the restless sea; at one point we passed
Where we had deposited Odysseus in Ithaca,
Now looked on in dreadful irony;
Then they skirted other islands until they came to a huge bay,
Up which they plunged headlong,
Like a mass of insects scurrying together across some floor.
At the apex of the bay was the outlet of a river,
Into which the ships entered, one after another.
By now dusk had covered the sky,
And we could make out only the peaks of jagged mountains,
Stark and bare, around us. Then, in utter darkness,
With no moon or starlight to assist us, the ships
Continued without let along the river;
All we could hear was the seething of the water
As it slipped under our prows, and a growing noise
Of rapids as we continued up the river,
The oarsmen straining in their places,
But the ships continuing on unabated.
Finally, exhausted, all slept, even those
Manning the oars; yet the ships surged on.
Then, as Dawn rose majestic from her sable bed,
The ships slowed, and the oarsmen, awake again,
Guided them into the banks of the river
That flows not far from here.

We found ourselves in this valley,
Surrounded by harsh peaks on each side,
And, as we found in exploration later,
With no way in or out except by the river
Or by a perilous climb over the huge ranges.
We had landed by good fortune beside a large meadow;
And quickly each ship was unloaded
And tents raised to shelter the many people.
It was mid-spring when we arrived; at night
The air was chill, and we had quickly to cut wood
To make the fires that both would warm us
And provide the means to cook our food.
After the first day of setting up our means
Of living, we began to explore: the massive slopes
Of the mountains were clothed partway up
With forests of both dark trees and others
Whose leaves had still the light green tint
Of their new-born state; on the floor of the valley
Meandered the river, which near to us
Arrived in the valley through a cleft
In the mountainside and roared farther down,
Where it slowed as it moved among rich fields
And abundant woods. Over the next few weeks
We made our fragile camp as comfortable as we could
With what we had brought with us;
But it was necessary to find food to sustain us,
And so fields were sown with grain brought with us,
And we searched out the groves of olive trees
And some fruit trees, for the climate was not
So mild as the one to which we were accustomed.
Wild game we found in abundance, and fish in the river.
Finally, in one sortie through the valley, we spotted
A herd of wild horses—but not the small unkempt ones
That range in the outer reaches of a country.
These were magnificent creatures, proud and swift,
And we could but think that the Gods had given them
To us, and we therefore made sacrifice to them,
Using mountain goats that lived on the precipitous slopes.
Our problem, however, was that, although we had
Been commanded to use horsemanship,

None of us were proficient in the art,
For ours was a country of seamen.
It took the rest of the spring and part of the summer
Before we could capture and corral the herd;
And even then we did not know how to break them in,
But had to learn painfully the lessons of man with horse.
We also had to learn to provide the gear by which
The horse could be guided and led, as well as
How we would sit on the beasts.
But Alcaios with his great strength helped to subdue them;
And the princes Halius and Clytoneus showed
Their skill in movement in their work with their steeds,
As did Phrixos and Evaristos with theirs.
Finally, as leaves grew red and grain was harvested,
At least some of the herd had been trained,
And our horsemen spent time learning what they could do
With their mounts, and others had to learn
How to groom and feed them.
That first winter was hard, hard for us all,
Dealing with cold and snow while living in the tents.
The fleeces that we brought with us were insufficient,
And we had to hunt to find the furs to clothe ourselves
To keep warm, as well as forage for food
While stumbling through the snow that on the slopes
Grew deep. All suffered from the pangs of hunger
And some from starvation, even with the efforts of the king
To share what we had amongst each other.
When spring came, we were no longer the carefree people
Of our former isle; now we were much hardened and inured
To deprivation. But over the next year the court and people
Worked hard to provide for the winter;
The horsemen became more adept, and more learned horsemanship.
Still, no training in combat took place, for it had been ordained
That Odysseus, warrior hero of the Trojan War, would come
To train us for the ordeal to follow. And so we waited,
As a second winter came around, then early spring,
And then those closely watching the river
Saw a body wash through the cleft, unconscious,
And then Lord Laodamas and Alcaios themselves
Braved the raging current to drag it to shore,

Where it was found to be Odysseus, barely alive;
And here he is before us now, and the prophecy
Will be fulfilled."

And Demodocus, exhausted, sank down to his chair
As the last thrum of his lyre played against the sounds
Of the river nearby and the crackling of the fire.

For a time no word was said, but all faces turned upon Odysseus,
Who sat like stone, stunned by what he had just heard.
Then he raised his head and spoke quietly,
Though his words could be heard plainly among the group.

"As usual, Demodocus, you excel all other bards.
I sit in wonderment at what has befallen you all,
Subject, as I am, to Poseidon's wrath, but
With far worse consequences. I can see an end
With my quest fulfilled, but you know little other than
You will be exiled to the westernmost isles,
There to battle with a monstrous race; and
It is also worse for you as the God's own children,
Forsaken by him for doing good to humankind.
I wish, with all my being, that all will finally
Turn out well for you—and I will indeed train you,
To my utmost, in the art of war, for I feel
That I was the crucial means by which the God was stirred."

And he lowered his head and covered it with his cloak
That they would not see his grief.

Then Alcinous laid his hand upon the arm
Of the slumped form of the sorrowing Ithacan.

"Good Odysseus, we do not blame you for what has happened.
We had been warned by my father of Poseidon's feelings
For the way we helped other races, but we ourselves
Dismissed it as an old wives' tale, and also because
We could do naught else but help those who
Needed our aid. Our race has been beset before,
The Cyclops harrying us until that first migration;
Now we shall move again, but this time stand up
Against those who might oppose us.
As well, my friend, you may have in your own way

Helped us, for if you had not been the one on whom
Poseidon frowned, the prophecy would have been fulfilled
As it first stood, and we would have been imprisoned
On our island by the mountains that Poseidon
Would have thrown around our harbour,
Cutting us off from the world itself.
Now at least we shall be abroad, even if it means
In the westernmost isles and in battle.
Is it not better to fight to keep alive and free
And not give in to bitter isolation and imprisonment?"

The weary Ithacan raised his head to look
At Alcinous. Even in the uncertain flaming light
He saw again new lines of care in the king's face
And darkness behind his eyes, although,
Noble as he was, he stood here steadfast.

"You are right, royal Alcinous. We must
Endure what the Gods ordain for us
And make the best of what we can."

But he shivered as he thought,

*A race such as this? The children of the God himself?*
*And placed in durance by him only to salve*
*His own arrogant sense of his power?*
*How can we find any solid place to stand*
*When we are but the Gods' playthings,*
*With them sometimes patrons, sometimes destroyers*
*According to their whim?*

But he was stirred from his brief reverie
As the Phaeacian king exclaimed,

"But now, enough of history and prophecies!
Let us drink now, and thank the Gods
That we still live to enjoy such things."

And he himself took a golden pitcher
From his attendant and filled Odysseus's silver goblet.
The rest of the night became a blur
To the exhausted warrior; Alcinous and others
Spoke to him and toasted him, and he saw

Before the huge fire, its sparks ascending to the night sky,
The two princes Halius and Clytoneus dance as they had before,
But this time their movements were not astounding
In their jumps and quickness, but slow, stately,
And the dance expressed the grave life in which
All now found themselves, and Odysseus
Was moved to tears by their heartrending gestures
And the graceful tortured movement of their bodies,
So that for the rest of his life he would not forget
Them silhouetted against the flames, lyre and flute and drum
Mournfully in conversation with them.

When Dawn rose gracefully from her consort's bed
Odysseus wrapped furs about himself to step outside his tent.
As the snow-topped peaks first grew pink
And then glistened white, he walked to a small rise
To look about him. Far beyond him he saw
A forest of trees, but before it he observed
A forest of tents that stretched out to fill the bottom
Of the valley up to the river that he saw not far
From where he stood. He could also see the two ranges
That enclosed the valley and marched off into the distance.
His bruised body still ached, but he walked to the bank
Of the river and looked back up it. A distance away
He saw the cleft through which the water rushed
To its present course, and he marvelled that he had
Somehow travelled through that gap and been safely found.
Now again he turned his attention to the neat row of tents,
Where he found small fires already burning before each,
And people slowly making ready for the day.
He recognized a square of ground where the fire
Had blazed the previous night, and on several sides
The royal tents, from one of which he saw Laodamas
Emerge and stride toward his own tent. He walked back
To intercept him, and the prince smiled.

"Well, mighty Odysseus, would you like to tour
Our new city and see its many wonders?"

Odysseus smiled back, and together they ranged
Through the streets of tents, as Laodamas pointed out
Where the smithies were, the rough-hewn stables

And the stockades for the horses, and all the other places
Where skilled artisans and others worked to keep them
As they wished to be. Then they moved past the huge camp
To look at the fields and woods and slopes that lay beyond,
And at the river Odysseus saw, lined up at the bank
As far as the eye could see, the sleek black ships,
Which seemed themselves to be leashed but eager
To move off again, slipping effortlessly through
The turbulent waters.

"When we board our vessels again, it will be
For the last time, as it is ordained,"

Said Laodamas grimly.

"But we still have much work before us. How long
Do you think you will need to train us?"

"I will not know until I see your men at work.
It is not only a matter of learning the skills
Of the sword, the spear, and the bow;
All of these armaments must be manufactured first.
As well, we must hold council on the arts of war—
Strategies and tactics, both for those on foot
And those on horse; and although you may lose
Your ships when you land, it does not mean
That you cannot fight with them until that time.
There is thus much to be done."

Laodamas nodded his agreement but said,

"In one sense we have anticipated you, for our smiths
Have been hard at work on such weapons,
And we now have enough to supply most of us properly.
As for the rest, we leave that in your hands."

Then they returned to the royal tents. By this time
The sun had driven high into the sky,
And with the royal family they feasted sparingly
On bread and wine and fruit. Odysseus wasted no time,
But talked throughout the meal of what he would need
And the schedule to be followed. As he did so,
A basket of bread was offered to him; he looked up,

And to his surprise he saw it proffered in the hands
Of Nausicaa herself.

"My gracious and beautiful princess, why do you
Do that which your attendant should?"

She blushed and said,

"Great Odysseus, it is the least that I could do
For the hero who will save our people."

Odysseus gently took the basket from her hands.

"Thank you for your generous consideration.
I did not have the opportunity last night,
But now I must thank you also for your ministrations.
Again you have helped to save me in a time
Of watery distress."

                    Both smiled at his words.

"As you asked, I have not forgotten you
Over these past two years, nor will I forget
In future years how much I owe to you."

At this she blushed and lowered her eyes
But continued to stand beside him.

"Do sit with us while we eat, I beg you."

Nausicaa quickly looked over to her father,
Who nodded to the request; a chair was brought
For her, and she sat at Odysseus's side.
By this time the clear-eyed Ithacan had noted
That the Phaeacian court had brought its rich appointments
With it, the chairs delicately covered with ivory
And silver decoration, even though they still must now
Live in tents as if in a camp of war.
Nausicaa sat quietly, nibbling on some bread,
Her eyes on Odysseus but averted when he looked at her.
Odysseus chatted with her and the king about
Inconsequential matters—the vivid scenery about them,
The new warmth of the spring air and with it
The budding of the trees and vegetation—
But then he turned to her.

"It is now two years since we last met, Princess Nausicaa,
And you are even more lovely now than before.
But you are not yet married, I see—
Are there no Phaeacian nobles who are worthy of you?"

At this she flushed deeply; but her father said,

"More than enough, I fear, who would be eligible
And who woo me to let them wed her.
We hope that before our next migration
She will make up her mind, for time presses for all of us."

As he listened, Odysseus noted strain
In both Alcinous's smile and voice;
The Ithacan wondered what it meant,
But put it aside to consider later.

"Surely there is one here who could meet your favour?
I know from when I was here that there are many
Who would be worthy."

Nausicaa's eyes glistened, and for a moment again
She averted her face and half-heartedly nibbled her bread.
But then she appeared to make up her mind,
Turned toward Odysseus, and looked him in the eyes.
He saw the directness of her stare and realized
Who had taken her heart. Then she glanced away
As he, shaken, realized that what before had appeared to him
To be admiration was truly passion for him.
For a moment he did not know what to say;
Then, turning to Alcinous, but keeping Nausicaa
In the conversation, he said,

"My gracious king, last night I told you of my adventures
Since you delivered me to my island, but let me now
Tell of my home."

And he told them about the island of Ithaca,
Rugged and sparse of land, but the place he loved;
And of his palace and the bedroom in which he had
Constructed his large bed from the living tree
That had grown through it; and of his wife Penelope,
Who had so faithfully waited for him for twenty years—

He saw Nausicaa colour at this reference—
And of his son Telemachus, who had grown up
While he was away; and of the impending marriage
With Polycaste, daughter of King Nestor, now dead,
Which would take place when he returned from his quest.
They all sat, spellbound by his heartfelt words.

As he finished, Nausicaa rose.

"My father, and noble Odysseus, you must excuse me,
For I feel somewhat ill."

And she hurriedly left, her father
Watching anxiously her demeanour.
Odysseus quickly turned the conversation
Back to the schedule for the training,
And by the time they rose it had been established.

That afternoon the Phaeacian men met with him.
Among them were those whom he had met before:
Alcaios, son of fortunate Kallicrates—only Laodamas
Was more handsome and powerful than he—
Who was the champion wrestler of the Phaeacians;
He had mocked Odysseus for his reluctance
To join in the sports when he observed their games,
And he it was who was rebuked by the king for doing so,
And then apologized with warmth to Odysseus,
Giving him a sword rich in silver, ivory, and bronze;
Phrixos, son of generous Gennadios
And the champion jumper of all the Phaeacians;
Arsemios, famous for his mighty arms,
The greatest discus thrower; the graceful Prochorus;
Evaristos, noted for his great charm;
And Euthymios for his ebullience;
Popular Pamphilos; Eutropios,
Clever in strategy; formidable Zoticus;
Eustathios, of all the Phaeacians
The most dependable; and Hilarion, the most cheerful
Of them all. This day Odysseus explained to them
What they would be practising to start with: swordsmanship.
All had such weapons and some rude knowledge of them,
And so Odysseus undertook to see their skill.

"Mighty Alcaios, attack me with your sword."

Alcaios grinned and rushed at him, his sword raised high
To sweep down at the Ithacan warrior, who remained still
As he approached. Then, before he knew it, Alcaios
Found himself past his quarry, his sword knocked from his hand,
And when he turned, he found the point of Odysseus's sword
At his throat, for the skilled swordsman had stepped aside
From the blind rush before using his own sword to advantage.
All who had watched gasped at the swiftness and strength
Of the dexterous instructor.

"As with all our weapons, strength must be assisted
By the skill of anticipating the opponent's intention
And his weakness, as well as by your dexterity.
I could have killed you in different ways—piercing
Your side or stomach as you swept by, stabbing
Or slashing your back after you passed,
Cutting your throat as you turned, or at the least,
Hacking your hamstrings so that you would fall
And then be an easy prey. You are a powerful man,
Alcaios, and a champion wrestler—but you know
That wrestling is not a matter of pure strength,
But of tactics and strategies, of knowing your adversary
And his moves."

Alcaios, who had been stunned by what had happened
And shamed by his ignominious defeat,
Suddenly understood what his instructor said;
His eyes lit up and a grin crossed his bluff face;
He nodded and stepped back with a bow of respect
To stand with the others, who now showed
A much deeper respect for the Ithacan veteran.
All afternoon he had them learn how to parry,
How to thrust and slash and cut and stab,
Practising each move over and over;
And that night all feasted, tired but exhilarated
By what they had learned, including
The royal family, who also trained with their men.
Each day, morning and afternoon,
Odysseus instructed them patiently and long.

As they became adept with their short swords
He added shields, and they learned how to use them
Against swords. Then, as they showed that they
Were now conversant in this art to practise on their own,
He turned to the spear, showing them how to throw it
Accurately and long—Arsemios showed himself
Most adept at this—how to use it as a weapon in the hand
To aim accurately at those parts of the body
Where armour was weakest or was not found,
And adding their shields for protection,
Both when in individual combat and then when
Shields could be used to form a common wall.
Finally he showed them the use of the bow,
How to aim and where to aim, the need to use
Arrows wisely and sparingly; their use both
At a distance and against a moving target;
And their strength when massed together
To send volleys of arrows toward their foes,
And how the bowmen could be protected
By a wall of shields before emerging for each volley.
Finally, he turned to the most intimate weapon,
The dagger, showing all its deadly attributes
And when to use it to slit the throats of sentries
To prevent warning of an excursion.

Throughout all these the Phaeacians watched in awe
Odysseus's skill in using all these weapons,
But most admired his great skill with the bow,
Both for his strength in easily drawing their strongest bow
But also his uncanny accuracy in hitting any target
That they placed before him.
At night at the feasts they also listened, spellbound,
As he related in detail the Trojan battles,
Not only narrating the action, but carefully examining
The tactics and the strategies employed by both sides,
The triumphs and the failures of all.
Their horsemanship he also examined, and helped them
To understand and train their beasts so that
Man and horse worked as one; and when
They had mastered this art, he had them use

The skills that they had learned to do combat
On horse with their weapons, whether
With sword or spear or bow.

When high summer had arrived, Odysseus
Reviewed all that they had learned, and
He found that the Phaeacians had become adept
In all the martial arts and could be
A formidable fighting force. They now organized
Their own training sessions; his discussions
With the royal family on tactics and strategy
Revealed how clever they could be in this respect.
During all this time, he noticed that Nausicaa
Avoided him at all meals; but he also found
That he would catch glimpses of her watching him
As he trained the men, and his keen eyes noted
That she was thinner and looked more drawn.
One day, after the afternoon training,
Queen Arête called him to her tent.
He found her there, her spindle in her hand,
Her silver bowl of wool at her feet.
She gestured to him to sit by her side,
And for a moment she continued to spin in silence.
Then she spoke, her agile fingers still swift.

"I have not thanked you personally,
Noble Odysseus, for all that you have done for us."

He demurred politely, but she shook her head.

"No, it is true. I do not know what we would have done,
If the prophecy that you would come
Had not been fulfilled. For you have given us
Our pride and respect again, and hope that
We will succeed in the struggle which has been ordained."

For a moment she became silent, struggling with her emotions,
Then turned again to him, and in a quieter voice,
But one filled with strain and worry, said,

"You know how our daughter, the princess Nausicaa,
Feels about you?"

Odysseus could see that the mother knew too well
The passion that her daughter felt for him
And decided that speaking truly was needful.

"We both know, gracious Queen Arête,
That she holds me dear in her heart.
You have seen that I have not encouraged this,
Telling her—and you all—about my home
And my relationship with my dear wife and son."

The queen nodded her head.

"I know, good King Odysseus, that you have acted
At all times with honour and circumspection.
But she cannot overcome her passion for you.
Two years ago, when she was still immature,
We thought that her feelings for you were
Nothing but a first flush of feelings for a man—
And a great hero like yourself"—

And Odysseus, startled, saw that the queen
Had not been unaffected herself, but she
Collected herself and then went on.

"But now we realize that her passion was real
And steadfast, and now, in the impossibility
Of the situation, she pines away,
And I am afraid that if she continues
In this way, she will die."

And Arête could not contain herself longer,
But wept in anguish before him.

Odysseus, moved by the queen's distressed state,
Yet did not know how to reply, but said,

"I pity you and your daughter, good queen.
But, as you know, not only must I fulfill
My pilgrimage but also return home to my wife,
Who, as you have heard, has been faithful to me
All these years. What can I do to help?
Is there no Phaeacian lord worthy enough
For her hand?"

The queen regained control and sighed.

"There are some whom we consider right for her.
But she refuses to acknowledge them."

Then she placed her hand on Odysseus's arm, saying,

"She is my only daughter; my five sons
Will continue our line, but our hopes also lie
With her—for wherever now we go,
We will stay apart from other races
And therefore have only ourselves to propagate
Ourselves. I fear that sometime in the future
We will have bred among ourselves too much
And therefore will begin to sink in quality."

A haunted look; Odysseus now remembered
Alcinous's expression from before.

"And Apollo has prophesized as much,
Ordering that for each generation
At least one of our women must bear
The child of a great stranger to our race.
I have talked to my husband of this problem,
And we had thought you best for this purpose,
The perfect match to fulfill His order,
A fine union between royal families.
Then we heard from your own lips of your own
Marriage, your own family, and our hope
Vanished. We never again will see you.
So now I ask you, What can we do?
Our best hope gone, Apollo's charge
Left unfulfilled. Can you, who are so wise,
Give us advice in this dire circumstance?"

Odysseus stared at her and could not speak,
So moved was he by her revelation.
They both sat still, the queen in desolation.
Finally he stirred and gently spoke.

"Queen Arête, I am stirred deeply by your plight
And that of your daughter and your race.
I must admit that I have known other women

While returning from Troy, but always under duress,
As with Calypso, who had God-like powers over me.
Never was I truly unfaithful to Penelope—
And, in fact, refused Calypso's gift of immortality
So that I could stay with my beloved wife.
But this matter is more serious, for
I am not coerced nor have some good advice."

Arête raised her head, her face a tragic mask,
And he went quickly on.

"And yet I understand that two dark results
Can rise if I do not yield to your wish—
That your daughter can, in fact, die,
A tragic end for so young and lovely a woman;
And your race will not be enriched with
A different blood. Give me until tomorrow,
I entreat you, to consider this matter
More deeply, and then perhaps we may meet
With both you and the king."

Queen Arête looked at him, her face strained,
But she nodded to him, and he bowed and took his leave.

Later, after the evening's banquet—during which
Odysseus watched carefully but secretly
Nausicaa, who sat close with the royal family
But neither ate nor drank; nor did she look
In his direction, but he could sense that she
Felt his presence strongly—he wrapped furs about him
And went to the bank of the river, where he sat,
Listening to the babble of the current and thinking.
For the first time since he had fully arrived here
He felt weary, unutterably weary; for a time
His mind wandered back over the journeys
He had made—his adventures in the Peloponnesos
With Orestes and Menelaos and Helen
And Nestor's funeral; the Delphi expedition;
All his old companions from the war;
His son and Pelagia and Polycaste;
Thoas and Aetolia; his slavery; and now
The ill-fated Phaeacians—and how through them all

He had had to solve problems, think strategically,
And find his way through the maze that surrounded him.

*And now this—how can I satisfy this girl*
*And her family and her race and still*
*Preserve the sanctity of my marriage?*

But his mind balked at the dilemma, and he
Walked slowly back to his tent, flung himself
On his pallet, and fell into an exhausted sleep.

*White sanded beach*
*Limitless sea*
*The sun orange*
*Sinking below the waves*
*Leaving for this moment the sky*
*Brilliant with the last glowing rays*
*She comes to me sitting there*
*Calypso's mantle silvery*
*Reflecting the sun's rosy admiration*
*Trailing gently in the sand*
*Her golden belt about her waist*
*Her veil misting her radiance*
*Her long slender hand*
*Reaches for mine*
*The current in the hand*
*Led back across the beach*
*Tracked with our bare footsteps*
*And the sinuous trailing of her robe*
*Into the coolness of the cave*
*The feast incomparable*
*The divine nectar*
*Firing the blood*
*Led again to her bed*
*My clothes flicked away*
*Her robe slips from her*
*The utter radiance*
*Of her white body*
*Her unearthly beauty*
*Her eyes blazing*
*Desire*

*So wild*
*Limitless*
*The curious hunger*
*For a human body*
*Male*
*Instilling the power*
*Desire within me*
*Irresistible*
*My hands exploring her body*
*As hers do mine*
*As if for the first time*
*The wild entrance*
*The glory limitless*
*And wet*
*Exhausted*
*Spent*
*Lying beside the immortal body*
*Forever young and unutterably beautiful*
*Feeling its alien energy*
*Even in rest*
*And all the while*
*I see*
*Penelope*
*The next night*
*All renewed*
*And Penelope*
*And the next night*
*And another*
*And another*
*Each always new*
*But Penelope*
*Always in the mind*

*Pelagia*
*Polycaste*
*Artemisia*
*Nausicaa*
*All would be*
*Of ages that my daughters*
*Could have been*

*Daughters*
*I never had*
*So young*
*So vital*
*So ready*
*For love*
*For conception*
*So vulnerable*
*My son*
*A concubine*
*A wife*
*Myself*
*A wife*
*My wife*

Early the next morning
Odysseus again mused by the river,
And after he had breakfasted with the royal family
Odysseus invited Alcinous and Arête
To walk with him along the river's bank.
The sky was blue, the sun warm upon them,
And summer was lush in its full glory
Around them. They sauntered until they found
A place where the current lowered its voice
And they could talk without effort,
And as they moved slowly there,
Odysseus opened the conversation.

"I have thought deeply of what you propose,
Queen Arête."

She blushed, and a tiny frown creased
The king's forehead, but neither said a word,
Waiting to hear Odysseus.

"What you ask is council from me
Without what you had hoped for in your heart,
An enduring bond between two families
That would solve the problem of the prophecy."

As his words sunk in, Arête's face paled,
Tears broke the dam of her strained composure,

And Alcinous held her tightly to him.

"As I said to you, gracious queen, I am moved
Both by the plight of your daughter and of your race,
And time has only deepened such feeling for me.
For me to respond is at a cost, a cost
That is not reckoned in material things
But in my devotion to my wife Penelope."

They looked at him, alarmed.

"Yet, because you have twice rescued me
And done such favour to me as to
Cause such distress to you, I cannot
Deny you in this matter."

Both looked relieved, yet puzzled.

"For me there will be only the memory
Of what I do here, for I will never see
You or your lovely daughter again;
But she must live with you and, if all is well,
Bear the child you and she hope for.
What, then, will be her position in your society?
She is a princess. She cannot be a concubine
Or worse. How will she, without a husband,
Live with respect?"

The parents looked at each other and nodded.
Odysseus realized they would not let this happen
Despite their daughter's need. Then he went on:

"I do not know the customs of your country,
Noble Alcinous. But it seems to me that
You could wed us here without my own marriage
Becoming void, for it would apply to your country only,
And to none other, for, as I suspect, you wish
No traffic with other peoples. But we can speak
Further on this matter at another time.
I suggest that you find a way to do this.
As well, once I leave, never to return,
You might decree that she is, in essence,
A widow, and eligible to be wed again.

For it would be a pity if she remained alone,
Only her child to comfort her, for the rest
Of what should be a long life.
How she will deal with our separation
I cannot tell as yet. It will not be easy for her,
But it is inevitable."

He finished, and then stood staring out at the river,
Giving the couple time to consider what he had said.

The two moved slightly away and conversed
Urgently about his proposal; then Alcinous
Approached him and gravely said,

"Noble Odysseus, you perpetually amaze us
With your wisdom and with your understanding.
With what you say we cannot disagree:
Our daughter's need cannot sacrifice her honour,
And your proposal both legitimizes your union
And prepares for your departure.
We accept it but have no means to express our gratitude."

Then he grasped Odysseus's hand; but when he let it go,
His wife, with a sob, tightly embraced the startled man,
Crying with her relief.

For a moment all three stood thus;
Then Odysseus gently disengaged himself
From the still weeping queen, and said,

"Now you must prepare the ground for this union.
Tonight have Nausicaa sit by me,
And do the same for the meals tomorrow.
On the next day I will walk with her,
And, if she proves then to be ready,
Before her will ask you for her hand.
You then can make the announcement,
And at a time deemed decent by you,
Celebrate our wedding. Now let us return,
For I have some training yet to do!"

And they all returned to the tent,
Much different from what they had been before.

At the noon meal Odysseus talked and laughed
With Laodamas and his brothers, but he noted
Still the mute and forlorn Nausicaa,
And he contrived near the end of the meal
To speak briefly to her, to which she responded
With confusion, for she had prepared herself
Never to speak to him again. That night
She found herself sitting next to him;
Gently he talked to her and led her into conversation.
Like a bud that slowly unfolds its petals
As the sun begins to shine upon it,
So Nausicaa shyly began to respond to him,
And as she found his attention upon her,
And sensed that he not only listened to her
But seemed aware of her physical presence,
She became first confused, then as he continued
To respond to her, began to speak and act more warmly.
Odysseus himself began to look at her more closely.
She was indeed lovely, and as she became more open,
He found that she was intelligent and observant.
At the feast's close as they parted Nausicaa
Felt Odysseus's eyes upon her, and she flushed
Under his appreciation. That night
She tossed restlessly, the emotions which she had
With such effort suppressed rising irresistibly,
With the last image of Odysseus and his appraisal
Graven deeply in her mind. The next morning
She found him again at her side at the meal,
Attentive to what she said; and again at noon;
And at the evening feast, and at each she
Responded more, their conversations at times
Cheerful and gay, at other times more serious,
Her face now no longer guarded but open
And radiant, and it became obvious to everyone
What she felt toward the Ithacan king.

The next day, between the afternoon session
And the evening feast, Odysseus walked with Nausicaa
Along the bank of the river. The sun still shone
Above the peaks on either side, the valley

Bathed in its glorious light; to one side of them
The river declaimed its low sibilant dialogue,
And on the other the air was filled with the songs
Of birds and the rustle of animals through
The woods and fields. For a time they walked
In silence, listening to the sweet cacophony of nature,
Nausicaa acutely aware of the man close to her side.
Then Odysseus stopped and turned to here.

"Fair Nausicaa, I have known for some time
Of the feeling you bear toward me"—

She flushed and turned her head away to study
The river, but he could see that she could not deny
That she was deeply in love with him—

"You are indeed beautiful and desirable"—

And looking at her now, her lustrous golden hair
Touched by the winds to move gently
Around her slender neck, her face now defined
Softly with a fine structure, and her eyes,
Full and expressive, intelligent,
And her young vibrant body—
He felt the erotic power that she possessed
But knew little of, and his heart twisted—

"And any man would willingly give his heart to you."

She turned to look at him directly, and her gaze,
So vulnerable and passionate, tore at him again.

"You know that I still have a wife at home,
My beloved Penelope."

Her face twisted with pain and longing.

"But I cannot leave you in your present state,
Alone, unfulfilled and, until two days ago,
In despair."

She looked at him still, and he saw that what
He had said was true, and he felt her relive
That pain, but also her eyes showed puzzlement
At what he said.

"Nor would I be like some vile man,
To take advantage of your feeling
And seduce you, leaving you forsaken and shamed."

She now looked bewildered and apprehensive.

"You are a princess and deserve the respect
Of your position and must not relinquish it
Or your honour."

She made to speak; he could see that she would
Throw away all to be with him, but he placed
His hand upon her lips and continued.

"Your race is apart from those of humankind about you,
And I suspect will remain so in the future.
I feel that because of this different state,
I can say what I am about to say."

She looked at him wonderingly.

"If I ask your father for you as a bride,
Will you accept me?"

In astonishment she cried out, then
Melted into his arms and sought his lips.
He responded, feeling those soft young lips on his,
Surprised by his own surge of feeling.
The first kiss was long; and when she broke it,
Breathless, she spoke for the first time:

"All that you have said is true—I have loved you
Since I first saw you over two long years ago
And thought of nothing but you since then.
When you came back so suddenly, and in the same way
As you had arrived the first time, on our island,
I had thought that you were destined for me by the Gods,
But then, when you talked of your home and son and wife"—

For a moment she had to stop, her eyes filled with tears—

"I could see no hope that we could be together,
And I felt then that life held nothing for me

And I was willing to die to alleviate the
Dreadful longing and loneliness I felt without you."

And she looked into his eyes, her face shining.

"Yes, I will have you, whether my parents consent or not."

She was about to kiss him passionately again,
But Odysseus gently held her away from him.

"You must understand that our liaison cannot last:
I must fulfill my quest, and you must stay with your people."

She looked at him, her desperate longing unconcealed,
And said, deeply affected,

"I know that you will leave me, and that all I have
Will be the memories of you and me together;
But rather that brief moment of happiness
Than to endure the loss of you altogether!"

And this time she pressed close to him
And kissed him with all her being,
And he could not resist her.

After a time he stood with her in the embrace,
His cheek beside hers, and quietly said,

"If we are fortunate, you may have a child
In which our memories can live."

She moaned slightly as the thought lived in her,
And they remained close for a time more.

"Now we must go to ask your parents."

They walked back to the tents, her hand
Never leaving his.

*How different from my marriage to Penelope*
*All arranged*
*A trade-off*
*Negotiation*
*I was with her like this*
*Only after she learned*

*She would be my bride*
*But the same age*
*Perhaps a year younger*
*And I not much older*
*And that first marriage night*
*Like two strangers*
*But she gave herself to me*
*Willingly*
*And I have loved her*
*Ever since*

The meeting with Alcinous and Arête
Was a joyous one, as they knew it would be,
And that night at the feast Alcinous
Announced the betrothal and that the wedding
Would take place in a week's time.
Many of the young Phaeacians were disappointed,
And some were on the verge of anger,
But they all realized the quality of Odysseus,
Even as they wondered at the fact
That he already had a wife back in Ithaca.
The royal sons were startled but not surprised,
For they had noted for a long time
Their sister's feelings for the Ithacan,
And they congratulated the two of them heartily.

Two days later Alcinous invited his fellow king
And prospective son-in-law to hunt with him.
They rode up the valley and into a forest
That spread up the slope of the great range,
Followed by the king's sons and followers.
It was another warm summer day, but
It was cool in the shade of the tall trees
That stood densely together. A boar was sighted,
And as it charged, Odysseus quickly speared it
Expertly through the heart, and it fell dead at their feet.
The others watched the killing in admiration
And praised him for his hunting prowess.
Then, as the boar was taken up to provide the feast
That evening, Odysseus and Alcinous rode back
A distance behind the others. For a time they chatted

About the progress of the training; and then
Odysseus said,

"My fellow king—and soon to be my father"—

Both men smiled—

"Within less than a week now I will wed your daughter.
Now, tell me if you will, what you intend to do
When you reach the westernmost isles?
Until now you have managed to remain on your island,
Helping other peoples with your black vessels,
Having migrated there to avoid the Cyclops's aggression.
But now you have been forced to this retreat,
Forced to learn the arts of war,
And you have mentioned that you will have
Little or no contact with other races.
How, then, do you intend to live?"

Alcinous rode along in silence for a time,
Then replied, his face grave:

"Our future appears uncertain.
You have heard the song of Demodocus,
But our priests also had visions,
Which they have told me in secrecy,
For what they say is strange and terrible.
So far we know that we will be taken
To those islands, about which we know nothing,
There to fight first a race more brutish
And less civilized than ourselves—barbarians
Crude and in appearance hairy and ugly,
But one that came not long ago from Thrace.
If we win against them—and the priests
Feel we will gain the upper hand, though
At a hard loss to ourselves—
Then later we must again battle against
A monstrous race from the sea, huge,
Hideous and deformed, although some
Are handsome and beautiful as well—
A strange and disconcerting mixture.
Also—and this has begun, but again secretly—

The magic that pervades our black ships
Is growing through some of our objects,
And our priests begin to feel new powers
To use as well as our new force of arms.
I do not know what these powers are,
And they disturb me, but I have neither will
Nor strength to know or to fight them.
The priests tell me that they will be vital
To our distant future, but other than what
I have told you, the near future is clouded
With uncertainty and anxiety."

For a short time they walked on in silence;
Then the king burst out,

"For our whole history our people have
Worked for the good of others and for
Their own good. We are not warlike,
We have not lusted after land nor power,
And have migrated away from those
Who feel that way. And in our sailings
Around these seas, we have seen
That all countries but ours covet such things.
That is why this migration is so hard for us,
For we must conquer others to survive ourselves,
And what might then occur to us can make me
Despair!"

And he stared down the river at the long, long line
Of black ships resting on its banks, and at
The vast congregation of tents that spread
Across the valley.

*That great sweep of ships on the banks*
*Just as the thousand ships on the shores*
*Near Troy*
*And the multitude of tents*
*Like our Greek camps*
*All*
*All for destruction of others*
*Even this race*
*So civilized*

*These golden people*
*Who now must survive*
*Through conquest*
*Using their new skills in arms*
*And in dark arts*
*All brought on*
*By the whim of the Gods*
*Will this race be lost*
*As were the Trojans*
*And how will my presence*
*Change the course of their fate*
*So many trained*
*Those that I took in charge*
*They training others*
*Who train others still*
*Now thousands*
*Who can kill with skill*
*And other ways less known*
*And more to be feared*
*To help in conquest and death*

Odysseus put his hand on the shoulder
Of the brooding king.

"Noble King Alcinous, your people and yourself
I admire without let. Yours is the only race
That I have seen that would forbear power
And deadly conquest. I grieve that you
Must now follow that bloodstained path,
But I hope that at some distant time
You will be able to remove yourselves
From such terrible ways and live in peace,
Showing your true selves and way of life."

The king put his hand on Odysseus's arm
And smiled gratefully at him; but the
Clear-eyed Ithacan saw that even this noble man
Began to show the stains that the need for power
Foster and grow, and he pitied him.
Conversation ceased; and the two kings
Strode back to the tents once more.

The day of the wedding finally arrived,
And the union was solemnized with
The great mass of people in their paeans
And shouts in praise of the Gods bombarding
The valley and the slopes, which echoed in return.
Priests made the sacrifices as the fiery pyres
Sent their flames and smoke high into the mountain air.
The famed dancers moved with grace and passion,
Along with other companies who showed the skill
Of this race in dance. Odysseus was dazzled
By the beauty and the warmth of the race,
And even more so by the sight of his bride,
Unutterably beautiful and radiant at his side.
On that nuptial night, Odysseus undressed Nausicaa
As she did him, and he marvelled at her young
And perfect body, while she traced with her finger
The white welts that sent trails across his body
From wounds and from the whippings he had received.

*I had forgotten the beauty of a young body*
*And that first exploration with Penelope*
*Who traced my body as Nausicaa does now*
*But who did not find the history of my battles*
*And my misfortunes etched there as they are now*

Then began the long sweet journey to fulfillment

*Her eyes open so wide*
*With the sensations of my hands*
*On her body*
*So new*
*Now they begin to glaze*
*As she becomes aroused*
*And now they close*
*Her mouth slightly parted*
*The shock of entrance*
*The gasp*
*And then for her all lost in the moment*
*And for me all lost in the moment*
*All lost*

The next two weeks were occupied,

By day with the final training of the warriors,
By night with Nausicaa, who grew
More passionate with each union.
Now in this high summer time
He became more restless, his pilgrimage
Weighing on his mind, and he spent each night
And at the meals each day, talking to Nausicaa,
Helping her to understand his past and he hers,
And preparing her for the inevitable parting.

One evening at the feast, as Demodocus began
A song, he gasped and seemed to enter
Into a trance, then sang ecstatically:

"Sing praise to Apollo, Lord of Song and Prophecy;
Sing praise to Poseidon, dread father of us all;
Give them obeisance, and let the fumes
Of our sacrifices rise to reach them on Olympus.
Now the God of Song sings to me
And I sing his divine wisdom to you.

    'Odysseus must leave within three days
    To continue his pilgrimage; find him the way north
    From the valley so that he can make his arduous way
    To his goal, and from there reach my sacred shrine
    In Dodona. As for you, the fated Phaeacians,
    Prepare carefully for your departure
    And wait for the sign to go. You will not sail
    Directly to your ordained destination;
    Instead you must let your swift ships speed down
    Your river, past deep gorges and high mountains,
    Until, free on the sea, skim north, skirting
    The western shore of fertile, white-stoned Leukas
    To penetrate the passage pinched by lands
    That guard the entrance to the Ambracian Gulf,
    To the entrance of the river Arakhthos.
    The fleet will anchor in a safe enclosed harbour not far away
    While one sleek ship will race up the swift winding waterway,
    Wend north at its junction and keep with its main stream
    North of the towering range found there.
    Finally, in a tall pine on one of its steep banks

Two eagles will sit, and it is there that Odysseus will be found.
The ship will return with him to the fleet,
And then all will return south by a new route,
Skirting the islands of Othronus and Malthabe,
And speeding in the open sea itself
Until they reach Ithaca, where Odysseus will say farewell
To you for the last time.'"

Demodocus sank into his chair, exhausted,
As a migrant bird descends to a tree after a long flight,
And all wondered at his words, but none more so
Than Odysseus and Nausicaa. He knew
His need to find Dodona once his quest was done;
But he knew little or nothing of the river and
The country where he was foretold to be,
Although he shrewdly guessed the oracle
At Dodona would bring forth his next task.
Nausicaa was dismayed at the bard's ecstatic words:
She knew now what she had tried not to think about,
That her loved one would leave her very shortly,
And that she would see him only once more again,
But just long enough for the voyage to Ithaca.

The king, who had paled at hearing how soon
Their trials would be upon them, nonetheless
Stood and spoke in a voice that carried over them,
His echo returning from the mountain slopes,

"Let us make libation to the immortal Gods,
Who speak now through our bard,
And let us sacrifice again this night, especially
To the lord of the song and bow and prophecy,
Phoebus Apollo, and to our own dread lord
And father, the mighty God Poseidon,
And let us do so as well for the next two nights,
Before noble Odysseus must leave us."

Libations were poured on to the ground and
Drunk as well, and the beasts were sacrificed,
While Nausicaa, her eyes wide with apprehension,
Clung close to her husband's side.
That night she made frantic love to Odysseus

Until he gently helped her to relax,
And through the night he murmured to her
To allay her fears and her anticipated loss.

For the next two days patrols of Phaeacians
Prowled the northern reaches of the valley,
Looking for a pass or some way for Odysseus
To pass across the craggy mountains
That opposed his way. Finally, just before
The last day was spent, they found, high up,
Where snow still clothed the barren peak,
A ridge which seemed to lead to a way
Through the forbidding range.
When they returned and told the two kings,
Odysseus immediately began to prepare
For his next journey, while Nausicaa watched him
Despairingly, but also found him warm clothes
And furs and footwear for his dangerous trek
Over the mountain. He made sure that the clothes
Did not mark him as noble, but he also determined
That they would not be so lowly as the ones
He had used as a disguise through Aetolia.

As he was preparing, Laodamas came to him.

"When we found you, you had strapped to your back
An oar. It was damaged and needed repair:
Here it is, renewed for you."

And he gave the surprised Odysseus the refurbished oar,
Which had been made to look as new.
Odysseus thanked him warmly, but this time
He would not conceal it in a cloth case
But keep it strapped to his back or carried
By hand, resting on his shoulder. He also made sure
His sword and its scabbard had been seen to as well.
For food and other things essential for him, Nausicaa
Made for him a bag to fit across his back, sewn of furs
And strong hide. All this he made ready the day
Before he left. On his final night, at the evening feast,
After the sacrifices and ceremonies were completed,
Alcinous spoke to those assembled:

"People of Phaeacia, we must bid farewell tonight
To one who may be known to us through our days
As the saviour of our race, teaching us the arts
Of war so that we may fulfill what is ordained for us.
We grieve at his departure, both as our hero,
And as the husband of my daughter, Nausicaa,
Who, after the future journey of the ship to Ithaca,
Will see him no more."

Nausicaa's eyes filled with tears, but she composed herself
And sat, steadfast, her eyes on Odysseus as if to
Keep every part of him cast in her memory.

"We thank him for all that he has done for us,
And we wish that his pilgrimage will find its goal
And that his life thereafter will be filled with peace
And that he will live in comfortable prosperity
To a great age in Ithaca. We drink to you, great Odysseus!"

And all there shouted, with all their hearts,
                                    "Odysseus!"

And the sound was such that it reverberated
Through the valley and echoed to the heavens.

Much moved, the Ithacan king stood up to speak,
And his voice, as it did at such times, could be heard
Clearly to the uttermost person that listened there.

"Noble Alcinous, gracious Queen Arête,
Lord Laodamas and all your brothers,
And my dear wife Nausicaa,"

And he took her hand and held it,

"I thank you for what you have said more than
You can imagine. Twice you have saved my life,
Twice shown me your generosity and hospitality,
And you have given me as well a wife without compare
In beauty and intelligence.  I am proud and grateful
To have helped you for your final migration,
For you have learned well the arts of war and those
Tactics and strategies so needed for them.

But before I must leave you—forced, as you know,
By what is ordained for me—I must in all truth
Tell you this: of all races that I have seen in this world
And in my life, you have shown yourselves to be
The most admirable, serving others in right fashion,
Generous among yourselves, adept in sports and arts,
Truly civilized. You go to face an unknown future,
But whatever may befall, I beg you not to lose
Your shining ways but act by all means to the good
And keep your deep integrity. You are descended
From a God, and God-like you are in appearance,
Full of grace and beauty, but you are still human
As well, still mortal, as are we all. May you continue
In this fashion for all the years to come."

He finished, and a roar arose from all as King Alcinous
Embraced him, then the queen and Laodamas, and
Finally his wife, now weeping openly at his fine words.

The feast went on yet longer; then Odysseus led his wife
Back to their tent; and there they made love repeatedly,
As if the world would end when they did. But Dawn arose,
As she always did, and her rosy light shone through the tent.
Reluctantly the two arose, and Odysseus prepared himself
To go, Nausicaa assisting where she could. A last meal
Was eaten with her and the royal family; and then a troop
On horseback awaited him. He embraced the stricken
Nausicaa, saying in her ear,

"I will see you again on the black ship."

Then he mounted and rode off with the others.
Alcinous led his wife and grieving daughter
To a vantage point on a slope not too far away;
And there they watched the troop disappear
Into woods, then reappear on the far-off slopes,
Becoming smaller and smaller, until they
Dwindled to dots on the slope at the end of the valley,
And disappeared completely.

# Canto 15
## ITHACA

Pelagia stood, wrapped tightly in her cloak
Against the still chill air, before her new home.
Below her the hill sloped away through the groves
To a sandy beach below; and across the bay,
Caught in the first rays of a fresh dawn,
She saw the palace glint against the mountains
That loomed around it and the bay.
Behind her the newly constructed house
Nestled against the hill, sheltered against
The north winds at its back, face toward
The south and the sun. To her left
Ran the wall that enclosed her new garden,
Still bare of plants in this late winter season.
As she watched the dawn give way
To the sun's majesty, she saw glint change to glow,
And she shivered, not from the vanishing chill.

*Only two days ago I saw this place,*
*Newly finished, from the palace, tiny*
*Against the hill and mountains behind it.*
*And now ...*

       She wrapped her cloak tighter
And through her surged a sense of utter isolation,
Cut off from those few that she now knew,
Despite the slaves who cared for her,
Despite the ever-present Amunet.
Just before Dawn had revealed herself,
Telemachus had left, riding back to the citadel.
She knew that this is what her days would be—
Telemachus with her through the night,
Gone through the day—and when he married—

She exclaimed and turned away—
She would seldom see him, and then against
The turbulence of his relationship with his new bride
And herself. Inside her she felt a stirring
And she was lost in the feelings of the being
Inside her body and walked back to the house,
Slightly more secure.

*The child will bring him*
*Back to me more than he comprehends.*

Soon it became warm enough to work the garden,
And she was busy moving between the two gardens,
Supervising the removal of the flowers and herbs
And all other flora, and making sure that they
Were planted properly and where she wished,
Under the tutelage of Amunet.
During this time Telemachus was with her
As much as he could manage, and he wondered
At her authority and knowledge as the garden
Flourished around them. And at night, while they lay
Together, he would feel her growing roundness,
Her fingers lightly on his as they explored,
And tenderly they loved.

During the past months Amunet had trained her well,
And now they could explore more exotic lore.
During this time her clients found their way
To her new place, and she treated them
With the dried herbs and potions that made up
Part of the warren of her workshop and storage spaces.
Far from driving off those who wanted her help,
The distance from the town enhanced her reputation,
Particularly since it took few hours to get there,
And she found herself busier than before,
But despite those who constantly came and went
She found herself desperately yearning
For Telemachus's return, even though few hours
Separated them. Many days he was forced
To feast with the queen, and Pelagia saw him
Grow in maturity as he took on the tasks

That his father would have done and that
His mother made sure he knew. During
The winter months neither of them spoke
Of Odysseus, but on those infrequent visits
To the palace that she was allowed to make,
Pelagia could see that the queen was under strain
And that Telemachus bore deep concern for
Both his father and his mother. As well,
The two lovers avoided mention of the summer
And the marriage now beginning, like a
Malignant moon, to rise on the horizon.

Winter sidled quietly away to let spring reign;
The garden was a riot of blooms and scents,
And its trees echoed the groves below it
In the greening of the leaves. Pelagia was now
In her last trimester; for some time she had
Not been able to ride or to practise arms,
And she chafed at the lack of such action
And worked harder in her garden
And amongst her pestles and potions.
She could feel the child now active in her,
And she became sensitive to all about her,
The growing morning breezes, the warmth
Of the sun on her skin, the beauty of the dusk
With the fading tints on the bay, and the gleam
Of the moon spreading on the quiet water,
And her attention grew more and more obsessed
With the imminent birth and what the child would be.
She could now see the growing worry
In the faces of Telemachus and his mother,
Even though no mention did she hear of Odysseus.
In her heart she half hoped that he would not return
And that the wedding would not take place,
But she knew that even if he did not come back,
The marriage would still at some time come to pass,
And she also knew that Odysseus would protect her
More than Queen Penelope. But, despite her forebodings,
When she came to the feasts, she made sure
That both drank wine drugged to make them

Peaceful in their minds and hearts; and she noticed
That she began to be invited to more feasts.
Penelope also treated her more solicitously,
Particularly as she was now so heavy with child,
And there were evenings when they talked together,
The queen asking of her former life, of which at first
She was reluctant to speak, for the pain
Still remained strong for her loss; but gradually
She spoke, first hesitantly, then in a flood, of
Her childhood and her parents, the mountains
And her friends, her training in horsemanship
And arms; the forests she loved, thick with evergreens,
The ground a carpet of needles and vegetation,
The light slanting through the high boughs;
And the birds, of whom she loved best the eagles
That soared above forest and crag and down
To the valley below. When she related these things
Her face glowed with memory and happiness,
And the queen was deeply moved by this young woman,
So ripe for birth and life, whose life had been wrenched
From her and twisted into new paths. Penelope
Found herself now beset with concerns—would
Her beloved Odysseus return, or would he remain away
As he did for years before, or, worse, not come back
At all; what would the new bride be like, who would come
Whether he returned or not, so young, untravelled,
Away from home, and unaware that her new husband
Had a concubine and child; and Pelagia herself, whom
The queen liked more and more, but who must remain
At distance from the family. Only when Pelagia visited,
And they feasted and talked, did she feel more at peace,
And she made sure that Pelagia came almost daily.

As her time grew near, Pelagia, now ripe with child,
Made preparations for the birth. Each day
At the small altar in her garden she sacrificed
Young lambs and goats, and each day she left there
Gifts for the two Goddesses to whom she prayed.

"Radiant Artemis,
Lovely daughter of Zeus and Leto,

Who helped give birth to your own twin,
Glorious Apollo, great God of healing,
Goddess of light,
Protector of women,
Compassionate in childbirth,
Be with me in my own time of birthing;
And gracious Eileithyia,
Gracious daughter of Olympian Zeus and Hera,
Gentle Goddess of childbirth,
Come to me when I am in labour,
Help me in my arduous time
To endure the pain of my child's delivery."

And she made sure of her preparations,
Both at her own house and at the palace,
Having on hand olive oil and provision for warm water,
Soft sponges from the sea for cleansing her,
Woollen cloths to cover her parts,
Soft swaddling bands for the newborn infant,
Pillows and stools and a proper place
For the birthing bed and delivery,
And herbs and fruit and vegetables
For her to smell and to help revive her
As she laboured. She made such things
For both places, even as she hoped the time
Would be at the palace.

But, as it turned out, Pelagia was at home
When her waters broke and Telemachus
Had not yet come. A servant was quickly sent
To inform the palace, but she was still attended
Only by servants, frightened and inexperienced
In these matters, and by Amunet, who gave her potions.
Her labour pains increased far more than she had thought;
She tried to control her cries, but began to call
For Telemachus as they increased. Then
He arrived, and with him the old nurse Eurycleia,
Who as an experienced midwife quickly took charge.
And Amunet silently left the room.
From the time that she first met her,
The old woman had been disturbed by Pelagia,

But as she saw her work with herbs and drugs,
And as Pelagia courted her, listening to her attentively,
Asking her questions about remedies and healings,
She grew more fond of the girl, even though
She was now recognized as concubine to the prince,
Something that had not happened before
In her experience. Now she felt secure as midwife,
And found everything in place as she would wish,
Had the servants heat water, had the labouring girl
Pray again to the two Goddesses, had her breathe in
The fumes of the herbs she had provided, along with
Lemon and quince to keep her alert and strong.
Telemachus came to her side to hold her hand
And give her reassurance, but Eurycleia quickly
Shooed him away.

"I did not permit your father
To be present at your birth, nor will I now
Let you be here!"

As it turned out, Pelagia's labour was not so long
As they feared; and in an orgasmic effort,
The child was born, and the mother, seeing her new son,
Lay back, exhausted and happy as Telemachus,
Hearing his son's first cry, burst into the room.

"A male child!"
                    cried the old woman joyfully,
Showing him the baby, now swathed in wool,
And he touched it in wonder, then swiftly moved
To Pelagia, who smiled wearily at him.

"You have now a son, my beloved prince."

Moved, he knelt to kiss her; then, without speaking,
Stayed with her as she fell asleep, his hand
Always in hers.

Spring now grew into glorious summer,
And both mother and child flourished
As did her garden. But as the summer matured
To its height, the mood in the palace darkened.

No word of Odysseus; no fleet ship from other lands
Brought word of him; no traveller knew anything.
Penelope grew anxious and restless; particularly
When a messenger arrived from Pylos, asking
About Odysseus.

"Please inform the royal family
That we have had no word of him yet, and
Ask them to be patient: as soon as we hear
From him, we will send our fastest ship
To tell you, and plans for the wedding
Can commence. In the meantime,
Send my own warm welcome to Polycaste
And her gracious mother, and say that
I hope that we will soon be together."

The messenger left, his disappointment
Unable to be concealed. Penelope grew more worried;
She feared another twenty years before she saw her husband,
Or even worse. Pelagia, who now stayed overnight at the palace,
The queen enjoying her new grandson, worked hard
To alleviate her concern, making sure that drugs helped
To assuage the doubt that lurked to attack the queen
When she least expected. Telemachus, although concerned
As well for his father, spent his time revelling in
His new fatherhood, but also helped his mother more and more
In all aspects of statehood. For a time it appeared
That the remaining parents of the slain suitors might
Attempt to overthrow the palace; but Telemachus kept
The men who had accompanied him on the last adventure
Fully in training, and all feared to confront that
Formidable force.

And so the summer heat beat down, while each day
Penelope kept watch on the bay, or at times
Travelled to see the ocean dark before her;
And at night she looked out when the moon shone
At its rays glistening on the surface of the bay,
And on some nights those same rays found
The tears glistening on her cheek.

# Canto 16
## THE PINDOS MOUNTAINS

For some time Laodamas led his troop up the far slope,
For he it was who wished to accompany Odysseus
To the final farewell. Although summer was at its height,
The trees soon thinned and petered out, and the horses
Now had to trudge through the snow that covered the summits
Of these towering mountains. No pass revealed itself to them,
But onward they went, concern mounting that the king
Would be forced to climb over the summit
That towered precipitously above them.
On they went, the sun now past its apex in the sky,
The snow yet deeper, the horses now struggling.
Then the alert Ithacan saw ahead that behind
A mound a distance before them, a slight shadow
Betrayed a more distant slope. Pointing this out
To the group, he had them struggle to reach,
Then move around, the impediment; and there
They saw, reaching before them, the steep slopes
That led to the roots of the two embracing mountains.

"Here I must leave you, noble Laodamas and friends,
And leave also my mount that cannot traverse
What I must now cross."

              And he dismounted
And carefully took the bundle and the oar
And arranged them on his back. Then he embraced
And said farewell to the prince and the troop,
Who, sad-eyed, watched him as he pushed his way
Through the snow and disappeared around the bend.

As he struggled through the snow, Odysseus
Glanced at the high mountains that towered about him.

Where he was they appeared patched in white,
But through the snow their mighty grey stone thrust,
And he shivered, not only with the cold, but with
His sense of these forbidding peaks.
Gradually he began to descend, and as he did
The snow thinned as he came to the frontier of the trees.
Along and down he went through the thick forest,
And as he did so he could feel the sun again
Bringing life to the slope. As he progressed farther,
He came to brief meadows, now alive with green grasses,
And as the sun began its descent behind the mountains,
He stopped at one of these and made ready for the night,
Eating a sparse meal and finding water in a stream nearby.
That night he piled up boughs around him near the fire
Which he had started from a glowing ember that he
Had brought with him. As he lay there, looking up
At the clear cold sky, the stars dancing in their multitudes,
He thought back on the events of the past few months—
His captivity and slavery, his escape, and the months
With the Phaeacians, and finally his marriage
To Nausicaa. Even as he thought of her,
A surge of desire swept through him as he remembered
Her young body; and then, without pause, the memory
Of Penelope and their love came into his mind,
And he found himself caught between the visions
Of the two women. Then, as the sound of the flames
Crackling in his fire, and the sounds of animals and
Night birds in the forest dark merged with those of the fire,
He gradually fell asleep, still haunted by the memories
Of those so intimate with him.

*Sputtering of the fire*
*Another sound*
*Piercing through the fire*
*Buzz*
*Nothing*
*Penelope looks at me*
*Her face*
*The care burnt in*
*Still stops my heart*
*But she stares at me*

*Then beside me*
*Standing there*
*Nausicaa*
*Penelope knows*
*Her face*
*Betrayal and grief*
*Nausicaa*
*Melts into me*
*Then walks away*
*Smaller*
*Smaller*
*Gone*
*But Penelope still stands*
*Looking at me*
*Now sad beyond hope*
*Then turns*
*And walks away*
*Smaller*
*Smaller*
*Gone*
*Alone*
*Only chill wind a companion*
*I acted honourably.*
*Helped a people*
*Helped a girl to live*
*But*
*But*
*No woman left*
*No Nausicaa*
*No Penelope*
*No one*
*Nothing*
*So empty*
*Barren*
*Like the shade*
*Of my mother*
*Like my shade will be*

Morning light crept upon his face
And he awakened, stiff under the boughs,
His fire, embers and ashes. He arose painfully,

Found water to drink and with which to cleanse,
Then gathered his belongings and set off again.
He gradually trekked downward, through forests
And small clear spaces, watching carefully
The peaks of the mountains about him
As he kept descending. In this time of summer
He could hear the calls of birds increasing,
And around him at times he could make out
The rustle of animals as they paced quietly
Through the undergrowth that now became
More plenteous. Finally he reached the roots
Of the mountain, a clear stream rushing along
Steep banks on either side as the two mountains
Nudged closely to each other at their bases.
Above the turbulent waters he trudged with care,
Then stopped at a small plateau to eat and drink.
In all this time he had seen nothing that revealed
That humans had passed this way, and deer
And other animals came near to him, unafraid.
But while he rested after his sparse meal,
He searched among the peaks that now soared
High above him. He noticed that farther on
There appeared to be a range that reared up against
The mountains beneath which he travelled.
Soon he arose and started out again,
Keeping careful note of the mass ahead.
But as the afternoon wore on he realized
That the distances he saw were much farther
Than he had thought. And that night,
Finding a place where he could secure himself
And keep a safe fire, he made his bivouac
And warmed himself against the quickly chilling air.
As he prepared for sleep again, the sibilance
Of the stream below was stronger than
His fire's voice, and to that swift music he succumbed.

*Phaeacians*
*Massed before my eyes*
*Like a plain of statues*
*All frozen in positions*

*Alcinous and Arête*
*Their arms clasped about each other*
*But each looking in other directions*
*Her look of anxiety and fear*
*His look fierce and protective*
*But his wise face now twisted*
*Toward secret plans and tactics*
*Laodamas*
*Strong and intelligent*
*Seated on his horse*
*His spear raised threateningly*
*But in defensive posture*
*And his open face now closed*
*More secretive and crafty*
*So all the others*
*Who crouch or stand defiantly*
*Or hold their horses*
*Or keep their arms before them*
*All with expressions veiled*
*Eyes suspicious*
*And in their midst*
*The women hold their gowns*
*Tight about them*
*And on their faces unutterable sadness*
*And in the centre of them*
*Nausicaa*
*Heavy with child*
*Her face a mask of calm despair*
*And then as one*
*On the whole plain*
*The statues' heads come to life*
*To turn to look at me*
*Their eyes*
*Their eyes*
*And a pang spears through me*
*Of such desolation*
*That I cannot bear it*

And Odysseus awoke, sweat running from him
Despite the chill night air, the sky dark above him.

He groped to the dying embers of the fire
And renewed its life, then sat for the long remainder
Of the night, brooding on what he had dreamed,
Not willing to return to sleep, where he might revisit
That terrible scene.
Dawn arose from her nocturnal bed,
But her soft fingers did not touch the deep ravine
In which Odysseus dozed, his fire almost dead again.
Sighing, he packed and started out more,
Following the steep banks of the rushing stream.
At midday he stopped and checked his supplies,
Only to find that he had little left. Hungry,
With his knife he cut smooth a slim branch
And shaped a sharp point on one end; then
He clambered down the bank to a place where
Stones broke the surface of the swift current,
And, poised there, he watched for fish to pass.
Twice he lunged and missed; but on a third try
He impaled a silver shape that gleamed as it
Writhed on his pole. Another fire made, he gutted
And cleaned the fish, then grilled it on a pole
Supported by two y-shaped boughs that
He had fashioned. He ate fully, savouring the flesh,
And tidied the space, packed once more, and
Started out again. For three days thus he travelled,
Spearing fish and trudging toward the great range
That loomed ever closer.

Finally he came to a space where the roots ended
Of the mountains he followed, and he emerged
To see the huge range that ran north and west
As far as he could see. Now before him he found
A valley that was enclosed on one side by the range
And on the other by more mountains, equally immense.
At his end the valley was hidden by a thick forest,
Through which he now worked his way. For some time
He trudged, and as the sun began to slide behind the peaks
He looked for a space where he could camp for the night.
At last he found a small clearing, and there
He made a fire and cooked what remnants he had left

From the fish that he had caught earlier that day.
As he prepared boughs again for a sleep that he dreaded
But needed after his effort, he heard, not far away,
The howl of a wolf, to which others replied.
Quickly he rearranged his camp, making sure
That behind him were trees and a barricade
That he improvised, and before him his fire,
For which he made sure there were ample supplies of fuel.
Then, his back to a tree trunk, he sat and waited,
His sword across his lap, his knife by his side.
No further howls were heard; but the sharp-eared warrior
Could hear the sounds of movement in the trees around him.
Then, as he watched closely, he could see yellow eyes
Gleaming in the dark just beyond the flames.
He waited, motionless, alert. Then, a sudden leap
Behind his tree and barricade, and a yelp
As a body thudded against his shelter and was pierced
By the pointed sticks he had carefully arranged
Among the heavy branches and foliage.
Now he saw the wolfish shapes trotting around his camp,
Looking for some means of entry.
Quietly, as a shadow slowly rises on a wall,
He rose, and stepping to the fire, reached for a brand.
As he did so, a wolf leapt by the edge of the blaze
And at him. The blur of his blade, and the wolf's
Head dropped at his feet. Now others began to jump
At the same place; but he now had placed himself
So that as they jumped he sliced them with his sword
Or with the brand pushed them onto the flames.
A maelstrom of bodies, shadows leaping in all directions,
Snarls and yelps, and the warrior at battle worse
Than that he waged at Ilion. An eternity of brief time,
And then silence fell again, except for Odysseus,
Breathing heavily. At least half of the pack had been
Killed or wounded, the others slinking off into the dark.
Odysseus checked each body, slaughtering those
In wounded or burnt agony. Finally he tossed the bodies
On the fire, built it up to new heights, and wiped his blade
Clean of the blood and fur. Making sure his barricade
Was rebuilt to ward off any further attack, he sat

Against the massive trunk again to rest.
In exhaustion his head dropped forward and he slept,
But in a deep dreamless sleep.

The sun was bright above the peaks when he awoke.
And the fire burned only faintly, the wolves' bodies
Consumed but for occasional bones and skulls.
He packed his few belongings, adjusted his oar
Upon his back, then cautiously set out through the trees,
Wary of the remnant of the pack. But he could not sense
Them near; and he plodded on. Now thirst beset him,
And he looked along the way for signs of a stream,
Yet none he saw. But as he foraged on he found a small trail
That now wound through the forest, and he realized
That he must be near some human habitation,
And he hurried on, his tongue thick and dry.
The trail continued on, and soon the trees began to thin,
And at last he saw ahead a clearer space.
Breaking from the verge of the forest
He saw before him a valley with immense peaks
On each side and at its far end enclosing it
In such a way that it seemed sealed away
From access to any other place—and this
He could confirm from his own ordeal
In penetrating its barrier past the woods
Of those mountains he had with pain traversed.
Immediately in front of him he saw a field of grass
In which cattle browsed contentedly; and
Just beyond he saw a field of lush grain
Now turning gold for their future harvest.
On huge flanks of the rearing mountains
He saw groves of olive trees, and even
Here and there, other trees bearing fruit.
Farther down the valley, but indistinguishable
From where he stood, he could see smoke rising.
He wished to reach there as soon as he could,
But his thirst forced him to search for a stream.
The observant Ithacan carefully watched
The beasts grazing before him and noted where
Some of them seemed to gravitate;

Following them, he shortly came to
A wide stream that meandered down the valley.
He dropped down before it, giving a silent thanks
To his immortal patroness, Pallas Athena,
And then drank long and deep. His thirst now slaked,
He stripped and, hiding his clothes and possessions
Under a bush at the water's edge, he plunged in,
Gasping at the water's chill, then enjoying
The exhilaration. His ablutions finished,
He returned to the bank next to his things
And lay in the warm bright sun to dry himself,
Letting the sounds of the cattle and the chattering birds
Drift over him. For a time he dozed, content
To be as one with all about him; then, hunger
Now reminding him, he fetched out his possessions
And with his knife fashioned another spear,
With which he stood patiently in the quiet current,
Then finally speared a fish whose silver scales
Flashed in the bright sun. A small fire quickly made,
The fish roasted, a prayer made to the Gods,
He feasted; and, hunger assuaged and vigour renewed,
He put out the fire, carefully tidied the place,
And started out again, this time along
The low bank of the stream. Trees straggled beside
Him on either bank, and he saw birds and their nests
Occupy them. As he walked he noted also
That on the lower slopes he could see,
As well as groves, meadows and pasture land
On which cattle, sheep, and goats all grazed,
And there he saw as well houses and huts.
By now he had passed the grassy field and
Strode at the edge of the field of grain,
Which was larger than he had envisaged;
But when he came to its end he found a trail,
Wide and well-trodden, and he left the bank
To follow it. Now he saw on either side
The small farms with groves and animals and fields,
All of which seemed well tended; he also saw
Figures out in the fields, but they did not see him,
Or if they did, they gave no sense that they had.

Then, a distance ahead, he saw a cluster of buildings,
And he made for them. They were too few
To compose a town or village or a hamlet,
But they appeared to be the only clustered
Habitation in the valley. As the trail
Moved between them he saw that the buildings
Were part of several farms that fanned out
On either side. As he travelled between them,
The trail sending up small puffs of dust from his feet,
He saw several men, clad in garments of wool and fur,
Who watched him in amazement. He nodded to them
In greeting, but they quickly moved away
To field or building. Somewhat disconcerted
He strode onward; but behind him in the clear air
He could hear animated discussion, and his sharp ears
Noted that despite the strange archaic dialect
He could still make out words and understand the sense.
What he concluded was that they knew all who lived
In the valley, and therefore, both from that fact
And from his clothes, so different from theirs,
He was a stranger—and strangers were unknown here.
In fact, they had no such word: "someone
Not seen before" was how he was described.
But still he continued on, for no one had greeted him,
And he hoped that soon a man passing him
Would stop and greet him as the prophecy foretold.
But here no one did so, and he passed through
And on along the trail. More fields of grain
And grass and cattle ranged on either side,
And the groves and meadows still spread up the slopes.
By now the sun was creeping close to the western peaks.
Hungry again and thirsty, at a field of grass
He veered off the trail to search for river or stream.
For some time he walked, the eastern flank now
Slightly closer. Finally he saw a row
Of trees and shrubs, and his pace quickened.
There he found the stream's bank, and as before
He fashioned a spear and impaled his fish.
A fire built, the fish roasted and eaten,
A careful camp made near the bank, he then

Could rest and think as dusk grew thick
Around him. Like a boulder solid in the earth
He sat, still and immoveable, as he considered
What next to do.

*This valley shows no sign*
*Of travel from afar that I can see—*
*The route I took to get here is hard*
*And tortuous, and I see nothing to suggest*
*Any came that way before me. And those*
*That I have seen so far seem amazed at*
*Strangers in their midst. As well there appear*
*No means or place for defence. Yet this land*
*Seems prosperous and fruitful, with well-tended*
*Fields and groves, with numerous beasts, and all*
*Their clothing is obtained from what they have*
*About them. Fortunate it is that*
*Their language, strange to my ear, still lets me*
*Understand somewhat. I pray to the Gods*
*That it be here that the quest is fulfilled;*
*But still I must meet on the road the man*
*To ask the fateful question.*

Darkness now
Shrouded the valley, and, building up his fire,
He lay down and drifted into sleep.

*The current whispers quietly*
*Water slipping over rocks and pebbles*
*Then*
*Underneath*
*Buzz*
*Buzz*
*Lifted high above*
*Snow encrusted peaks*
*The cold clear voice*

   "Dodona"

*The slopes and lakes*
*The sacred shrine*

*Altar blazing*
*Before me*

    "Come soon
    Soon"

And his eyes opened to the night stars
Above him, a quiet breeze rustling leaves
Around him, and the whispering gurgle
Of the stream next to his camp. Awake now,
He lay gazing at the constellations
Creep slowly above him in that infinite sky,
Until, before the first tinge of the dawn
He fell exhausted into deep black sleep.

When he awoke the sun had cleared the peaks
And he again performed the rituals
Of fire, hunt, and feast, and ablutions
And striking of his camp. Then he retraced
His steps through the field and back to the trail,
Which he soon found turned abruptly to come near,
Then follow, that path of the stream. He trudged
Along, shaded by trees along the bank,
Seeing on the other side of him more fields
And beyond the stream the nearer slope studded
With groves and meadows and low houses.
He could see as well still some way ahead
The end of the valley; but soon he came
To marshy ground and the trail veered again
Away from the running water. Then through
Some bushes he caught sight of a lake,
Its waters crystal clear, with narrow beaches
Now on its shoreline, and more marshes on either side.
Herons he saw among the reeds, still and poised
As they searched about for their prey,
And ducks and many other birds swam or
Flew about the lake and shore. The sun was now
At its height in the harsh blue sky, the tips
Of the peaks bright with dazzling snow, the slopes
Ablaze with all the colours found in grove
And meadow, flower and bush. Odysseus moved on,

Noting that on the lake he could see boats
With fishermen. The trail continued along the verge
Of the lake; finally the tired Ithacan
Took rest under a tree with leaf-laden boughs,
First slaking his thirst, and there he stayed
For a short while, watching the sun creep over
Its apex, and noting the slope far beyond the lake.
It looked nothing like the slopes beside it:
A vast smooth wall was left where most of
The side, in a cataclysmic slide, had
Sliced away so that at the mountain's foot
Huge piles of rubble littered slope and valley.
Now he began to understand clearly
The isolation of the valley: the slide
Must have sealed off any pass or gap;
And the way he had come was too difficult,
With its devious route along such banks
Precarious, the danger of wild animals,
And no way without hard effort to clear
A road to the next valley, hidden itself.
Somehow this race had become self-sufficient.
But how? And when? Still, tantalizing as
These questions were, more assuring still
Was its isolation for the success
Of his quest. The thought spurred him on; he rose
And continued along the trail beside the lake.
He could now see that the water crept near
Either side of the valley, although where
He travelled there were more woods to be seen.
As the afternoon wore on, he managed
To come near the end of this side of the lake,
Where he found the trail bifurcated, one
Leading away back along the valley,
And the other skirting still the lake.
Without a thought he took the lake route
And found on one side the lake now marsh strewn
And at his other shoulder woods thick with
Trees and bushes. This way seemed less trodden.
As dusk approached, he found a place to camp
At the wood's edge, then again fashioned a spear

And crept into the marsh, where he crouched in wait.
After a while a duck swam through the reeds
And he swiftly and with deadly aim speared
The hapless fowl. Back at his camp he made
Ready, preparing and roasting it. Then,
With thanks to the Gods, he ate it with relish,
Piled high his fire, fashioned his bed from boughs
Soft with foliage, and lay there, watching night
Darken and the stars adorn the black sky.

*Hills at dusk*
*Hills in a new land*
*Unknown*
*Men on horseback*
*Grim*
*Weary*
*Familiar*
*So familiar*
*Then*
*Laodamas*
*Clytoneus*
*Halius*
*No Alcinous*
*But others*
*Alcaios*
*Arsemios*
*And many more*
*They wait*
*Then Laodamas raises his sword*
*And before him*
*The hill*
*The hill opens wide*
*And glorious light*
*Golden*
*Blazes forth*
*And in that unearthly light*
*Towers and palaces*
*And fair streets*
*All shine in the light*
*And the horsemen*

*Canter into that light*
*And down the thoroughfare*
*And as the last enters*
*A deep rumble*
*A deeper roar*
*And the hill*
*Majestically*
*Seals behind them*

Dawn with her slender delicate fingers
Lightly touched his eyelids, awakening him,
And he finished the duck's remains, bathed,
Broke camp, and started on his way again
As the sun broke free above the peaks.
While he walked along the trail faint with use,
Shadowed on one side by the tall black trees
And on the other reflected in the lake's crystal liquid,
He saw across the farther end of the lake
That the moraine that seemed so near before
Was much farther off, and that much, much time
Had passed since its fall, for the lower debris
Was softened by trees and vegetation
To make an approximation of a plain,
Rough and bumpy as it may appear.
On he continued, and by midday he
Found himself more than halfway down the length
Of the lake. He stopped, slaked his thirst, rested
In shade, protected from the sun high above,
Then again proceeded on his journey.
As the afternoon neared its end, he found
Himself at the lake's end. The meager trail
Led through some trees and bushes to more open ground,
But because the day was soon to draw to a close
He returned to a space near the lake, and
As he had done before, made camp, hunted, and ate.
Then, his faced reflected in his fire's blaze,
He sat and thought more about what he had seen.

*That landslide is much older than I thought.*
*These people could have been here a long time,*
*For many generations. And all this time*

*Cut off from any contact elsewhere.*
*Their dialect seems old as well, though I*
*Can, with effort, understand it. But soon*
*I will reach the end of this valley, soon.*
*Not much opportunity is left here*
*In this place of hope for me—Athena,*
*Great Goddess and my patron, I pray*
*To you to aid me to fulfill my task!*

Then, exhausted, he lay on soft boughs and slept.

*On Ithaca*
*I stand at the cliff's edge*
*And look across the sea*
*Tall ranges of mountains*
*Tipped with white*
*Then*
*Over them*
*Small specks appear*
*Then darker clouds*
*Make their way*
*Along the ranges*
*Across the countries*
*That I know*
*Across the sea*
*Toward me*
*Now nearer*
*Eagles*
*Eagles in their thousands*
*And their harsh cries*
*Pierce my heart*
*And on the mainland*
*Fires rise on the slopes*
*And on Ithaca*
*Fire rises around me*
*Everywhere*
*And I see all*
*Consumed*

Early the next morning, his rituals
Done, Odysseus started forth again.

The trail, now very faint, led him away
From the lake and wound across the rough plain.
An occasional small field of grain he saw,
But most of the ground seemed suitable for
Meadow, and indeed he saw cattle and
Sheep and goats dotted throughout, all grazing.
He walked on, finding the ground sloped upward,
And after a time he stopped to look across
The lake and down the valley. He was surprised
To see more farms and buildings than he
Had assumed; and when he turned back and looked
Over the plain, he saw there dwellings as well,
And high above where he had begun his trek
He now saw among the moraine a cave
That seemed to be an opening to a mine,
With men leading carts of ore to a nearby
Shed, where smoke belched forth.

*They mine and refine metal.*

And he became more intrigued with
This lost land and its inhabitants. Soon,
In fact, he came to a place where a branch
Of the trail led back and up to the diggings,
But he chose to keep to the main trail,
Such as it was. By now the sun had reached
Its zenith in the clear blue sky. He moved on,
With each step more anxious that he would not
Meet anyone. Ahead he saw, still far off,
The destroyed face of the mountain seal off
All exit from the valley, just as he
Had seen on its other side. Whatever
Happened in the valley, he knew he must
Still travel north somehow across that vast
Barrier. He winced; then up the way he saw
A young man, who hitherto in a grove
Had been unseen, step across a field
On to the road and walk toward him.
Each closely eyed the other as they approached.
The young man was on this hot day wearing
Only a loin cloth of soft fringed leather

And leather sandals on his feet; over
His shoulder he had slung a young lamb.
His face appeared open and genuine
Under his curly dark hair, his eyes bright
And inquisitive, and at this moment
Wide. When they met the young man stopped and greeted
The travel-worn king, as surprised as the other.
Odysseus found the dialect even stronger
Than the one heard farther back in the valley
But still understood and answered in kind.
The other was equally puzzled by
The Ithacan's words but also could make out
What he said. For a short time they spoke of
Things inconsequential—the weather, the trail—
Like two dogs who sniff at each other
To determine friend from foe. Odysseus
Quickly saw that the other did not travel
Much in the valley and did not see him
As someone alien to this land,
But the young man did look curiously
At the stranger's clothes, and then he could not
Restrain himself further—he asked, so far
As Odysseus could tell,

> "What is that you
Have upon your back? Is it a tool for
Winnowing the wheat?"

> For a moment
The astounded king could not believe what he
Had just heard—then with a joyous shout he
Embraced the astonished youth, and taking
The oar from his back and holding it
Upright, Odysseus knelt in the dust and
Called out,

> "Thanks to you, great Lord Poseidon,
Who has given me this sign to fulfill
Your prophecy. Here will I set up this oar
As you commanded, as a shrine to your glory."

Then he arose and told the dumbfounded youth
The story of the prophecy and his quest.
He in turn, now looking at Odysseus
Almost as a God, offered his lamb
For sacrifice. Close to the trail there was
A mound that acted as a small promontory
Above those who travelled below. Up to
This place Odysseus climbed with the oar
And his new follower, and together
They planted the oar firmly in the ground,
Then around it built a cairn of good stones
For which they searched carefully everywhere
On the slope. When the shrine was completed
To Odysseus's full satisfaction,
He built a fire before it; with the help
Of the youth he placed the terrified lamb
Below the shrine, then prayed to the God.

"I hymn to thee, Poseidon,
Brother of Zeus, dread hurler of the lightning,
Thou Ruler of Earth and Sea, whose majesty
Is seen in the illimitable waters
And the tall peaks that you have reared up
To the heavens; whose awesome power we see
Unleashed in great tempests where our ships
Are tossed helpless and ripped into small slivers,
Ourselves sinking into your unknown depths
As morsels for your underwater creatures;
Or when with your terrible fist you strike
The earth and mountains crumble, cities tossed
Into great chasms to perish utterly.
Still now, mighty Lord, your power and your wrath.
With this dedication to you, done at your command
To expiate me from my sins to you,
I ask you, as it is foretold, now
To release me from your dread enmity
And let me return to my native Ithaca
To live the days I have in peace, at home.
And to your honour and just accord
Here we sacrifice to you this lamb

Brought fatefully to do you service,
And as promise of the greater sacrifice
Of the best ram, bull, and boar."

And as he finished praying he drew
His dagger and with a swift stroke sliced open
The lamb's neck and let the blood pour upon
The ground, seeping in pools before the shrine.
For a moment there was silence and
A stillness over all; no bird could now be heard,
Nor any wind nor breeze; then, deep below them
Came a rumble that grew louder, and
The earth began to move and shake, boulders
Began to tumble down from the moraine;
And to the far side of the slope, against
The neighbouring range, grinding shrieks erupted,
And another vast slide rushed down, plunging
To the plain. The two men were thrown down
And they watched with horror as huge boulders
Roared down from above; some bounced high over them;
But neither they nor the shrine, whose rocks remained still
And firm, were touched or harmed. Time seemed to stop;
And then the jolts and noises ceased, and all
Was as before, except for the mountain's new gash.
They remained there on the shaken ground, dazed
But unhurt, the lamb's corpse beside them.
Then Odysseus cleared his head and arose,
Helping the other up.

                    "Have you family near?"

The young man nodded.

                    "Do they have animals,
Rams, bulls, boars?"

                    A reluctant nod.

                    "Have them
Bring the best of each, so that obeisance
Can be made."

This time a look more disturbed.

"Only then can the God be appeased and kept
From greater destruction."

                     The boy, white-faced,
Gaped at the dreadful possibility.

"Hurry, bring them here with the beasts to join
Us in our feast and celebration—and
Any wine you have!"

                    A nod, and he passed back
The way he had come. While he was away,
Odysseus prepared the carcass to roast,
Muttering a prayer as he threw the entrails
On the flames where they sizzled, sending smoke
And the prayer up to the Gods. By the time
The young man returned, the lamb's parts roasted well.
With him he brought an older couple, the man
Lean and deeply tanned, his face lined, his hair,
Curly as his son's, now touched with grey;
Beside him his wife, tall and worn from work.
Both wore clothes of home-grown wool, but their feet
Were bare. Beside them was a girl, lissome,
In her late teens, dressed like her mother, and
With her a younger boy, dressed like his brother,
The women herding before them the ram and bull,
The men staggering under the weight
Of a large boar, stunned and trussed to a pole.
All approached him wide-eyed, still stunned from what
They had endured in the massive earthquake
And fearful from what the older son had told them
Of his meeting, the building of the shrine,
The prayer and sacrifice and the prompt,
Earth-shattering response, and now the sight
Of the Ithacan dressed in clothes so strange
To them. Odysseus greeted them warmly
And led them to where the lamb was roasting.

"I thank you for the gift of this fine lamb
To offer in sacrifice to the sacred God

Poseidon, who, as you can see, has answered
My prayers. Let us here feast in his honour,
Once we have completed the sacrifice."

The father nodded but said nothing, both
Because of the shock of the mention of
The God, and the present loss of his precious
Animals. But now to the fire they went,
Where the woman from her pouch now produced
Herbs which she sprinkled on the roasting lamb.
Then he had them bring the beasts to the shrine,
Where each in turn he slew, separating
Head from body with swift mighty strokes of his sword
To the family's fearful amazement,
And completing the prayer to the awesome God.
Perceptive Odysseus, who noted that
They had brought a wine-skin, now prepared
A libation to the Earth-Shaker, and
All drank from the skin. Then from the lamb
He cut choice pieces and gave them to each
Of the family even as the other victims
Began to roast. At the impromptu feast
All relaxed before the warmth of the food
And drink and fire and the king's charm.
Gradually he drew from them the story
Of the valley.

       "A long time ago,"
                       said
The father, gazing into the flames,

"A time our fathers heard from their fathers,
Who had in turn learned of it from their own,
And so kept it alive through generations,
Our people travelled here from a land far
In the north—so far that none knows where it
Truly was or what it was like, only
That they crossed through valleys and through passes
Between towering peaks. But at last they
Found this valley, void of people but teeming
With wild life, and with fertile soil, and here

They settled to live happily. Sometimes
Trade took place with others in distant valleys,
But few came here, and all of us lived in peace.
But, it is said, we lost contact with the Gods,
For we had no priests and lost the habit
Of sacrificing. Then one fateful day
A man of dour disposition, of mean spirit
And vile mouth, cynical and bitter too,
Blasphemed, saying that our Gods were but tales
Told to frighten children and make us fear
At night. No sooner had he spoken this
Than all sounds of animals ceased here—
Birds were silent, cattle remained motionless,
And dogs crept on their bellies into places
Secret. A terrible stillness lay upon
The valley. Then a faint rumble started
Deep, deep in the earth. It grew in strength, and
As it did so, the ground began to shake and
Move and ripple; houses of stone crumbled;
Cracks and crevices ravaged the earth, into which
Whole fields were swallowed and families fell
Screaming. Then, at the height of this dreadful
Movement people shouted and pointed to
The mountain upon which we sit. Slowly
A long, long crack appeared high up, and with
A grinding roar, much of the face broke off
And rushed down the slopes, the fierce avalanche
Carrying all before it, with whole forests,
Farms and people obliterated. What
Was left you see before you now, but long
Since vegetation has covered some of the scars.
Afterwards, those who had survived explored
The extent of the damage and found all
Passage from the valley sealed off, old passes
Blocked. It was then that our forebears understood
Two things: we had been isolated from
The rest of the world, with no means of contact,
And this was our punishment from the Gods
For our blasphemy. The man responsible
Could not receive our anger, for he and

His family had been swallowed up in
The catastrophe. But since so few were left
No temple nor no priest could be created,
And so in each home a shrine was built,
And each day every family prays
In contrition, and sacrifice is made—
In fact, the lamb we eat was intended so.
And so you see us here today—all things
Made by us or grown or hunted by us.
Our mines and quarry give us metals
And we have managed over the long years
To live in some comfort and in peace."

With that he stopped and smiled wanly at
Odysseus, who had listened intently
To all he had said, adjusting his thought
To the archaic speech. But before
He could reply, the man said,

"But stranger—for we now understand you so—
Tell us how you came here, and why, and what
This shrine and sign for the God portend."

"I will do so with great pleasure,"
                                        replied
The clever king.

                 "But first, I notice that
The sacrifice you season with fragrant herbs.
I seem to know most of them—no salt,
However, did I see you use. Can you
Tell me why?"

                 The others looked at him
In puzzlement; and then the wife, who had
Not spoken until now, asked,

                              "Good sir, what
Is this herb that you call *salt*? We know not
What it is."

               Odysseus carefully took
From his bag a small pouch, carefully opened it,

And from it took a small pinch of coarse-grained
Salt.

    "Perhaps you know it as a spice?"

Each tasted it, but all shook their heads
Wonderingly. The grateful king with pleasure
Sighed.

"Then, good people, I will tell you
My story."

        And he told them all—his part
In the Trojan War; his hard struggle
To journey home for yet another decade;
His angering Poseidon on that voyage;
The prophecy that forced him to the quest;
And his journeys through Hellene to gain
What he pursued.

         "And here is the end of it—
Here with you, and the Earth Thunderer
Has given his sign of approbation."

He ceased; now it was dark, but in the flames
Of the large fire he saw the look of awe
On each face before him.

         "And he may smile
Upon you as well. In the morning let us
Explore what the fallen rock reveals."

They nodded acquiescence, their expression
A rich mixture of both hope and wonder.
Then the father invited Odysseus,
Now looked upon as one half divine,
To sleep at their house. He gratefully
Accepted, and they stumbled to the farm,
Tripping on, or having to travel around,
The new stones and boulders that now littered
Their way. But finally they arrived, and
The weary Ithacan lay upon soft fleeces
That were carefully arranged for him.

That night he slept without event, but when
He awoke in the crisp dawn air, a strong
Urge came upon him, an urge to move on.
He resisted long enough to eat with
The others; then, as soon as was appropriate,
He packed his few possessions and, no longer
Hampered by the long oar he had carried
On his back over all these mountain ranges,
He led the father and his two sons
Across the new-torn face of the ravaged
Mountain. But first, looking around them,
They marvelled at what they saw: new debris
Littered the wounded side, and vast heaps
Of moraine farther on and below had
Obliterated forest, farm, and even part
Of the lake, now murky with rock and dirt.
But most they were in wonder that their own
Farm and house had been spared despite the rocks
And boulders that had confronted them.
They also saw, far off in the valley
And at the mountain's foot, small groups of men
Moving toward the new created gash.
But Odysseus, impatient to get on,
Led them forward and up the new terrain.
For a time they moved across raw rock
Exposed from that which had been ripped from it,
And below they could see the huge remains.
When Helios had lashed his great horses
Half across the sky they found themselves
Still some distance from where the mountains joined,
And Odysseus, despite the mighty urge
That had grown since he awoke, had them stop
To eat provisions that the wife had packed
For them and to drink a cooling draught
From their wineskins. Then, after this brief time,
They started out again. No sound could they hear
Of birds or animals—only a slight breeze
And their own movements. Beyond them they saw,
More clearly now, the tangled remains that
Had shaken loose between the two mountains.

They were still too far away to see
In greater detail. Odysseus quickened
Their pace, and by mid-afternoon they came
To the meeting of the slouching giants.
At their roots another huge pile of rubble
Lay, and they found themselves at the edge
Of a new steep cleft. Where it cut into
The mountains' flanks they could not tell; its side
Was precipitous, and the man and his sons
Drew back from it, unwilling to attempt
Its steep face. Odysseus saw their hesitation;
To allay their fears he said,

              "More of you
Will be needed to explore this new
Possibility. But let me try it
On my own. If I return you will know
That the valley is sealed still; if I do not,
Then you know that once again you will have
Access to the outer world."

              He did not
Mention that if he did not return he
Might also have died in his attempt,
But all there understood this as well.
Now the others pressed upon him what was left
Of their provisions and also a stout rope;
These he accepted with grateful thanks. Then,
Saying farewell to them, he swung round
The cleft and started the slow and dangerous
Descent. For a time they watched him as best
They could until he disappeared behind
An outcrop and they saw no more of him.

# Canto 17
## DODONA

Intrepid Odysseus clambered down the huge gash,
Among boulders towering above his head,
Stepping with care among the pebbles on
The still unsettled mountain's wound. Once
His foot slipped and he caught himself from falling,
But below he could see the rocks that he dislodged
Tumble down, gathering speed and debris as they went,
Until an avalanche roared down into the rift below
Sending up clouds of dust which made him stop
To cover his face with his cloak against the choking haze.
His whole attention on the ground where he trod
Now so gingerly, he had no time to see where he went,
But only knew that he must continue down,
Zigzagging around the huge obstacles obtruding
In his path, and avoiding small crevices that waited
To devour him if he was inattentive.
Slowly he continued on and down, fighting
With all his will a terrible urge to race on
That had grown slowly since the creation of the shrine.
Time disappeared in his fierce concentration,
And when he finally found himself at the base
Of the gigantic rupture, he became aware
That the sun had already made more than half
His journey. Looking back up where he had come,
He realized just how enormous the earthquake had been:
The whole side of the mountain had been sheered away,
With its rubble filling the fissure in part
And devastating the sides of the valley
Where now he found himself.
But he had no time to consider the awesome sight;
The urge to move pushed him on despite his weariness,

And he followed the broad slopes of his new way,
Skirting the broken trees and crushed vegetation
As he moved north, the valley long and curving.
Finally, with dusk settling, he found a stream
With waters unpolluted by the cataclysm,
And there he drank and rested and made camp
For the night. It was only then he realized
That from his descent and trek until he came to this grove,
Now beyond the devastation, he had heard no sound;
Even the air had been still. But now a slight breeze
Stirred the branches of the trees, and birds again
Began to chirp among themselves, and the stream
Sang its gurgling melody, and the fire that he made
Spat and crackled comfortingly, and he fell asleep
Without further preparation, even where he sat before the flames.
Early the next morning, just as Dawn stretched to leave her bed,
He started out again, moving urgently and swiftly.
Sometime along the way, as he saw far ahead
The valley curving farther north, he saw below him
A trail that meandered through the meadows and the woods.
Quickly he moved down to examine it: it was old
And appeared to have been unused for a long time.
But he felt grateful for it and trotted along.
When the sun had reached its zenith he found another stream
And there, fighting the compulsion to move on,
Drank, ate from his meager provisions, and rested briefly.
As the afternoon progressed he came to the curve
And discovered that the valley bent around a ridge,
Then narrowed to the opening of a lake,
Here filled with marsh and rushes. As he moved along
The pungent shore, he suddenly found, drifting among the reeds,
An old boat. He waded out and brought it ashore.
It was still serviceable, even still had oars,
And it reeked of fish.

                 *A fisherman's small craft,*
*Probably broken away from its mooring in a storm.*

He thanked Athena and Apollo for his good fortune,
Shoved off, and climbed into the small boat.
Then he started down the lake, his mighty arms

Straining to speed the vessel faster.
Soon he discovered that the lake was larger than he thought,
For at his end it had narrowed, and now he saw its full width.
Nonetheless he drove forward, prudently keeping it near
But at a safe distance from the shore. Twilight had now come,
And he was forced to come ashore, where he hid his boat
In some reeds, and moved to where he could see it
And yet himself be hidden, and there he ate and drank again
And, exhausted, slept. Nothing untoward happened in the night,
And just before dawn he started out again,
This time making for the middle of the lake and driving straight north.
By noon he could see in the distance the shore,
But then realized that the lake was curving,
And he rowed closer to the shore to see where it would go.
What he saw did not reassure him: mountains descended
As great cliffs to the water's edge. But as he skirted the shore
He saw a small channel opened there, and he made for it.
Beyond he thought he could see more water,
And accordingly he rowed up it, to discover a second,
Narrower lake, but long, and into it he rowed;
But the demands of weariness and hunger forced him
To find a beach where he could land to rest and feed.
His shoulders and body ached from the strain to which
He put them; but he stolidly ate, then rested,
Making sure his boat was secure and that he could not
Be surprised; for in the other lake, when he was far out,
He saw boats fishing closer to the shore, and he was not sure
Whether they had seen him as well. But now he leaned back
Against a tree and rested, fighting any need to sleep.
For an hour he remained this way, gathering his strength;
Then, through the channel he saw several boats appear.
Quickly he left the shore and rowed swiftly down the lake,
But behind him he could see the three boats gaining on him,
With several in them rowing. He strained the more,
And for an hour or so he kept distant from them,
As the distant end of the lake grew closer.
But even his mighty sinews could not continue at this rate,
And seeing that they were now gaining on him more swiftly,
He made sure his boat veered in such a way that he could still
Swiftly move but could land at an appropriate spot.

Soon he could see them clearly and hear their shouts of anger,
And he searched the shore for an appropriate place.
Ahead he saw it: a small beach backed by a small cliff.
He made for it, and reached shore with the boats now close
Behind him. Quickly pulling the boat up the sand,
He moved with his back to the cliff
And waited for them, his sword and dagger now in his hands.
As they drew nearer, he hailed them.

"I am here in peace and on a pilgrimage;
I ask you to honour the sacred task I have."

They snarled at him and beached their boats,
Then stood before him. There were nine in all;
Short and burly, with knives and fish hooks grasped
To make short work of him. As they paused to group,
He spoke again.

　　　　　"I warn you not to attack me;
If you do so, prepare for the reward you will receive."

One of them, apparently the leader, gave a harsh laugh
And rushed at him, the others following.
As a shark within a school of fish creates havoc,
So did the veteran warrior deal with this mob.
Swiftly he sidestepped and slashed open the leader,
Kicking him into the way of some of the others,
Then with deadly swiftness and accuracy cut down the rest,
Some with throats cut, others hamstrung, another stabbed in the heart
Even as he passed by. Within a minute all were lying on the sand,
Now blood soaked, and passing among them, he slit the throats
Of those who still gasped in pain. For a time he rested,
Sitting against the cliff and looking at the bodies scattered before him.
Then he arose, cleaned the blood from his blades,
Slipped his boat from the beach,
And wearily rowed away. All along the edge of the lake
He saw nothing but cliffs; but just as he began to despair,
He found another opening through which a river quietly ran,
And steering for it, he rowed against the slight current
Until the way opened up again to another lake,
This smaller and narrower; and, now utterly exhausted,
He found another small beach beneath a cliff,

Grounded his boat, and, with night quickly sweeping overhead,
Collapsed into a dreamless sleep.
The next morning the sun had already started its race
Across the sky when he awoke. His body aching still,
He drank and ate what food he had left,
Then began the voyage down the long length
Of the narrow lake, on either side of which
Steep-sided slopes and cliffs plunged into the water.
He travelled the length of it by the time the sun was at its height,
And at the end, on the north side, he spied
A stream emptying into the lake. Quickly,
Impelled by his urge to leave the boat there,
He walked along the current's narrow banks,
The slopes of the mountains looming on either side.
By late afternoon he had reached a place
Where another stream joined his, and there he stopped,
Famished and weary. Gathering his strength,
He cut a spear from a bush close by,
Then, after several attempts, he impaled a fish,
Its silver sides flashing as it writhed,
Made a small fire, and cooked his catch,
Drinking copiously from the streams.
He carefully made his bivouac among the bushes,
Well out of sight of anyone, and again
Fell into a deep exhausted sleep.
The next several days his impulse urged him
Along streams that gradually led him north and west;
At one point a valley opened that led northeast,
But he was impelled to continue along the banks.
It was hard for him to understand what he was walking through,
For the slopes on either side of him were too steep
To see other than a glimpse of the mountains towering above,
But finally he broke through to a large valley
In which a plain was circled by high mountains.
Across the plain, covered with sweet grasses and trees,
He walked, refreshed by the feeling of more space;
And by the end of the day had reached the northwest side,
Where huge mountains brooded again, and made his rest there.
Then again he found himself in the twisted roots of the hulks
Around him, and he had to trudge this way and that

As the streams wound around, first the way he had come,
And then, as he reached higher ground, to the west.
Several days went by; then he found himself descending slopes
To a large plain. Where before he had seen no human life
And wondered at it, here he saw the plain dotted with fields
And groves of trees and herds of animals
And he felt his urge press him more strongly to head north
Along the fertile land. Farmers looked at him curiously
As he passed along the road, but he smiled at them
And continued briskly on his way. However,
Even as he proceeded up the plain, he was impelled
To veer to the west, and he found himself on trails
That led him through passes and then down again
To a valley that led north, winding among the ranges
And narrowing before breaking onto another plain,
Broad and fertile. Two days had been spent in this
Latter journey, but, tired as he was, his urge
Was now so powerful that he could resist it no longer,
And he almost trotted across the fields,
His tired legs in agony, then climbed up steep slopes
Where he found a well-used trail, and now a second day
Without sleep, he staggered up the trail, where before
Him now stood the place he had striven for;
And there he collapsed on the verge of Dodona.

*Buzz*
*louder than before*
*louder than ever before*
*grating din*
*black masses before my eyes*
*eyes iridescent*
*flurry away*
*his face again*
*enigmatic smile*
*cold*
*divine*
*no word*
*now his body*
*dazzling*
*his arm raises*
*points*

*Troy as before*
*splendid in its towers*
*the court*
*Andromache*
*so young    so lovely*
*smiling as she presents her son*
*Hector's son*
*beside her*
*Cassandra of the haunted eyes*
*and her brother Helenos*
*They breathe*
*vibrate together*
*Helen with Paris*
*a mask of beauty*
*incomparable and unreadable*
*Helenos's eyes always watching her*
*memorizing her flesh inch by inch*
*lost in her*
*Cassandra's eyes always on her brother*
*reading his story with fear she tries to mask*
*not towers but*
*Mount Ida*
*Helenos caught*
*lost in his desire for Helen*
*thwarted*
*vengeful*
*tells me all I need to know*
*to break the towers*
*The flames*
*Andromache's face*
*as her son plunges from the cliff*
*dragged away by Neoptolemos*
*later*
*her face*
*like the slave Thoas keeps*
*Flames so bright*
*so bright*

Odysseus, the warmth of the sun on his eyelids,
Awoke and opened his eyes to squint against

The late afternoon sun. The weary Ithacan,
Sore and stiff, found himself on a thin pallet
Resting on the earth. As he shifted his aching body
To sit up, beside him, still as a hawk watching a prey,
A man sat watching him.

                    "My lord Odysseus,
Welcome."

Odysseus stared at him for a moment,
Then looked about to see where he had come.
A grassy slope descended before him
To a valley buttressed by a mighty mountain range;
Behind him rose the majestic twin peaks of ...

"Mount Tomaras. Yes, my lord, you have reached
The shrine of Dodona as was prophesied."

Odysseus, now fully awake, looked at the man
More closely: one of the Selli, the sacred priests
Of this shrine of Zeus Naios, equal in its fame
To that of Delphi. The observant king noted
The stained and unwashed feet, and instead of
A rich hymation or an impressive priestly robe,
The man wore a slight chiton, equally stained
With grass and earth.

               *They do sleep upon the ground.*

The priest smiled at him in a friendly way,
But Odysseus looked at his eyes that seemed to glitter
And move in that way of wild beasts as they tread lightly
Through their forest haunts.

"How long have I been here?"

"Noble king, we found you collapsed here a day ago,
And you have slept till now. Permit us, then,
To offer you food, but still rest here."

The priest nodded,
And Odysseus saw that there were others not far off
Who left and shortly returned with a simple meal
Of bread and wine. Once Odysseus had made libations

To the Gods, he ate ravenously, and whether because
Of his exhaustion or because of the nature of the wine,
He soon lay back and slept again, and in his mind he saw
Once more, but in wavering images such as are formed
When still water, mirroring what surrounds it, is touched
Lightly by a gentle breeze, the same as he had seen
In his last, incomprehensible, dream.

The next morning he woke again, now more refreshed
But still with his body recovering from its harsh ordeal.
Again he was fed a simple meal, but this time when he
Was finished he thanked his host and asked permission
To explore the slope.

        "You may walk where you will,
But not within fifty paces of the shrine itself,"

                         the priest
Politely said, and pointed to where it was some distance away.

All that Odysseus saw was a huge oak tree, ancient and gnarled,
Whose limbs overspread a small grassy knoll.
But no altar stood within its shade; no stones
Defined its limits; only, suspended from a fine chain,
A bronze gong hung from its largest bough,
And standing beside it, motionless, a priest
Dressed in a spotless robe, holding a scourge.
The host priest smiled at Odysseus's confusion.

"Tomorrow you will understand the nature of the shrine."

Odysseus thanked him, and, like a panther too long confined,
Moved restlessly around the slope. He noted that
Although the priests lived in the open, there were huts
In which food and objects were stored, and he saw as well
That there were areas where camps had been set up.
But at the moment none stood there, and he could look
Down into the valley and trace back his journey,
And he shook his head in disbelief that he had made
His way here through such country. That night
He sat with the priests around a fire, eating and drinking
With them, but they said little, although he saw
Some of them look at him with wondering eyes.

Again he felt himself weary after the meal,
And he lay upon his pallet and let the quiet God
Hypnos lull him to sleep.

*Buzz*
*a roar*
*Again the face*
*again the gesture*
*again Troy*
*Andromache*
*Cassandra*
*Helenos*
*the cliff*
*the fire*
*but now*
*Andromache and Helenos together*
*the shadow of a boy holding their hands*
*and behind*
*silhouetted against the sheet of flame*
*another shadow*
*larger*
*in armour*
*Achilles*
*And the fire passes them*
*and clouds of eagles*
*sweep like black smoke*
*over the mountain ranges*
*and the fire follows them*
*and I stand in Ithaca*
*and watch the great sheet of flames*
*above the sky black*
*with lightning writhing always*
*through the murky flame-ridden sky*
*Zeus is busy*
*And the flame starts to cross the water*
*toward me*
*but the flies blacken out the sight*

Odysseus awakened, covered in sweat,
Shaking, to see the Selli stand before him.
They brought him food and drink, then led him

To a spring where they cleansed him
And clothed him in a soft robe with his feet bare,
Then led him just outside the limit of the shrine,
Where he could see above him the ancient oak
Looming over the sacred earth. Then the high priest
Spoke to him.

        "Know, King of Ithaca, that
Zeus Naios does not reveal the future at this shrine,
But only correct actions to be done. We will
Lead you onto the sacred ground. Say nothing
At any time. We will pray and then wait for His word.
But before we interpret what he has said,
You must promise to do what he commands."

Then the Selli surrounded the king and led him
To a space beneath the oak. He now saw how truly
Large and ancient it was as it spread its boughs
Over the ground as a roof covers a citadel.
Until this point all had been silent, the only sound
The soft slip of naked feet on the meadow grass.
Then a soft prayer whispered from the lips of the Selli.

"Zeus Naios, King of the Heavens, Lord of Dodona,
You who live on cloud-capped Olympus
But command our rugged mountains
And especially here the twin-peaked Mount Tomaras,
Whose white dove announced your founding
Of this sacred shrine, and whose words come to us
Through the shifting leaves of your immortal oak,
Whose devoted priests we are, the Selli,
Always connected to your holy earth
By our own human skin, we beseech you here,
Come to us now and deliver to us what action
You desire Odysseus, King of Ithaca, to take.
And here he promises to obey your divine command."

They signalled to Odysseus to nod acceptance,
And he gravely bowed his head in acquiescence.
Then there was silence, and all stood motionless.
Time passed until Odysseus lost sense of it;

Then he felt a slight brush of air against his face,
And a quiet wind began to stir the oak's leaves.
As it did so, the guardian of the brazen gong
Let his scourge sway in the slight breeze
And touch the metal. A deep low note began to sound,
Quiet but penetrating and continuous,
In counterpoint to the new rustling of the leaves.
Like an animal whose ears shift to hear the slightest sound,
Who lets its whole being respond to what it hears,
So the Selli, their faces upraised, absorbed,
Took in the murmuring on the oak's boughs.
Odysseus felt a curious shiver pass through his body
As the sound of the leaves and of the brazen vessel
Mingled in a continuous drone, hypnotic, unceasing.
Then he became aware that the breeze had died down
And that the sounds, leaf and instrument, slipped away
Into the air, and silence enveloped all again.
Then the Selli began to whisper to each other,
Creating their own hushed cacophony,
None of which Odysseus could understand.
Finally the high priest nodded, and all fell silent
And moved to the perimeter of the shrine,
Leaving Odysseus and the priest facing each other.

"Odysseus, hero of the Trojan War, King of Ithaca,
Zeus Naios, Lord of All, has spoken to us.
This is what he commands you to do:
That what is told you by those whom you will meet here
You must tell no one—neither family nor friend,
Neither ally nor fellow king—not now nor as you die,
But take your knowledge with you even into death.
This you have promised; this you must obey,
Or incur the wrath of Zeus the Thunderer."

Intrigued and confused, Odysseus responded,

"I have promised to do so, and I will keep my promise.
But from whom will I hear what I must not speak of?
You are the only ones here."

The priest smiled.

"This very afternoon you will find out,
For that is when the meeting will take place."

Then he led the perplexed king from the shrine,
And he was given back his clothes and weapons,
And they ate a simple meal together quietly.

That afternoon, as the priest had said,
Odysseus saw horsemen arrive below the slope,
And soon a procession wound its way
On foot up to the shrine. From a distance
Odysseus could make out a troop
Of spearmen, whom he knew were famed in Epirus,
But until they were nearer he could not make out
Those who led the procession, which,
Like a bristling black and yellow caterpillar
Slowly crawled its way farther up the slope.
Then he gasped in astonishment, for now he made out
Two that he knew well—Helenos and Andromache,
Whom he had seen in his latest dreams; and between them
A boy of under ten, who strode briskly with them.
With foreboding in his heart the Ithacan king awaited them.
Finally they came to a stop a short distance from him,
And for a moment there was silence, on one side
The armed procession behind the three before them,
On the other, Odysseus in front of the still-robed Selli,
As each side studied those opposite.
Helenos, Odysseus saw, was now in his forties,
And still retained the gauntness that he shared with his twin sister,
Although the beauty that he had shared with her still stayed.
His face looked older, now lined and furrowed,
But his mouth was still full and curved like a girl's;
The eyes, now more haunted like those of his sister,
Remained as Odysseus remembered them,
Particularly at Mount Ida.
Andromache, who had been so young those long years ago,
Still in her late thirties looked beautiful;
But her eyes betrayed much pain, and she looked at
Odysseus with these eyes now masked from meaning,
Although he could still make out the grief and hate
She yet nurtured within her.

Then Helenos greeted him.
"Welcome, King Odysseus, destroyer of Troy"—

Sharp-eared Odysseus noticed the bite
In the other's voice despite the quiet way
In which he always spoke—

"We have been expecting you."

Odysseus could not help showing his surprise
At this statement, for he knew that no one,
Not even his son and his retainers, knew where
He might be at present. Helenos's lips
Curved at his response.

"You forget, Odysseus, that I was trained
By my sister in the art of prophecy."

Then, studying the Ithacan once more,

"But I see you have been through much
Since we last met. Let us relate our tales
At a feast which we will host tonight,
When all will be revealed."

He smiled again,
And Odysseus, still puzzled by this unexpected visit,
Saw that the smile was not pleasant, and he wondered
Uneasily what that feast had in store.

Helenos motioned to his spearmen to move forward
To accompany Odysseus, but before they could start,
The Selli closed ranks around Odysseus.

"The King of Ithaca has come as suppliant here,
And while he remains in these precincts
He is under our care and protection,"

Proclaimed the high priest. Helenos's face darkened,
And for a moment his spearmen appeared ready
To attack the priests, who stood there motionless.
Then, glancing at the oak towering behind the priests,
He motioned to his men to fall back.

"Well, then,"
$\qquad$ he said smoothly,
$\qquad\qquad$ "what shall we do?
We wish to honour King Odysseus at our banquet.
But it is at our camp below, for such things
The Selli"—
$\qquad$ he nodded respectfully to them—
"Do not permit so close to this sacred place."

The high priest did not respond to his words,
And again a silence fell with the impasse.

Then Odysseus himself spoke.

"Helenos, I thank you for your invitation,
Which I wish dearly to accept. However,
Let me speak first to my hosts, the Selli.
As I have witnessed, is it not true that the oak
Is the central place of your shrine?"

$\qquad\qquad$ A nod.

"Is it not true as well that it is not alone
The sacred vehicle of Zeus Naios, great lord
Of the thunder, giver of commandments,
But that the earth that nourishes the tree
Partakes of his sacredness?"

$\qquad\qquad$ Again a nod,
But also a slight puzzled furrow of the brows.

"And because of that, do not you, his ordained priests,
Remain in contact with that soil always
Through your naked feet and through your sleep
Upon that very earth?"

$\qquad\qquad$ More nod, more furrow.

"And because you keep in contact always through
This ground, do you never break your union
With the great God?"

$\qquad\qquad$ Thoughtful, then a nod.

"And is the earth not continuous, without
A break or crevice in this plain and below it?"

Another nod, but with growing comprehension.

"And therefore, would you not say that anywhere
You trod here with your feet sanctified by Zeus,
Does him honour and no shame to you?"

With greater understanding, a nod again.

"Therefore, would it not be proper for you
To accompany me to this camp, and there
Attend the banquet in honour of the God"—

Before the priest could protest—

"Not partaking of the rich meats and wines
Served there, but accepting as your due
The simple bread and water that is your
Ordained sustenance?"

              Full comprehension,
And a grave smile of acknowledgement.

"There, Helenos, the issue is resolved.
When you are ready for us, send a messenger,
And we will come as a group, the Selli
Sitting with me as we feast and talk."

Helenos shook his head with a wry smile.

"I had forgotten how gifted you are
At untying knots of discord. All will
Be done as you suggest."

              And, bowing
To the Selli, he and his procession returned
Down the hill.

Odysseus turned to the high priest.

"I thank you for your courtesy to me,
And for the protection which you can afford me."

The high priest gravely looked at him.

"It is our task to help you fulfill your obligation,
And you have smoothed the path for us.
Now rest here until the messenger returns."

And the Selli left the veteran to ponder
What the appearance of Helenos and Andromache
Meant, and how such was connected to his dreams.

In the time just before Helios reaches the limit
Of the earth and must stable his fiery steeds,
The messenger came to Odysseus, and he
And the Selli followed him down the hill
To where the camp of Helenos sprawled
To the bottom of the valley. Odysseus noted
As they passed fields in which cattle grazed
The huge hounds that guarded them, famed
In this region for their strength and viciousness,
And as they passed the dogs set up a violent
Clamour which rent the heavens with their baying.
Passing through the ranks of tents, Odysseus's group stopped
Before Helenos's tent, in front of which a large area
Was found, and on it a large fire. Helenos
And his entourage stood outside his tent
To greet his visitors, and then his priests
Brought forward white bulls dedicated to Zeus,
And these were, with great pomp, sacrificed
And their pieces brought to the fire for roasting.
Around the flames and smoke soaring up
To provide a succulent repast to the Gods,
On chairs rich in woods and inlaid metals,
Their seats covered with fleeces dyed purple,
The groups sat, with the Selli preferring
To sit upon the ground around Odysseus's feet.
Bowls of wine were brought in to fill the goblets
Now held by the banqueters. Odysseus noted
That some of the chairs, the bowls, and goblets,
Seemed familiar, and then he realized that
He had seen them before, at feasts in Troy itself.
For a moment he could not tell whether he was
In the past, for here he sat with two of the Trojans
Themselves, Helenos and Andromache,

But, holding back his wonder, he waited for his host
To reveal more of what this meant.
Libations were made, and wine drunk, with talk
Of Dodona and the valley. Odysseus sat between
Helenos and Andromache, and beside her sat the boy
Whom Odysseus had seen at the shrine. He could see
In the boy's lineaments proof of Andromache's blood;
She was his mother, he was sure; but he could see
None of Helenos's attributes there, although he thought
That there was still something familiar about the boy,
But nothing yet that he could grasp. Quietly he held
His tongue, waiting again for the host to speak.
Finally, as the evening light quickened and
The meat was almost ready, Helenos turned to him.

"Now, King Odysseus, we must hear your story.
We have heard tales about you, but from your own lips
We wish to hear what happened to you after Troy's fall"—

Andromache almost began to weep, but with effort
She retained her self-control—

"And how you came to appear here, out of nowhere,
After these long years."

Odysseus nodded, then said,

"I shall be happy to do so, Prince Helenos"—

He noted Helenos's wince—

"But I will do so only if you will reciprocate
And tell me your own story, and how here
Andromache, still lovely, comes to sit."

Helenos chuckled.

"I will do so readily, have no fear."

Odysseus prayed silently to his patron Goddess,
Athena, to assist him in his speaking,
And then told again the story of the struggle
To return home after the fall of Troy,
The massacre of the suitors for his wife,

His winning of the civil war, and the two years
He spent in strengthening his island kingdom.
Then he told of the edict of Poseidon
To perform the quest of penitence;
How he had, with his son Telemachus, travelled
Through the Peloponnesos assisting
Orestes—at his name Helenos and Andromache
Looked at each other guardedly—in his conquest
Of Arcadia; his visit with Menelaos and the death
And funeral of ancient Nestor and the future
Marriage of Telemachus with Nestor's daughter,
And then his journey to Aetolia and Thoas
And the shrine there, where the oracle ordained
That he must come to Dodona, and
Where he left his son to return home to Ithaca;
And his final ordeals through the mountains
Of Aetolia and Epirus to the place
Where he fulfilled his original quest
Before continuing on to Dodona.
But he was careful in his recount not to mention
Pelagia, nor how he had slipped away from Thoas,
Nor his imprisonment as a slave.
When he had finished in the hushed space,
With only the crackling of the fire to accompany
His tale, there was silence, as all looked at him
In awe at what he had accomplished.

"Truly,"
          said Helenos at last, reluctantly,
"You have lived a life that no other man
Could have survived, and deserve your fame.
Let us all drink to your exploits."

And he raised his goblet, and all with him drank as well.

"Now we will tell you the story of both of us,"

He said, nodding toward Andromache, who lowered her head.
For a moment he paused, collecting his strength,
And then he began as the flames reflected in his face,
Night having spread his ebony cloak over all.

"When our great city, the wondrous Troy, fell,
Andromache and I were given to Neoptolemos,
Son of Achilles, as you know. He returned here
To Epirus, which in the past he had conquered,
Myself as his advisor, and Andromache"—

Odysseus saw her face still lowered and unseen,
But a shudder passed through her at the name—

"His concubine. For several years he kept us
In this state, finding my advice useful, and
In his union with Andromache fathering three children"—

Odysseus's ears perked up on hearing this,
For from Hermione he had heard of only two—

"One of whom you see here now, the eldest,
Molossus. Then he became enamoured
Of Helen's daughter, Hermione, whom he claimed
Menelaos had promised to him in marriage.
He brought her here, unhappy as she was, but no child
Issued from her. But at that time Neoptolemos
Began to be tormented by strange dreams
In which the mighty God Apollo threatened him
For his demanding reparation for his father's death.
He approached me as to what to do; I advised him
To travel to Delphi and stay there until he had won back
The God's favour. He saw the strength of this plan
And shortly sailed off, leaving me to govern in his place.
It was some time later that word reached us of his death
By Orestes, and soon the murderer arrived and carried off
Hermione, leaving us here in charge until such time as
The boy Molossus reaches his maturity to govern.
Since that time I have fulfilled one dictate left me
By Neoptolemos, and founded on the coast
The city of Buthrotum. As well, Andromache
And I, praise to the Gods, married, and she
Has given me a son, Cestrinus."

"And praise to you, Andromache,
For your fruitfulness,"
                            interrupted Odysseus.

Andromache raised her head to look at him sharply,
But he looked back at her without guile,
And again her head was lowered.

"Then, not long ago, I had a vision from Apollo
That warned that you would be coming to Dodona,
And commanded us to see you here."

Odysseus, who now felt an urge to know why
The God had ordained this meeting, asked
Involuntarily,
        "Why did he do so? Do you know why?"

Helenos rose and moved to stand with one hand
Resting on Andromache's shoulder, the other
On the boy's.

        "Let me start with news you may not
Wish to hear. Several years ago Trojan ships—
Trojan!—sailed into the harbour of Buthrotum,
And on the wharf I greeted Prince Aeneas."

Odysseus gasped. After the sack of Troy
The Greeks had neglected to determine
What Trojans had escaped. Aeneas had led
A charmed life; Odysseus realized that it continued.

"He and his followers were sailing west after
He had left Carthage by order of the Gods,
There to set up a new colony of Trojans."

Now he gazed at Odysseus triumphantly,
And it became clear that Apollo was now
Speaking through him.

"Although the Trojans have lost their country,
They will ultimately win this war with
The Achaeans. Look at us here, two Trojans
Now united; and look at this boy, son
Of a Trojan woman and with the blood of Achilles
Flowing in his veins, greatness from Trojan and Greek,
Who someday not far off will command
This country. He and his descendants will

In these generations to follow sweep down
Upon the lands of Greece and destroy the states
That conquered us. You and I will not see it,
But your son's sons will, and they will fall with the rest.
And the new colonies in the west will also spawn
A greater kingdom than that known by Troy,
Until all that Achaeans have done will be
Reduced to ashes."

Odysseus was dumbfounded by this revelation.
Now he began to understand the full import
Of the visions in his dreams—and, worse,
He realized that he could not break his promise
And therefore could not warn his fellow kings,
Even if it had no effect on such a terrible prophecy.

But he had little time to contemplate,
For Andromache, who had been listening closely
All this time, rose quickly to confront him.

"Think of these things, you who destroyed Troy,
You who killed my son, Hector's child, basely.
May you go to your death with these things
On your conscience and with foreknowledge
Of the doom of your own family!"

At this outburst, Odysseus could be patient no longer.
He rose himself, and carefully choosing his words
Despite his anger, spoke in his most compelling voice.

"Andromache, widow of the great hero Hector,
Who has lost grievously and endured much,
Think again of how that war came to be.
Was it not the abduction of Helen,
Loveliest of women, that began it all?
And who tried to find a way to peace
Through embassy but myself?
But when in arrogance Troy refused our offer,
Then only one course was open to us all:
War, to the delight of the rapacious God Hades.
For ten long years our two sides struggled—
Ten years filled with death and tragedy,

As you know from your own conduct, Helenos,
Who, though the dear son of Priam and wisest
In council, still fought bravely with your brother
Deiphobos, slaying Deipyrus and staying
On the field until Menelaos himself wounded
Your bow hand and you had to retreat,
Your hand hanging down and the spear
Trailing after you."

              Helenos without thought
Touched the hand, on which two white scars were stitched.

"You call me, both of you in the same words,
Destroyer of Troy, and indeed I was an instrument
In its downfall, as was my duty to my side.
Yet as you know, Helenos, only too well,
I could not have prevailed without help.
Let us remember, then, your own story.
After Paris was killed, you vied with your brother
Deiphobos for the hand of Helen, and when
He was preferred, in anger you left your city
And your father, and went to live on Mount Ida.
There I found you and captured you, bringing
You back to the Achaeans, and there it did not
Take much to have you aid us, for you prophesied
On whatever we wished to know. Was it not you
Who instructed us that in order for Troy to fall,
One of the bones of Pelops must be brought—
Which we failed to do when our ship sank
Returning with it—to fetch Neoptolemos from Scyros;
To persuade Philoctetes, possessor
Of the Bow and Arrows of Heracles, to come from Lemnos;
And to steal from the city the sacred Palladium,
The wooden statue once fallen from Heaven, without which
Troy could not survive, which I myself did,
Disguised as a beggar. Did you not aid us
In all of this against your homeland,
Either because of your thwarted love for Helen,
Or because you knew from prophetic vision
What would happen?"

On this last remark
Helenos, before white-faced, flushed.

"And were you not so sure of your predictions
That you willingly gave yourself over
To execution if your prophecies proved false?
You it was who set up the destruction of your city
And your family; I was only the agent,
The Trojan Horse the last instrument
In the downfall of Troy and its people.
And, yes, Andromache, I was responsible
For the death of your son, for the prospect
Of another war under him in the future
Haunted us. Yet here you are, having borne
Children of the son of the slayer of your husband,
Neoptolemos, so that, as Helenos has prophesied,
Achilles's progeny will return to haunt us still."

Andromache had listened to him, wide-eyed;
It was clear to Odysseus that she had not known
Of Helenos's contribution to the destruction of her people,
And when he finished, she wailed with grief,
Pulling her hymation over her head and weeping.
Stricken, Helenos stood frozen behind her,
His hands still on the two shoulders, while the boy
Glared in hatred at Odysseus, who could see
Already the promise of power
That surged through him. For a moment
There was a hush as both kings glared at each other,
Each tensed for battle. Then the high priest
Of the Selli stood and raised his hand.

"Both of you have now fulfilled what Zeus Naios
In his wisdom has ordained. You, Helenos,
Have given the prophecy with which he filled you;
You, Odysseus, have heard what was prophesied
That you should hear, and are now constrained
Never to speak of it again to anyone. You must
Now separate in peace—you, Helenos, to return
To your city, and you, Odysseus, to accompany us
Back to the sacred shrine."

He nodded; and
The Selli quietly surrounded Odysseus
And led him from the camp, away from the roar
Of the fire and the snarling of the dogs.
When they reached the edge of the sanctuary
The Selli stopped, and the High Priest spoke softly.

"King Odysseus, our great Lord Zeus Naios
Did not speak to you only. We also have received
Instructions from him. There is a possibility
That Helenos will do harm to you. Therefore,
We have been commanded to lead you to the river
That you have seen below in the valley,
And that we do so tonight, in the darkness,
So that no one will know where you have gone.
What will happen to you at the river we do not know;
But these are the wishes of Zeus Naios,
And we will obey them."

Then he nodded to a priest
No longer dressed in a white robe, but in a dark chiton.
Around his waist was tied a rope, one end of which
He handed to Odysseus.

      "Keep the rope taut
Between us,"
     he said quietly, and without other words
They started along the plain. Although it was pitch dark,
Odysseus realized from the incline of the ground
That they were not descending toward the camp
But crossing farther north. As they went,
The ground began to slope more steeply, and
Odysseus was thankful for the rope and
For the cautious but sure-footed way the priest
Led him. Down they went, veering slightly
To the east. At one point they had to crawl down
A steep face along a narrow path, and
Then finally, they reached more level land,
And the priest led him along a more travelled path
In the midst of what seemed to be a large forest.
Ahead Odysseus could hear the sound of water,
And soon they came to the banks of the river.

"May you fare well, and Zeus Naios protect you,"

The priest whispered, then slipped quietly away
As he had come. And in the darkness there
Odysseus sat with his back against a tree,
Waiting for the black ship to come,
And as he did so he heard faintly in the distance
The fierce baying of the hounds.

# Canto 18

# ITHACA

Pelagia moved about her garden in the first rays
Of the sun, tending to this plant and that,
Taking what she needed to work on in the house,
Creating her potions. She loved this early time,
When all was still, dew still glistening on the leaves
And blossoms, the birds finished with their first round
Of song, and a time before she now looked forward to
With eagerness, her breasts warning of their fullness
And her baby waiting for his nourishment against her.
She had returned at night to her now familiar home,
Intent on harvesting the crop that needed her attention,
Telemachus accompanying her—he still lay asleep,
Not to be wakened until they could breakfast together.
Finally she took the basket of her gleanings and returned
Inside, leaving it in her workroom and hastening
To her baby, who eagerly received what she offered.
As he lay there at her breast, she marvelled at how much
He had grown these last two months; how that small
Mewling face now showed signs of awareness;
How character began to appear in his expressions
And his actions, and how the first explorations of sound
Began to shape the tiny mouth. No thought could penetrate
Her mind; all her being was focused on the small creature
Feeding from her, warm and close to her, and she revelled
In the sensuous experience. Finally they both were finished,
And, the infant given to his nurse, Pelagia made her way
To Telemachus and looked at him lying there oblivious
To the world. All about his young body was relaxed.
And that face, now so strong and thoughtful when awake,
Looked peaceful and innocent and young, so young,
And her heart gave a pang as she looked at him.

For a long moment she stared at him, absorbed,
And then, collecting herself, she touched him lightly.

"Telemachus,"
                    she called softly.

He stirred, then woke,
Within an instant alert. Then he felt her hand
Upon his face, softened and turned to her.
She bent down and kissed him softly; he reached up
To pull her down to him, but she smiled and shook off
His embrace.

"Time for that tonight,"
                         she murmured,
Straightening up. He sighed, but then he rose,
And together they went to have breakfast
In a place where they could see her cultivated land
And also the bay. They sat there happily, eating
And conversing about nothing in particular; the baby
Was brought in, and Telemachus played with him
For a time, Pelagia laughing at the spectacle
Of her two men making faces. After a time
The nurse took him away again, and they
Finished what repast they were taking.

As they were doing so, Telemachus looked out
At the bay and stiffened. Coming into view
Was a sleek vessel that he knew from before.

"Another ship from Pylos!"
                            he exclaimed;

Pelagia gasped, and they looked at each other
With apprehension.

                    "I must get there
Before it docks,"
                    he said. She nodded,
White-faced, and he quickly prepared to leave,
An attendant bringing his horse.

                              Before
He could speak, she said,
                              "I will stay here tonight
And do not expect to see you."

                              His eyes darkened,
But he nodded, kissed her passionately, and leapt on
His horse, galloping away at full speed.
Pelagia sighed, foreboding in her heart,
And went to distract herself in her workroom,
Working alongside silent Amunet,
But always the image of the ship stayed in her mind.

On the road Telemachus passed a messenger
Hastening to him, and together they sped to
The palace. Penelope herself, anxious and disturbed,
Had prepared to travel to the dock, the ship
Fast approaching; she was relieved when she saw
Her son, and together with counsellors they arrived
Just as the ship reached the dock.
When the first man leapt from its deck,
Telemachus cried out joyfully,

                              "Pisistratus!"
And the two friends embraced happily.

"What brings you here at this time, my friend?"
Telemachus asked quizzically.

                              "Ah, well you
May ask!"
                    responded Pisistratus,
                              "but first
Please introduce me to this beauteous woman,
Who can be no other than the famed Penelope,
Your queen and mother."

                              And the gallant
Youngest son of Nestor knelt at her feet.
Penelope raised him up, flattered and not immune
To the charm of the young man, smiling.

"Who is this charming young warrior with whom
You are so familiar?"

                     She asked her son.

"One of the finest princes of Pylos: Pisistratus,
The youngest son of noble Nestor, and worthy of him."

Nestor's son grinned.

                  "Yes, Queen Penelope, it seems
That being youngest is itself worthy."

All laughed at this, including those who had been
At Pylos, and then the queen, still chuckling,
Said,

     "Let us hear what you have to say
At our palace, where it is more comfortable
And where, I'm sure, you and your people
Will not be unhappy to feast later on."

"We look forward to it, gracious queen, for
Your son has told us wondrous tales of your feasts,
And we wish to make sure that what he said is true!"

More laughter, and in this amiable mood
The procession strolled up the hill to the palace,
Attendants busy to unload or help the crew of the ship.
Penelope found herself continually charmed
By the young prince's banter and the true affection
Held between him and her son, and she began
To feel more hopeful of the coming marriage,
If the others of Pylos were like him.
In the palace, once provision had been made
For the guests, attendants scurrying about
To prepare accommodation for them,
Penelope led them into the hall, where chairs
Were found for them, made comfortable
With soft fleeces, and attendants brought wine
And some bread to cure their thirst and hunger
Until the later banquet.

Once seated
And the refreshments served, Penelope
Gestured for the attendants to leave the hall,
And now, the company alone, she turned to the young prince.

"Now, good Pisistratus, tell us why you have come."

The son of Nestor looked about, then said,

"I do not see the great Odysseus. He has not
Yet returned?"

           The faces of both the mother
And the son clouded.

         "Not as yet,"
                Penelope answered.
"We watch daily for his return."

"As do we,"
       said Pisistratus gravely.
"His quest is fraught with danger, as all here
Well know, but if any man can fulfill
Such a task, it is he, and may the Gods
Protect him!"

        And all poured a libation
On the dirt floor in the Gods' honour.

"As you know, we had sent a previous ship
To learn if he had returned, and we saw
The time was not yet ready, either for his return
Or for the wedding, although I must say
That my sister thinks otherwise, as you know,
Telemachus."

        He grinned at the Ithacan prince,
Who grinned wryly back.

         "But others also
Wonder at his return, and they are less
Optimistic than we are. You are aware
That this marriage is not only for love"—

Telemachus flushed at this—

                       "but also
To forge an alliance among us all.
Elis is not happy with this union,
For they are hungry for our land,
And with no word of Odysseus's return,
They have become restive. Thalpios,
Polyxeimos, and Automedon are
Spreading rumours that Odysseus is dead,
And that the wedding will not take place.
And in this atmosphere we have learned
That they are quietly preparing to invade
If soon Odysseus does not appear
Or if the wedding does not take place.
I have come, therefore, to hold counsel with you,
To determine what we must do,
For we must act soon, if not now, to forestall
A coming storm."

Silence in the room as the news was digested.
Then Halitherses spoke.

                    "My gracious queen,
May I speak?"

Penelope nodded, herself not sure
Of what to say.

"First, let us examine together
What we should do, not excluding the noble son
Of Nestor, but listening as well to what he says,
For I have known him to be wise and honourable,
And will respect his opinion."

                    Penelope
Looked at her advisor and seer in surprise,
But knowing his wisdom, nodded again.

"I agree with Prince Pisistratus that there now
Is urgency that the wedding take place.
Odysseus feared, I know, that if he could not
Return in time, this might occur.

But even if the wedding does take place,
Without Odysseus the Elisians might still
Have courage to attack, despite their knowledge
Of Prince Telemachus's own exploits."

                                    And
He nodded respectfully at the prince, who sat
With furrowed brow.

                    "But I also say—I also know—
That Odysseus will return, and soon."

He spoke this in his seer's voice, which many there
Knew, and it gave them new comfort in this
Disturbing time.

                    "Therefore I suggest this:
Send back your ship, Prince Pisistratus, with
Word that Odysseus will soon be back
And that preparations should go forward
For the wedding. But you, good prince, should stay
With us, and the word your ship brings back
Should say that you stay here to greet the king
And to make such arrangements for the wedding
As are necessary in Ithaca, to where the bride
Will soon travel with her husband, and that
In seven days the wedding party and yourself
Will leave Ithaca for Pylos."

The others listened to his plan in wonderment,
And for a time there was silence as each pondered
The implications of what he had said.
Then Pisistratus spoke.

                    "Your plan is audacious,
But I can see the truth in it. I know
You feel that Odysseus will return,
And you seem to think that it will be
Within these next few days; but suppose that he does not
Appear at this time? We will have made public
The wedding day, and there will be expectations
That he will appear. If he does not, what then?"

Halitherses looked at him.

"We do not
Have much choice. If Odysseus is not there,
At least the wedding and alliance will
Occur, and if the Elisians venture to attack,
Telemachus and you can call to our allies
For help, which they have sworn to do."

Both Pisistratus and Telemachus
Looked dubious at this possibility.

"Yet I feel strongly that Odysseus
Will return before we leave, and that he
Will be at the wedding."

Then he turned to
Penelope.
"What think you, my queen?"

Penelope had sat listening to this plan
With foreboding. She knew what a gamble
It would be to have the wedding without
Her husband, and yet there seemed to be
No other choice if such invasion would occur.
But she also knew that Halitherses
Was not a gambler and did not speak his mind
Without having weighed all elements;
And she knew his powers as a seer. When he
Prophesied that Odysseus would return
In these coming days, she had felt her heart
Leap up, and now, keeping that feeling fresh,
She said,

"Your words, as always, Halitherses,
Are wise, and we do well to heed your counsel.
I think that we must act as you say,
For if Odysseus does return, the matter is resolved,
And if he does not, we can do no better
Than what you say and hope for relief.
Do you agree, my son?"

Telemachus nodded gravely.

"And you, Prince Pisistratus?"

For a moment he did not speak, and then,
His eyes glistening, he replied.

"I knew the quality of your illustrious king
And of his son, my dear friend. But I did
Not realize the courage and generosity
Of Ithaca, its counsellors, and its queen.
I agree, and I am grateful that my sister
Will marry into such a fine people.
Yes, I agree."

          And he knelt again before the queen
And took her hand and kissed it. Then he arose
And embraced Telemachus with deep emotion.

"Then it is settled,"
               the queen said huskily,
Moved by the prince's response and now
Even more reassured of the family that would
Unite with theirs.

          "And now I suggest that
You all draw up the plans for preparations
For the wedding and the return of the happy couple."

She arose and swept from the room,
Leaving them to work out the details of the fateful
Voyage, the wedding, and the return.

That evening the sacrifice was made of a fine bull,
Libations were poured, and all settled in the great hall
Where Penelope kept her precious chair and sat
Where she could listen to her son and his friend talk.
For a time they bantered back and forth
About their prowess and accomplishments,
And then Telemachus hesitantly said,

"And how is your sister, my bride-to-be,
The beautiful Polycaste?"

To his surprise, Pisistratus did not make a joke,
But instead looked serious.

"A year makes a great difference in a young girl,"
He said.
          "She is even more beautiful
Than when you saw her, but now she knows what she
Will be—a bride and wife—and that she must wait
For you to come; she has become less the girl
She was, and more a young woman. She asks her mother
Many things; then she takes long walks along
The beach, and finds places where she can sit alone
And think. I can no longer tease her as my
Little sister; when she asks me something
About you, it is not silly but more searching.
I cannot believe how much she has changed.
But I can tell you that her love for you has deepened;
No longer does she think only of her passion for you,
But wants to know more of you as a person."

Penelope had listened closely, saying nothing;
But she took note how much the young girl had matured,
And felt relieved that the marriage would be
More substantial than she had feared.

The next day Pelagia saw the ship slip from the dock
And sail away, and she was beset both with
Hopes and fears—hopes that the message that it brought
Had been inconsequential, and fears that it presaged
Worse things. The whole day she went about her work
Abstractedly; even the infant could not bring her peace;
And when Telemachus did not appear that night
She tossed restlessly and slept little.
The next day, late at night, he finally came.
Nothing was said at first, for he took her in ardour,
And only when they both lay exhausted
Did he tell her what had happened.

"I cannot come except late in this fashion,
For Prince Pisistratus remains as our guest
And I must be with him until we part at night."

And then he told her of the crisis in Pylos
And of the plan to leave within seven days,
Hopefully with Odysseus having returned

As Halitherses thought he would, and that
The wedding would occur when they arrived,
Whether the king was with them or not.
As he told her this, Pelagia grew cold,
For what she had hidden from herself,
Drowning instead in their love and in the child,
Now emerged from its hiding place—but worse,
For she feared that despite the wedding
There would be war, and Telemachus could be killed,
And this, not the wedding, which still cut through her
Like a knife, was what she feared most.
That night she clung to him in love and desperation,
And when he left before dawn had arisen
She lay there still and sobbed as she had never done before.

The days passed swiftly, with feverish preparation,
Both for the journey, and to prepare the palace
For the return of the newly married couple.
Pelagia now lived only for the moment when,
The night long dark, Telemachus arrived
And they had a few brief hours together.
He himself, hurled this way in preparations
And in his hunting and hosting of the prince,
And that way with his passionate hours
With Pelagia, with little sleep, became exhausted,
And Penelope, seeing his condition, forced him
To rest in the heat of the afternoon
While she engaged Pisistratus in conversation,
Asking him many questions about Pylos
And his family, and particularly Polycaste.

On the sixth day Odysseus had not returned,
And with a heavy heart all prepared to leave
Early the next morning. Telemachus
Excused himself early and left the prince
To make his own preparations for the morn.
He came to Pelagia just as night's black sable
Covered the island. For a time the two
Played with their son, whom Pelagia then nursed
As Telemachus sat with them in rapt
Attention, as if to pack into his memory

Every movement of this time together.
Then, the baby given to its nurse,
They talked long into the night of what
Was to come, but with the future murky,
They could not make special plans;
And then they made love as if it would be
The last that they might make; and then they clung
Together, not daring to sleep,
As the dark hours crept slowly by.

# Canto 19
# THE BLACK SHIP

As Odysseus sat patiently in
The pitch black of the pines amongst which
He found himself, he coolly estimated
How far away the distant halloo of the hounds
Must be, and how, even with torches
To light their way, Helenos's spearmen
And his dogs would still take some time to find him here.
Having come to this conclusion, he let
Himself think upon what had occurred.
He understood too well the irony
Of knowing with dreadful clarity
The future conquest of his Hellas
And the fall of the Achaean kingdoms,
Yet restrained by his own word to warn
Even his own family; nor could he see
A purpose in doing so, for the prophecy
Allowed no room for any outcome
But disaster. Perhaps, like Aeneas,
Some might escape far to a colony
In some distant place, far from their Hellas,
So beloved; but the loss of country, loss
Of all so hard-won and cultivated,
Would bear heavily in the hearts of those
Who might survive. And he remembered
Weeping for the wrack of Troy, and now,
Sometime in the not-so-distant future,
His own people would suffer the same fate,
And his heart almost broke in his grief.
Then he thought of the Trojan lady, now
Slave to Thoas's whims, and Andromache,
Forced to bear children of a man whose father

Had killed the husband she adored; and Pelagia,
Her citadel destroyed, herself a concubine;
And all the towns that he himself had pillaged
For spoil and slaves; and he thought,

*What is this world we struggle in, where death*
*And greed drive us all, and Gods,*
*Immortal and all-powerful, force us*
*To do their will, or trap us in deceitful*
*Webs, or destroy us without a blink,*
*All for their pleasure and to feed their lust*
*To glorify themselves?*

                    And for a while
He lowered his head and wept bitterly.
Then he realized the night was in its deepest depths
And that the baying was much closer,
Though he could not yet see torches flickering
Through the woods. His hand closed on his sword;
But then, above from his tree, came the harsh cries
Of eagles, and just around a curve downstream
In the river, he saw light brighter than any
That he had ever seen, which let him know
The river's curve was there; and as he watched,
Stunned, a ship, jet-black, sleek and powerful,
Glided effortlessly against the strong current's flow
And came to stop beside the bank where
He had now leapt up. At the same time he heard
The baying much louder, and not far away
Torches danced among the trees, and men shouted.
Before he could determine more, strong hands
Grasped him and dragged him on board, and in that
Instant the blazing radiance, a brilliant sun
In its own right, snuffed out, and the ship
Drew away from the bank, turned sharply around,
And sped swiftly down the river in the utter dark.
For a moment he looked back and saw
That the torches had reached the place where
He had waited, but then arms turned him back
And soft lips sought his. He could not help but
Respond to Nausicaa's embrace,

And they stood locked together in the dark.
Finally, putting a finger to his lips,
She took his hand and led him quietly
Along the deck to a small cabin
Located at the stern. A door opened
To a lighted space into which they entered.
Odysseus was disconcerted to find himself
In a spacious room, far larger than the ship
Should be able to accommodate,
In which chairs rich in carving and fleeces
Were arranged comfortably, and a table
On which goblets and a bowl of wine
Were placed. Sitting there with some of the
Lords of Phaeacia was Lord Laodamas,
Who rose to embrace the startled Ithacan.

"Welcome, noble Odysseus and kinsman—
I see as usual that adventure follows
Wherever you go."

        The king murmured
His acknowledgement.

         "You must be thirsty
After your ordeal."

        And a lord poured
A goblet which he received gratefully.

"Let me toast you and your new exploits,
My husband,"
      said Nausicaa huskily,
And a goblet was brought to her as well.

"To you, whose fame is brighter after your
Success in this last quest, and to you,
My love, whom I will remember all my life."

They both drank, their eyes on one another.
Odysseus was intrigued by what he drank,
Which he found both heady and exhilarating.
They both sat together among the bright-eyed
Phaeacians and sipped their beverage.

Odysseus was about to speak when
Laodamas forestalled him with a smile.

"I know what you are about to ask.
How could we make a light so bright as that
With which we found you? And how could this room
Be larger here on the inside than out on the deck?"

Odysseus nodded but said nothing, listening
Carefully. Laodamas now smiled wryly,
His eyes bright in the room's light.

                                "In the way
You may well ask how our black ships sail
On their own, without our need to guide or
Provide any oars to move them."

Nausicaa took another sip, and Odysseus,
Without thinking, did the same.

                            "You must know
That we have been given powers which we
Have not had need to use until now, nor
Wished to show you until this last voyage
With you."

               Odysseus wondered that his wife
Showed no grief at this, but instead drank again,
And he followed automatically.
The light now seemed to cast a glow around
Everyone, and the king, whose body
Still endured the wear of his exhausting trek,
Began to feel his veins and muscles acquire strength;
But this he ignored, fascinated by what
The Phaeacian had to say.

                    "But now,
My kinsman and one who has done so much
For our people, I want you to see what
We now become as we start our new life,
Which we know will involve great hardship
Out of which we must forge our own peace."

His eyes shone even brighter, and Odysseus
Saw that a new, darker light was in them,
More haunted and less compassionate
Than before. But before he could think more,
Laodamas said,

>                 "But we must not waste
Your time with your wife present. Please, enter here."

He gestured to a door that the king now saw
At the end of the room; Nausicaa drained her goblet,
And he without thought did likewise; then they
Both entered the room that awaited them.
The room was smaller than the other, but
Reason said that it should not exist at all;
Yet, here it was, and Odysseus saw that
It was a bedroom in which a large bed
Covered with fleeces filled most of it.
Around the edges of the rooms were stands
With dim candles, and from which incense rose
In fragrant smoke. Odysseus now found his
Blood sang with life, and he became aware
That he was young again, with his muscles
Rippling with his former strength; and then,
As he turned to Nausicaa, he felt the rush
Of that first youthful desire now long past,
And he could see she felt the same way.
Quickly he removed her clothes, and she his,
And then they embraced and fiercely kissed,
The feeling of their bodies pressed so hard
Together unleashing more desire.
Never had he felt such an explosion of emotion,
Neither as a youth, nor when Circe used
Her arts to entice him to ardour. They fell
On to the bed, and each explored the other
As if they had never touched before, and
Soon they both cried out passionately as
Their love consummated, and then they
Lay together briefly, and again were ignited,
And so the next hours passed in continual
Adoration and fervent lovemaking,

Until at last, they lay quietly together
And murmured to each other in the scented
Dimness. Then a knock came, and they knew
That they must part, and each shared a tender kiss,
Then both arose and dressed and passed through
The other room and out onto the deck.
It was still dark, but as the sleek ship sped
Along the sea, the wind ruffled their hair.

Laodamas came to them at the railing.

"We will shortly be at Ithaca; make
Ready to disembark. We will take you
Into the harbour, but to the beach beside
The docks, for we must not be seen."

In the sky the first faint glimmer of light
Could be seen, and with it the profile
Of the island appeared darkly against it.
Around them he could now see the great fleet
Spread across the sea speeding with him,
Then hanging back as they turned to the island.

Nausicaa clung tightly to him.

"Remember me!"
                          she breathed in his ear,
"And I will remember you in our child."

Odysseus looked at the graceful form
Against him, the face in the first glimmer
White as a ghost's, and his heart went out
To her.

          "I could never forget you,"
                                    he said
Into her ear,
               "and I will pray that the Gods
Will protect you and your people in what
You must do."

          They kissed again for an
Eternity; then a hand touched his shoulder,

And Odysseus looked up to see his harbour
And his beach speed quickly into sight.
The ship seethed unto the beach; he jumped down;
And standing on the sand he saw the ship slip
Smoothly from the beach and turn, and he watched
As the figure on the deck kept her arm raised
As the ship swiftly sped from the harbour
And from his sight.

# Canto 20
## ITHACA

As the sun's new-born rays began to streak
With gold the walls of her airy bedroom,
Penelope arose, exhausted from
A long sleepless night in which the harsh winds
Of apprehension raged through her mind.
Even as she did so, a shout arose
From the gates of the palace; she moved
To see from the window what had occurred,
But before she could look out, the old nurse
Eurycleia burst into the room, breath
Short from her haste to come.

"Queen Penelope,"
                          she gasped as the queen
Herself supported the tottering woman,

"He is back!  He has returned!"

                                   And she
Broke into sobs of happiness. No doubt
Shadowed Penelope's mind; only one man
Could affect her nurse this way, and her heart
Beat fast. Turning the now feeble woman
Over to a servant who had just arrived,
Without a care for her appearance, she
Raced toward the hall, just in time to meet
King Odysseus himself as he strode in.
No words were said; they met in close embrace
And stayed thus while time tiptoed quietly
Away. Then, still together locked, they fed
On the face of the other, devouring
Greedily each feature—eyes, brows, forehead,
Hair, cheeks, nose, chin, and mouth—and each thought,

*How worn the face, how tired the expression,*

And again without a word they embraced,
This time allowing their bodies to relax
Into each other.

         Finally, still close
Against her lord, Penelope spoke to him
Huskily, breathing words into his ear,
Their cheeks still united.

         "Oh, dear husband,
How we have yearned for your return and feared
That you had been lost."

         As she was about
To sob in relief, a chuckle vibrated
Between their bodies.

         "Have I not always
Returned—even if it took me a while?"

She had to smile at this, and for a moment
Pressed closer to him. Then she pulled away
To look more closely at him. She saw him
Much thinner than before, with evidence
From his scars that he must have endured much.

"Oh, my poor Odysseus, what has happened
To you?"

         He shrugged and then countered to her,

"I may ask the same of you, Penelope."

She suddenly remembered the journey
They must make that day. Quickly she told him
Of the need to travel to Pylos for
The wedding, with danger there imminent.
He quickly took in the situation.

"I must bathe and eat, and you must prepare
As you intended. While we do so, call
Our advisors together for council.
Where is Telemachus?"

Even as he
Spoke his name, his son had dismounted and
Strode in. Astonished and relieved to see
His father, he embraced him, deeply moved,
Then stepped back to look at him more closely.
Perceptive Odysseus, observing him as well,
Laughed.

"I see all three of us seem somewhat worn."

Telemachus smiled wearily.
"These weeks
Have been hard on us, as have preparations
For the wedding."

Odysseus stopped smiling.

"Your mother has told me the details. Go
And get ready, for we will meet before
We sail."

And without another word off
He went, the others following behind.
Within an hour Halitherses and Medon,
Both ready for the journey, and Mentor
Had arrived, overjoyed to see their king.

Telemachus himself had searched out his Pylian friend
And both hurried to this last conference,
Where Pisistratus, awe mixed with relief,
Greeted the Ithacan king:

"Hail, hero,
Not only of Troy, but now of more deeds
For bards to sing of in our future days!"

Odysseus smiled and grasped the prince's arm.

"I see you watch well over your sister's affairs,
Prince Pisistratus,"

and all chuckled at
The playful jibe. Then the meeting started.

Odysseus heard the full story of what
Had happened, thought briefly, then asked them,

"Were invitations sent to Orestes,
Menelaos, and the rest?"

                              Shocked, they looked
At each other before Telemachus
Replied,

          "No, father, we were so concerned
About the situation that only
Our own preparations were kept in mind."

His father sighed but did not chastise them.

"Send messengers at once to invite them
To the wedding, which must now take place
Four days from now."

                    Telemachus, puzzled,
Asked,

          "But what will they think in Pylos, where
They expect the wedding tomorrow or
The next day?"

              Odysseus smiled.

"I'm sure that when I am there and they know
Who will be coming, they will not refuse.
I will tell you my adventures on board."

Pisistratus laughed and nodded at this
And Odysseus ended the conference.
Then he swiftly checked with Mentor about
His governance of Ithaca while they
Were away; and all business done, they
Went to the ships, where already one was
Preparing to take the messengers to
The mainland, and boarded their own ship,
Which slipped from the familiar dock
On its voyage to Pylos; and as it sped
From the bay, Pelagia left her baby

With the nurse and rode to Laertes's farm
To tell him of the return of his son.

She found him as before, tending his vines.
He glanced at her as she came to him
But worked on, his knife between his gnarled fingers.

"King Laertes,"
               she said carefully,
"I bring you news"—

                   "that my son has returned?"
He said, cutting away a dead tendril.

                       "You know?"
She said, surprised.

                    "I know more
Than you suspect. He returned just before morning,
On a black ship that then joined many others.
I kept watch myself, high on this hill."

As light suddenly bursts into a darkened room,
Showing all within with utter clarity,
So Pelagia now realized that the old man
Throughout the year, in frost or rain, harsh sun
Or deepest night, had kept his own vigil
For the return of his beloved son, on his own;
And she understood as well that he was
Conversant with more than others were aware,
And she acquired new respect for him.

"But it was good of you to come to me."

"And now they have sailed off for the marriage."

"Ah, and you have been left with the child,"

For he saw the shadow that crossed her face
Before she could suppress it, and he knew
That she could that moment find no reply.

"You must bring him to me someday soon,
My little great-grandson."

     His fingers continued
Their busy work. Unaware that she did so,
She gasped at this recognition of the child.

"Did you not think that I would see him,
My grandson's boy?"

    She looked at him speechless still.

"I know that it will be hard for you"—

Another swift sure slice—
      "Concubine
That you are"—

    she stiffened at the word
As if he had slapped her hard, but he continued,
Unperturbed—

    "and your best times will be few
Once the bride gets here"—

     her face now white—

"But you have two rare gifts to ward off
Ill fortune. First, your skill in healing arts,
Now found indispensable here. Then,
The infant, whose blood belongs to my line"—

He spoke with fierce satisfaction—
      "so that
I will protect him so long as I live."

He gave a gravely laugh.

    "Bring him to me
When you have need, and we will have some time
Among my restful trees, and in a few years
I will show him the rows of vines and trees
That I will name for him."

    Before she could
Stammer out a word, he brusquely barked,

"Now, go."
    And he turned his head back to his work.

Astonished at what she had just heard,
Pelagia silently turned away
To mount her horse and start her journey home.
As she rode along, making her way
Across the rugged countryside, she marvelled
At the secret depths of the strong old man,
And she understood for the first time
His wisdom and powerful character,
What an impressive king he must have been,
And how both Odysseus and his fine son
Had inherited his best qualities.

At home she plunged again into her tasks
Working beside Amunet until the day
Grew weary as herself; but in the night,
With no Telemachus close by her side,
She shifted restlessly, her mind caught up
In the turmoil of her thoughts about the future.
The next morning as she nursed her baby,
She looked at him with fear over what might
Befall them, and then she thought of the bride
With Telemachus, so that the child, disturbed
By her anguish, cried out. Immediately,
In remorse she comforted him, and as
He began to suck again, she spent all
Her attention upon him. But, when sated
He fell asleep, she gave him over to the nurse,
And, when ready, joined Amunet to work.
For a while they worked in silence, for they
Had over the months, like the joins of fine carpentry,
Become indistinguishable in tasks together.
But Amunet saw her mistress's growing
Agitation and finally said,

                    "Perhaps
We should take a drink and rest for a while."

Pelagia, startled, put down her pestle,
And together they went into the garden,
To a corner shaded by a young tree
And sat on a stone bench, sipping their cool beverage.

For a time neither spoke, letting the breeze,
Light and fragrant with the scents of herbs
That in their beds surrounded them, waft
Over them, to their sensuous pleasure.
Finally, Pelagia, who heavy lidded,
Had studied the silent figure with her,
Spoke lazily.

    "You were a gift
To Helen?"

     The figure remained still,
Her face expressionless, and turned toward
The garden.

     "Yes."

      "From the queen at Thebes?"

"Yes."

   "Is that where you learned your skills"?

        "In part."

At this reply, Pelagia's eyes opened fully.

"Where did you begin your training, then?"

A pause, as a sudden gust of anguish
Swept across Amunet's face.
      "With my father."

Pelagia could see her no longer still,
Her breathing uneven as she struggled
To contain feelings that had been buried
Deep within her.

     "Your father? How could a ..."

"Slave?"
    Exclaimed Amunet, her voice bitter,
Her anger barely suppressed.
      "He was no slave."

"But how?"
             began Pelagia, but
She was stopped by a gesture that revealed
Such authority she was shocked into silence.

"Know, then, that you are not the only one
Cast into servitude."

             For a moment
She struggled with the emotions that raged
Within her, and then her powerful will
Took charge, she became still and quiet,
And finally, after a long-drawn breath,
She continued.

             "I am not from Egypt,
But Phoenician, from the great city Tyre,
Where my father was respected for his skill
In medicine."

Catching the blank look
Of her listener, she sighed and explained,

"Tyre is a wealthy city, powerful,
The jewel among our cities. It rests
On an island just off the sea's coast,
And but a day's sail or so from Egypt.
It is ideal for our sea-faring trade,
With two fine harbours, one found in the north,
The other in the south, of the island,
With a canal that links them in such a way
That ships can move easily from one harbour
To the other to shelter from a storm."

Now lost in her memories, she smiled.

"The city is well fortified, impregnable,
But is limited in space, its buildings
Rising high rather than spread out, but with
Squares and parks amongst its labyrinth
Of streets, all on different levels. We lived
High up in one of these, with my father's

Workrooms below, and farther down, where
He met his clients. From one of my windows
I could see across to the coast and watch
The ships passing through, their sails sun-brightened."

For a moment she was caught up in the vista
Of her memory, and then she returned.

"I was my father's only child; he had no son;
And my mother had died at my birth.
I was very close to him"—

                     her eyes filled
With tears, but she ignored them and went on—

"And he treated me not only as a daughter
But as a son, starting with me early
In my life to train me in his art
And pass on to me his vast knowledge.
I proved, as you know, to be adept
And he grew proud of my accomplishment.
But when my girlhood was finished and I
Was newly a woman, he told me
What he now intended: that we would move
To Thebes, in Egypt.

                'There the ruler
Favours the medical arts, and with my skills
I can teach there, and you would have a chance
To become a physician, for women
There can do so, whereas here you would have no chance.'

"I did not know what to say, for I loved
My city, with its pillars white and brown,
The lively square in front of our house,
The small park, green and cool in the summer,
And from its battlements the view of the sea
And its changing colours day by day.
But I realized the wisdom of my father
And his plan—for if I stayed in Tyre, all
I could expect would be marriage and loss
Of my skills in the domestic life
Of household and children and family.

"Now my father made his final preparations.
To his apprentice, a young man some years
In service to him, he gave his practice,
Our servants, and our house, for in Tyre
We had no relatives, those alive
Located far up the coast, and with whom
We had had no contact for many years.
As we left, many tears were shed among us,
For these slaves had been my own family
Since my infancy, and our farewells were prolonged,
Much to my father's wry impatience.
But now we had made ready, packing all
We needed and could use, and at the dock
Boarded a large ship packed with much freight.

"It was my first time on a ship at sea,
But I proved to be a true Phoenician—
I never felt ill with the sway and chop
Of the boat but revelled in the glory
Of sun-glittering waves and the bracing breeze
Ruffling my hair and my clothes, tingling my skin.
The boat moved swiftly in the wind, and that night,
Having sailed since dawn, we were landed at
A small dock at one of the arms of the Nile
In its huge delta. My father, leaving me
To guard our possessions, searched along the dock
For a sailing vessel while I endured
The looks of those passing by. Finally,
After much haggling, he acquired a boat
That seemed equipped to make the journey
Up the river, providing tents and what
Was necessary for meals. Since it
Now was nearing dusk, we camped on a beach
Near the boat. The crew put up our tent, and
The captain invited us to eat with him
At his fire. He seemed amiable,
Keeping a brisk conversation going,
But I noticed that he asked many questions—
Where we had come from, what we would do
At Thebes, and particularly questions

About me, and I became uneasy
With the way he looked at me, appraising
My age and my appearance, and when he listened
To my father, his eyes seemed always searching
For something, and when we took leave of him
I glanced back and caught his gaze, speculative
And hard. As we lay in our tent I whispered
To my father my misgivings, but he
Laughed and told me that I had the silly
Fears of a young girl, and after a time
Listening to the strange new noises
Of the night birds and animals and insects,
I fell asleep. But in the morning, cool and fresh,
My worries were submerged in the sun's glory,
And after a sparse breakfast, and all packed
Aboard, we set sail, the morning breeze filling the sail,
And the boat drifted along the small river,
Pushing against the lazy current's protests.

"All was for me new born, the flatness of the land,
So different from my island view of coast and sea,
The lush green along the banks, the groves glimpsed
Of the soaring palm trees and the verdant fig,
And hint of rippling fields of grain beyond the banks.
That night we camped again beside the river,
But this time the captain left us alone,
And my father and I sat quietly,
Gazing among the stars fixed above us
In the clear night air. Another day passed
In the same manner. The day following
We cleared the delta, entering the Nile itself.
The river widened, our boat sailing as on
A lake, but the captain kept it closer
To the eastern bank. The landscape began
To change, rising on either side, first hills,
Then cliffs, their sandy brown a reminder
Of the tall buildings' stones at home in Tyre.
As the day wore on, the country grew wilder,
More rocky, and human habitation
Seemed to disappear. That night we camped
On barren ground where the bank moved slightly back

From the forbidding cliff that brooded over it.
As before we sat looking out at the dark mass
Flowing quietly by, and at the stars
Peeking over the huge shapes beyond us.
And then we moved into the tent and slept.

"Suddenly I was shocked awake by hands,
Rough and powerful, that grabbed both my arms
And jerked me up in time to see my father,
His head yanked back, receive a slash across his throat
And his dying body shoved to the ground.
I screamed in horror at his murder, done
By his killer as efficiently
And dispassionately as one would slaughter
A bull; and then my screams changed to terror
As the men, four in number as I now saw,
Dragged me out of the tent. The fire there that
Had died to embers they built up again;
Two men, still grasping me, dragged me to where
In the pitiless flames I could be seen clearly.
Then one of the others ripped what slight clothing
I wore from me, and for a long, long moment
They studied my naked body as I stood,
Shocked into silence. But they did not leer,
As I thought they would, but with hard eyes looked
At every inch of my person. I stood
There held immobile but shivering violently,
Locked in apprehension and in grief.
Suddenly they hurled me to the ground,
And before I could respond, two pinned my arms
To the earth and another forced my legs apart
And held them there. The fourth knelt between them,
And slowly began to caress my body,
Stroking my neck, fondling my breasts, moving
Down to caress my belly, then my legs
And thighs, then his hand entered me, worked there,
And finally he came down on me, and
The real rape began. I could scream no longer,
Only cry out with the pain. When he was satisfied
He left me, and another took his place,
Following the same procedure; four times

I was thus raped, nor could I find the peace
Of fainting; and when they had finished their work
They tied me, whimpering and shuddering,
To a pole, where, exhausted, I hung and lost
Consciousness. The next morning they freed me
But then bound my hands to a lengthy rope
Which one of them held as he rode before me
On a donkey. Down a trail I stumbled
After him, my naked feet now bruised and cut
On the rocky path. I still was too distraught
To think, my body sore and aching, and
All my thought on following the donkey—
Once I did stumble and fall and was dragged,
My body cruelly scraped before he heard my cry,
For I was still unclothed, and the sun beat
Upon me unmercifully. As well,
My thirst and hunger grew unbearable,
For I had had nothing since the night before,
And only when I fainted did they stop,
Let a few drops pass my lips, and then rest.
But now they gave me a thin covering
To shield my body and my head from the harsh rays.
Yet still they forced me to stumble behind,
My feet now bleeding and in agony.
At last, my moaning now continuous,
They placed me on the donkey, where, semi-conscious,
I could barely keep my balance, and once
At least I did fall off, at which they bound
Me firmly to the donkey's back. The rest
Of the day I have no knowledge of, nor
Of the trail or landscape; but in the evening
They made camp, let me drink and gave me food,
And let me rest while the dusk sank into the night.
Then, but this time in the dark, once more
Each repeated the dreadful ritual
From the previous night, while I, aching,
Exhausted, submitted without struggle,
Numb and uncaring in my misery.
Over the next several days they changed again,
Clothing me in the Egyptian fashion,

Letting me ride atop the donkey
So that my feet could heal, and feeding me.
And my training continued, although during that time
I did not recognize it as such, for
They now forced me to make their meals, beating me
If I made mistakes, for I had not cooked
Until now. During this time my mind cleared
Somewhat, especially while I rode,
But when they saw this happen, at night they
Forced me to drink a liquid which was drugged,
Which I knew from my own skills; despite my will,
Pleasant sensations infused my body
And when each came again to lie with me
My body responded to each touch and thrust,
Even as my mind was detached, witnessing
As if from a distance these eroticisms.

"Another week passed in this fashion,
By which time I had but little will left;
And as we entered Thebes, they were satisfied
I had been broken in as the slave
They had intended. During all this time
I had taken little note of the land
Through which we had travelled, and now the bustle
And the crowds of the busy city
Bewildered me as they brought me, now dressed
In the garb of an Egyptian slave,
To a merchant who inspected me, heard
From them of my skill, although they knew
Little of that lore, and then purchased me.
For several days, he tested my skills
With herbs and drugs; then, satisfied, he brought me
To the king's palace, where, after they
Had examined me further, I was then bought.
For a time I did menial tasks but
Also learned from Egyptian practice new
Substances and applications. One day,
When no one else was available,
I made a potion for the king's wife
That eased some discomfort that she suffered,
And she noticed me. I soon became a favourite,

Much to the envy of my fellow slaves,
And I learned from my mistress I could hope
To be freed, for in Egypt there exists
The possibility to acquire
A position in this art, even as a woman,
Just as my father had foretold."

                Silence
For a moment, as the memory of her father
Made her falter, but then she gained control
And continued.

             "It was with such new hope
That I went on. But shortly after,
King Menelaos arrived with his wife,
Queen Helen"—

              an edge came to her voice—

"Who, learning of the fame of our house in this art,
In her boredom at being marooned in Egypt,
Asked my mistress if she could acquire learning
Of the discipline. She agreed and sent me
To teach and to assist her. The queen was pleased
With me, and when the time came for them
To depart for Sparta she requested me
As a gift. My mistress could not help but agree,
And so I lost all chance of position,
Especially in Hellas, and here I am today,
Your teacher-slave until sent back to Helen."

But Pelagia could see her still form
Suffused with rage and grief barely controlled
By a granite will, polished by the years
Of servitude. Only the hum of busy insects,
The whisper of leaves stirred by an infant wind,
And a bird's occasional call were heard.
Then Pelagia, who had with fascination
And with horror listened to her account:

"We are sisters in our dismembered lives,"

And she told Amunet in full how she
Came to be here, and at the end she took
Cloth, covered her head and face, and rocked in grief.
Amunet could no longer restrain herself
And likewise covered her face; then both rocked
And gave vent to their mutual anguish,
The sound of their pain flooding the garden.
When they in exhaustion subsided, again
The garden's small disturbances returned,
And they sat, spent, in the time-wrenched space.
Then, as both rearranged their clothing quietly,
Pelagia spoke.

          "I can think of you
As slave no longer. Always I respect
Your knowledge and skill as a teacher, but
Now, our lives in wreckage though on different roads,
We must be closer while we still have time,
And I ask you to be my friend, my teacher."

She took the other's unresisting hand,
Who, direct gaze to direct gaze, nodded.
For a short while, now calmer after the storms
Of feeling that had afflicted them,
They talked of inconsequential matters
Until Pelagia with sudden curiosity:

"You are Phoenician, and yet your name
Appears Egyptian—why is that, if I
May ask?"

        Amunet smiled grimly, then said
Ironically,

         "My mistress in Egypt,
When out of shame I would not tell her my name,
Gave me this one, based on that of her god
Amun, a deity she had adopted
As patron of our healing arts."

           She stopped
Pelagia before she could speak.

"I will keep the name, especially
Since it is the one by which Helen knows me,
And also because I will never use
My birth name again."

                        Then she rose.
"And now we must get back to work, must we not?"

And the two returned to the workshop,
But Pelagia now felt comforted
By her new friend, and the atmosphere had changed,
Even as both knew that when Telemachus
Returned with his new bride, Helen would claim
Amunet, who would be shipped back to Sparta
To live her life out no higher than a slave.

# Canto 21
## PYLOS

On the tall wall of the citadel stood
Polycaste, looking out toward the sea
As she had since the messenger returned.
The breeze stirred her hair and her gown, adrifting
About her. Her eyes were somber and showed
The effects of her sleeplessness and her
Constant vigil. She stood as a statue
Would stand, motionless, as Thrasymedes
Gained the platform and watched her, oblivious
To his presence. What he saw confirmed his
Belief in how she had grown up: she had
Matured in the year that so soon had passed;
Her eyes were still those of a doe, violet
And large, but her face was now more sculpted
And though still soft, more defined in a way
Which made her even more lovely than before,
And her body, which before was still ripening,
Was now in full bloom, causing men to gasp
At her extraordinary beauty. He
Saw as well that her deepening character
Gave her a more thoughtful mien, her passion
Contained as she stood patiently, waiting
For the arrival of her betrothed.

                              "Come, rest,"
He said, putting his arm around her.

She looked at him gravely.

                              "The seventh day
Has come,"
                 she said.

                              "This is the final time
That he can arrive."

"And he will, I know,"
Hastily her brother said.
                              "And with him
Will be the queen his mother, Penelope."

"Yes, he will come,"
                              she said without doubt.
"I will watch here for his sail."

                              He saw she
Would not move from there; he sighed; a quick hug
And he left her there, still gazing far off.

She still stood there as her shadow shifted
And grew slightly longer through the journey
Of Helios. Then, as she watched, she thought
She saw a flicker on the horizon;
Then, the possibility of a sail;
And finally, the tiny ship sped closer,
Until she could see its shape and its sail;
And she turned and raced from the wall even as
The watchman shouted his recognition.

"He is here!"
                    she cried; and the family,
Overjoyed, quickly made preparations
To greet their visitors; and by the time
The ship slid its prow into the yielding sand,
They were all on the beach before it.
Telemachus was the first from the bow,
Leaping from it; his bride met him halfway
Between the ship and her family, and
Embraced him fiercely. They remained locked
Together even as the Ithacan
Delegation disembarked to be greeted
By their hosts. Penelope herself was
Disconcerted by the break with protocol,
But Odysseus firmly steered her toward
The family, who had advanced to greet them.
Pisistratus moved to embrace the group
Warmly, but the Ithacan king first grasped
Thrasymedes's arm.

"Welcome, Odysseus,
King and hero,"
warmly exclaimed the prince.

"As you can see,"
Odysseus replied,
A smile on his lips,
"I have returned
As I promised."

And the family broke
Into laughter to allow their surprise
To evaporate. Then Odysseus
Introduced great Nestor's family to
Penelope.

"My queen, you have already
Met the youngest son of noble Nestor,
Pisistratus; and this is Thrasymedes,
The senior prince; and his brothers,
Echephron, Stratius, Perseus, and here
Aretos. And finally, the lovely
Mother of the bride—who presently,
As we all can see, is occupied—
Aristomachê,"

who moved forward
To acknowledge the Ithacan queen.
Penelope looked at her searchingly, as
Did Aristomachê her. The queen saw
A woman of extraordinary wild
Beauty and strong character, a few years
Younger than herself, and determined
Quickly that she was both ambitious
And clever, not one to antagonize,
And one to watch carefully. For her part,
Nestor's wife saw a stately queen, sharp eyed
And intelligent, and knew without more
Study that she would be formidable
To cross.

They smiled at each other, and then
The Pylian spoke in a rich voice,

"Please forgive my daughter for her actions—
It has been so long since her betrothed
Left, and she is somewhat impetuous,
As you can see."

Penelope smiled and nodded,
And Aristomachê called out to her
Daughter,
"Polycaste! Please come to meet
King Odysseus and his queen Penelope."

Telemachus gently pulled away from
The now breathless girl, and they moved toward
The party awaiting them. Penelope
Almost gasped when she now saw her son's bride.
She had heard of her beauty, and she had
Seen the mother's own attractiveness, but
She was unprepared for the unparalleled
Loveliness of the girl she saw there, who
Now stood gravely before her, her eyes
Still shining from her intimate encounter.
All the Ithacan men were equally
Stunned, for the young girl they had met before
Was now a young but mature woman in
Full blossom. Penelope looked at her for
A moment longer, then turned to her son,
Who himself had not till now truly seen
His beloved.

"My queen and mother,"
he stammered,
"My betrothed, Nestor's daughter, Polycaste."

And the girl gracefully made obeisance
To her future mother-in-law. The queen
Smiled again and said to her prince,

"You have

Chosen well, my son."

All present sighed with
Relief at this, while Odysseus said,

"Gracious Polycaste, you have grown even
More lovely since last we met."

She lowered
Her eyes and gracefully inclined her head,
But said nothing.

Telemachus could not
Tear his eyes away from his betrothed, but
Pisistratus, laughing, took him by the arm.

"Come, my friend, you will have time enough later
To look at your bride. But now I suggest
That we return to the palace in triumph!"

All smiled at this, and his suggestion taken,
Echephron leading the way before them,
Odysseus in arm with Thrasymedes,
Penelope and Aristomachê,
The Ithacan queen asking questions of
Aristomachê about Pylos,
Telemachus walking with Polycaste
And Pisistratus, and the other brothers
And attendants following behind them,
As back at the ship the crew unloaded
Their cargo, helped by the Pylians.

At the palace, quarters were assigned
To the royal Ithacans, and spaces
For the crew and for the other nobles,
Halitherses and Medon, all swept clean,
With soft fleeces laid. As the sun now ran
Its last course in the sky, steaming baths
Were poured, and attendants helped visitors
In their ablutions. Then all met again
For the evening feast, the pure bulls brought
And sacrificed, and fumes as they roasted
Ascended to the Gods. There at the banquet
Sat Odysseus; with space left for his queen

On one side, and noble Thrasymedes
On the other. Soon the men gathered,
And platters heaped with breads and fine tidbits
Were presented to them as a libation
Was made and wine poured into bronze goblets.
As this was completed, the women made
Their entrance, and all were captivated
By their beauty—even that of Penelope,
Whose grace and dignity complemented
The ravishing beauty of the Pylian
Mother and daughter. Penelope took
Her place beside Odysseus; Aristomachê
Sat beside her, then Polycaste, and
Then Telemachus. As the wine flowed
And all nibbled in anticipation
Of the coming meat, the women chatted
With Telemachus and amongst themselves,
Penelope learning more of Nestor
And his marriage to the young captive,
And then the first visit of Telemachus
As he searched through Greece for his father.

"And that's where Polycaste first laid eyes
On our young hero"—

                    Pisistratus, sitting
On the other side of Telemachus,
Exclaimed jovially—

              "all of him, for
She was the one that bathed him that day!"

Polycaste blushed and reached across her
Betrothed to lightly slap her brother's hand,
While the two queens smiled; but Penelope
Made note of the incident, and knowing
The two years that had passed, now understood,
As had Odysseus, how the girl's passion,
Her infatuation, had been fanned
By her mother and the family
To provide for this possible marriage.
But as she watched the way in which the girl

Gazed at her son, she knew as well that
Her love was genuine; and her poise
And intelligence further convinced the queen
That the match was suitable, though, hidden
In the labyrinth of her mind, the thought
Stirred of Pelagia, and she wondered
What would happen, not only when the bride
Discovered the relationship and the child,
But what her mother would think, or, worse, do.
But she closed the door on that thought for now,
And continued to learn more about Pylos
And in turn spoke of Ithaca's past.
In the meantime, Odysseus was deep in talk
With Thrasymedes, who was glowing with relief.

"It is evident that Poseidon has

     Forgiven me,"
said Odysseus wryly,

"For I returned just as the ship prepared
To disembark."

    Thrasymedes chuckled
In sympathy and wonder. But, leaning
Toward him, the astute king said,

      "In haste,
I had to do something which I did not
Have time to discuss with you. Messengers
Have been sent to King Menelaos, to
King Orestes and his friend Pylades,
To attend the wedding four days from now."

Thrasymedes looked at him, astonished.

"It is important, I think, that they come
To reinforce our strength in the sight of
The Elisians—and I suggest that you
Send a messenger to them with the same
Invitation, but also telling them
That the kings will attend."

Thrasymedes's brow furrowed.

                              "How do we
Know that they will indeed attend, wise
Odysseus?"

               The Ithacan king chuckled.

"Oh, they will come, have no fear—they want to
Witness what we promised last year, which is
To their advantage strategically."

Then Odysseus turned to the events that
Must come before the wedding, and afterwards.

"Normally Telemachus would host the feast
The day following, but given how far
We are away, we must borrow your palace
For this duty, if you will permit us."

"We would be honoured if you do so,"
Said Thrasymedes enthusiastically.

"And we will provide the music and the dances."

"We thank you,"
                   said the relieved Ithacan,

"And when you visit us, we will return
The favour multifold."

                   As he spoke,
The great joints of beef were brought in and carved,
And the attendants brought around huge platters
Heaped with the succulent meat. Then again
Spoke the Pylian prince.

                  "Great Odysseus,
We all are waiting anxiously to hear
You recount what has happened in your quest
For this past year. Please, we beg you to speak
Of this for all our gratification,
For it must be wondrous what you have done
To return as you have."

All those at table
Raised their voices with his to beseech
Odysseus to do so. He raised his hand
To silence them.

"Noble Thrasymedes,
I will be happy to fulfill your request,
For I returned so suddenly that even
My family has not heard my account.
But before I begin, I beg you to
Have your wonderful bard, Euphranor,
Attend here and hear my story, for he
Is the one who should sing of it at
The wedding feast."

Thrasymedes, pleased
By this request, summoned the singer, who
Was placed at a table and given food
And wine and bade to listen carefully.
Then, as the shadows sprawled longer and
The torches flared brighter, King Odysseus
Related his tale, and as he did so
His wife and son noted how worn he looked,
Older, and in his eyes there glimmered a light
That they had not seen before nor could
Understand, and as his tale progressed, they wept
At the hardships he had undergone. But
He was careful to leave out any mention
Of the Phaeacians and how he returned.
When he finished, a silence so deep that
Only the sound of the torches' flame could
Be heard, and then a deep sigh issued from all
The feasters and even the attendants
Who had paused in their work, rapt in his tale.

Then Telemachus rose with tear-stained cheeks.

"My noble father and great king, truly
You have made the greatest journey that we
Have heard—greater than Jason with his crew
Of Argonauts, for you have done all alone,

Without the help of any other hero.
And I here praise you for your great labour."

And the prince knelt to embrace the knees
Of his heroic father, who, moved, raised him
Up and embraced him, each wet with tears,
As were Penelope and many others.
Polycaste watched with enormous eyes,
Awed by Odysseus's accomplishment, and
Deeply moved by the love she saw among
The family.

        Then Odysseus turned to all
And said,
        "Now let us make proper obeisance
To Lord Poseidon, who has forgiven me,
And praise his name."

        A libation was made,
And wine spilled upon the floor, and then he
Had Euphranor lead all in a hymn
To the dreaded lord:

"I sing in praise of Poseidon, mighty God,
Disturber of mountains and the barren sea,
Majesty of the Deep. To you, Earthshaking Lord,
Have been apportioned two different tasks:
Tamer of the wild horses, and Saviour of ships.

"Hail, Poseidon, blue-haired cradler of the Earth:
O blessed God, to us show kindness:
Help those who venture in ships upon the sea."

Halitherses had joined in with glowing eyes
And at the end looked at his king with pride.
Little talk followed the hymn; and soon all
Arose, with Telemachus and his betrothed
Forced to part, Polycaste's mother with
The reluctant girl, and Pisistratus
Engaging his friend in conversation.
Penelope and Odysseus retired
To the room allotted them, in which
The exhausted king immediately fell

Fast asleep upon the soft fleeces. His queen
Studied him as he lay there—his worn face
Showing the hardships through which he had passed,
The new scars upon his body—and she
Considered the new look betrayed in his eyes,
That seemed to show him haunted by knowledge
That he had gained and by what he had seen.
Moved and disturbed, she lay close to him, her
Arms about his body, protecting him
As if he were a child, and in such way
She fell asleep, his head upon her breast.

As the next day Dawn arose to brush the earth
With her glowing fingers, so in the palace
Life stirred again, and within a short time,
Like ants in incessant movement in their
Colony, or the bees at work in their
Busy hive, the palace sprang into action
As preparations were made for wedding
And visitors. A messenger was sent
To nearby Elis with the invitation,
And attendants rushed about in their need
To have things ready. For the Ithacans,
The time was not so precious, and they ate
With their Pylian friends, revelling
In the leisure that they had this day.
But even in Time's sanctuary
They still went quietly about their tasks.
Penelope visited Aristomachê
And they talked pleasantly about what must
Take place before and after the wedding;
Odysseus met with Thrasymedes and
His brothers to discuss what to look for
Politically with the different guests,
Particularly the Elisians,
Who the crafty Ithacan was sure
Would attend; and Telemachus walked with
Polycaste and told her the adventures
He had undergone. She listened, her eyes
Shining with admiration and love, and
The prince was pleasantly surprised by her

Questions, which were to the point, intelligent
And searching, increasing her stature in
His eyes, as her mature beauty attracted
Him far more than last time. As well, she showed
No longer the impetuous passion
That she had unleashed before, but conversed
And walked with him without yielding to
The attraction that she so clearly felt.
After the meeting with the Pylians
Odysseus held conference with his own
Advisors, who had also attended.

"Well, my councillors, what do you think?"

Medon replied,
                    "So far, all could have not gone
Better. It will depend on the responses
Of the kings and the Elisians as to
What the outcome will be."

                              The king chuckled.
"You are right, of course. It is up to me
To prepare our allies so that all will
Be well."

          They discussed some details about
What he might do, and then he dismissed them.
However, Halitherses stayed after
Medon had left, and Odysseus looked at him
Quizzically.

          "Yes, old friend?"

                              The wise seer
For a moment said nothing, but studied him
Closely. Then he sighed.

                    "My lord, more took place
Than you have recounted. May I ask you
To tell me more?"

          Odysseus looked at him
And sighed, his face more worn and his eyes
More haunted than before.

"Ah, my great seer,
I knew you would see through what I have said.
You may ask, but forgive me if I do not
Reply."

Halitherses looked closer yet
And then gravely replied,
"I see under
Some constraint, but I will yet continue.
What did the Lord Apollo reveal to you?"

"Alas, Halitherses, I have sworn an oath
Never to reveal what was prophesied
To me."

The seer studied him more closely
Yet, and then shuddered and turned away.

"I cannot determine what you learned, but
What it was I am chilled to touch. Let me
Ask, then, a different question. How did
You return? You make no mention of it."

Odysseus smiled helplessly.
"Again,
My peerless seer, I cannot tell you."

Halitherses looked at him sharply, then drew in
His breath.

"You have done something, I cannot
Tell, that will have future consequences.
What it is, is veiled from me; only the sense
Of it I can feel. I will ask no more."

Odysseus smiled and acknowledged him, but
The Ithacan seer could see clearly the king's
Troubled eyes that seemed to remove him from
The present; and, disturbed himself, he bowed
And left his presence. Wise Odysseus thought
For a time, and then he walked slowly to
His room, where he found Penelope waiting.

"My lord, have you had rest enough?"

                                    He knew
What she meant and moved to her, undid
Her gown, and studied the form revealed—
So familiar, and still lovely after
The years, and his heart lurched within him
As he lay again with his wife and made love
To her and felt his age and hers against
The youthful passion spent but two nights since,
And with all his being accepted
Their mortality.

The day before the wedding
Dawned with everything prepared, and by noon
The first guests arrived, with Menelaos
Thundering up to the palace, Helen
By his side and his entourage behind,
Their helmets and spears glittering in the sun.
Standing before the palace were Pylian
Brothers, Odysseus, and Telemachus.
In his usual fashion, Menelaos
Leapt from his chariot and heartily
Embraced his fellow king.

                        "By the Gods,
You have returned, just as you promised!
I look forward to hearing your story
At the feast."

                    He clapped him on the back, and
Turned to Thrasymedes.

                        "Your invitation
We had to accept, given the circumstances.
And my wife, lovely Queen Helen, insisted
That she come as well."

                        Helen was helped
From the chariot and gave a dazzling smile
To all the men there.

                        "Well, King Odysseus,
The famed wedding is about to take place.
My congratulations! And you, good prince,

Have mine as well. I look forward to meeting
Your young bride."

            Father and son bowed to her
And Telemachus introduced her to
Thrasymedes and his brothers, who were
Awed by the legendary queen of whom
They had heard so much and who in real life
Excelled all that had been said about her.
They all then entered the palace and their room
Assigned, and Helen was taken away
To meet the other ladies and the bride.

In the meantime, as was his wont, Odysseus
Took his old friend for a walk upon
The palace hill. As they trudged along farther
Up the hill to where they were quite alone,
Menelaos reminisced about the last time
They had met there.

            "Much has occurred since then—
Orestes's road is almost finished—be sure
To compliment him on it. And he has
Kept Arcadia under his thumb,
As we had hoped."

            By this time they had reached
A small plateau where they could look back and down
At palace and beach and sea, and here they stopped.
Menelaos now spoke more seriously.

"You have heard, I suppose, that because
You had not been heard of, the Elisians
Make plans to invade Pylos while it is still weak?"

Odysseus nodded.

            "My son has told me all.
And that is why at this wedding we must
Show that we are all united, and that
Any show of force against one of us
Will bring down the wrath of all upon those
Who dare to do so."

Menelaos remained silent for a moment.

"I know we had made our pact last year,
But do you really think we should do thus,
Despite the marriage of your son?"

Clever Odysseus, who knew well his friend's
Changeability, remained patient.

"What better time to show your combined force?
It would make clear who controls the land,
And its example would keep other factions
From attempting their own forays."

Menelaos thought again, and nodded
Reluctantly.

       "And what would be even better, and keep
War from breaking out, would be to show here
How unified we are, and how determined
Not to let any violate our borders."

A sigh.

      "Well, my friend, as usual you
Can talk me into anything. I'll follow
Whatever you say or do. Now let's go
Back and prepare for Orestes and for
Tonight's feast."

         Odysseus laughed and clapped
His friend upon the back, and the two
Descended to the palace, Menelaos
Chatting as they went.

As the sun still blazed upon the earth in
The afternoon, a large troop arrived,
Their dust and noise apparent in the distance.
At the head was King Orestes, splendid
In armour, and with him in the chariot
His wife, Queen Hermione. Beside them
Was the chariot of Pylades
And his wife, Electra. Behind them,
As a forest may appear upon a plain,

The tree tops numberless to count,
A great multitude of spears flashed brightly
In the afternoon sun. The kings dismounted,
Pylades smiling and quickly grasping
Odysseus's arm.

              "A wonder it is to
See you again—reports said you vanished
And were nowhere to be found."

Odysseus smiled.

                "I had indeed dropped
From sight. But you will hear more of this
At tonight's feast—as will you, Orestes,"

He said, turning to greet the Mycenaean
King, who gravely nodded in acknowledgement
And replied,
            "All of us should have known that
You would return unharmed, good Odysseus,"

And the two grasped arms in comradeship.
As the queens descended from their chariots,
Telemachus introduced them to the Pylians,
Who had already greeted the familiar kings.

"My congratulations, Prince Telemachus,
On your coming marriage,"
               murmured Hermione,

"I look forward to meeting your bride, whose
Fame for her beauty has spread through Attica."

Electra smiled slightly in acknowledgement
Of her fellow-queen's compliment, and the prince
Bowed to them both; then all proceeded to
The palace, where quarters were apportioned
To them. As at King Nestor's funeral,
Below the palace numerous tents were raised,
With areas where the men could eat.

While all prepared for the pre-wedding feast,
The kings met quietly together.

Odysseus, acknowledged by the others,
Took charge.

          "My gratitude for your
Coming—and thanks to you, wise Orestes,
For the troop that you brought with you today."

Orestes nodded, but he did not smile.

"All here will witness this marriage, which will cement
Our alliance, as we affirmed here last year."

A moment. Then Menelaos nodded, and
The others followed.

          "The question is, what
Will the Elisians do? We must keep
United during the festivities,
Whether they attend or not. And your troop,
King Orestes, helps greatly for this time."

Now Orestes spoke.

          "What you say, my friend,
Is wise as usual. I have brought this number
For two reasons: first, as a show of force,
To dissuade those who would consider here
As a treasure to be looted; second,
To show our strength throughout all our countries
And let the news of it reach those more distant."

All nodded at his wisdom, although
Menelaos wondered to himself
Whether the show was also directed
Toward himself and Sparta. Even as
They met, an attendant came with news that
The Elisians had arrived with a large force
Of their own. Thrasymedes, apprehensive,
Looked, as did the others, at Odysseus.

"We will make them welcome, of course, and praise
Them for the honour they have bestowed you
By coming in such numbers. I will
Come with you in support—and let us place

Their troop lower on the hill, below and
Apart from King Orestes's forces,
So that no friction can occur during
The festivities."

        Turning to Orestes,

"I think sentinels should quietly be placed,
Made inconspicuous as possible,
Do you agree?"

        King Orestes nodded,
A slight smile on his face at the cunning
Tactics.

        Then Orestes went with the Pylian
To greet the Elisians, who were seen
Approaching along the beach, thick forested
With spears. By the time their leaders approached
Them, the Ithacans and Pylians had
Gathered to greet them on the beach.

        "Welcome,
To you all—good Thalpios"—

        he made curt
Acknowledgement, unsmiling—

        "and also
You, great Polyxeimos"—

        a brief nod and
Surly look—

        "and you, mighty Automedon,
Peerless driver of chariots"—

        this time
A more gracious nod, but the observant
Ithacan could see the giant of a man
Noting carefully all about him.

"My personal gratitude to you all
For attending my son's marriage, and for
Doing us such honour by your numbers.
Prince Thrasymedes will have attendants
Show you where you may camp."

                    The prince added
His own thanks for their arrival, invited
Them to the pre-wedding feast that night,
Let Telemachus and his own brothers
Join in the greeting, and then all separated.

Since he had arrived, apart from his tasks
In greeting guests on this day, Telemachus
Had spent time with Polycaste when she
Herself was not busy with the wedding
Preparations. He noted again how
She no longer showed the adolescent
Impulses of the previous year, but,
While still showing her love for him when they
Kissed for long moments, she spent much of the time
Questioning him about Ithaca, Penelope,
His father, and where they would live. At last
He laughed and said,

             "You would do better to
Ask my mother most of these questions, for
She is the one who will order our lives for
The next while."

          She smiled thoughtfully and said
No more on the subject, but chatted
About Pylos and the guests at the wedding.

"You know the queens?"

           "Not well,"
                    he said diffidently,
And told her about the adventures that Electra
And Hermione had endured. As he
Related these, she became even more
Thoughtful and listened closely.

             "And what of
Helen?"
     she asked.
          "Her daughter is beautiful,
But none surpasses the queen of Sparta."

And he told her of what Helen had done
Following the Trojan War to the present,
And how she was now expert in the use
And knowledge of drugs.

        "I must get to know
Her more—and the others,"
            murmured his bride.

Telemachus became uneasy
On hearing her desire, for he remembered
Helen's training of Pelagia, and
He did not want Polycaste to know
Of his concubine and her child until
Much later, when they had been settled in
Ithaca for some time. He decided that
He must ask his mother to make sure that
No one mentioned the relationship.

When he left his bride's side, he sought out
His mother, sending an attendant for her.
Penelope came to him shortly after.

"Yes, my son?"

He opened the conversation carefully.

"Now that you have met my bride, what do think of her?"

His mother smiled.

        "She is very beautiful,
And from what I have seen so far, should have
A good mind and seems to be mature. I
Think she is a good choice, and I congratulate
You for this match."

        Relieved, Telemachus
Then went on:

        "I am glad you approve, mother.
But there is something that we need to think on.
Queen Helen knows Pelagia well—
She taught her the skills that have been useful

In Ithaca. But I am concerned that
She will reveal to Polycaste and
The queens that Pelagia is my
Concubine."

"That could indeed be a problem,"

Replied Penelope, watching her son
Carefully. Uncertainly he asked,

"Did you know Helen before?"

"Oh, yes,
I knew her."

"Do you think that you could speak
To her and ask her not to tell anyone else
Who is here?"

His mother sighed.

"I have already
Considered the problem and agree. Yes,
I will see her privately as soon as possible.
But I cannot be sure that she will not tell."

Penelope found Helen alone
On the hillside above the palace,
Studying and gathering herbs and plants.

"Well, Penelope, it has been long since we met,"

Glancing up from having placed something
In her basket.

"Yes—over twenty years,"
Replied the Ithacan queen quietly,

"As you were being courted by so many.
I can thank you for Odysseus as my
Husband."

Helen smiled.
"And for keeping him
From you for twenty years."

"Yes, that also
Is true."

"And now here we are, my daughter
Married and your son about to do the same."

"Yes."

"And you have come to ask me to keep
Silent about Pelagia, have you not?"

"Yes. Will you?"

The Spartan queen laughed.

"Of course.

I have no intention of disturbing
The marriage, particularly if it
May put Pelagia in harm. She is
Interesting, is she not?"

"Yes. And she now
Has a child, a boy."

"Ah. The situation
Is becoming more complicated all the time."

"It is."

"Well, I will not make it more so.
I will tell neither the bride nor her mother—
Who seems ambitious for her, does she not?"

Penelope ignored the question.

"I find the girl herself to be suitable."

"Yes, indeed—very beautiful, and from what
I've seen so far, with character.
I hope that she will learn to live
In the circumstances she will find herself."

"So do we all."

Penelope was about
To leave when Helen put her hand upon
Her arm.

"Stay a moment longer?"

She paused.

"You are the only one to whom I can
Truly talk here—my daughter and Electra
Are severely formal with me in a way
That only hate can show. But you and I
Share so much from the past, with our lives so
Intertwined."

"If you wish."

A pause.

Then Helen burst out,
                "Can you not say more?
Why are you so quiet?"

A grim smile.

"Was I not quiet then as well? You were
The one who led the conversation
Even then, and I would listen and
For the most part agree with what you said.
You were never really interested in what
I might have to say."

                "But we were so young,
Both of us."

                "And you were so beautiful,
Always the centre of attention."

"But I should not be held to blame for my
Beauty, over which I had no power.
And look what misery it caused for us both!"

"No, I cannot blame you for those catastrophes.
The men were the cause, helpless by your sight.
But for the rest of us, who did not have
Such graces, you took away our respect
For ourselves as we saw them drift away
From us to you. Odysseus chose me
Only because you rejected him."

Helen softly said,

        "Yet he came to love you
So deeply that he endured for twenty years
To return to you. And I know that when
I saw him in Sparta I could not turn
Him again toward myself. And now here
You are, with a fine prince about to wed
A lovely princess, your husband truly
A great hero; and I myself estranged
From my daughter and envied by many
And hated by more for what I am."

Silence, while about them a breeze sifted
Through the grasses and herbs. Then Penelope
Took Helen by the shoulder

        "Both of us
Have suffered over the years. I do not
Blame you for your younger arrogance—
Too much has happened to overshadow
Those brief glittering moments. Let us now
Speak as we should to each other and hope
That our future days will shine more than
Those past."

        And the two queens embraced without
A word for a long moment, and then both
Walked down the hill toward the palace,
Chatting about Sparta and Ithaca,
To join the stiff cold younger queens.

But now the time came for the pre-wedding feast.
Along the beach and hillsides huge fires blazed
As if mirroring the stars yet to come out
Overhead. A small herd of bulls were brought
And sacrificed through the camps, and in
The high hall the kings and their lords began
The banquet. Libations were made; bowls filled
With breads and delicacies to provoke
The appetite were served by the busy
Attendants, and as wine started to be
Consumed, the women arrived to join the feast.

The men were stunned; never had so many women
Of unparalleled beauty been seen in
One place for a feast. Helen still shone as
The brightest star in their brilliant heaven,
But Polycaste almost equalled her
In loveliness, and the others were not
Dimmed in their grace and dignity. They took
Their places beside their husbands and groom,
And soon the walls of the hall echoed
With the bright sounds of conversation.
Finally the gifts of the bull's body
Were brought, carved, and served, and all in earnest
Began the feasting. As they did so,
Odysseus arose.

    "My dear friends and comrades,
All the seasons have passed once since we ate
Together here. At that time I told you
Of the quest that I was obliged to fulfill,
And tonight you shall learn of what happened
In this eventful year."

    Like the sound of current
As it fought its way through the pebbles of
A stream, so did a surprised babble
Reverberate into the high rafters.
Odysseus raised his hand for silence
And all quieted.

    "But I will not speak
Myself of this—instead, I invited
Euphranor, the superb bard of Pylos,
To sing of my journey, and he agreed."

Odysseus gestured, and the singer rose
From his place at the side and moved forward
With his lyre, and to King Odysseus
He bowed and then began.

"I sing of the hard travails and exploits
Of Odysseus, King of Ithaca,
Famed hero of the War with Ilion,

Whose long journey back from that fateful place
Has been sung across Attica to praise
His courage and renown. It was here, at
The funeral of our great King Nestor,
After praising him for his wisdom and
His prowess, a man surpassing more
Generations than any mortal here,
That the Ithacan King informed us
Of his son's betrothal to Polycaste,
Lovely and beloved daughter of our
Late king, and also told us of his quest
To appease Lord Poseidon, Shaker
Of Earth and Mover of Seas. From here he
Crossed the land of Attica and sailed to
Aetolia, land of jagged peaks and
Feuding warriors. There, after he had
Enjoyed the hospitality of his
Old friend, King Thoas, at Calydon, he
Prayed at the Laphrion sanctuary,
Sacred place of Artemis Laphria
And her brother, Apollo Laphrios,
Dazzling children of Leto and Lord Zeus,
And there received divine instruction,
If clothed in mysterious words, of where
He must go. Faithful to their instruction,
He left his ship, disappeared from view,
To travel north through harsh mountain passes
Amongst wild animals and peoples.
As he crossed one valley, a rough band
Wounded him almost to his death, and when
He had recovered, as a slave he was kept
And beaten through the cold winter months.
But in the spring he killed the ruler
With his bare hands and miraculously
Escaped. Over more ranges he struggled,
Until at last he found a valley sealed
From other men, where they knew no salt,
And here he met the man who asked if the
Oar on his shoulder was used to winnow wheat;
And there he planted it in the ground, as

Had been ordained, and the dread God himself,
Poseidon, there shook the mountains roughly
As a sign that he was appeased, and thereby
Opened a new pass to let him through; and then,
Still with a struggle, for to keep his life
He battled to the death nine men at a
Lake's side before he reached where the prophecy
Ordained—the shrine of Zeus at Dodona,
Where he received final inspiration
And found his way back to Ithaca and
His home. And now here he is among us,
Blessed by the Gods after his long travail.
All hail to thee, great King Odysseus—
No man has undergone what you have lived,
And no man now deserves greater praise."

Here he finished, tears in his eyes, as for all
There, who rose as one to shout,

"All hail,

Noble Odysseus!"

Odysseus, weeping
Himself, humbly acknowledged their praise, then
Himself carved a choice morsel and gave it
To the singer, along with a gift
He had brought for that purpose—a scabbard,
Exquisitely wrought and small, designed for
The dagger that he had given him last year.
The feasting continued for some time, many
Coming forward to greet the Ithacan
And personally compliment him.

Then the women rose and excused themselves,
Took Polycaste back to her quarters,
Where she was dressed in virginal white
And took a decorated box which was
Already full, and the women escorted her
To the temple of Artemis, located
To the side of the palace, where it
Commanded a view of the hillside, beach

And sea. At the altar on the ground
Outside the pronaos they gathered, as
A lamb was brought to it by priestesses,
And as the main priestess raised her knife,
The women sang their hymn to Artemis.

"We celebrate Artemis of the shining hair,
Beloved of both her father Zeus
And her twin and brother, Apollo,
Whom she helped from her mother's womb
Into the world.
Hail to you, radiant Artemis,
Giver of light in the midst of darkness,
Protector of children and of women,
Great huntress, deadly in aim,
Instiller of courage and compassion,
Hail to you, splendid in your glory!"

And the knife descended and the white wool
Of the feebly kicking lamb was spattered
In crimson. Then the priestess left the offering
For her acolytes and gave her knife
Now clean, to Aristomachê, who came
To her daughter, now kneeling, and cut
A lock of the bride's hair and gave it to her;
Then the priestess raised and led Polycaste
Through the pronaos of the temple
Into the cella and before the tall statue
Of Artemis. The girl shivered as she
Stood in the high shadowy room lit by
Torches that in their flickering light seemed
To bring the statue alive. At the feet
Of the Goddess was a plinth, and on it
Polycaste began to place from her box
The objects of her childhood.

        "Dear Goddess,"
She barely breathed,

          "accept, I beg you, these
My most precious mementos of my youth."

She first took out her toys, with which she had played
So many times—a small wooden top; balls,
Also of wood, their paint now faded, worn;
A horse mounted on wheels, polished smooth
By her touch; small clay bulls and sheep and dogs;
Her knucklebones, with which she had played
The game so merrily—then her dolls, some
Made of rags and wax; and then her daidala,
With its jointed and moveable limbs,
Whose features had always fascinated and
Disturbed her. Finally, she brought out her
Childhood clothes, now so tiny to her; and
As she placed each at Artemis's feet,
She felt her childhood leaving her, piece by piece;
She wept, her tears falling on her hands as
She held each object, and a feeling of
Loneliness and vulnerability
Overcame her as she finished, and she
Knelt before the feet and sobbed without let.
At last the priestess came forward and placed
Her firm hand on the distraught girl's shoulder;
Her sobbing subsided; she wiped the tears
From her eyes and clothes; composed herself, rose,
And walked from the temple as a woman,
Her childhood left behind her.

Back in the hall, the men feasted and drank on.
Odysseus carefully nursed his wine, for
He watched carefully how the Elisians
Would act at this time before the wedding.
Menelaos sat near them, retelling
Stories of their exploits in the long war,
And reminding them of jokes of that time.
At times they chuckled, but as the night grew
They became more silent and sullen, with
Their goblets filled more often. The Spartan
King finally gave up talking to them
And returned to Odysseus, who during
This time had been congratulated by
Many of those at the feast.

                              "I can talk
No further with them,"

                         Menelaos grumbled.

"Don't worry—at least for tonight,"

                                   wily
Odysseus replied.

                   "I suspect that they
Did not expect to see Orestes bring
Such numbers with him, given the short time
For the invitation. Watch them for now,
And you will see them come to no decision
And then leave."

              And as he had predicted,
The Elisians muttered together
For a time, and then with a curt nod to their hosts,
Arose and left the feast.

                    "Tomorrow should
Bring no problems; it will be the next day
That the matter will come to a head."

                              Then
As the torches flickered lower, the kings
Left the feast for their spouses and their beds.

The wedding day began as the sun rose
High in the sky. A procession of women,
Led by a child, wound its way up into
The hills to a clear spring that gushed forth
From a small cleft around which bushes and
Fragrant flowers bloomed. Here the child, dressed
In a chiton of pure wool, drew water
Into his loutrophoros, and then, assisted
By another on the other handle,
Carried the heavy-laden vase, painted
With images of Eros, back to the palace
As flutes and drums echoed through the hills.
Inside, while the queens stood by the side
To witness, the water was poured into
The already steaming bath. Then the bride

Came forth, clad in a filmy gown, which was
Removed ritually by the two mothers,
To reveal her lovely, unblemished body,
And she was helped into the ritual bath
And bathed, then dried, and her body rubbed
With precious oils, and scents applied to hair
And body, and dressed carefully in her
Wedding clothes, but without her veil for now.
Silence was kept during this time, but
The queens noted to themselves how beautiful
She was, and each remembered back to her
Own marriage and its rituals, and all
Were moved as each thought of that past day.

In the late afternoon, as the sun still
Arced across the sky, outside in a great space
The wedding took place, with the bride now veiled
And both wearing fresh bright garlands, brightening
All around them. Thrasymedes, taking
Great Nestor's place, moved to the altar
With Polycaste, there to be met by the groom
For the Engyésis, the betrothal.
Thrasymedes, with solemn face, gestured
Toward the bride.

                    "I bestow upon you
This bride, who, within this bond of wedlock,
May bring forth your children into this world."

With equal gravity, Telemachus
Replied,
            "With gratitude I accept this woman."

Then Thrasymedes spoke again.
                            "With her
I agree to provide a dowry of half
This kingdom, joining our two lands in peace."

And Telemachus responded,
                            "This gift
I accept as well, with pleasure and with hope
That both countries will prosper from this."

Then Polycaste was taken to stand
By her groom before the altar there, with
Pisistratus standing on the other side
Of Telemachus as his paranymphos.
Then the priest placed upon the altar
A young lamb, whose blood soon dripped upon ground,
And the women sang to Hera:

"Of Hera I sing, Mother Rheia's daughter,
Seated in loveliness upon her golden throne,
Queen of all the immortal Gods on Olympus,
Incomparable in her radiant beauty;
Hera, sister and wife of deafening Zeus;
Magnificent Goddess, whom those sacred
On towering Olympus honour and revere
As they do her husband and brother Zeus,
He who revels in the thunder's reverberation;
Hear our prayer and bless this mortal marriage,
So dear to you, lover of all true marriages;
Let this wife be fecund and give birth to sons
And daughters to enrich the bounty of this couple."

More hymns were sung, to Eros and to Aphrodite,
His immortal mother, and to Artemis,
And finally the ceremony ended,
And bride and groom separated again,
Thrasymedes taking the veiled girl back
To the palace, while the guests followed
To the aula of the palace for the feast.

When they were all in place, the veiled bride came
To them; wine was poured, a libation made,
And then the bride stood before her groom, who
Now took away her garland, removed the veil,
And placed again the garland on her hair,
To the shouts of the guests. The roasted lamb
And other meats were now served, and the guests
Entered into the revelry with gusto,
Comments shouted across the hall in glee,
And responded to with laughter and quips.
The sun was now in full retreat, torches

Blazing around the walls, just as attendants
Brought forth large flat cakes of pounded sesame
Seeds roasted and mixed with pungent honey.
Then at last Aristomachê rose, taking
Her daughter's hand in her own, placing
It in the groom's hand to pass her over to him.
Polycaste looked one last time at her mother
As Telemachus, accompanied by his
Best man, Pisistratus, led her outside
To where a chariot with four horses
Awaited them. Her mother and the others
Followed them, Aristomachê now raising
High a torch to walk behind them as they
Mounted into the chariot, Pisistratus
Taking the reins and the guests ranging behind,
All with torches as well to keep well lit
The couple. Off the procession went,
Down the hill and along the beach thronged
With those of the camps who had feasted there
As well, and who now shouted to them their
Fair wishes amid laughter and the sound
Of music and marriage cries—

"Ho, Hymen! Ho, Hymen! Hymenaios! Lo!"

Then up the hill went the chariot, to where
A villa loaned for the occasion waited,
And there they dismounted as blossoms snowed
Upon them. As well more delicacies
And wine were provided by sweating attendants
To the happy throng. Then Polycaste
Daintily ate a quince, glancing at her husband
With mischievous eyes as all applauded
And pelted them with fruit and nuts to aid
In the fertility promised by the nibbled fruit.
Then the two passed into the villa, while
Their friends and family sang to them
An epithalamion.

"Eros, deadly archer
Of passionate aim,

See through the bright window,
Moon-flooded the figures
Lying there on soft fleeces,
With clear white-tinted flesh
In fingered exploration.
Draw carefully your bow,
You keen-sighted hunter,
Search out the exposed place
To increase the man's pain
And loose your arrow there.

"And you, Aphrodite,
So irresistible,
Glide your finger along
The curving shape with him
To bring to her desire
And increase her allure
That Eros's arrow may
In its wound work its way
For their mutual coupling.

"And Hymen, Guardian
Of the soft marriage bed,
Protect them here from all
That may disturb their peace,
And let what Eros and
His mother have begun
Be fulfilled fruitfully."

Now Telemachus and Polycaste,
Laughing and flushed, had searched throughout the house
And finally found the room allotted them,
In which a single sweet candle flowed
Beside thick fleeces, and the scent of flowers
Filled their nostrils. Now they grew quiet, as
They listened for a moment to the song
Outside and looked at each other fully
For the first time without any hindrance.
In the soft dim light Telemachus saw her
In the mist of her clothes, wreathed with flowers,
As if in a dream, her eyes enormous,

Looking at him as if at a stranger.
He moved toward her to embrace her and found
Her trembling, although she did not move back,
And her breath had quickened. Gently his hand
Touched her cheek; she flinched but again stood still.
Then he softly kissed her lips, which remained
Unresponsive for a moment, as if
She were feeling his kiss for the first time;
As his kiss remained and became urgent,
Her lips began to respond, her trembling
Increased, until, as the kiss grew passionate,
She melted into his embrace without
Restraint, and they remained locked together,
One shape in the candle's glow. Then the need
To explore took hold, and each undressed
The other and for a moment stood again
To gaze without restraint. Telemachus
Had never seen so lovely a woman
As his bride in her naked glory, and
His desire for her surged; but even as
He moved to embrace her again, he could not
Help remembering the first sight in moonlight,
Clear and cold, of Pelagia, and as
He moved, he saw in Polycaste's eyes
That she also held the image of him
In that bath so long ago. But now they
Came together once again, feeling warm
Flesh, and soon lay upon the soft fleeces,
Where Eros and Aphrodite played their part.
And even now, aroused and urgent,
Telemachus could not stop comparison
With that other first time, for Pelagia
Had joined with him fearlessly, accepting
The short pain in complete union with him;
But with Polycaste, filled with desire
But uncertain of what was expected,
He worked more carefully, bringing her to
An agony of need before helping
Her to accept him fully. But then

All remembrance vanished, and through the night
The two found out their complete union.

The next morning, as faint light seeped through
The room, Polycaste awoke first, and
For a brief moment was lost in her sight
Of the strange room and the man sleeping there
Close beside her. Then her world shifted back,
And she rose on her elbow to look at him
As he lay there, breathing evenly,
Relaxed. She gazed at his face, now peaceful,
And realized how much older he had
Become; and as she inspected his body,
Shivering slightly at the memory
Of the night before, she discovered scars
That had not been there the last time she saw
His naked body, and she knew that he
Must have fought in battles, and again she
Realized that she knew little of this man
With whom she would spend the rest of her life,
And for a moment she felt chilled and lost; then,
As she studied him again, her feelings
For him welled up again, and she snuggled
Close to him, willing to let his warm flesh
Melt away her fears, and fell asleep again.
Later in the morning, both awakened to
Another epithalamion sung
Outside. Hastily Telemachus dressed
And went outside, where Pisistratus and
A crowd of others hailed him with boisterous
Cries and laughter.

    "What, are you alone?"
         laughed
His new brother-in-law, who had also
Secretly sent in Polycaste's slave
At another entrance to tend to
Her mistress's needs.

    "Poor man, has she already
Left you?"

Telemachus punched him playfully,
Saying,
   "At least I have a wife—why are you
Still without one?"

     And all around them laughed
And bantered. While they did so, attendants
Set up places there to eat and drink,
And when all seated themselves, wine was poured
And libation made. Then Polycaste
Appeared, radiant and lovely, to sit
By her new husband as all joked and made
Comments to which she blushed, increasing
Her attractiveness to all there. And so
Morning passed away, all there happily
Entertained, and the newly married couple
Closely attentive to each other.

Back at the palace the queens had their own
Breakfast together, away from the men,
Who were on a boar hunt with the leaders
Of the visiting groups. Aristomachê
As hostess placed herself in the midst,
As they sat in a circle, the attendants
Offering them breads and other viands.
On her one side was Penelope,
On the other Helen, with Electra
Beside Helen and Hermione
Next to Penelope. The atmosphere
Was chilled at first, with the younger queens
Saying little at all and suppressing
As best they could their hostility to
Helen, who ignored their stiffness and led
The conversation, asking her hostess
About Pylos and her marriage to Nestor.
As Aristomachê answered proudly,
Penelope studied the others quietly.
Three of them, she saw, were extraordinarily
Beautiful—only Electra and herself
Were attractive but less lovely than

The others. Helen, sitting there composed,
In her mature beauty, still with her
Exquisite face and hair and unrivalled
Body, her graceful fingers gesturing
As she spoke, still outshone her daughter, who,
Dressed in a delicate gown that displayed
Her form to advantage, brought all the
Attraction of youth to the fore, but who
Presently remained silent, studying her
Mother closely; and Aristomachê,
Darker and more exotic, more sloe-eyed
Than her daughter, with a vibrant and wild
Energy that must have captured the old king's
Love, with long fingers that played with her gown,
Gorgeous in colours and fringed girdle, or
Gestured in arcs and complex designs, rapt
In her awe of Helen and her reputation—
All three like birds of paradise against
The more modest plumage of Electra
And herself. She smiled slightly as she
Watched and listened to Helen do what she
Had always done, to dominate the group.
Finally, as the attendants circled them
Once more with offerings, Helen, weary
Of hearing about Pylos and the old king,
Turned to Electra.

                    "Tell me about
Your husband, King Pylades, whom I find
The most charming man here."

                              "Apart from
Your own husband, King Menelaos, I
Presume?"
                    said Penelope mischievously.

"Oh, far more charming than he!"
                              Helen laughed
With a sound like the chiming of wind bells.

"But come, Electra, tell us about him."

Electra looked uneasy, unwilling
To speak, when Hermione quickly
Interceded.

      "Mother, Electra and
I are not used to gossip in your way,
Especially about our husbands."

For a brief, brief moment Helen looked at
Her daughter, the tiniest of frowns
Slightly creasing her brow, and the others
Grew still as they felt the tension between
Mother and daughter. Then Helen relaxed
And smiled.

      "Of course. Both of you have been through
So much, I cannot blame you."

      And she turned
To the surprised Electra.

      "Forgive me,
I beg you. All of us have been affected
By that war so long ago."

      She looked at
Penelope as she said this, and
The Ithacan queen saw that Helen
Was reminding her of their meeting
The day before. For a moment they all
Thought back to that time and how their fates
Had been changed by that immense turmoil.

But then Hermione could contain herself
No longer.

      "And we know why that war began!"

All froze, stunned both by the attack and by
The ferocity with which she uttered it.
Helen looked at her daughter, her eyes black
With anger, and for a long moment they
Glared at each other. Then the look faded
In Helen's eyes; she became very still,

Breathed softly several times, and then,
As lioness will pad to an errant cub,
Gently placing its ruff in her great mouth
And taking it to a safe place, Helen
Now spoke quietly to her daughter.

"Yes, we do. I was kidnapped, with no means
To help myself and forced to live with
Another man without choice, leaving you,
Hermione, my only child, who
Was sent to your aunt, away from me and
Lost to me from then. And your man,"

        turning
To Penelope,

     "who won you with his
Ingenuity in working out the pact,
Because of it lost to you for twenty years.
And you, Electra, enduring the murder
Of your father because of his
Supposed sacrifice of your sister and
The slaughter of your mother by your brother.
And you, Aristomachê, who became
King Nestor's wife at the price of your town
And family, ravaged and destroyed by him.
And here we are today, sore with the wounds
Still festering in our bosoms despite
The brightness of the day and the marriage
Of the son and daughter of you two here.
Can we not lay these griefs aside for this
Brief happy time?"

     A long silence, each deep
In the swirling currents of their memories.
Then Hermione spoke, looking with eyes
Still in pain,

     "You speak wisely of what we
Should do, and I will do my best to keep
Alive the spirit of this time. But
I lost you, my mother; and I also

Had to endure the body of Achilles's son
Without recourse, and neither of these
Injuries can I forget or forgive.
So let us try for this while to remain
At peace; but I hope never to see you
Again after this."

        Helen stared at her,
And Penelope could barely endure
The pain that she saw in those shadowed eyes,
As the Spartan queen, without a word, nodded.
They all ate and drank without enjoyment,
And then they finished and each went her
Separate way.

In the afternoon, before the palace,
The wedding couple with the families
Attended the epaulia. A procession
Of guests wound down the hill before them,
Each bearing a gift, and in front of them
Arose a large mound of what was presented:
Golden combs, fragrant vials of perfume,
Goblets richly painted with scenes that showed
The revelries of Hymen, jewellery
Made of rich metals and precious stones,
Vases filled with young trees and shrubs and buds
Of exotic flowers, closely woven baskets
Designed for food or household objects,
Chairs made of ivory with golden ornament,
And pots of all sizes and shapes that were
Empty or filled with perfumed oils—and all
The objects glittered there, and their scents
Pervaded the air about the space. Last
To appear were the Elisians, with
Sumptuous gifts as well. At their end came
The huge figure of Automedon, and
Before the couple, beside whom were
The Ithacans Odysseus and his queen
And his seer Halitherses, who watched all
With care, the Elisian placed a lion skin,

Large but old and worn, and as he did so
He spoke.

"Offspring of illustrious
Families, we present you here with gifts,
But this one is the most precious. This skin
Was one worn by our ancestor, immortal
Heracles. We give it here as assurance
That we of Elis will be at peace with you
While you live."

He inclined his head to the astonished
Group, with Telemachus stammering
His thanks, and then as he turned to leave, he
Looked Odysseus in the eye. With a chill
The king suddenly understood that
The Elisian had now received the same
Vision as he had experienced at
Dodona, and as he had this insight
He saw that Automedon himself
Now realized that Odysseus also
Knew what he had discovered; he looked at
The shaken Ithacan with a grim smile,
Then moved off. Odysseus watched him go
And turned to Halitherses to find that
His seer had turned white with shock, for he
Now realized the vision that the two
Warriors shared, and its immensity
Overwhelmed him.

Odysseus quickly caught
The tottering man, and whispered to his son,

"Finish the ceremony with grace, but
Quickly—Halitherses is not well."

Telemachus, startled, did as his father bid,
And the family moved back into the palace.
Odysseus had attendants support
Halitherses to where he could lie on
Soft fleeces. Telemachus and others

Crowded around, anxious about their seer,
But Odysseus waved them away.

                 "He will be
Better in a while; leave the two of us."

And his son went, reluctantly, but he knew
Well to obey his father, who must have
Something in mind. After they left, the king
Bent close to the stricken man.

               "Can you speak?"

Halitherses nodded, his eyes still filled
With the horror of what he had seen.
Odysseus whispered, not more than a breath,

"You saw what dwelt in his eyes?"

                  His seer nodded
And breathed back.
          "You saw it as well?"

                  "As you know.
That is why there will be no invasion
In this next generation."

           "But in some
Generation following?"

           "You saw in
His eyes what will be."

The prone man shuddered.

            "Yes. A terrible
Fate for our peoples!"

          Then he looked closely
In Odysseus's eyes.

         "This is what you learned
From the Gods at Dodona, was it not?"

Odysseus looked at him grimly.

                    "I am
Constrained not to reveal what I underwent.
But I did see what you saw in his eyes."

Halitherses gripped his arm, his whisper
Harsh in the king's ear.

                 "What can we do? How
Can we go on, knowing what we do?"

Odysseus raised him up so that they sat
Close.

         "What can we do but go on? What choice
Have we? The Gods can speak and we cannot
Change the fate they give us, just as those we
Conquered suffered. And in the end our death
Must come, whatever we might do. Only
How we endure is our own choice and need."

For a long moment they were silent, while
Odysseus let his friend absorb what he
Had said. Then he spoke again.

                "But we must
Not tell the others of this distant fate.
They must live out their lives as best they can,
Just as I have tried to fulfill what choice
I had by my wits, hoping that the Gods
Permitted me to do so. And so, compose
Yourself and rejoice in the celebrations
This night."

        Halitherses, his face strained,
Nodded but could not yet speak. Odysseus
Warmly gripped his arm and then left him there,
Lying on the fleeces, his mind aflame
With the other fires that he had envisioned.

That evening the groom's banquet was held.
Odysseus had reassured his son that
The seer was recovering, and all was made ready.
Throughout the camps priests sacrificed their bulls

As hymns again were sung and danced to Hera
And Eros and Artemis and Aphrodite,
And the fires blazed high, their smoke and aromas
Ascending far into the deepening sky.
At the palace the same sacrifice and
Rituals were performed, and the guests came
To Nestor's high-ceilinged hall, where chairs and
Tables awaited them, and attendants
Poised to serve them. Soon the kings and the groom
Arrived, libations were made, and then the bride
And the queens arrived, and also fair young women,
All dressed in soft gowns of fine linen, all
Wearing upon their heads garlands of fresh flowers,
So that they were lovely to behold.
The women seated themselves appropriately,
Polycaste beside her husband, and
Attendants brought forward rich baskets of
Bread and delicacies to whet their appetites
Before the great haunches were carried in.
Telemachus proved himself a gracious host,
Responding to calls from his guests and to
His new mother-in-law, seated on his
Other side. Odysseus sat next her, and
Then Penelope, with Menelaos and
Helen on Polycaste's side. Pylades
Sat beside Penelope, with his wife,
Orestes and Hermione making up
That group, and the Pylians interspersed
On both sides. Menelaos was charmed
By Polycaste, with Helen making sure
That their conversation flowed as it should.
With Pylades attentive to Penelope
And Aristomachê distracted
By Telemachus, Odysseus found that
He did not need to force himself to make
Conversation, for which he was grateful;
Like someone in a dream who is in the midst,
Yet seems to witness each action detached,
So the Ithacan king found himself at
The feast. When he spoke to anyone, he

Felt as if he could see himself as he spoke,
And in this strange detachment he observed
The people as the attendants now served
The succulent slices to all there, as
If he could sense them anchored in time's stream
But with their destinations clear to him.
Orestes he saw with but few years left
To him, buoyed up by the death of the king
Of Arcadia, but heading then to
His inevitable death from the snake bite.
Could Pylades, he wondered, despite his
Cleverness, control Tiryns and Mycenae?
How would Menelaos deal with such a
Catastrophe? How firm would the union
Hold amongst them? Before he thought more, he
Heard the sound of music, for Euphranor
Had arrived to play his lyre while they ate,
And Odysseus let himself listen and
Feast. The musician did not sing this time,
But let the rich sound of his notes throb through
The hall against the cacophony of
Those speaking animatedly. Weary,
Odysseus found himself, weary of what
He had struggled to accomplish, weary
Of his knowledge of the distant, dreadful
Future, and weary of the complex pattern
Of the lives around him. But as the lyre
Spread its sweet sounds, he found the music
Crept into his consciousness and with its
Shifting tones soothed him more than he had thought.
Now the time had come for more of the cakes,
Flat-rounded, honey-soaked, to delight and
Enrich their palates, and as the feasters
Nibbled at these, more musicians arrived
To play with Euphranor, and a space was cleared
In anticipation of the new events.
Polycaste and her mother arose,
Along with the young women at the feast,
And they moved into the new space to dance
The Imeneos, the bride's dance. Once there,

They formed a ring, and new sounds rang out,
With the rhythmic noise of cymbals, the tympani,
Shell instruments, and the reinforcement
Of the lyre with the kithara and
The shriller sounds of wind instruments,
The avlos and the syrigs. The women
Joined hands and stepped rhythmically around
In their circle, their bodies twisting gracefully;
Then they broke hands and each circled, arms raised
Attractively. Again they took hands and
Repeated their steps, but as they did so
The music quickened, and their twists and turns
Became swifter and swifter as the rhythm
Accelerated, until they were a blur
Of sweeping gowns and arms and feet, until
At last the dance slowed and they returned
To the graceful beginning. All who had
Not danced applauded them enthusiastically;
Then Polycaste, flushed, her eyes flashing,
Reached out for Telemachus, the others
Reaching as well for men for the Hormos.
The men came into the space, each with
Their golden daggers on silver straps,
Their bodies lightly oiled, wearing woven tunics.
Telemachus led the chain, with Polycaste
Linked to him as were the others in the chain,
And the music began again, this time
With the beats stronger and the shrill sounds
Louder. Telemachus started with quick steps
As his body twisted to and fro; Polycaste
Took what he did and modified it,
The steps as quick but more delicate,
The body graceful in its twists; the men
Repeated their leader's dance, and the women
Theirs. Then Telemachus's steps grew bolder;
He leapt strongly in a martial stance, his arms
In strong gestures; and Polycaste again
Found a way to make the movements more feminine.
And so the dance progressed as the two
Invented more ingenious changes

That all who watched marvelled at and cheered
When the dancers, hot and gay, returned
To sit and drink. But then more dances
Were performed, sometimes by the men alone,
Doing martial and acrobatic steps;
Sometimes by women, both slow and stately
And wilder; and sometimes by both happily.
Odysseus sat with Penelope as
The dances went on. Some of the other
Queens joined in the dances, as did Pylades,
Who moved like a sleek panther, his quick feet
Sure and skillful, his leaps high as the beast
Would leap, without apparent effort and
With light landing, that all watched with admiration.
Both Helen and Hermione also
Danced exquisitely, their gowns flowing like
Water around their beautiful forms and limbs.
But Aristomachê and her daughter
Entered most into the spirit of the
Music and the dance, their bodies glistening
As they twirled and circled like the sure spin
Of their spindles in their domestic tasks,
And when the dance required it, they leapt
With wildness and passion, bacchante like,
Their gestures sweeping the air around them,
And their long legs creating lovely arcs,
Their eyes flashing from the power of the beat,
Their heads flung back in ecstasy. The groom
Now began to understand the woman
He had married and realized that
His relationship with two passionate
Women would not be peaceful; but as he
Watched her superb movements, her fine colour
High, he lost himself in her beauty, for
Truly she showed herself the most desirable
Woman in the hall, exceeding even
Helen herself and her daughter, and he
Could hardly wait until they were alone
Again. But Odysseus, who noted all
This, found himself both affected by the

Music and dance, yet again detached, as
He pondered, despite himself, the future
Of those of his family about him.

*This generation will be safe, and perhaps*
*The next. But we must deal still with the present.*

His mind went back to when they left Ithaca:
He stood braced upon the swift ship's firm deck
As the prow seethed through the swells black in the sun
On their southward journey, the breeze fondling his face,
And his queen, son, and seer came to him,
The Pylian prince out of earshot.

Halitherses spoke first:
                              "My noble king,
The prince must inform you of a matter
We thought should be told you without Pylian ears
To hear."

              The seer nodded to Telemachus,
Who, troubled but no longer diffident,
Spoke at once, and he was pleased to see
His son's growing maturity, but puzzled
By his look:

              "Father, we have not yet talked
Of Pelagia."

              And he, now alert,
Replied,
              "Indeed we haven't. And how does she fare?"

"Extremely well, my father and king.
Her skills in healing have made her welcome
Throughout Ithaca."

                    He then looked at Penelope.

"She has been accepted by us all,
And I find her a woman worthy to meet
And to converse with, and one who, despite
Her position, has gained a place in our family."

He was startled by his wife's response, for he
Believed that she would have been outraged by
A concubine for Telemachus. She
Saw his look and smiled.

                "You know, my husband,
That I do not like the thought of a concubine
Among us, but Pelagia has earned
Both our respect and friendship—and your son
Truly loves her."

           Her look at their son confirmed
What she had said, and Pelagia's worth
Rose again in Odysseus's estimation.

But with his mother's look, Telemachus
Again spoke:

          "What my mother says is true—
I do love her; and now, even more."

With eyes narrowed, he waited to hear more.

"Not only has Pelagia proved her skill
As a healer, but she has given us a gift as well."
He took a breath and, settled, then went on:
"We have a son—your grandson, my father."

He had suspected this, and so replied,

"I congratulate you both—and I can see
Your mother pleased as well"—

                for his wife's eyes
Glowed at the mention of the child—

                  "but how
Will this affect your coming marriage, for
I'm sure the bride and her family will not
Appreciate both a concubine and child
As part of the marriage settlement."

Penelope, who knew so well his mind, spoke:

"We have anticipated this as best
As we can. She now lives in a place built
For her across the bay, with her garden there
As well, and people are now accustomed
To visit her there. We must try to keep
Knowledge of her from his bride until a time
That is appropriate."

                    He slowly
Nodded, looking at her searchingly.

                              "And
When will that be, do you think?"

                         At this point
Halitherses interjected, his voice
That of the seer.

                    "My king, I will try this
To divine and will inform you when known.
In the meantime I advise that any talk
Of Pelagia deal with her as a healer,
And that those wedding guests who know of her
Relation to your son be warned not to speak
Of it before the family."

                    Again, he
Nodded

                    "I agree. Let us speak of this
Again at some other time as well."

                              Then
He embraced his son.

                    "I wish you the best,
My prince, in both your wedding and with
Pelagia, and I share your joy in
Your new son."

                    Laughter and shouting brought him
Back again to the festivities where
He sat in his reverie. For a time
He watched, but his thoughts arose again.

*The issue of Pelagia will be*
*More than delicate, I can see now,*
*Particularly with the child. We all*
*Must deal with this carefully, for we could*
*Be caught between the concubine and*
*Aristomachê, who will not be pleased,*
*Given the complications that could occur.*
*And I am not sure about Pelagia*
*Herself. She gave me her word not to harm*
*Any in the family, and I believe she*
*Will keep it. But can she find means to change*
*What might happen? With a son, she might think*
*Toward the future. What if Polycaste*
*Gives birth to no heir, but only to girls,*
*Or no children at all? And will Pelagia*
*End up as has the mother of the sons*
*Of Menelaos, exiled, and Helen*
*In hazard herself if her husband dies?*
*The future, whether in Ithaca or*
*Elsewhere, is like mists shifting in the fog.*

He looked out at the dancers, gay and strong,
And his heart twisted as he felt their youth
And life and joyousness, blind to their fates.
For a moment he almost wept, but then
His will, indomitable, held sway, and
He cleared his mind again; and as a dance
Began, he took Penelope by the hand,
And together they joined the dancers' chain.

That night, as the stars glittered overhead
And the moon peered with her cold face through
The windows, each of the kings lay with his queen,
And Telemachus with Polycaste,
And each in his own way made love, some wild,
Some tender, some for their own gratification,
Some in full union with their mate, and thus
The wedding days and nights found their end.

Early the next day, like ants streaming from
Their colony, the camps broke up and marched

Away, their leaders making a last farewell
To their Pylian hosts and the Ithacans.
Polycaste, who had found time to talk
To the queens, discovering not only
What they told her but also the quiet
Tensions among them, herself bid each
A private farewell. Hermione was
Charming and less distant than before,
And wished the young bride with full heart that she
Would have a happy marriage; Electra, more
Reserved, wished her well simply, but with deep
Feeling—the bride could sense that she had suffered—
Helen spoke to her warmly and recommended
That if she was ill she should visit one
Who had trained with her in drugs and herbs.
Then came the formal goodbyes at the palace gates,
As each king and his followers made their
Exit—the Elisians first, with few
And formal words; then Pylades, who embraced
Warmly Odysseus and Telemachus,
Spoke gaily to the Pylians, then rode off;
Then Orestes, more formal, but with a
Look of respect to Odysseus; and
Finally Menelaos, who again
Embraced his old comrade and his son and
Gave a speech which Helen quietly made
Him stop; and off they went into the dust
Raised by the marches of the other troops.
A final feast at midday among
The two families while attendants toiled
To load the Ithacan ship with the gifts
And the rest of the cargo. Then a tearful
Farewell between Polycaste and her mother,
And promises to visit from the Pylians.
Then down to the beach, and aboard, where
Odysseus stood at the sharp-pointed prow,
His eyes already fixed on the limitless
Horizon of the sea as the sleek ship
Whispered from the sand and headed from the bay.

# Notes

These "notes" are fuller descriptions of some of the characters. Only those who are not more fully treated in the text of the cantos are included.

## AGAPENOR

Son of Ancaeus, grandson of Lycurgus,
Arcadian king, yet another suitor
Of Helen, received sixty ships, when war
Began, from Agamemnon, and brought there
The unruly tribes of his rough kingdom.
He was in the Trojan horse; he helped sack
The doomed citadel. But when his fleet sailed
Triumphantly from that distant shore, it
Was caught with other Greek fleets in the storm
That overtook them and carried it far
To Cyprus, where he stayed to found Paphos
And to build Aphrodite's famous shrine.

## AGASTROPHOS

A Trojan warrior, son of Paeon,
His genealogy noted, and, too,
His fatal error: leaving his chariot
And his team reined at the side of the fight
As he advanced, tight packed in the front ranks,
Grinding on until the spear hurled at him
By Diomedes smashed through his hip's joint
And he lay, dying, trampled, helpless.
No fast escape for him, error rectified,
As Diomedes stripped the brawny fighter,
Ripping from his chest the burnished breastplate,
His shouldered shield and helmet heavy-crested,
As the man's eyes darkened and went out.

## AUTOLYCUS

A fitting man to be ancestor to
Odysseus, whose very life was wondrous—
Conceived in the touch of a virgin's face
By the agile God Hermes, Chione
Giving birth to this new demi-god, who
Himself sired two daughters: Anticleia,
Mother of Odysseus; and Polymede,
Who bore the hero Jason. When the prince
Was born, Eurycleia, coming to him,
Laid the babe upon his knee and then spoke:

"Autolycus, search yourself for a name
To give to your child's own child; for be sure
He has long been prayed for."

For a great time
He studied the small creature on his knee
And then he said, with a sigh and wry smile,

"You will bear the name Odysseus and wreak
All that it implies."

And so it was.
"Lone Wolf" was the meaning of the man's name,
And Lone Wolf he was. Hermes in his touch
Bequeathed him his skills, particularly
The art of theft, ability to trick,
Talent to play the lyre, sing gracious songs.
He loved, it is said, to make black of white,
And white of black, portray a hornless beast
With horns, a horned one unadorned. As well,
Hermes gave him the gift that his thievery
Could not be caught by anyone—the herd
Of Sisyphus he stole right from under him.
He could prove both a blessing and a bane:
Heracles from him learned the art of wrestling;
But·when the wily thief stole some cattle
From Euboea and Eurytus,
It was Heracles, accused of the deed,
Who went mad from the accusation,

Killed them and, much to Autolycus's grief,
One of his sons, Iphitus. For these crimes
Heracles for punishment had to serve three years
To repent for the murders. But Autolycus
Continued on, and his grandson loved him
And showed himself such gifts passed on, but with
The wisdom to use them carefully.

## DEIOPITES, THOON, ENNOMOS, CHERSIDAMAS, CHAROPS HIPPASIDES, SOCOS

These Trojans were the ones who ringed about
The valiant Odysseus, who taunted him,
And who paid dearly for their presumption,
For he knew well their names and wrote their death:
The spear slicing into the shoulder of
The lord Deiopites; the sword tasting
The blood of Thoon, of Ennomos, and then
Chersidamas leaping from his chariot
Split to the navel and left there writhing
In the dust, hands scrabbling the earth; while on
Odysseus went, confronting the two sons
Of Hippias, fine trainer of horses,
Wealthy and bold—the first, Charops, impaled
Upon his sword—then, Socos, who, insults
Screaming from his mouth, wounded Odysseus,
Only to be boasted at and speared
Through the back and out the chest as he ran.
Never take for granted a cornered wolf.

## DOLIOS

What mysteries this old slave hints at!
When much younger, a present to
Penelope from her father
Icarius when she was given
As bride to Odysseus, not by him
But by Tyndareus, her uncle.
Why this slave to tend her garden?
Had she known him when as a child

She played amongst the lush foliage
Of Laconia as he tilled
The verdant soil? Had he played with her,
Talked with her, become her friend?
Does his name, "the crafty one," tell,
As Hermes, called the same word,
Would have wielded persuasion,
How he could have enticed the girl
To wish him with her wherever
She may find herself?

And when they sailed to Ithaca,
Dolios learned to work the rocky ground
To make her sojourn sweet,
And a servant bore him six boys.
As time passed and Odysseus
Was but a wisp of memory,
Laertes took Dolios and his sons
To his farm to work for him there,
And the old servant tended them both,
And her sons. Then, when the hero
Returned, old Dolios still kept
Faith with the family, aided
The intrigue, the slaughter, civil war;
Then two of his sons sailed off with
The king and prince on the next quest.
And he and his progeny returned
To working the soil and vineyards,
And keeping watch that all stayed well,
As he rose stiffly from the vines
To see, far off, his queen, his girl,
Peering out from the high window,
Out toward the sea and Greece itself.

## ELEAN ITYMONEUS

The enmity between Elis and Pylos
Was long-standing. In defence of his cattle
Nestor felled Itymoneus, son of Elean
Hypeirochos, and routed his rural troops;
Then the Pylians gathered much booty

In retaliation, taking large herds
Of cattle, along with goats, sheep, mares
And pigs, driving them at night to Pylos.
When morning came, heralds summoned creditors
Of the Elisians. Neleus took a flock
Of sheep and a whole herd of cattle
To settle a notorious debt—four
Champion horses with their chariots,
Which had been sent to Elis and been detained
By Augeas. But shortly the army
Of the Elisians, in reprisal seized
The Pylian town of Thryoessa.
Out again the Pylians marched to fight
And routed them, inspired by young Nestor,
Who captured an enemy chariot
And with it destroyed almost the entire
Elisian chariot force. Only two
Escaped—the youthful Molion twins, whom
Later Nestor met in a chariot race
At the funeral games of the Elisian
Chief, Amarynceus. And so the conflict
Continued, whether peaceful or in war.

## ERINYES

Resting in Erebos, the dark, the shadowed deep,
They wait until awakened by the sound,
An awful shrillness, blood-piercing, the curse
Echoed by the Moirae from some riven victim
To avenge the crime against him; for these,
The dreaded Erinyes, inflict punishment
For crimes against the order of nature—
Blood-drenched homicide, ripping away life;
Betrayal of woman by man, man by woman;
Through unfilial conduct, wrenching bonds
Intimate; acts against the Gods by word
Or deed; or the twisting of truth to lie
By devious perjury. But for them,
These three infernal ones, the powerful,
The curse closest to their hearts, was the cry

Of the murdered parent against the child
Who took such caring life; for they themselves
Had been born of such a crime when Cronos,
Lurking hidden, with his sickle, sliced off
His father's genitals and sent Ouranos,
His mutilated parent and God of the Sky,
To darkest oblivion. Drops of blood
From the shorn flesh fell upon Gaia,
Goddess of the Earth and discontented
Wife of the Sky God, who months later bore
The three sisters. Now the cry sounds, in wrath
They rise, terrible to behold, dressed to hunt,
As might huntress-maidens, but with their hair,
Their arms, and waists entwined with snakes,
Writhing and poisonous, their eyes blood dripped,
Gripping torches or harsh whips, their vast wings
Swiftly thrusting them up to earth and air—
Alecto, the troubled one, Megaera,
The one infused with implacable hate,
And Tisiphone, the wrathful avenger
Of murder, the deities of vengeance.
Their wrath revealed itself in many ways—
Murderers may endure illness or worse,
Agonizing disease. Nor could a nation
Harbour such a criminal, for it could
Suffer drought and with it famine, disease.
But their worst fury was directed at
A patricide or matricide, on whom
They inflicted dire, tormenting madness.
These dreadful guardians of stern justice
Confronted Orestes, even as his blade
Still dripped with the blood of those before him,
His mother and her lover, slaughtered there.
Nor could he escape them, for fleeing was
Impossible, and their torments ended
Only in madness or in death. Thus he
Was whirled through the maelstrom of flight, madness
Pursuing him always, until at Athens
He was permitted his trial, Apollo
By his side, Athena the judge, and the three

Hovering before him, now clad in their
Long black mourning robes. The trial's outcome
Was uncertain, for Erinyes refused
To recognize the Gods' authority,
Who were subject to their will as also
To those of the Moirae, the Fates themselves.
But they honoured and esteemed Zeus himself,
Who had avenged them by castrating Cronos,
His own father; and after he intervened
With Athena when Orestes had clearly
Acknowledged his killing, done by order
Of Apollo, and sought expiation,
To be cleansed, the first to do so among
The whole line of the Atrides,
They bowed to the wisdom of the high God,
To become their other selves, Benign Ones,
The Eumenides, protectors of those
Supplicants to them, after offerings
Of black sheep sacrificed and nephalia,
That sweet drink of water interfused with
Honey. And Orestes, the first suppliant,
Was made whole through this ritual purification
And the tortures he had before endured.

## ESCALIOS

Corinthian ally who fought
With Menelaos for those ten
Long years until the fateful night
When Troy was ravaged and destroyed.
Only then was he cruelly wounded
In that last moment of victory,
When in the flickering light
Of the burning city, when none
Could be identified, a prince
Unknown of the doomed city
Fought with him in the uncertain
Light and caught him below the shield,
His leg hacked through and lost from him.
Now he sits in pain in Corinth,

On a throne as ruler of this
Citadel, but the memory
Of the war still twists at his flesh.

## EUCHENOR

Polyidos's son learned to bear
A terrible prophecy
Uttered to him by his tranced father
Grieving as he croaked the words.
For him a choice unthinkable:
To die in pain, in his bed,
Of fever unendurable;
Or to join with Menelaos,
In the Laconian forces,
Sail to Troy, and there be stricken
In the inevitable battle.
He chose a warrior's death,
The least worse choice, with honour
The dure badge of his unsought demise.

## HIPPODAMAS and HYPEIROCHOS

Two Trojan warriors who fought together
And in the end died together, killed
Within moments by the swift Ithacan
With his relentless sword, and armour stripped.
But how in all the turmoil of the battle
Those fighting in their thousands recognized
Their foes, called them by name, and when they killed,
They took the armour of the new fallen
Both as spoil and as a last souvenir.

## ILOS DARDANIDES

The tomb of Ilos, son of great Dardan,
And grandfather of King Priam of Troy,
Crowned with pillars in reverence and state,
Near which the battles rang against the still
Sides of the resting place, and where Paris,
Lurking there, could unleash his deadly arrows.

## MANTILIOS and DORINDOR

Two of the six sons of Dolios,
The old slave working for Laertes,
Who now, having been blooded at home,
Look eagerly toward adventure
With Odysseus and Telemachus
On this second quest of the king.
No longer slaves but warriors,
They revel in their hard-fought gain,
Learning the disciplines of war
But already hardened by their toils
In the fields and orchards at home.

## MERIONÊS

As a suitor of Helen, he was forced
To join the others against Ilium
And with Idomeneus led eighty ships
From Crete. A formidable warrior,
Who among innumerable others
Killed seven Trojans prominent in Ilium,
He was famed for his skill in archery.
In Achilles's contest between the Cretan
And King Teucer as to who could transfix
A pigeon and not the string tethering it,
Teucer's arrow severed the string and let
The pigeon fly free; but Merionês took aim
And caught the bird in full flight, who fell to earth
And won him the prize of ten double-edged,
Sharp axes. He it was as well who helped
With the two fierce Ajaxes to defend
The body of Patroclus, carrying it
From the field to the grieving Achilles.

## MOIRA / MOIRAE

Each person in this life, however great
Or mean, is allotted his or her moira,
One's portion in life or in destiny,
By the infernal Moirae, the ancient crones,

Guardians and directors of eternal fate.
Remorseless and unfeeling, stern, severe,
Inflexible, the three work together:
Clotho, the Spinner, spins the thread of life
From distaff to spindle; then Lachesis,
Drawer of Lots, with her measuring rod
Determines the length of the thread of life
Allotted to each person; and Atropos,
She Who Cannot be Turned, inexorable,
Chooses the manner of that person's death,
And when that time has come, with her dread shears
She cuts off the life-thread. Independent
Of the Gods, who feared them, guiding necessity,
They watch that the fate assigned to everyone
By eternal laws must take its course with
No obstruction. And so they follow each man's steps
And direct the consequences of his actions
Accordingly. But even acting in this way,
They do not interfere directly in affairs
Of humankind, using causes more distant,
Determining the lot of mortals
Conditionally, so that even man
Himself was allowed a certain freedom
To exercise some influence upon them;
And Zeus himself, if he saw fit, exercised
His power to save even those already
On the point of being grasped by fate's doom.
In keeping to the eternal laws, they
Assigned to the Erinyes their right
Function, to inflict punishment for evil deeds,
So that with them they directed fate according
To the laws of necessity. Powerful
As they were, they could still be defeated
In battle, for when they fought with the Gods
And Heracles against the Giants, they won
Only because Heracles fought with them;
If he had fought on the side of the Giants,
The prophecy would have been fulfilled that
They would have been defeated. As it was,
They fought fiercely with bronze maces, killing

The Giants Agrios and Thoon. As well,
As Goddesses they could be placated,
Brides in Athens offering them locks of hair.
And women swearing by them—for among
Mothers, who would not pray to them to gift
The destiny of their new-born child? Thus
It is that they appear as Goddesses of Birth,
Spinning the thread of life and foretelling
The fate of the newly born, their companion
Eileithyia; but also can they be
Seen as Goddesses of Death, appearing
With the Erinyes and the Keres,
Those female spirits of violent or cruel death,
Found in battle, accident, murder, or
Ravaging disease, who craved blood, gorging
Upon it after they had ripped a soul
Free from the mortally wounded body
And sent it on its way to Hades.
Thus the three sisters help shape the things
Of the world and hover over it
Continually.

## MYCONIDES

Aoidos in the pinnacled citadel,
High at Corinth, in the great hall at night,
At day rooting for the tales let slip from tongues
Foreign at the quay, ears quick to pick up
Even fine shreds of possibility
To weave together, then tuned to his lyre
In preparation for the evening's feast.
Then, quiet at the side or close at hand,
To rise at the bidding, lyre at his side,
Pick the first notes that set the story's mood,
And let it fill his mind, fingers, and voice
So that it lives, in his imagination
Vibrant, surging forward like the horses wild
From the career of chariot among
The flashing swords and thrusting spears of war,
Trampling the prone men in agony

Or, gored and screaming in their whinnies,
Plunging to the bloodied earth to release
Their crazed fear and life; and so his song
Soars to its end and he blinks, back among
Those rapt by what they have experienced;
Then receives his praise and delicacies
And returns to his anonymous place.

## PALAMEDES and NAUPLIOS

Son and father, gifted more than most men,
Who changed the fate of all Achaeans
In the Trojan War—for Palamedes,
Wise in knowledge, inventor of letters
For the alphabet, cleverly exposed
Odysseus's feigned madness to avoid
His part in the coming war (having been
Foretold that if he did so, his companions
Would all perish and he would take long years
To return), and it was the Ithacan
Who ultimately shaped the victory.
But Palamedes, brilliant though he was,
Did not reckon with the enmity
That he aroused in the bitter warrior,
And later paid with his life unjustly,
When Odysseus's trap closed tight around him.
He was slain as a traitor, and his father,
Nauplios, raging, lost his strong plea for
Satisfaction and had to return home,
Unsuccessful. But enmity breeds more;
And Nauplios was no common man:
His father was the god Poseidon, and
His mother a Danaid, and he had served
When younger as an Argonaut. Revenge
He worked in many ways, persuading
The wives of the absent Achaeans
To be false to their husbands—Clytemnestra
With Aegisthus, Diomedes's wife with
Cometes, the wife of King Idomeneus
With Leucus—to the later ruin

Of their husbands; and on the rugged cliffs
He placed false beacons that led many ships
Returning from the war to be dashed
Against the rocks, all hands lost. He himself
Later suffered the same fate, drowning when
His ship was led astray by such a beacon.
So both child and parent, great in themselves,
Inventive in letter and word, persuasive,
Were engulfed in the maelstrom of the war
Along with so many others from their little world.

## POLYIDOS

Sing of the seer Polyidos,
Wise in divination's tangles,
Cunning in adversity.
He it was whom Minos, fell King
Of Crete, ordered to find his child
Glaucis, a shadow vanished.
His sacred vision let the seer
See the boy, chasing a mouse,
Fall into a honey jar
And drown. On the grief-stricken plea
He applied to the useless corpse
An herb and pried the boy from death.

But when after a time the seer
Wished to depart for Argos,
Minos, jealous of his powers,
Refused to let him go
Until he had taught Glaucis
Divination's mysteries.
Under compulsion the seer
Taught until Glaucis could show
The powers of foretelling,
And Minos, satisfied, released him.
But as he was about to sail
Polyidos bade Glaucis
Spit into his mouth. He did so,
And in that moment all he learned

And practiced in divination
Vanished completely from his mind.

Yet though he himself sired children,
The two daughters, Manto and Astycratea,
Themselves blessed with the gift
To purify, and his son,
Euchenor, beloved by him,
His own power betrayed him,
For he divined two deaths for his son,
And his son chose that of honour.
Nor could the seer's powers change
Such fate, nor could he use herbs
To return to life his only son,
And that grief lay with him till his end.

## RHESUS

How unfortunate, King Rhesus of Thrace.
When the messenger, breathless, exhausted,
Announced the attack on Ilion, and
Pled for assistance to Troy, he agreed.
But then another messenger arrived
To warn him that Scythia had attacked
Thrace itself. First, then, he battled at home
To defeat the invading hordes, to drive
Them back, smarting, to their own boundaries.
Finally he set sail for Ilium,
Arriving as the battles had matured.
Hector welcomed him gladly, and found him
A space which the Trojan prince assured him
Was safe, secure. Accordingly he camped
There, finding a place for his warriors
And for his famed horses, white as snow and swift
As the wind, then setting up his own tent,
Spacious and rich, with his captains around it,
And there he settled in that night, asleep
In supposed security, but never
To wake again, killed in the stealth of night
By Diomedes and sly Odysseus,

Who stole both his life and his fine horses.
"Better never than late" should be his motto.

## THYMBRAIOS and MOLION

Both thundered down the plain, exultant, buoyed
By their leader, Prince Hector's, fierce onslaught,
The tall Molion guiding the chariot,
Keeping the horses, slavering, in stride,
So that his war-lord and companion,
Thymbraios, could launch well his deadly spear
Or hack men down with his bright-driven sword.
The lord had answered famed Ilion's call
For allies, bringing his men and his best,
His aide-in-arms, and now the glare of war
Shone in their eyes, and they yelled victory
Songs—until before them stepped two foes,
Whom they barely saw before the one,
Diomedes, snatched the hapless warrior
From the chariot, and, gripping him tight,
Speared him through the left breast, while Molion,
Slashed by Odysseus, toppled to the ground,
Where the two dying men lay side by side,
Their blood mingling as they saw at the last
Their warrior friendship now completed.

## TIRESIAS

Most renowned of seers, blind prophesier,
Many generations old, descendant
Of the dragon-tooth-begot Udeaeus,
One of Cadmus's Sparti at Thebes's creation,
Blinded on sight of Athena's nakedness
But gifted by her as an oracle,
His ears cleansed to understand the birds' songs,
A staff of cornel-wood to walk as sighted,
Longevity, and when dead and in Hades,
His understanding left whole, undisturbed.
He it was at Thebes who foretold the fate
So terrible of Oedipus; he it was